P9-EKE-794

lonely planet

Moscow

"All you've got to do is decide to go and the hardest part is over.

So go!"

TONY WHEELER, COFOUNDER – LONELY PLANET

THIS EDITION WRITTEN AND RESEARCHED BY

Mara Vorhees,
Leonid Ragozin

Contents

Plan Your Trip 4

Explore Moscow 42

Understand Moscow 181

Survival Guide 225

Moscow Maps 257

JONATHAN SMITH / LONELY PLANET IMAGES ©

TOM COCKREM / LONELY PLANET IMAGES ©

JONATHAN SMITH / LONELY PLANET IMAGES ©

Left: Portrait artist at work by the Wall of Peace, Arbat (p114)

Above: Churchwarden at Upper St Peter Monastery, Tverskoy (p76)

Right: Shashlyks cooking at Noev Kovcheg, Basmanny (p140)

Tverskoy p73

Presnya p90

Kremlin & Kitay Gorod p46

Basmanny & Taganka p134

Dorogomilovo & Sparrow Hills p147

Arbat & Khamovniki p102

Zamoskvorechie p121

Welcome to Moscow

During any season, any hour of day, Moscow thrills visitors with its artistry, history and majesty.

Kremlin & Red Square

Moscow started in the 12th century as a triangular plot of land – a smallish fort – perched atop Borovitsky Hill. Surrounded by a wall for protection, the fort contained the earliest settlement, while ceremonies and celebrations were held on the plaza outside. The fort, of course, is the Kremlin, while the ceremonial plaza is Red Square – still at the heart of Moscow historically, geographically and spiritually.

Performing Arts

The classical performing arts in Moscow are still among the best and cheapest in the world. But New Russia comes with new forms of entertainment. Nowadays, even the most traditional theatres are experimenting with innovative arrangements and cutting-edge choreography, reviving lost favourites and hosting world premieres. Sometimes debauched and depraved, sometimes intellectual and inspiring, Moscow's performing arts are always eye-opening. And if you're not into that, there's always *Swan Lake,* which is lovely too.

Communist History

The remains of the Soviet state are scattered all around the city. Monuments remember fallen heroes and victorious battles, while museums attempt to analyse and synthesise the past. Some of the sites evoke whimsy, such as Art Muzeon Sculpture Park, where you can see Lenin and Stalin off their pedestals, or the All-Russia Exhibition Centre, which evokes a Socialist Realist fantasy. Other sites are deadly serious, such as the Gulag History Museum, remembering the millions who suffered in the labour camps. Nowadays, retro is all the rage in the capital's clubs and cafes, which allow their guests to relive the Soviet experience.

Nightlife

Night owls enjoy a dynamic and diverse scene out on the town – not only exclusive clubs, but also bohemian art cafes, underground blues bars, get-down discos and drink-up dives. You don't have to be a high-heeled glamour girl or a deep-pocketed man about town to enjoy the capital by night. Moscow has a club or a cafe for everyone, from nostalgia-rich retro to rocked-out indie. And no matter where you spend the evening, all are invited to gather in the wee hours to watch the sunrise over Moscow's golden domes and silver skyscrapers.

JOHN BORTHWICK / LONELY PLANET IMAGES ©

Why I Love Moscow

By Mara Vorhees, Author

Moscow surprises me every single time, and has done for more than 20 years. The Russian capital never ceases to inspire, confound, disgust or delight me in some unexpected way. This time I was thrilled to see how brave cyclists are taking to the streets and (not unrelated) how drivers have become more conscientious, when previously cars had the right of way, even on the sidewalk!

Over the years, I have witnessed impressive cultural developments in Moscow, including the tantalising restaurant scene, an innovative home-grown fashion industry and the incredible explosion of contemporary art and design. I certainly didn't see any of that coming 20 years ago.

For more about our authors, see p280.

Above: St Basil's Cathedral (p62)

Moscow's Top 10

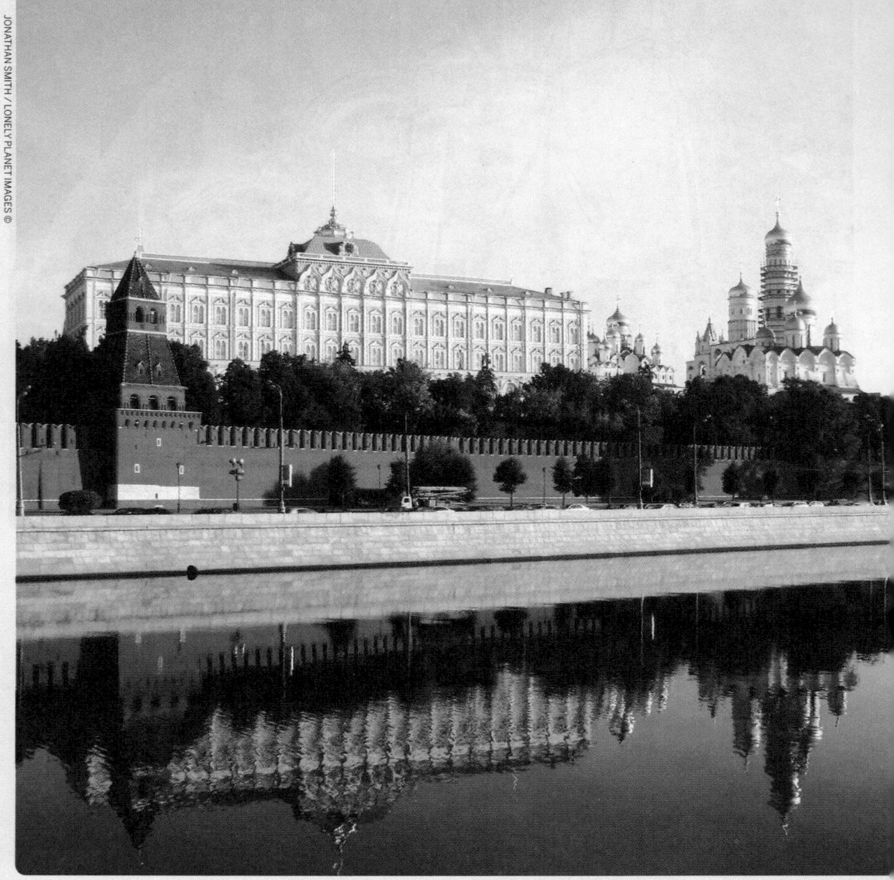

JONATHAN SMITH / LONELY PLANET IMAGES ©

The Kremlin *(p48)*

1 This ancient fortress is the founding site of Moscow and the ultimate symbol of political power in Russia. Within its ancient walls you can admire the artistry of Russia's greatest icon painters, gawk at the treasure trove that fuelled a revolution, shed a tear for Russia's great and tragic rulers and climb the Ivan the Great Bell Tower for an amazing panorama. On your way out, admire the bouquets left by newlyweds and scrutinise the perfect synchronicity of the guards at the Tomb of the Unknown Soldier. GREAT KREMLIN PALACE REFLECTED IN THE MOSCOW RIVER

Kremlin & Kitay Gorod

Red Square *(p62)*

2 Stepping onto Red Square never ceases to inspire: the tall towers and imposing walls of the Kremlin, the playful jumble of patterns and colours adorning St Basil's Cathedral, the majestic red bricks of the State History Museum and the elaborate edifice of GUM, all encircling a vast stretch of cobblestones. Individually they are impressive, but the ensemble is electrifying. Come at night to see the square empty of crowds and the buildings awash in lights. ST BASIL'S CATHEDRAL, RED SQUARE

Kremlin & Kitay Gorod

1

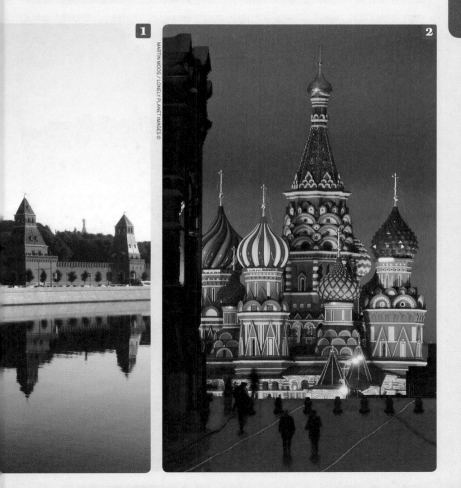

MARTIN MOOS / LONELY PLANET IMAGES ©

2

3

JONATHAN SMITH / LONELY PLANET IMAGES ©

5

JANE SWEENEY / LONELY PLANET IMAGES ©

SERGEY PETROV / SHUTTERSTOCK ©

Shopping at Izmailovo *(p138)*

3 It's a fine line between shopping and fun at the Kremlin in Izmailovo. Cross the footbridge and walk through the tent-roofed gate to enter a Disney-like medieval village, complete with wooden church, whitewashed walls and plenty of souvenir shops. Just as in times of yore, the best shopping is in the trade rows outside the kremlin walls. Wander among the stalls of the sprawling market to find an endless array of traditional handicrafts, as well as art and antiques, Central Asian carpets, Soviet paraphernalia and more. MINIATURE MATRYOSHKA AT A MARKET STALL

Basmanny

Ballet at the Bolshoi *(p85)*

4 After six years and $730 million, the world-famous Bolshoi Theatre finally reopened its doors in 2011. The newly renovated main stage sparkles even brighter than before, with expanded theatre space draped in rich red velour and glittering with newly gilded mouldings. Ever since its opening in 1824, the theatre has offered a magical setting for a spectacle. Nowadays the historic theatre is home to the Bolshoi Ballet – one of the leading ballet companies in the country (and the world).

☆ ***Tverskoy***

Suzdal *(p163)*

5 Gently winding waterways, flower-drenched meadows and dome-spotted skyline make this medieval capital a perfect fairy-tale setting. Under Muscovite rule, Suzdal was a wealthy monastic centre; in the late 17th and 18th centuries, wealthy merchants paid for the construction of 30 charming churches. Suzdal was bypassed by the railway and later protected by the Soviet government, all of which limited development in the area. Nowadays, its main features are its abundance of ancient architectural gems and its decidedly rural atmosphere. SAVIOUR MONASTERY OF ST EUTHYMIUS, SUZDAL

Day Trips from Moscow

Moscow Metro *(p38)*

6 The Moscow metro is at once a history lesson and an art museum (not to mention a pretty efficient form of transportation). Construction started in the 1930s and it continues today. The design of the stations and the direction of the expansion tell a story about Moscow in the 20th and 21st centuries. Even more intriguing is the amazing artwork and architectural design that characterises the stations, many of which are constructed out of granite and marble and adorned with mosaics, bas-reliefs and other detailing. KIEVSKAYA METRO STATION

Tour of the Metro

Tretyakov Gallery *(p123)*

7 The memorable Russian Revival building on Lavrushinsky per is Moscow's largest art museum, covering the span of Russian art history from ancient icons to avant-garde. (Indeed, the Tretyakov's second building on Krymsky val continues further into the 20th century with Supremetism, constructivism and, of course, socialist realism.) The Tretyakov is famed for its impressive collection of wonderful realist paintings by the Peredvizhniki. But the museum also contains show-stopping examples of Russian Revival and art nouveau artwork.

Zamoskvorechie

6

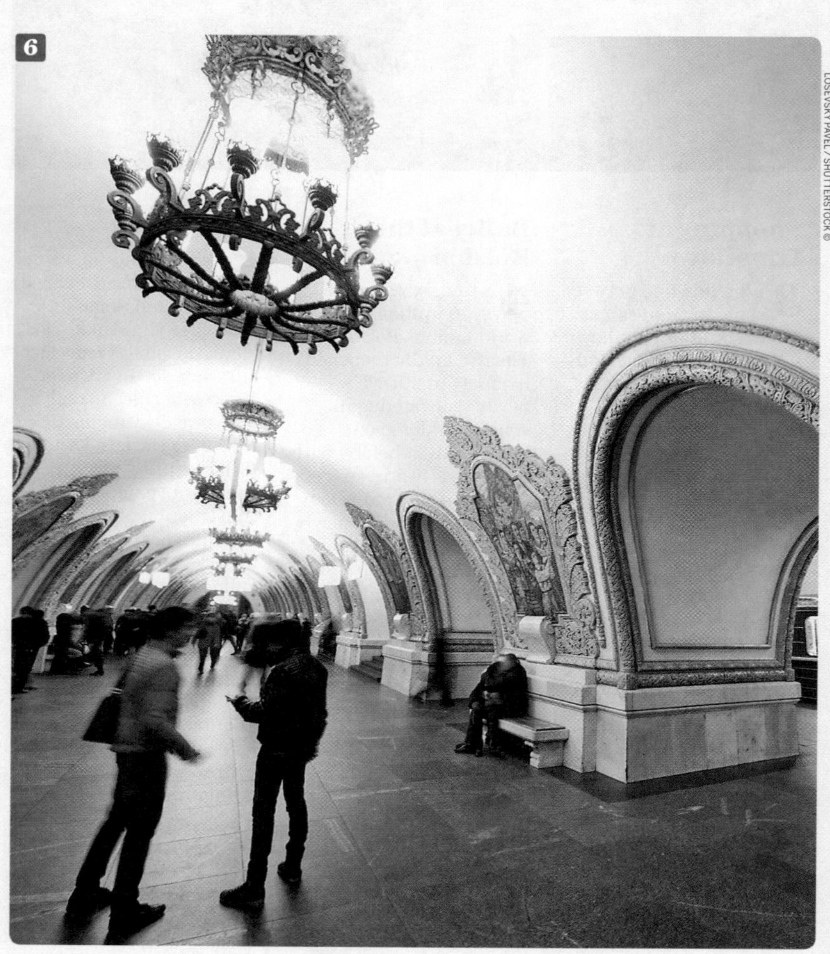

LOSEVSKY PAVEL / SHUTTERSTOCK ©

VLADIMIR ZHURAVLEV / DREAMSTIME ©

JONATHAN SMITH / LONELY PLANET IMAGES ©

Banya at Sanduny Baths *(p85)*

8 What better way to cope with big-city stress than to have it steamed, washed and beaten out of you? The *banya* is a uniquely Russian experience that will leave you feeling clean, refreshed and relaxed. Even in winter, the tension of constant cold is released by the hot, steamy bath, while a beating with birch branches helps to improve circulation. Sanduny is Moscow's oldest bathhouse – a luxurious setting to indulge in this national pastime.

☆ ***Tverskoy***

Moscow River Boat Tours *(p231)*

RICK GERHARTER / LONELY PLANET IMAGES ©

9 Avoid traffic jams, feel the breeze on your face and get a new perspective on the city's most famous sights when you see them from one of the ferry boats that ply the Moscow River. The 90-minute tour provides a wonderful overview of the city, cruising past Novodevichy Convent, Gorky Park, the Cathedral of Christ the Saviour, the Kremlin and Novospassky Monastery. Incidentally, the ferry can also be a useful form of transport from one sight to another. BOAT PASSING CATHEDRAL OF CHRIST THE SAVIOUR

Transport

10

TONY WHEELER / LONELY PLANET IMAGES ©

Pushkin Fine Arts Museum *(p107)*

10 For more than a century, the Pushkin Fine Arts Museum has anchored Moscow's art district, with its impressive collection of European art, spanning the centuries from antiquity to the modern era. The original location – now the main building – houses artefacts from ancient Egypt and Greece, as well as the celebrated paintings of the Dutch masters. Next door, the Gallery of European & American Art of the 19th & 20th Centuries contains exquisite pieces from the world's most celebrated Impressionist and neo-Impressionist painters. PAINTINGS BY GAUGIN, PUSHKIN FINE ARTS MUSEUM

Arbat & Khamovniki

What's New

Red October

The Red October chocolate factory has been reincarnated as the city's hottest art and entertainment centre. The Strelka Institute for Media, Design and Architecture is the centrepiece of the complex, while other factory buildings are being converted into clubs and cafes, art galleries and fashion boutiques. The transformation is ongoing, so the whole place has an edgy, post-industrial vibe that conveys the artistic energy of this creative hotspot. (p126)

Ivan the Great Bell Tower

The bell tower is almost as old as the Kremlin itself, but now you can go inside and climb to the top for incredible views of the surrounding city. (p55)

Great Wooden Palace at Kolomenskoe

Build, demolish, repeat. This amazing piece of architectural whimsy is a painstaking reproduction of Tsar Alexey's 17th-century palace; the original was demolished by Catherine the Great. (p127)

Moscow Planetarium

The Moscow landmark has reopened after 17 years, and it was worth the wait. The revamped facility has a huge stargazing hall and loads of interactive exhibits. (p93)

Gorky Park

The Park of Culture and Leisure is getting a makeover. Now owned by billionaire Roman Abramovich, the place is slated to become a family-friendly urban oasis, free of kiddie rides and other kitsch. (p126)

Kremlin in Izmailovo

The Vernisage Market has always been a drawcard, but now it's housed in a photogenic mock kremlin, complete with church, shops, restaurants and museums. (p138)

Icon Museums

Two new venues showcase this art form, with hundreds of examples from all eras of Russian iconography. Visit the Museum of the Russian Icon (p139) or Dom Ikony on Spiridonovka (p92).

Ostankino TV Tower

The tall tower in the north of Moscow was closed for years, following a fire in 2000. The observation tower is now open, along with a small museum and cafe. (p82)

Cosmonautics Museum

The renovated museum is bigger and better than ever, with a special 50th-anniversary exhibition in honour of Yury Gagarin's flight in space. (p82)

Tsereteli Studio

Apparently Moscow needed somewhere for Zurab Tsereteli to exhibit his work. It comes complete with a shady courtyard crowded with bronze and enamel sculptures. (p95)

Bicycles

Bikes have infiltrated Moscow city streets, whizzing past pedestrians and traffic jams. Rent yours at Gorky Park (p126), Vorobyovy Gory Nature Preserve (p150) or Oliver's Bikes (p230).

For more recommendations and reviews, see **lonelyplanet.com/Moscow.**

Need to Know

Currency
Roubles (R)

Language
Russian

Visas
Nearly all foreigners visiting Russia need a visa to enter. Details of the application process vary (eg costs) depending on where you apply and what kind of visa you need.

Money
ATMs widely available. Credit cards accepted by most hotels and restaurants.

Mobile Phones
Local SIM cards can be used in European and Australian phones; other phones must be set to roaming.

Time
Moscow Time (GMT/USC + four hours)

Your Daily Budget

Budget Less than R1500

- Dorm beds from R700
- Cheap, filling meals at cafeterias for less than R300
- Use student ID (if available) to get cheaper admission tickets to museums

Midrange R1500–R5000

- Double rooms from R2500 at minihotels
- *Prix-fixe* lunch menus for R200–500
- Two-course dinner with a glass of wine R600–1000
- Tickets to any theatre other than the Bolshoi from R500

Top End More than R10,000

- Double rooms start at R8000 and go all the way up
- Two-course meals from R1000
- Bolshoi Theatre tickets from R1000

Advance Planning

Two months before Apply for your visa.

One month before Check the schedule at the Bolshoi and other theatres; reserve your tickets in advance to ensure great seats and avoid language difficulties.

One week before Book any guided tours that you intend to take.

One day before Book a taxi from the airport, if necessary.

Useful Websites

- **Lonely Planet** (www.lonelyplanet.com/moscow) Destination information, hotel booking, traveller forum and more.
- **Expat.ru** (www.expat.ru) Run by and for English-speaking expats living in Moscow. Useful information about real estate, restaurants, children, social groups and more.
- **Moscow Business Telephone Guide** (www.mbtg.ru) A free bilingual phonebook.
- **Way to Russia** (www.waytorussia.net) Written and maintained by Russian backpackers.

WHEN TO GO

Standout seasons to visit Moscow are late spring and early autumn. Summer is also pleasant – though hot – and long hours of sunlight bring out the revellers.

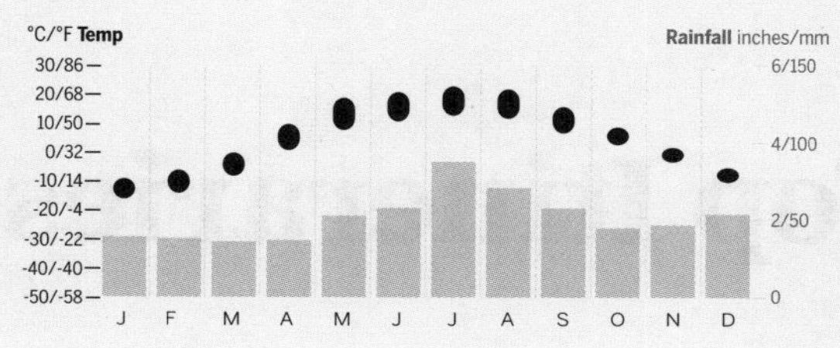

Arriving in Moscow

Airports All three airports are accessible by the convenient **Aeroexpress train** (☎8-800-700 3377; www.aeroexpress.ru; business/standard R550/320) from the city centre. If you wish to take a taxi (p227), book in advance to take advantage of fixed rates offered by most companies (R1000 to R1500).

Train stations Rail riders will arrive at one of the central train stations. All of the train stations are located in the city centre, with easy access to the metro. Alternatively, most taxi companies offer a fixed rate of R300 to R500 for a train-station transfer.

For much more on **arrival**, see p226.

Getting Around Moscow

➡ **Metro** The easiest and cheapest way to get around town. One ride is R28, or buy a multiride card for slightly cheaper fares. Tap your card on the magnetic reader, wait for the green light, and pass through the turnstile. Trains run every few minutes from 6am to 1am.

➡ **Taxi** Can be tricky to flag on the street, but easy to book 30 to 60 minutes in advance by telephone. The dispatcher will call back with the make and number of the car before it arrives to pick you up. Some companies have English-speaking dispatchers.

For much more on **getting around**, see p227.

Sleeping

Advance reservations are highly recommended, especially if you intend to stay at a minihotel or hostel, most of which only have a handful of rooms, which are often booked out. Weekdays (Sunday to Thursday nights) are especially busy due to business travellers.

Moscow has the world's highest average hotel rates. Five-star hotels offer fabulous service and amenities, but you will pay for them. Don't expect much value for your money at midrange hotels. Hostels, on the other hand, often offer friendly faces and loads of services for the price of a dorm bed.

Useful Websites

➡ **Booking.com** (www.booking.com) Often offers the best deals on rooms.

➡ **Moscow Hotels** (www.moscow-hotels.com) Descriptions of rooms and services, plus online booking.

➡ **Moscow Hotels** (www.moscow-hotels.net) Ditto.

For much more on **sleeping**, see p169.

FIVE VISA REQUIREMENTS

Your nearest Russian consulate will have precise details about the requirements for obtaining a visa. But all applicants will need to submit the following:

➡ **Passport** Valid for at least six months beyond your return date.

➡ **Two passport-size (4cm by 4.5cm), full-face photos**

➡ **Completed application form** With entry and exit dates.

➡ **Handling fee** Usually in the form of a company cheque or money order.

➡ **Visa-support letter or letter of invitation** Not required for a transit visa.

For more on **visas**, see p237.

Top Itineraries

Day One

Kremlin & Kitay Gorod (p46)

Arrive at the Kremlin ticket office at 9.30am sharp to reserve your times to enter the **Armoury** and **Ivan the Great Bell Tower**. Dedicate your morning to admiring the amazing architecture, gawking at the gold and gems and climbing the tower for sweeping city views. End your Kremlin visit with a stroll through **Alexander Garden** and a stop to witness the changing of the guard at the **Tomb of the Unknown Soldier**. Exiting Alexander Garden, jump right into the queue on Red Square for **Lenin's Tomb** before it closes at 1pm.

Lunch Have lunch at Bosco Cafe (p70); or at Stolovaya 57 (p70).

Kremlin & Kitay Gorod (p46)

If you eat at Bosco, linger as long as you like, ogling the Kremlin spires and St Basil's domes. If you wish to see what goes on inside the **cathedral**, you can do so after lunch. Otherwise, stroll through the **ancient streets of Kitay Gorod**, discovering the countless **17th-century churches**.

Dinner Dine at a restaurant on ul Petrovka, like Barashka (p79).

Tverskoy (p73)

Get tickets in advance to see a classic opera or a contemporary ballet at the world-famous **Bolshoi Theatre**. Or pamper yourself with a steam at the **Banya at Sanduny**.

Day Two

Khamovniki (p102)

A beautiful 17th-century bell tower is the beacon that will guide you to the historic fortress of **Novodevichy Convent**, which contains nearly five centuries of history. After admiring the art and architecture, head next door to the eponymous cemetery, where many famous political and cultural figures are laid to rest.

Lunch Indulge in a delicious sweet or savoury pie from Stolle (p117).

Dorogomilovo (p147)

Make your way across the river to Kievsky vokzal, where you can hop on board the **ferry** (p231) that cruises the Moscow River. The 90-minute trip takes you past Novodevichy Convent, Gorky Park, the Church of Christ the Saviour, Red October and the Kremlin, before turning around at Novospassky Monastery.

Dinner Sample scrumptious Georgian cuisine at Genatsvale on Arbat (p113).

Arbat (p102)

Imagine you are in a traditional Georgian mountain village – at **Genatsvale on Arbat** it's not so difficult to do, as the restaurant provides the setting, as well as the delectable Georgian fare. After dinner you can stroll along Moscow's most famous street – **the Arbat** – enjoying the talents of buskers and the atmosphere of old Moscow.

Day Three

Zamoskvorechie (p121)

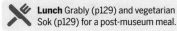

Get an early start to beat the crowds to the **Tretyakov Gallery**. Take your time inspecting the icons, examining the Peredvizhniki, marvelling at the Russian Revival and ogling the avant-garde.

Lunch Grably (p129) and vegetarian Sok (p129) for a post-museum meal.

Zamoskvorechie (p121)

After lunch, stroll over to **Art Muzeon Sculpture Park**, where you can stand eye-to-eye with the Soviet heroes and admire their more whimsical contemporary counterparts. Then head across the street to **Gorky Park** for an afternoon of bicycle riding or boat paddling. At the southern end of the park, **Chaikhona No 1** offers the perfect place to regroup.

Dinner Snag a table on the rooftop terrace at Strelka Bar (p130).

Zamoskvorechie (p121)

The former **Red October** factory is now the city's hottest nightlife spot, jam-packed with eating, drinking and entertainment venues. Let yourself wander, stopping here for drinks, there for dinner, and somewhere else for dessert. Explore the galleries. Rock the bar scene. Have fun.

Day Four

Izmailovo (p138)

Reserve the morning for shopping at the **Vernisage Market**, crammed with souvenir stalls selling everything from silver samovars to Soviet propaganda posters to modern pop-culture matrioshkas. Inside the **Kremlin at Izmailovo**, you can also learn about the art of making vodka (and sample the results) at the **Vodka History Museum**.

Lunch Izmaylovo market is famous for the grilled *shashlyk* (kebabs).

Izmailovo (p138)

For the afternoon, you have booked a tour of **Stalin's Bunker**, hidden away underneath the All-Union stadium. If you're not able to make these arrangements, you can head over to **Izmailovsky Park** for a picnic and a walk in the woods.

Dinner Reserve your table for an *haut russe* feast at Café Pushkin (p96).

Presnya (p90)

End your time in Moscow with an evening at **Pushkin Cafe**, Moscow's best place to sample old-fashioned Russian cuisine. Indulge in a multicourse medley that might include *bliny* (crepes) with caviar, a hearty soup, meat or fish in a rich sauce, and plenty of vodka shots. If you're still standing afterwards, enjoy an after-dinner drink and a fabulous vista from **O2 Lounge** in the Ritz-Carlton Moscow.

If You Like...

Architecture

Ascension Church at Kolomenskoe The first building that put a tent roof on a brick structure, creating a uniquely Russian style. (p127)

Church of the Trinity in Nikitniki An exquisite example of Russian baroque, concealed by hulking grey edifices. (p68)

Cathedral of Christ the Saviour The premier example of Russian Revival, even though it was built at the end of the 20th century. (p111)

Hotel Metropol An art nouveau masterpiece, replete with mosaics, stained glass and wrought iron. (p70)

Narkomfin The quintessential example of constructivist architecture, now in a state of disrepair. (p95)

Gorky House-Museum Shekhtel's whimsical fusion of Russian Revival and art nouveau. (p92)

Russian Literature

Tolstoy Estate-Museum in Khamovniki The Moscow residence of Russia's greatest realist novelist. (p113)

Bulgakov House Long an underground pilgrimage site, and now a cool cafe and literary hangout. (p95)

Gogol House The abode where Gogol spent his final tortured months. (p109)

Pushkin House-Museum A short-term residence for the national bard and his new bride. (p110)

JONATHAN SMITH / LONELY PLANET IMAGES ©

Bust of Lenin, Art Muzeon Sculpture Park, Zamoskvorechie (p126)

Dostoevsky House-Museum The birthplace and childhood home of St Petersburg's most celebrated author. (p78)

Contemporary Art

Garage Centre for Contemporary Culture An exciting contemporary-art venue housed in a former bus depot. (p78)

Winzavod A former wine-bottling facility, now containing Moscow's most prestigious art galleries. (p137)

Multimedia Art Museum Excellent photography and other multimedia exhibits in a newly revamped building. (p112)

Red October A former chocolate factory, now home to bars, cafes and a handful of galleries. (p126)

Bourganov House A working studio that displays the artist's creations as well as some examples from his private collection. (p111)

Tsereteli Studio-Museum A classical mansion filled with enamel artistry and a courtyard crammed with sculptures. (p95)

Moscow Museum of Modern Art An eclectic collection of works by artists from the 20th and 21st centuries. (p75)

Soviet History

Lenin's Tomb Pay your respects to the founder of the Soviet state. (p64)

Art Muzeon Sculpture Park Soviet heroes put out to pasture. (p126)

Bunker-42 A secret underground Cold War communications centre now open for exploration. (p136)

Moscow Metro A monument to socialism and populism. (p38)

All-Russia Exhibition Centre Formerly the USSR Economic Achievements Exhibition. (p82)

Contemporary History Museum Features an excellent selection of propaganda posters, amid other Soviet nostalgia. (p76)

Gulag History Museum A memorial to the victims of the harsh Soviet justice system. (p75)

Charming Churches

Ul Varvarka in Kitay Gorod A tiny street lined with 17th-century churches. (p69)

Upper St Peter Monastery Home of the lovely Cathedral of Metropolitan Pyotr. (p76)

Church of the Small Ascension A 17th-century beauty with whitewashed walls and carved detailing. (p92)

Church of the Nativity of the Virgin in Putinki An elaborate concoction of tent roofs and onion domes. (p76)

Church of St Nicholas in Khamovniki Colourful church of the weavers' guild, which was also the home church of Leo Tolstoy. (p113)

Church of St John the Warrior An 18th-century example of Moscow baroque. (p126)

Church of the Intercession at Fili A memorial church of mysterious origins, as all records were destroyed in a fire. (p150)

Iconography

Tretyakov Gallery The world's best collection of icons, including the revered Holy Trinity by Andrei Rublyov. (p123)

For more top Moscow spots, see

- Eating (p25)
- Drinking & Nightlife (p28)
- Entertainment (p31)
- Shopping (p35)

Annunciation Cathedral in the Kremlin Iconostasis featuring work by Andrei Rublyov, Theophanes the Greek and Prokhor of Gorodets. (p57)

Museum of the Russian Icon Thousands of examples from the private collection of a Russian businessman/iconophile. (p139)

Dom Ikony on Spiridonovka A museum designed to reignite interest in the underappreciated art of iconography. (p92)

Rublyov Museum of Early Russian Culture & Art A small museum on the grounds of the monastery where Rublyov was a monk. (p139)

Parks & Gardens

Alexander Garden A flower-filled space just outside the Kremlin walls. (p61)

MGU Botanical Garden An urban oasis with floral species from three different climate zones. (p137)

Vorobyovy Gory Nature Preserve The wooded hillocks overlooking a picturesque bend in the Moscow River. (p150)

Gorky Park Moscow's most famous green space, now an ideal spot for riverside strolls and bike rides. (p126)

Month by Month

TOP EVENTS

Winter Festival, January

Moscow International Film Festival, June

White Nights, June

Moscow Biennale of Contemporary Art, October

December Nights Festival, December

January

Though January represents the deepest, darkest days of winter, it is a festive month, kicked off by New Year's celebrations in the grandest tradition. Many offices and services are closed for the first week of January.

Winter Festival

An outdoor fun-fest for two weeks in December and January, for those with antifreeze in their veins. Admire the elaborate ice sculptures on Red Square, stand in a crowd of snowmen on ul Arbat and ride the troika at Izmailovsky Park (p138).

February

Maslenitsa marks the end of winter, but it seems premature. Temperatures are cold, hovering around -10°C for weeks. The city still sparkles with snow, and sledders and skiers are in heaven.

Maslenitsa

This fete kicks off Orthodox Lent. Besides bingeing on *bliny* (crepes), the week-long festival features horse-drawn sledges and storytelling clowns. The festival culminates with the burning of a scarecrow to welcome spring. Exact timing depends on the dates of Orthodox Easter.

March

The spring thaw starts at the end of March, when everything turns to mud and slush. It is Moscow's dreariest month: tourists tend to stay away.

International Women's Day

Russia's favourite holiday was founded on 8 March to honour the women's movement. On this day men buy champagne, flowers and chocolates for their better halves – and for all the women in their lives.

Moscow Forum

This contemporary music festival (www.mosforumfest.ru) features avant-garde musicians from Russia and Europe performing at the Moscow Tchaikovsky Conservatory (p101).

Fashion Week in Moscow

The capital's premier fashion event (www.fashionweekinmoscow.com) is the chance for Russia's top designers to show the world their sexiest stuff in the age-old halls of Gostiny Dvor (see p72). The autumn show takes place at the same location in October.

April

The days are blustery but spring is in the air. Moscow residents flock to sights and museums during this season, since there are not too many tourists.

Golden Mask Festival

This festival (www.goldenmask.ru) involves two weeks of performances by Russia's premier drama, opera, dance and musical performers, culminating in a prestigious awards ceremony.

Russian Fashion Week

This fashion event (www.mercedesbenzfashionweekrussia.com) attracts top-name fashion designers to unveil their new collections. The event takes place at the World Trade Centre in April and again in October or November.

May

Spring arrives! Many places have limited hours during the first half of May, due to the public holidays. Nonetheless, it is a festive time, as flowers are blooming and people are celebrating.

May Holidays

From May Day (1 May) to Victory Day (9 May), the first half of the month is a nonstop holiday. While many residents leave town, the city hosts parades on Tverskaya ul, as well as concerts and other events at Park Pobedy (p149).

June

June is the most welcoming month. Temperatures are mild and the days are long and sunny. Girls wear white bows in their hair to celebrate the end of the school year.

Moscow International Film Festival

This week-long event (www.moscowfilmfestival.ru) attracts filmmakers from the US and Europe, as well as the most promising Russian artists. Films are shown at theatres around the city. See also the boxed text, p217.

White Nights

Moscow does not have an official White Nights festival, but the capital still enjoys some 18 hours of daylight in June. Revellers stay out late to stroll in the parks and drink at the many summer terraces and beer gardens.

July

Many Muscovites retreat to their dachas to escape summer in the city. Weather is hot and humid. Hotel prices are down in July and August.

Outdoor Concerts

Though many theatres are closed, the concert calendar is packed, as local and international bands play at outdoor venues. Summer is also the time for outdoor music festivals, such as Nashestvie (www.nashestvie.ru). Estates like Ostankino (p82) and Tsaritsyno (p131) host classical concerts on their grounds.

September

Early autumn is another standout time to be in the capital. The heat subsides and the foliage turns the city splendid oranges, reds and yellows.

City Day

City Day, or *den goroda* in Russian, celebrates Moscow's birthday on the first weekend in September. The day kicks off with a festive parade, followed by live music on Red Square and plenty of food, fireworks and fun.

October

The mild weather and colourful foliage continue in October, though this month usually sees the first snow of the season.

Moscow Biennale of Contemporary Art

This month-long festival (www.moscowbiennale.ru), held in odd-numbered years (and sometimes in different months), has the aim of establishing the capital as an international centre for contemporary art. Venues across the city exhibit works by artists from around the world.

Kremlin Cup

An international tennis tournament (www.kremlincup.ru) held every October at the Olympic Stadium, near the Renaissance Moscow Hotel. Not surprisingly, Russian players have dominated this event in recent years.

December

Short days and long nights keep most people inside for most of the month. But many bundle up to admire the city sparkling in the snow and partake of the city's premier cultural event.

December Nights Festival

Perhaps Moscow's most prestigious music event, this annual festival (www.museum.ru/gmii) is hosted at the Pushkin Fine Arts Museum (p107), with a month of performances by high-profile musicians and accompanying art exhibits.

With Kids

Filled with icons and onion domes, the Russian capital might not seem like an appealing destination for kids, but you'd be surprised. In Moscow, little people will find museums, parks, theatres and even restaurants that cater especially to them.

Kid-Friendly Museums

Most sights and museums offer reduced-rate tickets for children up to 12 or 18 years of age. Kids younger than five are often free of charge. Look out for family tickets.

Art Museums

The Pushkin Fine Arts Museum (p107) and the Museum of Decorative & Folk Art (p77) both have educational centres that allow kids to create their own art.

Moscow Planetarium

The planetarium (p93) has interactive exhibits that allow kids to perform science experiments, taste freeze-dried space food and run around on the surface of the moon.

Central Museum of the Armed Forces

You might not let your children play with guns, but how about climbing around on tanks, trucks and missiles? See p79.

Outdoor Fun

Even in winter, there are plenty of chances to get outside for fresh air and exercise.

Parks

With over 100 parks and gardens, Moscow has plenty of space for kids to let off steam. Discounting formal gardens such as Alexander Garden, most of the parks reviewed in this book include playgrounds. Larger spaces like Gorky Park (p126), Vorobyovy Gory Nature Preserve (p150) and Izmailovsky Park (p138) rent bicycles and paddle boats and such.

River Cruises

Most little ones love a boat ride. This is the perfect way for kids to see the historic sights and appreciate the architecture. On board the river cruiser, there's no need to fight the crowds or linger too long in one place.

Moscow Zoo

Even toddlers will get a kick out of the *detsky zoopark* (p95), with close-up exhibits of animals that they will recognise from their favourite children's story.

Eating Out

Many restaurants host 'children's parties' on Saturday and Sunday afternoons, offering toys, games, entertainment and supervision for kids while their parents eat. See also 'Best for Kids' on p27.

Children's Theatre

Little ones can choose from animal theatre, puppet theatre and musical theatre, not to mention the circus. See also 'Best for Kids' on p34.

Transport

The metro might be fun for kids, but be careful during rush hour, when trains and platforms are packed. Detskoe Taxi (p227) will look out for your kids, offering smoke-free cars and child seats upon request.

Like a Local

There are upwards of 11 million people living in Moscow. Chances are that no matter what you do, there is a local doing it too. But just in case, here are a few tips for doing Moscow the way the Muscovites do it.

Leave the Centre

If you really want to see how (and where) locals live, take a ride out of the centre and into Moscow's sprawling suburbs. This is the idea behind the **Last Stoppers Club** (www.laststoppersclub.com), a friendly group of expats and English-speaking locals who meet the last Saturday of every month to find out what happens at the 'last stop' of a designated metro line. Anybody is welcome: last Saturday, last stop.

Go Out to Lunch

The midday meal is traditionally the largest meal of the day. During Soviet times, it was customary for the employer to provide this meal, so most workers would sit down to a big satisfying lunch in the company canteen. Nowadays, there is no such thing as a free lunch. But Muscovites still tend to take a break from their workday for a filling noontime meal. Most members of the workforce go out to lunch with their colleagues, taking advantage of 'business lunch' specials (usually three courses for a fixed price), affordable all-you-can-eat buffets or modern incarnations of the company cafeteria.

Go Metro

Perhaps you have heard or read the oft-cited statistic: over nine million people ride the Moscow metro every day. Most of them are locals.

Park on a Park Bench

Most Muscovites live in small apartments. They don't have their own bedroom; they don't have a backyard. As a result, the local parks and public places become an extension of their private living space. In any season, park benches are populated by youths drinking beer, lovers engaged in an endless kiss, babushkas pushing strollers, and locals of all ages meeting friends or talking on their mobile phone. If you want to experience Moscow like a local, spend some time in any of the parks in the listings, especially Gorky Park (p126) or Patriarch's Ponds (p93).

Like a Tourist

A recent poll found that 36% of Muscovites regularly attend museums, theatres and concerts in their home city. Locals know that their city is rich with cultural offerings, especially as these institutions keep them coming back with special exhibits and expanded repertoires. So if you want to act like a local, act like a tourist.

SECRET MOSCOW

A Facebook page set up by Muscovites for Muscovites to share their favourite local spots. There's nothing to stop you from checking it out, even if you are not a Muscovite!

For Free

The good news is that Moscow is no longer the most expensive city in the world; the bad news is that it's still pretty darn close. However, budget-minded travellers can find a few bargains if they know where to look.

Art Centres

Most of Moscow's post-industrial art centres are free to enter (though you may pay for individual galleries or special exhibits). Spend an afternoon browsing the galleries and admiring the architectural repurposing.

Churches

Many of Moscow's churches contain amazing iconography and eye-popping frescoes. The Cathedral of Christ the Saviour (p111) in particular feels more like a museum than a church.

Estates

At Kolomenskoe Museum-Reserve (p127) and Tsaritsyno Palace (p131) you pay to enter the museums, but seeing the beautiful grounds and churches costs nothing.

Lenin's Tomb

Don't pay money, just pay your respects. This is one of Moscow's wacky and wonderful things to do (p64).

Moscow Metro

So it's not quite free. But it only costs R28 to ride the metro, which is an amazing amalgamation of art museum, history lesson and mass-transit system (p38).

Free Museums

Gorky House-Museum

Sometimes you do get something for nothing, namely an interesting literary museum and architectural masterpiece (p92).

Museum of the Russian Icon

This is the private collection of a Russian businessman, who has put it on display – for free – in hopes of reigniting interest in this underappreciated art form (p139).

Sakharov Museum

Free political and artistic exhibits, as well as information about the life and times of the dissident (p137).

Free Tours

Walking Tours

Moscow Free Tour (www.moscowfreetour.com) offers a free walking tour, led by knowledgeable and extremely enthusiastic guides.

MOSCOW'S BEST BARGAINS

- **Museum Night** Free admission to museums all over the city (once a year, usually in May).
- **Wi-Fi** At hotels, restaurants and cafes all over Moscow, and almost always free.
- **Student Discounts** Most museums offer them, but sometimes only to students at Russian universities. Bring your student ID just in case.

Eating

In recent years Moscow has blossomed into a culinary capital. Foodies will be thrilled by the dining options, from old-fashioned haute russe *to contemporary fusion. Daring chefs are breaking down stereotypes and showing the world how creative they can be. They're importing exotic ingredients, rediscovering ancient cooking techniques and inventing new ones. And Moscow diners are eating it up. Literally.*

Dining Overview

Moscow is not an obvious choice for culinary travel; but restaurant lovers will have unlimited opportunities to enjoy diverse, delicious cuisine in elaborate and exotic surroundings. Whether sampling Russian specialities or testing out the latest trends, diners in Moscow will have no problem sating their appetites.

In many cases, the dining experience is as much about the setting as about the food. Some thematic restaurants go over the top to re-create an appropriate setting, whether a peasant village or an aristocratic mansion. Other venues offer contemporary cool, with a hip, modern decor to complement an inventive menu. Even Soviet-style cafeterias try to provide an interesting ambience, often reminiscent of Soviet-era dining.

Russian Specialities

Russian cuisine is strongly influenced by climate and class. Long winters and short growing seasons mean the cuisine is dependent on root vegetables such as potatoes and beets. Fresh produce has always been a rarity, so vegetables are often served pickled; fruit is frequently served in the form of compote. According to an old Russian proverb, '*shchi* (cabbage soup) and *kasha* (porridge) is our nourishment'. This saying emphasises the important role played by soups and grains in sustaining generations of peasants through cold, dark winters.

Russia is also famous for its caviar *(ikra),* the snack of tsars and New Russians. The best caviar is black caviar, from osetra or beluga sturgeon. However, due to overfishing, sturgeon populations have declined drastically in recent years, driving up prices and threatening the fish with extinction. The much cheaper and saltier option is red (salmon) caviar. Russians spread it on buttered bread or *bliny* (crepes) and wash it down with a slug of vodka or a toast of champagne.

Moscow Trends

FOREIGN CUISINES

Moscow is mad for sushi. You'll see it on almost every menu, even at traditional Russian restaurants. It seems a little silly (in this city that is thousands of miles from the sea), but it's a good indicator of the strong interest in exotic, international foods. When you tire of beetroot soup and beef stroganoff,

TRY IT, YOU'LL LIKE IT!

- **Seld pod shuby** Try the classic Russian salad, the so-called 'herring in a fur coat', a colourful conglomeration of herring, beets and carrots.
- **Bliny** Russian crepes can be sweet or savoury, rolled up with jam, fruit, cheese, meat or caviar.
- **Pelmeni** Russian comfort food: dumplings stuffed with ground beef and topped with a dollop of sour cream.
- **Solyanka** You'll slurp down this tasty meat soup with salty vegetables and a hint of lemon.

NEED TO KNOW

Opening Hours

Many eateries are open noon to midnight daily, often with later hours on Friday and Saturday. In this book, hours are listed only when they vary from this standard.

Price Guide

$$$	over R1500 per person
$$	R600-1500 per person
$	under R600

Business Lunch

Discounts of up to 25% are sometimes available for dining before 4pm or 5pm. Alternatively, many places offer a fixed-price 'business lunch' during this time. This is a great way to sample some of the pricier restaurants around town.

Booking Tables

Most of the fancier places require booking in advance for dinner, as well as for lunch or brunch on weekends.

Tipping

The standard for tipping in Moscow is 10%, while a slightly smaller percentage is acceptable at more casual restaurants. The service charge is occasionally included in the bill, in which case an additional tip isn't necessary.

Websites

➡ **Restoran.ru** (www.restoran.ru) Restaurant reviews, recipes and other news about food stuff in Moscow.

➡ **Moscow Times** (www.themoscowtimes/guides/dining) Publishes a dining guide that is searchable by cuisine, metro station and other restaurant features.

➡ **Menu.ru** (www.menu.ru) Listings (in Russian) of menus, maps and other logistical info for hundreds of restaurants, bars and clubs.

See also the Menu Decoder, p245.

you'll be able to find excellent European, American and Asian cuisine, as well as the rich cuisines from former Soviet republics such as Georgia, Azerbaijan, Armenia, Uzbekistan and Ukraine.

THEME RESTAURANTS

Because of the explosion of eateries in Moscow, restaurateurs are desperate to entice diners with 'something different' in terms of atmosphere and entertainment. Your dinner experience might include sharing company with farm animals, ogling at the grandeur of 'Versailles' or watching old TV programs in a cosy Soviet-style flat. The effect is sometimes classy, sometimes comical, but always interesting.

VEGETARIANS

The culinary revolution has opened up some new options for vegetarians and vegans. Most restaurants now offer at least one vegetarian choice. Additionally, there is no shortage of Indian and Italian restaurants offering meat-free options. During the 40 days before Orthodox Easter (*post*, in Russian), many restaurants offer a Lenten menu that is happily animal-free. For more suggestions, see p27.

Cooking Courses

If you love Russian food, you can learn to make it yourself. **Taste of Russia** (Map p272; ☎495-916 3708; www.tasterussia.ru; Kazarmenny per 3, bldg 4; 3hr course R2800, market tour R1300; Ⓜ Kurskaya) offers courses in English, as well as market tours, wine tastings and special children's classes. Courses take place in the evening, when you prepare the meal, then eat it together.

Lonely Planet's Top Choices

Delicatessen (p79) An eclectic and innovative assortment of eats.

Café Pushkin (p96) Moscow's long-standing favourite for traditional Russian delights in an aristocratic mansion.

Ragout (p98) A rare combination of inventive cuisine, trendy crowd and affordable prices.

Volkonsky (p97) Come for coffee and fresh-baked goodness in a cosy setting.

Barashka (p79) Sample exotic Azeri fare like lamb stew in a restaurant reminiscent of a cool, contemporary Baku courtyard.

Best by Budget

$

Stolle (p117)

Liudi kak Liudi (p140)

Soup Cafe (p99)

Prime Star (p83)

$$

Correa's (p98)

Botanika (p98)

Khachapuri (p97)

Mari Vanna (p97)

$$$

CDL (p96)

Nedalny Vostok (p99)

Dodo (p79)

Pavilion (p97)

Best by Cuisine

Russian

CDL (p96)

Varvary (p79)

Mari Vanna (p97)

Yolki-Palki (p80)

Ukrainian

Shinok (p98)

Korchma Taras Bulba (p80)

Caucasian

Khachapuri (p97)

Dzhondzholi (p80)

Noev Kovcheg (p140)

Tiflis (p115)

Central Asian

Vostochny Kvartal (p115)

Chaikhona No 1 (p84)

Uzbekistan (p80)

Kishmish (p115)

Best for Vegetarians

Avocado (p141)

Jagannath (p80)

Sok (p129)

Maharaja (p141)

Best for Kids

Starlite Diner (p98)

American Bar & Grill (p141)

Colonna (p116)

Il Patio (p117)

Best Meals with a View

Loft Café (p70)

Pavilion (p97)

Bosco Cafe (p70)

Darbar (p151)

Best Eat Streets

Ulitsa Petrovka (p79)

Spiridonievsky pereulok (p96)

Kamergersky pereulok (p80)

Tverskaya ulitsa (p80)

Best Sunday Brunch

Hotel Baltschug Kempinski (p177)

Correa's (p98)

Scandinavia (p97)

Starlite Diner (p98)

Best Quick Eats

Liudi kak Liudi (p140)

Prime Star (p83)

Grably (p129)

Yolki-Palki (p80)

Best Bakeries

Baltisky Khleb (p83)

Stolle (p97)

Bulka (p98)

Upside Down Cake Co (p99)

Best Over-the-Top Thematic Dining

Shinok (p98)

Turandot (p98)

Uzbekistan (p80)

Genatsvale on Arbat (p113)

Best Soviet Nostalgia

Pavilion (p97)

Mari Vanna (p97)

Petrovich (p142)

Glavpivtorg (p140)

Best for Artsy Eclectic

Art Clumba (p139)

Art Akademiya (p131)

Cafe Mart (p84)

ArteFAQ (p84)

Drinking & Nightlife

Back in the day, the local pub was the ryumochnaya, *which comes from the word* ryumka, *or 'shot'. This was a pretty grim place, serving up* sto grammov *(100 grams), but nothing else. Moscow's drinking possibilities have expanded exponentially (although there are still a few old-school ryumochnye around). Now, drinkers can choose from wine bars, whisky bars, cocktail bars, sports bars, microbreweries and more.*

What to Drink

VODKA

The word 'vodka' is the diminutive of the Russian word for water, *voda,* so it means something like 'a wee drop'. Most often vodka is tipped down in swift shots, often followed by a pickle. Russky Standard and Stolichnaya are two good brands of vodka that are commonly available.

BEER

Many visitors to Moscow are surprised to learn that *pivo* (beer) is the city's most popular alcoholic drink. The market leader is Baltika, which makes no less than 12 excellent brews. If you prefer your beer straight from the tap, head to one of the fine microbreweries.

VODKA, TRADITIONALLY

Vodka is served chilled. One person makes a toast, then everyone clinks glasses and knocks it back. If you need something to wash it down, you can chase with a lemon or a pickle. Women can usually get away with sipping, but men will be scoffed at if they don't drink up – at least the first round. Back in the day, vodka bottles rarely had resealable caps, which meant that once opened it had to be finished. Times have changed, however; these days, finishing off the bottle is not technically required.

SPARKLING WINE

Russians drink sparkling wine, or *Sovietskoe shampanskoe,* to toast special occasions and to sip during intermission at the theatre. It tends to be sickeningly sweet: look for the label that says *sukhoe,* or dry.

KVAS

Kvas is a mildly alcoholic, fermented, rye-bread water. Cool and refreshing, it is a popular summer drink that tastes something like ginger beer. In the olden days it was dispensed on the street from big, wheeled tanks. The *kvas* truck is a rare sight these days, but this cool, tasty treat is available by the bottle.

COCKTAILS

It may not be traditional, but trendy bars and restaurants around Moscow are now offering cocktail menus featuring some pretty exotic elixirs. The capital's official drink may well be the mojito.

TEA & COFFEE

Moscow's cafe scene is huge, with dozens of chains of gourmet coffee houses luring caffeine addicts with frothy cappuccinos and free wi-fi.

Where to Drink

Drinking is a favourite national pastime in Russia, and modern Moscow offers venues for every occasion, mood and season. Former factories have been converted into nightclubs; leafy courtyards contain beer gardens; and communal apartments now serve as cosy cafes. Moscow arguably is the most dynamic and diverse city for drinking and nightlife in the world today. There is not one area of Moscow where bars and pubs are clustered; indeed, the whole city is littered with such establishments, with more opening every day. Pedestrian streets like ul Arbat and Kamergersky per are hot spots for strollers and drinkers. The former Red October chocolate factory in Zamoskvorechie is now packed with diverse drinking establishments.

CLUB-CAFE

Some places are hard to categorise. The full menu would indicate that it's a restaurant, yet many people just come for drinks. There is live music in one hall and some people are dancing, but elsewhere people are playing board games or (gasp!) reading. Such diverse offerings under one roof have sparked a new concept in entertainment: the club-cafe.

NIGHTCLUBS

Moscow nightclubs are notorious for their fast pace and over-the-top excesses. Wild clubs open and close every week, each trying to outdo the last with glitz and glamour. To ensure the clientele enhances the atmosphere, many clubs exercise 'face control', allowing in only a select few patrons. Fortunately, for the rest of us, there are a slew of less discriminating clubs that also have great music, strong drinks and cool vibes. Most clubs start hopping after midnight and keep going until dawn.

SUMMER CAFE

Summer doesn't last very long in Moscow, so locals know they need to take advantage of the warm weather. That's why every restaurant worth going to opens a *letnoe kafe,* or summer cafe. They take over the courtyard, or the sidewalk, or the rooftop – because they know that people want to be outside.

ANYWHERE

Many visitors are surprised by the ubiquity of drinking, with people cracking open a beer anywhere. It is legal to drink in public places, so it's not unusual to see young people sipping beers on the sidewalk or in the park. Consuming alcohol on the metro is prohibited. It is also illegal to consume alcohol at or around national and historic monuments, so you might want to forgo that beer at Park Pobedy.

NEED TO KNOW

Opening Hours

Almost all bars and pubs double as restaurants. As such, they generally have the same opening hours as eating venues (from noon to midnight). Some hot spots stay open for drinking until 5am or 6am, especially on Friday and Saturday nights.

How Much?

Prices for alcohol vary widely, depending on where you are drinking. Expect to pay anywhere from R100 to R300 for a pint of beer or for 50g of vodka. At upscale clubs, cocktails can cost R500 and up.

How to Get Past Face Control

- Dress up: skirts and heels for women, dress pants and leather shoes for men.
- Arrive by car.
- Arrive in a small group, preferably with more men than women.
- Speak English. Foreigners are not as special as they used to be, but they're still pretty special.
- Smile. Show the bouncer that you are going to enhance the atmosphere inside.
- If possible, book a table. Unfortunately, at the more elite clubs this requires a sometimes hefty 'table deposit'.

Face Control

'Face control' is the common practice of denying entry to clubs and bars based on a person's appearance. It's not uncommon for nightlife hot spots to try to create an illusion of exclusivity, but Moscow takes the practice to a new level, arbitrarily barring access to half-full, midrange clubs and bars. The Western egalitarian spirit is easily bruised by the blatancy of face control – the naked appraisal of your jeans, your watch and, yes, your face when you step up to the door. Follow the tips (p29) to avoid rejection; and most importantly, don't take it personally if you are refused entry.

Lonely Planet's Top Choices

Petrovich (p142) Our favourite secret spot. Don't let anyone tell you the Soviet Union wasn't fun (and funny).

Bar Strelka (p130) Artistic atmosphere, creative cuisine and picture-perfect panoramas from the rooftop terrace.

Kvartira 44 (p99) Make yourself at home in the warmly inviting depths of apartment number 44.

Simachyov (p84) From funky decor to fabulous clientele, there's plenty to look at while sipping cocktails at this designer bar.

Best for Gays & Lesbians

Maki Café (p82)

Propaganda (p142)

12 Volts (p84)

Discoteque (p143)

Secret (p143)

Best Summer Cafes

Daddy's Terrace (p131)

Lebedinoe Ozero (p130)

Chaikhona No 1 (p84)

Bar Strelka (p130)

Best Club-Cafes

Art Akademiya (p131)

Cafe Mart (p84)

bilingua (p142)

ArteFAQ (p84)

Best Soviet Throwbacks

Vysotsky (p143)

Ryumochnaya (p100)

Zhiguli Beer Hall (p117)

Glavpivtorg (p140)

Best for Sunset Drinks

City Space Bar (p177)

Sky Lounge (p152)

02 Lounge (p173)

Daddy's Terrace (p131)

Best for Watching Sport

Liga Pap (p143)

Zhiguli Beer Hall (p117)

Kukly Pistolety (p84)

Radio City (p100)

Best for Dancing

Krizis Zhanra (p142)

Garage Club (p132)

Discoteque (p143)

Propaganda (p142)

Real McCoy (p100)

Best by Drink

Beer

Zhiguli (p117)

Glavpivtorg (p140)

Probka (p152)

Maximilian's Brauerei (p117)

Wine

Dissident Vinoteca (p71)

Les Amis de Jean-Jacques (p113)

Art Akademiya (p131)

Cocktails

Tema Bar (p142)

Rolling Stone (p131)

Soho Rooms (p118)

Cafe Didu (p143)

Coffee

Red (p142)

Coffee Bean (p131)

Coffee Mania (p99)

Art Lebedev Cafe (p99)

Gogol-Mogol (p118)

Best for Face-Friendly

Gogol (p84)

Krizis Zhanra (p142)

Tema Bar (p142)

Mayak (p99)

Worst for Face Control

Krysha Mira (p152)

Soho Rooms (p118)

Rolling Stone (p131)

Simachyov (p84)

Imperia Lounge (p101)

JONATHAN SMITH / LONELY PLANET IMAGES ©

Performers at the Nikulin Circus (p224)

Entertainment

Moscow's performing arts are a major drawcard: classical ballet, music and theatre are at the heart of Russian culture. For so long, that's all there was. Happily, times have changed, as directors, conductors and choreographers are unleashing their creative spirits. If you have your heart set on Tchaikovsky, you won't be disappointed, but if you're yearning for something innovative and experimental, you can find that too.

Performing Arts

The classical performing arts are one of Moscow's biggest attractions. Highly acclaimed, professional artists stage productions in elegant theatres around the city, most of which have been recently revamped and look marvellous.

OPERA & BALLET

Nobody has ever complained about a shortage of Russian classics at the opera and ballet. Take your pick from Tchaikovsky, Prokofiev, Rimsky-Korsakov or one of the other great Russian composers, and you are guaranteed to find him on the playbill at one of the major theatres. The choreography and staging of these classics is usually pretty traditional (some might even say uninventive), but then again, that's why they're classics. If you tire of the traditional, keep your eye out for more modern productions and premieres that are also staged by some local companies.

CLASSICAL MUSIC

It's not unusual to see highly talented musicians working the crowds inside the metro stations, often violinists single-handedly performing Vivaldi's *Four Seasons* and flautists whistling away at Mozart or Bach.

NEED TO KNOW

Tickets

The standard way to buy theatre tickets is from a *teatralnaya kassa* (theatre kiosk), several of which are scattered about the city. Or you can get tickets directly from the theatre box offices. You can also make arrangements for tickets through most hotels, but be prepared to pay a significant mark-up.

Prices

The classical performing arts remain an incredible bargain in Moscow, especially if you go anywhere other than the Bolshoi Theatre. Generally speaking, only the most expensive tickets, in front of the orchestra, can compare to what you would pay in the West for a similar performance. Happily, Moscow venues do not charge higher prices for foreigners.

Tickets to the Bolshoi start around R1000, while tickets to other theatres might be half that price. Prices vary widely for contemporary music, but the biggest names (Russian and Western stars) charge big prices.

Theatre Seasons

Unfortunately for summer visitors, many venues are closed between late June and early September.

While it's possible to hear a good show in the metro station, a visit to one of the local orchestra halls is highly recommended.

CONTEMPORARY MUSIC

Live bands and DJs travel from other parts of Russia and all over Europe to perform in Moscow's many clubs and theatres. Summer is an especially busy concert season. Check the schedules of local clubs or look for signs advertising the biggest names.

FILM

Russia boasts a rich cinematic culture, and Moscow is its capital. These days, most theatres show the latest blockbusters from Hollywood, usually dubbed in Russian, as well as the hottest releases from Mosfilm (p150). A few cinemas show more interesting Russian and foreign films, especially during film festivals.

THEATRE

Due to the language barrier, drama and comedy are less alluring prospects for non-Russian speakers than are music and dance. Nonetheless, Moscow has a long theatre tradition, which remains vibrant today. The capital has around 40 professional theatres and countless amateur theatres, staging a wide range of plays.

CHILDREN'S THEATRE

Cultural instruction starts at a young age in Moscow, with many companies and performances geared specifically towards young kids. Performances are almost always in Russian, but at that age the language of fun is universal. Performances are usually in the afternoons.

CIRCUS

The circus has long been a favourite form of entertainment for Russians young and old. Moscow has two separate circuses, putting on glittering shows for Muscovites of all ages. The shows performed by both companies usually mix dance, cabaret and rock music with animals and acrobats.

Spectator Sports

Russia's international reputation in sport is well founded, with athletes earning international fame and glory for their success in ice hockey, gymnastics and figure skating. Now the country is looking forward to the 2014 Winter Olympics, which will take place in Sochi, in southern Russia.

FOOTBALL

The most popular spectator sport in Russia is football (soccer), and five Moscow teams play in Russia's premier league (Vysshaya Liga). Currently, football is enjoying a boom, pumped up by large sponsorship deals with Russian big business. Lukoil has thrown its considerable financial weight behind **FC Spartak** (www.spartak.com), Moscow's most successful team. The team's nickname is Myaso, or 'Meat', because the team was sponsored by the collective farm association during the Soviet era. Since the start of the Russian League in 1990, Spartak has been the Champion of Russia nine times and runner up three times. Nowadays, Spartak plays at Luzhniki Stadium (p118), but construction is underway for a new dedicated stadium, which is expected to be complete in 2013.

Other Moscow teams in the league are two-time winner **FC Lokomotiv** (www.fclm.

ru), three-time winner **Central Sports Club of the Army** (CSKA; www.pfc-cska.com), **FC Dynamo** (www.fcdynamo.ru) and **FC Moskva** (www.fcmoscow.ru).

ICE HOCKEY

After the 2007–08 season, the Russian Super League was disbanded and replaced by the Continental Hockey League (KHL), which also includes non-Russian teams. Moscow's main entrant in the KHL is **HC CSKA** (www.cska-hockey.ru), or the Red Army team. HC CSKA has won more Soviet championships and European cups than any other team in history. They play at the CSKA Arena (p85).

BASKETBALL

Men's basketball has dropped in popularity since its days of Olympic glory in the 1980s. But Moscow's top basketball team, **CSKA** (www.cskabasket.com), still does well in European league play. Often called 'Red Army', CSKA made it to the final four of Euroleague in 2004 and 2005 (undefeated in the regular season), before winning it all in 2006 and again in 2008. Only Real Madrid has won more European basketball titles than CKSA. They play at the CSKA Arena (p85).

Activities

Ice skating, sledding and skiing are forms of entertainment that date back to the prerevolutionary period, and the capital is still a great place to engage in such traditional activities. Young Muscovites have also discovered the appeals of other more Western activities, such as cycling.

ICE SKATING

There's no shortage of winter in Moscow, so take advantage of it. Several indoor and outdoor venues offer the opportunity to rent ice skates and see where all those great Russian figure skaters come from.

SWIMMING & SUNBATHING

If you are interested in swimming laps – as in exercising – you can pay a visit to one of the public pools, which usually have dedicated times for lap-swimming. If you're interested in frolicking in the waves and perhaps soaking up some sun, there are places for that too, such as Serebranny Bor (Silver Forest), a series of lakes and channels on the Moscow River about 20km north of the city centre. Take trolley 65 from Sokol metro station.

CYCLING & IN-LINE SKATING

Cycling has become a popular way to get around Moscow (and avoid traffic jams). The crowded streets are not ideal for bicycles, but the city does offer some opportunities to go off-road.

BANYA

Nothing beats winter like the *banya*. Less hot but more humid than a sauna, the Russian bath sweats out all impurity.

Enter the steam room *(parilka)* naked (yes, the *banya* is normally segregated by gender). Bathers can control the temperature – or at least increase it – by ladling water onto the hot rocks. You might add a few drops of eucalyptus to infuse the steam with scent. Then sit back and watch the mercury rise. To eliminate toxins and improve circulation, bathers beat each other with a bundle of birch branches, known as *veniki* (or you might have a professional do this for you).

When you can't take the heat, retreat. A public *banya* allows access to a plunge pool, usually filled with ice-cold water. The contrast in temperature is invigorating, energising and purifying.

A *banya* is not complete without a table spread with snacks, or at least a thermos of tea. And just when you think you have recovered, it's time to repeat the process. Bathhouses all over the city offer this experience, although the most historic and luxurious is Sanduny Baths.

As they say in Russia, '*s lyokum parom*' (easy steaming).

EASY STEAMING

The dos and don'ts of the *banya:*

➡ **Do** take advantage of the plunge pool (or at least the cold shower, if there is no pool on site). It's important to bring your body temperature back down after being in the *banya*.

➡ **Don't** bother with a bathing suit. Most public *bani* are segregated by gender, in which case bathers steam naked. In mixed company, wrap yourself in a sheet (provided at the *banya*).

➡ **Do** rehydrate in between steams. Tea or even beer are common, but it is also important to drink water or juice.

➡ **Don't** stop at one! Most bathers will return to the *parilka* (steam room) several times over the course of an hour or two.

Lonely Planet's Top Choices

Bolshoi Theatre (p75) Watch the dancers glide across the stage in Moscow's most famous and most historic theatre.

Sanduny Baths (p85) Sweat your stress away at this luxurious *banya*.

Moscow River Cruise (p231) Feel the breeze, avoid the traffic jams and get a new perspective on Moscow's best sights when you see them from the river.

Moscow International House of Music (p132) The contemporary concert hall is an atmospheric place for some musical magic.

Kuklachev Cat Theatre (p152) These playful feline performers will charm cat-lovers and kids.

Fomenko Studio Theatre (p152) Moscow's most innovative drama in a brand-new theatre.

Best for Classical Performing Arts

Tchaikovsky Concert Hall (p100)

Stanislavsky & Nemirovich-Danchenko Musical Theatre (p86)

Moscow Tchaikovsky Conservatory (p101)

Gelikon Opera (p118)

Novaya Opera (p86)

Kremlin Ballet Theatre (p72)

Best for Contemporary Music

Masterskaya (p85)

Chinese Pilot Dzhao-Da (p71)

Rhythm Blues Cafe (p118)

Sixteen Tons (p101)

PirOGI on Maroseyka (p144)

Best Cinemas

Rolan Cinema (p144)

Dome (p132)

Illuzion Cinema (p144)

Dome Cinema (p86)

Best Drama Theatres

Moscow Art Theatre (MKhT; p85)

Taganka Theatre (p144)

Maly Theatre (p87)

Lenkom Theatre (p87)

Satirikon Theatre (p87)

Best for Kids

Obraztsov Puppet Theatre & Museum (p86)

Moscow Children's Musical Theatre (p153)

Durov Animal Theatre (p87)

Nikulin Circus on Tsvetnoy Bulvar (p86)

Best Cultural Events

Golden Mask Festival (p20)

December Nights (p21)

International Tchaikovsky Competition (p101)

Nashestvie (p21)

Moscow International Film Festival (p21)

Best Spectator Sports

FC Spartak (p118)

HC CSKA (p87)

BC CSKA (p87)

Kremlin Cup (p21)

Best Outdoor Activities

Ice skating at Gorky Park (p126)

Bike riding in Neskuchny Garden (p132)

Cruising on the Moscow River (p231)

Hiking in Vorobyovy Gory Nature Preserve (p150)

Best for Getting Wet

Kva-kva Water Park (p87)

Krasnopresnensky Bani (p101)

Luzhniki Sports Palace (p118)

Serabryanny Bor (p33)

Best Folk Shows

Russian Ball at Yar (p85)

Kostroma Dance Company (p82)

Shopping

News flash: Moscow is an expensive city. So don't come looking for bargains. Do come looking for creative and classy clothing and jewellery by local designers; an innovative art scene; high-quality handicrafts, linens, glassware and folk art; and unusual and exotic souvenirs that you won't find anywhere else.

Where to Shop

Whether bartering for trash and treasures at the local markets, practising shop therapy at the mall, or examining the quirky creations at the contemporary art centres, Moscow challenges you to shop till you drop.

MARKETS

We told you not to expect any bargains. But if you're going to find any, it will be at the market, or *rynok*. Moscow's markets used to be pretty sketchy places, where the wares were sold from outdoor stalls in varying degrees of disrepair. Nowadays, most of the interesting markets have been cleaned up, making for a more pleasant shopping experience (though perhaps fewer bargains). Besides the atmospheric food markets (p151 and p130), there are specific markets dedicated to souvenirs (boxed text, p138) and electronics (p153), among others.

SHOPPING MALLS

High-end shopping malls have opened on every corner, including the world's biggest urban mall (so add that to Moscow's list of superlatives). On the outskirts, more cost-conscious shoppers are flocking to mega-malls in search of cheaper goods. Most of the mall stores are international chains that you might find in cities all around Europe.

ART CENTRES

Moscow artists and art dealers have made it easy on their customers, displaying their masterpieces in cool, contemporary art centres, where you can see the works of many artists under one roof (or at least in one block). There are a few small galleries sprinkled about town, but venues like Winzavod (p137) and Red October (p126) have revolutionised the Moscow art scene for both producers and consumers.

FACTORY STORES

There are factories in Moscow (and environs) producing porcelain, glassware, bronze and more. Buy these beautiful, high-quality items straight from the source at the factory stores around town.

Fashion

Beware of sticker shock when you check out the up-and-coming fashion industry in Moscow. A few local designers have blazed a trail, inventing sophisticated and stylish fashions, which you can try on at boutiques around town.

EVENTS

Moscow hosts two major fashion events:

Fashion Week in Moscow (www.fashionweekinmoscow.com) Held at Gostiny Dvor at the end of March and again at the end of October.

Fashion Week Russia (www.mercedesbenzfashionweekrussia.com) Held at the World Trade Centre in April and November.

STREET FASHION

These days most Russians shop at the same stores and wear the same clothes as their counterparts in the West: blue jeans, business suits or anything in between. Of course there are Russian designers catering to the fashion-conscious among the masses, some of whom are very stylish indeed (see p37).

NEED TO KNOW

Opening Hours

Most shops are open from 9am or 10am until 8pm or 9pm. Large shopping centres stay open until 10pm or later. Hours are usually shorter on Sunday, from about noon to 8pm. Hours of operation are indicated in this book only when they differ from the norm.

Customs Regulations

Items more than 100 years old cannot be taken out of the country. Anything vaguely 'arty', such as art, musical instruments, antiques or antiquarian books (meaning those published before 1975) must be assessed by **RosOkhranKultura** (Map p272; ☎495-628 5089; Kitaygorodsky proezd 7, bldg 2; ⌚10am-5pm Mon-Fri; Ⓜ Kitay-Gorod). Bring your item (or a photograph, if the item is large) and your receipt. The bureaucrats will issue a receipt for tax paid, which you show to customs officers on your way out of the country.

FUR

Winter brings out the best or the worst of Russian style (depending on your perspective). Muscovites still see fur as the most effective and fashionable way to stay warm. Some advice from a local fashion connoisseur: 'Your protests that fur is cruel are likely to be met by blank stares and an uncomfortable shifting of feet. Don't come in winter if this offends you.' If you think you might want to do as the Muscovites do when in Moscow, stop by Yekaterina (p87) and pick out a fur hat.

Arts & Crafts

Moscow's prolific craftspeople display their knick-knacks and bric-a-brac at souvenir shops around town, as well as at Izmailovo market. Feel free to haggle, but don't expect prices to decrease more than five or 10%. The selection of arts and crafts is always changing and growing, as craftspeople unleash long-dormant creativity and collectors uncover long-hidden treasures.

WOODWORK

The speciality of Russian craftsmen is painted wooden knick-knacks. It starts with the *matryoshka* (nesting doll) and takes off from there. Traditional wooden dishes and utensils are painted in decorative, floral patterns. This style – called *khokhloma* – is named for its village of origin north of Nizhny Novgorod. Chess sets are available in all varieties of size and style, often with elaborate detailing and historical themes. Painted lacquer boxes – known as *palekh* boxes – are usually black with a colourful, detailed scene. Prices are directly proportionate to the detail and skill with which they are painted.

PORCELAIN

Gzhel, a village about 50km southeast of Moscow, has been known for its pottery since the 14th century, and nobody will leave Russia without forming a decisive opinion about *gzhel* porcelain, those curly white pieces with cobalt blue floral design. More varied patterns – some traditional, some less so– are produced by the Imperial Porcelain Factory out of St Petersburg.

Textiles

Welcome to Calico Moscow. Once famed for its textile industry, the capital still offers bargains on soft, rich linens and woollens.

LINEN

Russia's cool, moist summers and fertile soil are ideal for producing flax, the fibre used to manufacture linen. This elegant, durable fabric is respectfully known in Russia as 'His Majesty Linen'. High-quality linen products such as tablecloths, napkins, bed covers and even clothing are still manufactured in Russia – and prices are lower than their Western counterparts.

WOOL

Pavlovsky-Posad woollen shawls are warm even for Russian weather and their vivid floral designs are bright enough to break the bleak winter monotony.

Lonely Planet's Top Choices

Izmailovo market (p138) A sprawling souvenir market, now in fancy new 'kremlin' digs.

Respublika (p88) Look for books, add some coffee and wile away the rest of the day.

Transylvania (p88) No matter what you like to listen to, you can hear it (and buy it) here.

Ministerstvo Podarkov (p101) An artists' cooperative, selling many clever and quirky items that you always wanted, even though you didn't know they existed.

Tricotage Club (p144) Hand-knit socks, sweaters and gloves, plus more fun fashion.

Best Boutiques

Russkaya Ulitsa (p133)

Bukle (p118)

Odensya dlya Schastya (p145)

Yekaterina (p87)

Best Local Designers

Liudmila Mezentseva (p118)

Valentin Yudashkin (p154)

Denis Simachyov (p88)

Igor Chapurin (p120)

Vassa & Co (p120)

Alena Akhmadullina (p72)

Best for Books

Bookhunter (p144)

Biblio-Globus (p145)

Dom Knigi (p119)

Dom Inostrannoy Knigi (p89)

Best for Art

Artefact Gallery Centre (p119)

Central House of Artists (TsDKh) (p133)

Khudozhestvenny Salon (p73)

M'ARS Contemporary Art Centre (p76)

Best for Handicrafts

Salon Podarkov (p145)

Russian Gift (p100)

Skazka (p120)

Buro Nahodok (p119)

Best for Quirky Gifts

Shaltai-Boltai (p145)

Buro Nahodok (p119)

Karpov Chess (p89)

Russian Bronze (p89)

Best for Sex & Violence

Erotic Museum sex shop (p109)

Factory-Expedition (p146)

Bustier (p88)

Army Store (p120)

Best for Jewellery

K Faberge (p89)

Vladimir Mikhailov (p72)

Podium Concept Store (p88)

Russkie Chasovye Traditsii (p120)

Best for Food & Drink

Yeliseev Grocery (p88)

Chocolate Salon (p119)

Magazin Chai-kofe (p146)

A Korkunov (p146)

Confael Chocolate (p120)

Best for the Home

Vologda Linen (p72)

Russian Embroidery & Lace (p119)

Bel Postel (p145)

Dom Farfora (p88)

Gus-Khrustalny Factory Store (p72)

Best Shopping Malls

GUM (p72)

Evropeysky Shopping Centre (p154)

Okhotny Ryad (p72)

Best Markets

Gorbushka (p153)

Dorogomilovsky (p151)

Danilovsky (p130)

Salon Podarkov (p145)

Kievskaya metro station

Tour of the Metro

The Moscow metro is a marvel of urban design. Every day, as many as nine million people use the metro system – that's more than in New York and London combined. What's more, this transport system marries function and form: many of Moscow's metro stations are marble-faced, frescoed, gilded works of art.

JONATHAN SMITH / LONELY PLANET IMAGES ©

Statues at Belorusskaya metro station

NEED TO KNOW

The Moscow metro runs everyday from 5.30am until 1am. One ride costs R28, although you can purchase a card with multiple rides at discounted rates (eg, 10 rides for R265 or 20 rides for R520). The metro can be uncomfortably crowded at peak times, so the best time to take a tour is Saturday or Sunday morning or any evening after 7.30pm or 8pm.

Komsomolskaya

Start at Komsomolskaya, where the Sokolnicheskaya line intersects with the Ring line (Koltsevaya line). Both lines have stations with the same name: they are named for the youth workers who helped construct the first stations. In the Sokolnicheskaya-line station, look for the Komsomol emblem at the top of the limestone pillars and the majolica-tile panel showing the volunteers hard at work. The Ring-line station has a huge stuccoed hall, the ceiling featuring mosaics of past Russian military heroes, including Peter the Great, Dmitry Donskoy and Alexander Suvorov.

From Komsomolskaya, proceed anticlockwise around the Ring line, getting off at each stop along the way.

Prospekt Mira

Originally named for the nearby MGU Botanical Garden (p136), this station features elegant, white-porcelain depictions of figures planting trees, bringing in the harvest and generally living in harmony.

Novoslobodskaya

Thirty-two stained-glass panels envelop this station in art nouveau artistry. Six windows depict the so-called intellectual professions: architect, geographer, agronomist, engineer, artist and musician. At one end of the central hall is the mosaic *Peace in the Whole World*. The pair of white doves was a later addition to the mosaic, replacing a portrait of Stalin.

Belorusskaya

The ceiling mosaics celebrate the culture, economy and history of Russia's neighbour to the west. The 12 ceiling panels illustrate different aspects of their culture, while the

HISTORY OF THE MOSCOW METRO

When Stalin announced plans for *Metrostroy* (construction of the metro) in the 1930s, loyal communists turned out in droves to lend a hand. Thousands of people toiled around the clock in dire conditions, using pickaxes and spades and hand-pulled trolleys. Some 10,000 members of the Moscow Komsomol (Soviet youth league) contributed their time to building the communist dream.

The first metro line opened on 16 May 1935 at 7am. Thousands of people spent the night at the doors of the station so they might ride the first train on the Sokolniki line (between Park Kultury in the south and Sokolniki in the north). Two additional lines opened in 1938.

Construction continued during the Great Patriotic War, with the opening of two additional lines. Several stations actually served as air-raid shelters during the Siege of Moscow in 1941. The Ring line (Koltsevaya line) opened in the early 1950s.

Khrushchev's tastes were not as extravagant as Stalin's, so later stations employ a uniform, utilitarian design. But the metro continued to expand, and still continues today (as does Moscow itself).

JONATHAN SMITH / LONELY PLANET IMAGES ©

Central hall of Mayakovskaya metro station

floor pattern reproduces traditional Belarusian ornamentation.

Switch here to the green Zamoskvoretskaya line (where the Belarusian theme continues) and travel south.

Mayakovskaya

This is the pièce de résistance of the Moscow metro. The grand-prize winner at the 1938 World's Fair in New York has an art deco central hall that's all pink rhodonite, with slender, steel columns. The inspiring, upward-looking mosaics on the ceiling depict *24 Hours in the Land of the Soviets*. This is also one of the deepest stations (33m), which allowed it to serve as an air-raid shelter during WWII.

Teatralnaya

This station was formerly called Ploshchad Sverdlova in honour of Lenin's right-hand man (whose bust was in the hall). Nonetheless, the station's décor follows a theatrical theme. The porcelain figures represent seven of the Soviet republics by wearing national dress and playing musical instruments from their homeland.

Change here to the blue Arbatsko-Pokrovskaya line.

Ploshchad Revolyutsii

This dramatic station is basically an underground sculpture gallery. The life-sized bronze statues represent the roles played by the people during the revolution and in the 'new world' that comes after. Heading up the escalators, the themes are: carrying out and protecting the revolution, industry agriculture, hunting, education, sport and child rearing. Touch the nose of the border guard's dog for good luck on exams.

Take the Arbatsko-Pokrovskaya line west.

Arbatskaya

This shallow station was damaged by a German bomb in 1941. The station was closed (supposedly permanently) and a parallel line was built much deeper. Service was restored on this shallow line the following decade, which explains the exist-

Moscow Metro Overview

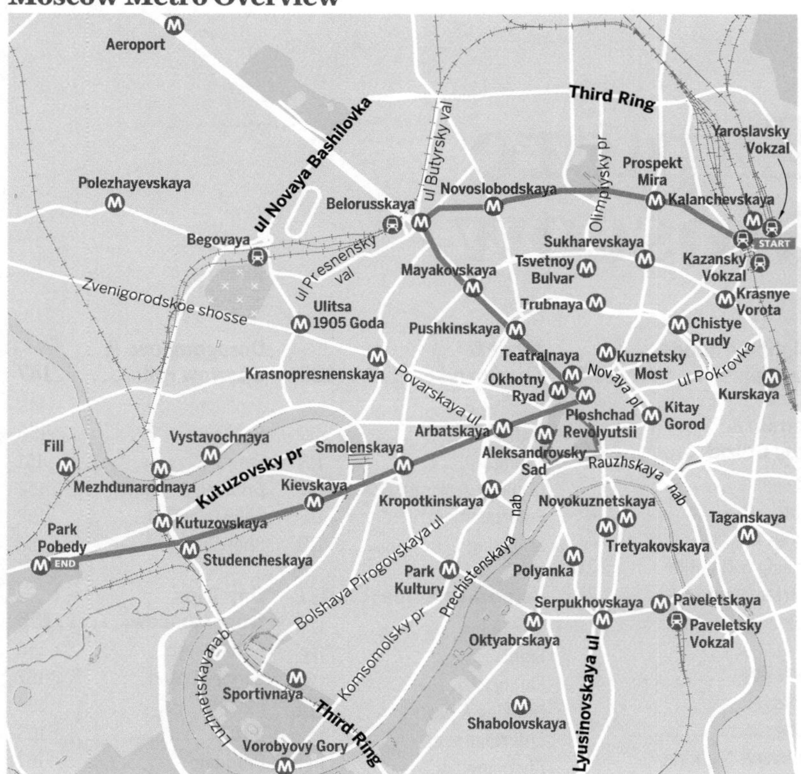

ence of two Arbatskaya stations (and two Smolenskaya stations, for that matter) on two different lines.

At 250m, Arbatskaya is one of the longest stations. A braided moulding emphasises the arched ceiling, while red marble and detailed ornamentation give the whole station a baroque atmosphere.

Kievskaya

This elegant white-marble hall is adorned with a Kyivan-style ornamental frieze, while the frescoed panels depict farmers in folk costume, giant vegetables and other aspects of the idyllic Ukrainian existence. The fresco at the end of the hall celebrates 300 years of Russian-Ukrainian cooperation.

Park Pobedy

This newer station opened after the complex at Poklonnaya Gora (p149), which commemorated the 50th anniversary of the victory in the Great Patriotic War. It is the deepest Moscow metro station, and it has the longest escalators in the world. The enamel panels at either end of the hall (created by Zurab Tsereteli) depict the victories of 1812 and 1945.

JONATHAN SMITH / LONELY PLANET IMAGES ©

Explore Moscow

MOSCOW'S TOP SIGHTS

Cathedral of Christ the Saviour *(p111)*

Neighbourhoods at a Glance

1 Kremlin & Kitay Gorod (p46)

Red Square and the Kremlin are the historical, geographic and spiritual heart of Moscow, as they have been for nearly 900 years. The mighty fortress, the iconic onion domes of St Basil's Cathedral and the granite mausoleum of Vladimir Lenin are among the city's most important historical sights. The surrounding streets of Kitay Gorod are crammed with churches and old architecture. This is the starting point for any visit to Moscow.

2 Tverskoy (p73)

The streets around Tverskaya ul comprise the vibrant Tverskoy district, characterised by old architecture and new commerce. Aside from being a cultural centre (home to 20-plus theatres and concert halls, including the

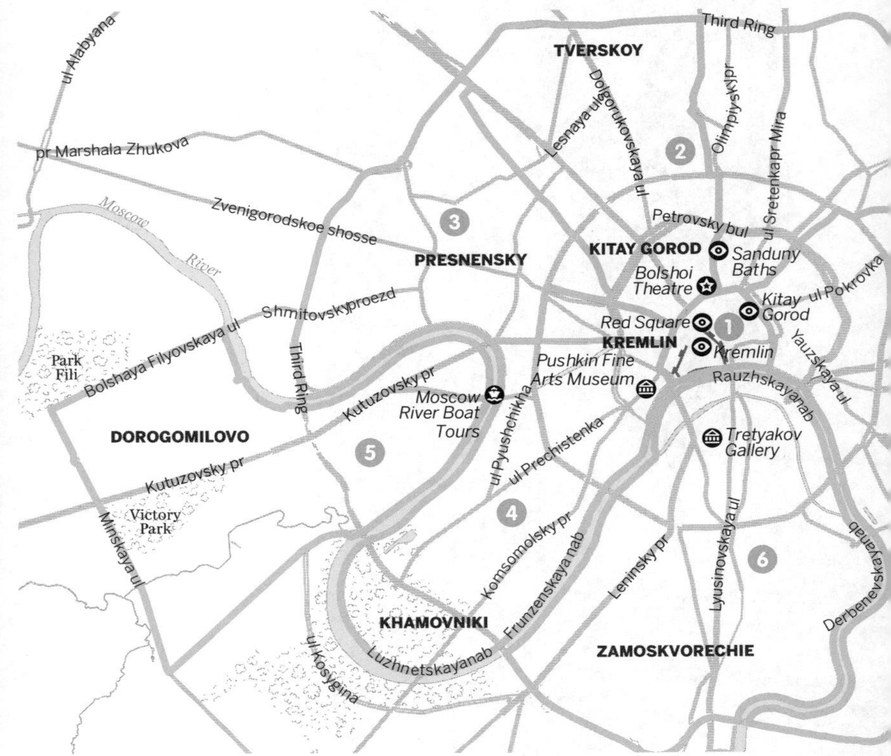

world-famous Bolshoi Theatre), Tverskoy is also the city's liveliest commercial district, its streets lined with restaurants, shops and other venues, such as the Banya at Sanduny.

3 Presnya (p90)

The vast, diverse Presnya district spans the centuries, taking in development from the last three centuries. The district's attractions are equally varied, ranging from traditional venues like the zoo and the planetarium, to the fantastical (and unique) Ice Sculpture Gallery. Presnya is also home to many of Moscow's top restaurants, including the highly lauded Café Pushkin.

4 Arbat & Khamovniki (p102)

These two side-by-side districts are rich with culture. Moscow's most famous street, ul Arbat, is something of an art market, complete with portrait painters, soapbox poets and buskers of all sorts. Nearby, the Khamovniki district positively sparkles, with the Cathedral of Christ the Saviour and Novodevichy Convent at either end. Stretching between these two landmarks, the streets are lined with world-class museums and galleries, including the Pushkin Fine Arts Museum, making Khamovniki one of Moscow's most vibrant art districts.

5 Dorogomilovo & Sparrow Hills (p147)

These outer neighbourhoods are set among the hills in southwestern Moscow. In Dorogomilovo, Poklonnaya Hill is the site of Park Pobedy, filled with museums and monuments dedicated to the Great Patriotic War. Further south, the Sparrow Hills (Vorobyovy Gory) are dominated by Moscow State University.

6 Zamoskvorechie (p121)

Zamoskvorechie – which means 'Beyond Moscow River' – stretches south from the bank opposite the Kremlin. This district is the site of Moscow's traditional art museum, the Tretyakov, as well as the capital's most exciting contemporary art and entertainment complex in the former Red October chocolate factory. Green Gorky Park lies further south along the Moscow River, while two ancient fortress-monasteries guard the city's southern flank.

7 Basmanny & Taganka (p134)

Basmanny and Taganka flank the little Yauza River in the eastern part of the city. The most central part of the Basmanny district is a bustling, atmospheric neighbourhood. Many of the industrial buildings in the outskirts now house innovative postmodern galleries and clubs. South of the Yauza, Taganskaya pl is a monster intersection that can be difficult to navigate, but the district is home to a few unusual sights such as Bunker-42 and the Museum of the Russian Icon, as well as a couple of ancient, atmospheric monasteries.

Kremlin & Kitay Gorod

KREMLIN | KITAY GOROD

Neighbourhood Top Five

❶ Wandering around the grounds of the **Kremlin** (p48) and exploring 500 years of artistic mastery, political power and spiritual devotion; gawking at the royal treasures in the Armoury.

❷ Marvelling at the multicoloured, multidomed spectacle of **St Basil's Cathedral** (p62).

❸ Paying your respects to Vladimir Ilych and other communist leaders at **Lenin's Tomb** (p64).

❹ Discovering the ancient churches hidden among the narrow streets of **Kitay Gorod** (p68).

❺ Watching ballerinas spin across the stage at the **Kremlin Ballet Theatre** (p72).

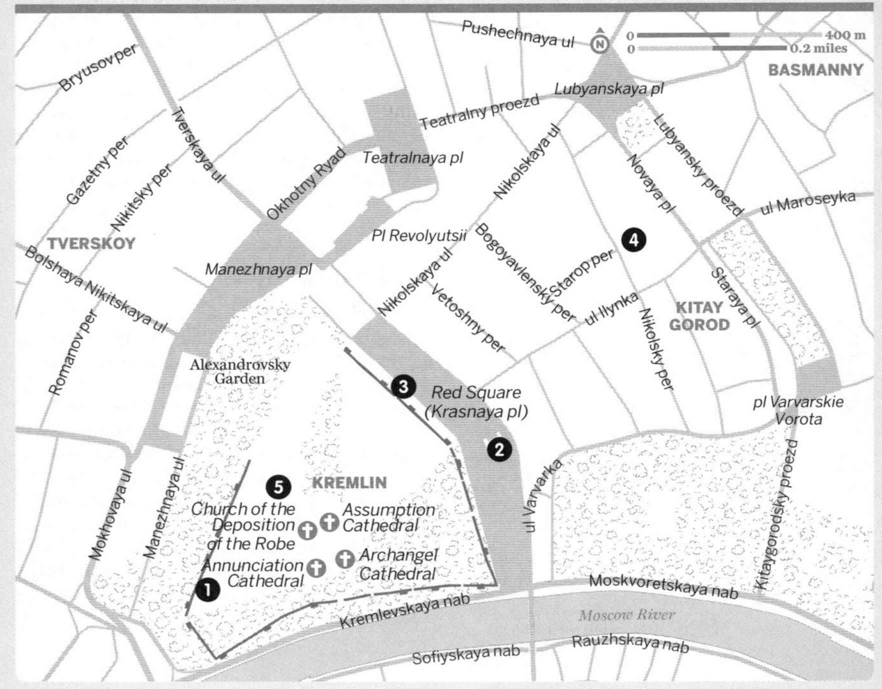

For more detail of this area, see Map p262

Explore: Kremlin & Kitay Gorod

If you have only one day in Moscow, you will probably spend it here. If you have more time, you might spend more than one day here, exploring the churches and museums and viewing at the trappings of power.

The neighbourhood's key attractions are clustered around Red Square and within the walls of the Kremlin. It doesn't matter which of these two you take in first, but try to leave time for both. Your visit to the Kremlin should be planned around admission to the Armoury and Ivan the Great Bell Tower: both require the advance purchase of tickets, which specify the admission times.

Besides being a major tourist attraction, Red Square hosts concerts, festivals, parades and other official events. As a result, the place is often packed with people. Come early in the morning or late in the evening to catch a glimpse of the square when it is sparsely populated, vast and majestic. Travellers with some extra time will enjoy wandering the medieval streets of Kitay Gorod, discovering ancient hidden churches and popping into shops and cafes. It is a welcome change from the hustle and bustle that dominates the Kremlin and Red Square.

Local Life

- **Parks** Muscovites don't often hang out on Red Square, but they do enjoy Alexander Garden, where they stroll among the flower beds, snap photos and (gasp) lounge on the grass.
- **Wedding Parties** The Tomb of the Unknown Soldier is Moscow's top destination for wedding parties, who snap photos and drink champagne while the bride and groom pay their respects by laying flowers on the grave site.
- **Shopping Malls** GUM is too expensive and too touristy for most Muscovites. But plenty of locals hang out, shop and eat in the underground Okhotny Ryad shopping centre on the opposite side of Manezhnaya pl. The shops are less interesting, perhaps, but there is a big food court with many affordable and fast eating options.

Getting There & Away

- **Red Square** At the very centre of Moscow. Three metro lines converge here. Teatralnaya station is on the green Zamoskvoretskaya line; Okhotny Ryad station is on the red Sokolnicheskaya line; and Ploshchad Revolyutsii is on the dark blue Arbatsko-Pokrovskaya line.
- **Lubyanka Sq** The red Sokolnicheskaya line has an eponymous station at Lubyanka.
- **Kitay Gorod** The orange Kaluzhsko-Rizhskaya line and the purple Tagansko-Krasnopresnenskaya line intersect in Kitay Gorod, with both stations sharing the name of the neighbourhood.

Lonely Planet's Top Tip

If you think Red Square is impressive by day, come back at night, when the crowds are gone and the lights cast a magical glow on the historic buildings.

Best Places to Eat

- Loft Café (p70)
- Stolovaya 57 (p70)
- Bosco Cafe (p70)

For reviews, see p70

Best Places to Drink

- Dissident Vinoteca (p71)
- Cup & Cake Cafe (p71)
- Club Che (p71)

For reviews, see p71

Best Soviet Relics

- Lenin's Tomb (p64)
- Lubyanka Prison (p68)
- Central Lenin Museum (p66)

For reviews, see p66

JONATHAN SMITH / LONELY PLANET IMAGES ©

TOP SIGHTS
THE KREMLIN

A 'kremlin' – or fortified stronghold – has existed on this site since Moscow's earliest years. In 1147 Yury Dolgoruky summoned his allies to this spot, which would have been occupied by a wooden fort. When the city became the capital of medieval Rus in the 1320s, the Kremlin served as the headquarters of the Russian Orthodox Church and the seat of the prince. From here Ivan the Terrible unleashed his terror, Napoleon watched Moscow burn, Lenin fashioned the dictatorship of the proletariat, Gorbachev orchestrated *perestroika* (restructuring) and Yeltsin oversaw the New Russia.

The ambition of Ivan III (the Great), who married the Byzantine princess Sofia Paleologue in 1469, was to build a capital that would equal the fallen Constantinople in grandeur, political power, achievements and architecture. In an effort to build the 'Third Rome', Ivan brought from Italy stonemasons and architects, who built new walls, three great cathedrals and other structures. Most of the present-day buildings date from this period.

Although Peter I (the Great) shifted the capital to St Petersburg, the tsars still showed up here for coronations and other celebrations. The fortress was captured by Napoleon, who inflicted serious damage before making his retreat in 1812. But still the ancient symbol endured. The citadel wouldn't be breached again until the Bolsheviks stormed the place in November 1917.

DON'T MISS...

- The view from the top of Ivan the Great
- The gilded cover of the coffin of Tsarevitch Dmitry in Archangel Cathedral
- The Crown of Monomakh in the Armoury

PRACTICALITIES

- Map p262
- www.kreml.ru
- adult/student R350/100, audio guide R200
- 9.30am-5pm Fri-Wed
- M Aleksandrovsky Sad

Visiting the Kremlin buildings and the Armoury is at least a half-day affair. If you intend to visit Ivan the Great Bell Tower, the Diamond Fund or other special exhibits, plan on spending most of the day here. If you are short on time, skip the Armoury and the

Diamond Fund and dedicate a few hours to admiring the amazing architecture and historic buildings around Sobornaya pl (Cathedral Sq), the central square within the Kremlin walls.

Entrance Towers

The **Kutafya Tower** (Кутафья башня), which forms the main visitors' entrance today, stands apart from the Kremlin's west wall, at the end of a ramp over the Alexander Garden. The ramp was once a bridge over the Neglinnaya River and used to be part of the Kremlin's defences; this river has been diverted underground, beneath the Alexander Garden, since the early 19th century. The Kutafya Tower is the last of a number of outer bridge towers that once stood on this side of the Kremlin.

From the Kutafya Tower, walk up the ramp and pass through the Kremlin walls beneath the 1495 **Trinity Gate Tower** (Троицкая башня), the tallest of the Kremlin's towers at 80m. Right below your feet were the cells for prisoners in the 16th century.

Government Buildings

The lane to the right (south), immediately inside the Trinity Gate Tower, passes the 17th-century **Poteshny Palace** (Потешный дворец), where Stalin lived. The yellow palace was built by Tsar Alexey Mikhailovich and housed the first Russian theatre. Here, Tsar Alexey enjoyed various comedic performances. In keeping with conservative Russian Orthodox tradition, however, after the shows he would go to the *banya* (Russian bathhouse), then attend a church service to repent his sins.

The bombastic marble, glass and concrete **State Kremlin Palace** (Государственный кремлёвский дворец), built between 1960 and 1961 for Communist Party congresses, is now also known as the Kremlin Ballet Theatre (p72). North of the State Kremlin Palace is the 18th-century **Arsenal**, commissioned by Peter the Great to house workshops and depots for guns and weaponry. An unrealised plan at the end of the 19th century was to open a museum of the Napoleonic Wars in the Arsenal. Now housing the Kremlin Guard, the building is ringed with 800 captured Napoleonic cannons.

The offices of the president of Russia, the ultimate seat of power in the modern Kremlin, are in the yellow, triangular former **Senate** building, a fine 18th-century neoclassical edifice, east of the Arsenal. Built in 1785 by architect Matvei Kazakov, it was noted for its huge cupola. In the 16th and 17th centuries this area was where the boyars (high-ranking Russian nobles) lived. Next to the Senate is the 1930s **Supreme Soviet** (Верховный Совет) building.

NO BAGS ALLOWED

Before entering the Kremlin, deposit bags at the left-luggage office, beneath the Kutafya Tower in Alexander Garden.

The Kremlin has been open to tourists since 1955.

TICKETS

The main ticket office is in Alexander Garden, just off Manezhnaya ul. The ticket to the 'Architectural Ensemble of Sobornaya pl' covers entry to all five church-museums, as well as the Patriarch's Palace. It does not include Ivan the Great Bell Tower, the Armoury or the Diamond Fund Exhibition. In any case, you can and should buy tickets for Ivan the Great and the Armoury here.

The director of the Kremlin museums is Elena Gagarina, the daughter of Yury Gagarin.

A DAY AT THE KREMLIN

Only at the Kremlin can you see 800 years of Russian history and artistry in one day. Enter the ancient fortress through the Trinity Gate Tower and walk past the impressive Arsenal, ringed with cannons. Past the Patriarch's Palace, you'll find yourself surrounded by white-washed walls and golden domes. Your first stop is **Assumption Cathedral 1** with the solemn fresco over the doorway. As the most important church in prerevolutionary Russia, this 15th-century beauty was the burial site of the patriarchs. The **Ivan the Great Bell Tower 2** now contains a nifty multimedia exhibit on the architectural history of the Kremlin. The view from the top is worth the price of admission. The tower is flanked by the massive **Tsar Cannon & Bell 3**.

In the southeast corner, **Archangel Cathedral 4** has an elaborate interior, where three centuries of tsars and tsarinas are laid to rest. Your final stop on Sobornaya pl is **Annunciation Cathedral 5**, rich with frescoes and iconography.

Walk along the Great Kremlin Palace and enter the **Armoury 6** at the time designated on your ticket. After gawking at the goods, exit the Kremlin through Borovitsky Gate and stroll through the Alexander Garden to the **Tomb of the Unknown Soldier 7**.

TOP TIPS

➡ **Lunch** There are no eating options. Plan to eat before you arrive or stash a snack.

➡ **Lookout** After ogling the sights around Sobornaya pl, take a break in the park across the street, which offers wonderful views of the Moscow River and points south.

MARA VORHEES

Tomb of the Unknown Soldier
Visit the Tomb of the Unknown Soldier honouring the heroes of the Great Patriotic War. Come at the top of the hour to see the solemn synchronicity of the changing of the guard.

Assumption Cathedral
Once your eyes adjust to the colourful frescoes, the gilded fixtures and the iconography, try to locate *Saviour with the Angry Eye*, a 14th-century icon that is one of the oldest in the Kremlin.

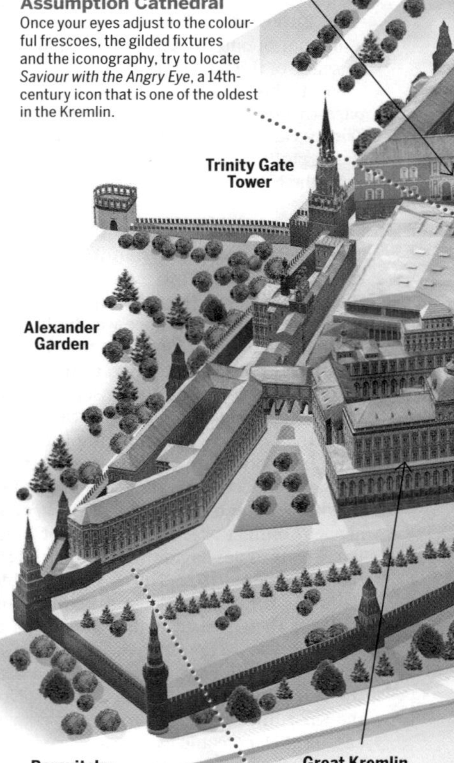

KREMLIN PRESS OFFICE

Armoury
Take advantage of the free audio guide to direct you to the most intriguing treasures of the Armoury, which is chock-full of precious metalworks and jewellery, armour and weapons, gowns and crowns, carriages and sledges.

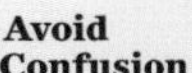

Avoid Confusion

Regular admission to the Kremlin does *not* include Ivan the Great Bell Tower. But admission to the bell tower *does* include the churches on the Kremlin grounds.

MARA VORHEES

Ivan the Great Bell Tower

Check out the artistic electronic renderings of the Kremlin's history, then climb 137 steps to the belfry's upper gallery, where you will be rewarded with super, sweeping vistas of Sobornaya pl and beyond.

Borovitsky Tower

Use the entrance at Borovitsky Tower if you intend to skip the churches and visit only the Armoury or Diamond Fund.

7

2

Patriarch's Palace

1

3

5

4

Sobornaya pl

Moscow River

Tsar Cannon & Bell

Peer down the barrel of the monstrous Tsar Cannon and pose for a picture beside the oversized Tsar Bell, both of which are too big to serve their intended purpose.

MARA VORHEES

Annunciation Cathedral

Admire the artistic mastery of Russia's greatest icon painters– Theophanes the Greek and Andrei Rublyov – who are responsible for many of the icons in the deesis and festival rows of the iconostasis.

KREMLIN PRESS OFFICE

Archangel Cathedral

See the final resting place of princes and emperors who ruled Russia for more than 300 years, including the visionary Ivan the Great, the tortured Ivan the Terrible and the tragic Tsarevitch Dmitry.

Patriarch's Palace

This **palace** (Патриарший дворец) was mostly built in the mid-17th century for Patriarch Nikon, whose reforms sparked the break with the Old Believers. The palace contains an exhibit of 17th-century household items, including jewellery, hunting equipment and furniture. From here you can access the five-domed **Church of the Twelve Apostles** (Церковь двенадцати апостолов), which has a gilded wooden iconostasis and a collection of icons by the leading 17th-century icon painters.

The highlight of the Patriarch's Palace is perhaps the ceremonial **Cross Hall** (Крестовая палата), where feasts for the tsars and ambassadors were held. From the 18th century the room was used to produce *miro* (a holy oil used during church services, which contains over 30 herbal components); the oven and huge pans from the production process are on display.

Now quiet, the palace in its heyday was a busy place. Apart from the Patriarch's living quarters, it had huge kitchens, warehouses and cellars stocked with food, workshops, a school for high-born children, offices for scribes, dormitories for those waiting to be baptised, stables and carriage houses.

The Patriarch's Palace often holds **special exhibits**, which can be visited individually, without access to the other buildings on Sobornaya pl.

Assumption Cathedral

On the northern side of Sobornaya pl, with five golden helmet domes and four semicircular gables facing the square, the **Assumption Cathedral** (Успенский собор) was the focal church of prerevolutionary Russia and the burial place of most of the heads of the Russian Orthodox Church from the 1320s to 1700. A striking 1660s fresco of the Virgin Mary faces Sobornaya pl, above the door once used

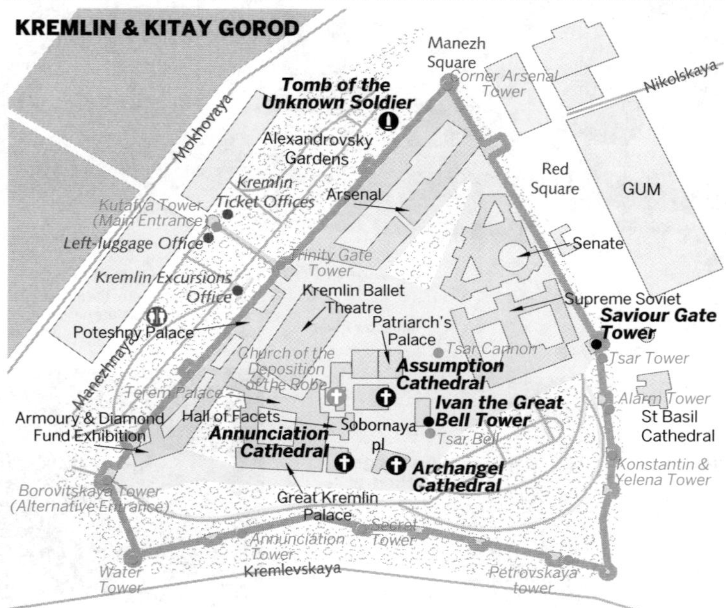

Inside Assumption Cathedral

for royal processions. If you have limited time in the Kremlin, come straight here. The visitors' entrance is at the western end.

In 1470 Russian architects Krivtsov and Myshkin were commissioned by Ivan the Great to replace the old dilapidated cathedral, which dated from 1326. As soon as the ceiling was put up, one of the walls collapsed. During Soviet times, history books said this calamity was the result of bad handiwork, but today revisionist history indicates that an earthquake caused the collapse. Either way, Krivtsov and Myshkin lost their jobs, and Italian architect Aristotle Fioravanti was given a crack at it. After the foundation was completed, Fioravanti toured Novgorod, Suzdal and Vladimir to acquaint himself with Russian architecture. His design is a more spacious version of the Assumption Cathedral (p159) at Vladimir, with a Renaissance twist.

In 1812 French troops used the cathedral as a stable; they also looted 295kg of gold and over five tonnes of silver from here, but much of it was recovered. The church closed in 1918. According to some accounts, in 1941, when the Nazis were on the outskirts of Moscow, Stalin secretly ordered a service in the cathedral to protect the city from the enemy. The cathedral was officially returned to the Church in 1989, but it now operates as a museum.

The interior of the Assumption Cathedral is unusually bright and spacious, full of warm golds, reds and blues. The west wall features a scene of the Apocalypse, a favourite theme of the Russian

The first stone structures in the Kremlin were built in the 1330s at the behest of Ivan 'Moneybags' Kalita. Only the Church of the Saviour's Transfiguration survived into the 20th century, but it was demolished by Stalin approximately 600 years after it was built.

STAND ON CEREMONY

Every Saturday at noon from April to October, the Presidential Regiment shows up on Sobornaya pl for a ceremonial procession, featuring some very official-looking prancing and dancing, both on foot and on horseback. The price of admission to the Kremlin allows access to the demonstration. Otherwise, on the last Saturday of the month, the demonstration is repeated for the masses at 2pm on Red Square.

In 1812 French troops used Assumption Cathedral as a stable.

KREMLIN TOURS

Let the professionals show you around the Kremlin:

Kremlin Excursion Office (Map p262; ☎495-697 0349; www.kremlin.museum.ru; Alexander Garden; Ⓜ Alexandrovsky Sad) Make arrangements in advance for the 'One Day at the Kremlin' tour.

Capital Tours (Map p262; www.capitaltours.ru; ul Ilyinka 4; adult/child R1550/750; ⏲2-5pm; Ⓜ Ploshchad Revolyutsii) Departing from the tour office in Gostinny Dvor every day that the Kremlin is open. Price includes admission.

Moscow Mania (www.mosmania.com; adult/child R600/300) Led by an archaeologist who participated in an excavation of the Kremlin in 2007. Advance arrangements required.

Church in the Middle Ages. The pillars have pictures of martyrs, considered to be the pillars of faith. Above the southern gates there are frescoes of Yelena and Constantine, who brought Christianity to Greece and the south of Russia. The space above the northern gate depicts Olga and Vladimir, who brought Christianity to the north.

Most of the existing murals on the cathedral walls were painted on a gilt base in the 1640s, with the exception of three grouped together on the south wall: *The Apocalypse (*Апокалипсис*), The Life of Metropolitan Pyotr (*Житие Митрополита Петра*)* and *All Creatures Rejoice in Thee (*О тебе радуется*)*. These are attributed to Dionysius and his followers, the cathedral's original 15th-century mural painters. The tombs of many leaders of the Russian Church (metropolitans up to 1590, patriarchs from 1590 to 1700) are against the north, west and south walls.

Near the south wall is a tent-roofed wooden throne made in 1551 for Ivan the Terrible, known as the **Throne of Monomakh**. Its carved scenes highlight the career of 12th-century Grand Prince Vladimir Monomakh of Kiev. Near the west wall there is a shrine with holy relics of Patriarch Hermogen, who was starved to death during the Time of Troubles in 1612.

The **iconostasis** dates from 1652, but its lowest level contains some older icons. The 1340s *Saviour with the Angry Eye (*Спас Ярое око*)* is second from the right. On the left of the central door is the *Virgin of Vladimir (*Владимирская Богоматерь*)*, an early-15th-century Rublyov school copy of Russia's most revered image, the *Vladimir Icon of the Mother of God (*Владимирская икона Богоматери*)*. The 12th-century original, now in the Tretyakov Gallery (p123), stood in the Assumption Cathedral from the 1480s to 1930. One of the oldest Russian icons, the 12th-century red-clothed *St George (*Святой Георгий*)* from Novgorod, is by the north wall.

The original icons of the lower, local tier are symbols of victory brought from Vladimir, Smolensk, Veliky Ustyug and other places. The south door was brought from the Nativity of the Virgin Cathedral (p163) in Suzdal.

Church of the Deposition of the Robe

This delicate single-domed **church** (Церковь Ризположения), beside the west door of the Assumption Cathedral, was built between 1484 and 1486 in exclusively Russian style. It was the private chapel of the heads of the Church, who tended to be highly suspicious of such people as Italian architects.

Originally an open gallery or porch surrounded the church; it was later removed and the church was connected with the Great Kremlin Palace for the convenience of the tsars. The interior walls, ceilings and pillars are covered with

17th-century frescoes. It houses an exhibition of 15th- to 17th-century woodcarvings.

Ivan the Great Bell Tower

With its two golden domes rising above the eastern side of Sobornaya pl, the **Ivan the Great Bell Tower** (Колокольня Ивана Великого; ☎495-697 0349; www.belltower.lagutin.ru; admission R500; ⏲10am, 11:15am, 1:30pm, 2:45pm) is the Kremlin's tallest structure – a landmark visible from 30km away. Before the 20th century it was forbidden to build any higher than this tower in Moscow.

Its history dates back to the Church of Ioann Lestvichnik Under the Bells, built on this site in 1329 by Ivan I. In 1505 the Italian Marco Bono designed a new belfry, originally with only two octagonal tiers beneath a drum and a dome. In 1600 Boris Godunov raised it to 81m.

The building's central section, with a gilded single dome and a 65-tonne bell, dates from between 1532 and 1542. The tent-roofed annexe, next to the belfry, was commissioned by Patriarch Filaret in 1642 and bears his name.

Ivan the Great is the site of the Kremlin's newest exhibit, a multimedia presentation of the **architectural history** of the complex. Using architectural fragments and electronic projections, the exhibit illustrates how the Kremlin has changed since the 12th century. Special attention is given to individual churches within the complex, including several churches that no longer exist.

The 45-minute tour ends with a **137-step climb** to the top of the tall tower, yielding an amazing (and unique!) view of Sobornaya pl, with the Church of Christ the Saviour and the Moskva-City skyscrapers in the distance.

The price of a ticket to Ivan the Great includes admission to the other churches (not the Armoury), so you don't have to buy an additional ticket to the Kremlin grounds.

Tsar Cannon & Bell

North of the bell tower is the 40-tonne **Tsar Cannon** (Царь-пушка). It was cast in 1586 by the blacksmith Ivan Chokhov for Fyodor I, whose portrait is on the barrel. Shot has never sullied its 89cm bore and certainly not the cannonballs beside it, which are too big even for this elephantine firearm.

Beside (not inside) the bell tower stands the world's biggest bell, a 202-tonne monster that has never rung. An earlier version, weighing 130 tonnes, fell from its belfry during a fire in 1701 and shattered. Using these remains, the current **Tsar Bell**

In 1600, Boris Godunov increased the height of Ivan the Great Bell Tower from 60m to 81m. Local legend says that this was a public works project designed to employ the thousands of people who had come to Moscow during a famine, but historical documents contradict the story, as the construction apparently did not coincide with a famine. The height was probably increased so that the belfry could also serve as a watch tower.

SPECIAL EXHIBITS

In addition to the permanent architectural exhibit inside Ivan the Great Bell Tower, temporary exhibits from the Kremlin collections are held on the ground floor of the Assumption Belfry.

Under Orthodox law, Ivan's fourth marriage disqualified him from entering the church proper, so he had the southern gallery of the Annunciation Cathedral converted into the Archangel Gabriel Chapel, from where he could watch services through a grille.

(Царь-колокол) was cast in the 1730s for Empress Anna Ivanovna. The bell was cooling off in the foundry casting pit in 1737 when it came into contact with water, causing an 11-tonne chunk to break off. One hundred years later, the architect Montferrand took the damaged bell out of the pit and put it on a pedestal. The bas-reliefs of Empress Anna and Tsar Alexey, as well as some icons, were etched on its sides.

Archangel Cathedral

The **Archangel Cathedral** (Архангельский собор) at the southeastern corner of Sobornaya pl was for centuries the coronation, wedding and burial church of tsars. It was built by Ivan Kalita in 1333 to commemorate the end of the great famine, and dedicated to Archangel Michael, guardian of the Moscow princes. By the turn of the 16th century it had fallen into disrepair and was rebuilt between 1505 and 1508 by the Italian architect Alevisio Novi. Like the Assumption Cathedral, it is five-domed and essentially Byzantine-Russian in style. However, the exterior has many Venetian Renaissance features, notably the distinctive scallop-shell gables and porticoes.

The tombs of all Muscovy's rulers from the 1320s to the 1690s are here, bar one (the absentee is Boris Godunov, whose body was taken out of the grave on the order of a 'False Dmitry' and buried at Sergiev Posad in 1606). The bodies are buried underground, beneath the 17th-century sarcophagi and 19th-century copper covers. Tsarevitch Dmitry (a son of Ivan the Terrible), who died mysteriously in 1591, lies beneath a painted stone canopy. It was Dmitry's death that sparked the appearance of a string of impersonators, known as False Dmitrys, during the Time of Troubles. Ivan's own tomb is out of sight behind the iconostasis, along with those of his other sons, Ivan (whom he killed) and Fyodor I (who succeeded him). From Peter the Great onwards, emperors and empresses were buried in St Petersburg, the exception being Peter II, who died in Moscow and is here.

Some 17th-century murals were uncovered during restorations in the 1950s. The south wall depicts many of those buried here; on the pillars are some of their predecessors, including Andrei Bogolyubsky, Prince Daniil and Alexander Nevsky.

Hall of Facets & Terem Palace

Named for its Italian Renaissance stone facing, the **Hall of Facets** (Грановитая палата) was designed and built by Marco Ruffo and Pietro Solario between 1487 and 1491, during the reign of Ivan the Great. Its upper floor housed the tsars' throne room, the scene of banquets and ceremonies. Access to the Hall of Facets was via an outside staircase from the square below. During the Streltsy Rebellion of 1682, several of Peter the Great's relatives were tossed down the exterior **Red Staircase**, so called because it ran red with their blood. (It's no wonder that Peter hated Moscow and decided to start afresh with a new capital in St Petersburg.) Stalin destroyed the staircase, but it was rebuilt in 1994.

The hall is 500 sq metres, with a supporting pillar in the centre. The walls are decorated with gorgeous murals of biblical and historical themes, although none are original. Alas, the building is closed to the public, although some special tours with Patriarshy Dom Tours (p231) allow access.

The 16th- and 17th-century **Terem Palace** (Теремной дворец) is the most splendid of the Kremlin palaces. Made of stone and built by Vasily III, the palace's living quarters include a dining room, living room, study, bedroom and small chapel. Unfortunately, the palace is closed to the public, but you can glimpse its cluster of 11 golden domes and chequered roof behind and above the Church of the Deposition of the Robe.

Annunciation Cathedral

Annunciation Cathedral

The **Annunciation Cathedral** (Благовещенский собор), at the southwest corner of Sobornaya pl, contains the celebrated icons of master painter Theophanes the Greek (Feofan Grek in Russian).

Vasily I built the first wooden church on this site in 1397. Between 1484 and 1489, Ivan the Great had the Annunciation Cathedral rebuilt to serve as the royal family's private chapel. Originally the cathedral had just three domes and an open gallery around three sides. Ivan the Terrible, whose tastes were more elaborate, added six more domes and chapels at each corner, enclosed the gallery and gilded the roof.

Many murals in the gallery date from the 1560s. Among them are *Capture of Jericho* in the northern porch, *Jonah and the Whale* in the northern arm of the gallery, and the *Tree of Jesus* on its ceiling. Other frescoes feature ancient philosophers such as Aristotle, Plutarch, Plato and Socrates holding scrolls inscribed with their own wise words. Socrates' scroll reads: 'No harm will ever come to a good man. Our soul is immortal. After death the good shall be rewarded and the evil punished'. Plato's says: 'We must hope God shall send us a heavenly Teacher and a Guide'.

The small central part of the cathedral has a lovely jasper floor. The 16th-century frescoes include Russian princes on the north pillar and Byzantine emperors on the south, both with Apocalypse scenes above them.

CAMERA SHY

Photography is not permitted inside the Armoury or in any of the buildings on Sobornaya pl (Cathedral Sq).

During the reign of Peter the Great all craftspeople, goldsmiths and silversmiths were sent to St Petersburg, and the Armoury became a mere museum storing the royal treasures.

ANNUNCIATION CATHEDRAL

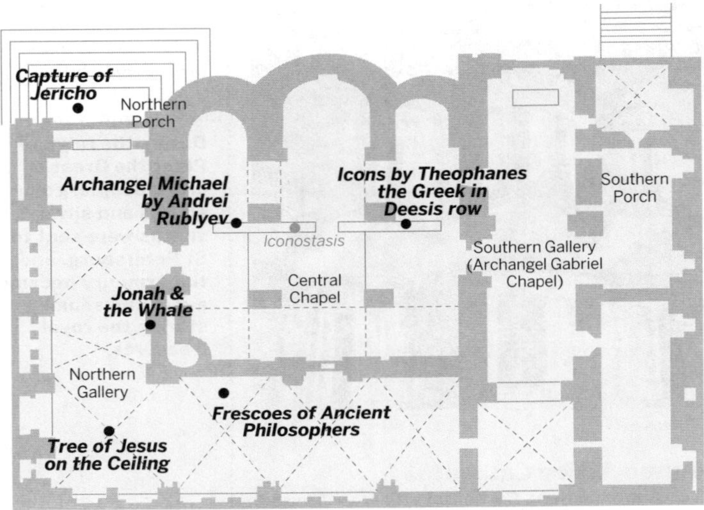

But the cathedral's real treasure is the iconostasis, where in the 1920s restorers uncovered early-15th-century icons by three of the greatest medieval Russian artists. It was most likely Theophanes who painted the six icons at the right-hand end of the biggest row of the six tiers of the iconostasis. From left to right, these are the Virgin Mary, Christ Enthroned, St John the Baptist, the Archangel Gabriel, the Apostle Paul and St John Chrysostom. Theophanes was a master of portraying pathos in the facial expressions of his subjects, setting these icons apart from most others.

The third icon from the left, Archangel Michael, is ascribed to Andrei Rublyov, who may also have painted the adjacent St Peter. Rublyov is also reckoned to be the artist of the first, second, sixth and seventh (and probably the third and fifth) icons from the left of the festival row, above the deesis (biggest) row. The seven icons at the right-hand end are attributed to Prokhor of Gorodets.

The basement of Annunciation Cathedral holds a permanent exhibit on the **archaeology of the Kremlin** – an appropriate place, as this is actually a remnant of the 14th-century church that previously occupied this site. On display are hundreds of artefacts – glassware, ceramics, tools and woodworks – that were excavated from Borovitsky Hill in the 1960s and 1970s. Archaeologists found around 30 'treasure troves', which included silver jewellery and coins dating to medieval times.

Great Kremlin Palace

Housing the Armoury and much more, the 700-room **Great Kremlin Palace** (Большой кремлёвский дворец) was built between 1838 and 1849 by architect Konstantin Thon as an imperial residence for Nicholas I. It is now an official residence of the Russian president, used for state visits and receptions. However, unlike Russian tsars, the president doesn't have living quarters here.

The huge palace incorporates some of the earlier buildings such as the Hall of Facets, Terem Palace and several chapels. Although vast, the building has never received great praise, being criticised as 'barrack-like' and 'pretentious'. Several ceremonial halls are named after saints, including St George, St Vladimir, St Andrew, St Catherine and St Alexander. St George's Hall is mainly used for state awards ceremonies, while major international treaties are signed in St Vladimir's Hall. To save you the trouble, the Great Kremlin Palace (apart from the Armoury) is closed to tourists, except those on an official state visit. From time to time Patriarshy Dom Tours (p231) brings tourists here.

Armoury

The **Armoury** (Оружейная палата; adult/student R700/250; ⌚10am, noon, 2.30pm, 4.30pm; Ⓜ Aleksandrovsky Sad) dates back to 1511, when it was founded under Vasily III to manufacture and store weapons, imperial arms and regalia for the royal court. Later it also produced jewellery, icon frames and embroidery.

To this day, the Armoury still contains plenty of treasures for ogling, and remains a highlight of any visit to the Kremlin.

The exhibit starts upstairs; your ticket will specify a time for entry. A one-hour audio guide points out some of the highlights in each room. Here's what you'll find:

Room 1 Gold and silver objects from the 12th to the 17th centuries, many of which were crafted in the Kremlin workshops. The most ornate designs were reserved for religious objects such as icon covers, gospels, censers and chalices – most crafted from the finest gold and encrusted with precious jewels.

Room 2 The renowned Easter eggs made from precious metals and jewels by St Petersburg jeweller Fabergé. The tsar and tsarina traditionally exchanged these gifts each year at Easter. Most famous is the Grand Siberian Railway egg, with gold train, platinum locomotive and ruby headlamp, created to commemorate the completion of the Moscow–Vladivostok line.

Rooms 3 and 4 Armour, weapons and more armour and more weapons. Don't miss the helmet of Prince Yaroslav, the chainmail of Boris Godunov and the sabres of Minin and Pozharsky.

Room 5 Gifts proffered by visiting ambassadors. Each piece of gold or silver was yet another reason why the average peasant trying to coax some

The obelisk in Alexander Garden was originally a monument to commemorate the House of Romanovs. In 1918 it had a dramatic change in mission when it was redesignated the Monument to Revolutionary Thinkers, in honour of those responsible for the spread of communism in Russia.

CHANGING OF THE GUARD

Every hour on the hour, the guards of the Tomb of the Unknown Soldier perform an perfectly synchronized ceremony to change the guards on duty.

The Tomb of the Unknown Soldier contains the remains of one soldier who died in December 1941 at Km 41 of Leningradskoe sh – the nearest the Nazis came to Moscow.

life out of a mouldy seed might get a little miffed. Ignoring the plight of the masses, you can enjoy the skill of the craftspeople who made these items.

Room 6 Coronation dresses of 18th-century empresses (Empress Elizabeth, we're told, had 15,000 other dresses). Other 'secular' dress is also on display, including an impressive pair of boots that belonged to Peter the Great. The robes of the churchmen are equally elaborate.

Room 7 Contains the joint coronation throne of boy tsars Peter the Great and his half-brother Ivan V (with a secret compartment from which Regent Sofia prompted them), as well as the 800-diamond throne of Tsar Alexey, Peter's father. The gold Cap of Monomakh, jewel-studded and sable-trimmed, was used for two centuries at coronations.

Room 8 Only the best royal harnesses and equestrian gear.

Room 9 Centuries' worth of royal carriages and sledges line the aisles. Look for the sleigh in which Elizabeth rode from St Petersburg to Moscow for her coronation, pulled by 23 horses at a time – about 800 in all for the trip.

Diamond Fund of Russia

If the Armoury hasn't sated your lust for diamonds, there are more in the separate **Diamond Fund Exhibition** (Алмазный фонд России; www.almazi.net; admission R500; ⏲10am-1pm, 2-5pm Fri-Wed) in the same building. The fund dates back to 1719, when Peter the Great established the Russian Crown treasury. The bulk of the

ARMOURY

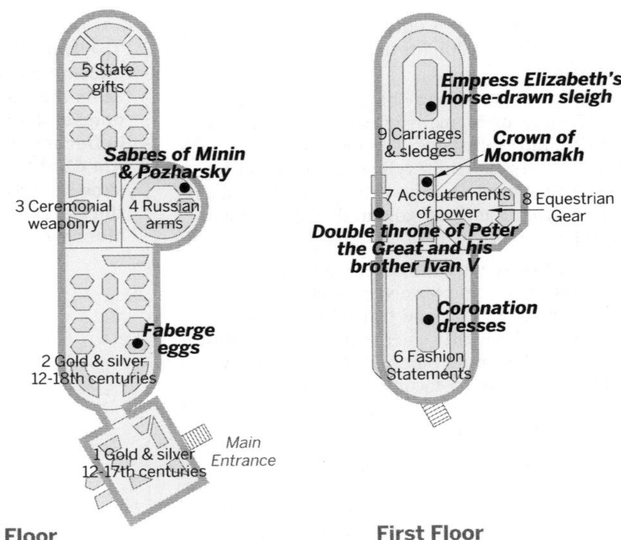

Crowns on display in the Kremlin Armoury

exhibit is gemstones and jewellery garnered by tsars and empresses, including the 190-carat diamond given to Catherine the Great by her lover Grigory Orlov. The Great Imperial Crown, encrusted with 4936 diamonds, was the coronation crown of Catherine the Great and successive rulers.

Alexander Garden

The first public park in Moscow, **Alexander Garden** (Александровский сад) sits along the Kremlin's western wall. Colourful flower beds and impressive Kremlin views make it a favourite strolling spot for Muscovites and tourists alike. Back in the 17th century, the Neglinnaya River ran through the present gardens, with dams and mills along its banks. When the river was diverted underground, the garden was founded by architect Osip Bove, in 1821.

The **Tomb of the Unknown Soldier** (Могила неизвестного солдата) at its north end is a kind of national pilgrimage spot, where newlyweds bring flowers and have their pictures taken. The inscription reads: 'Your name is unknown, your deeds immortal.' There's an eternal flame, and other inscriptions listing the Soviet hero cities of WWII – those that withstood the heaviest fighting – and honouring 'those who fell for the motherland' between 1941 and 1945. South of the tomb, a row of red urns contains earth from the 'hero cities'.

GETTING TICKETS TO THE ARMOURY

Visitors are allowed to enter the Armoury only at specified times (10am, noon, 2:30pm and 4:30pm). Tickets go on sale 45 minutes prior to each session. Try to be at the ticket window when the sales begin, as they sell a limited number of tickets for each entry time.

The Diamond Fund is managed by the Ministry of Finance, which retains a monopoly on the mining and sale of precious stones. As such, the collection includes many magnificent raw diamonds, some in excess of 300 carats.

TIM MAKINS / LONELY PLANET IMAGES ©

TOP SIGHTS
RED SQUARE

The first time you set foot on Red Square (Krasnaya pl) is a guaranteed awe-striker. For starters, the vast rectangular stretch of cobblestones, surrounded by architectural marvels, is jaw-droppingly gorgeous. In fact, in old Russian '*krasny*' was the word for 'beautiful', and it does live up to the original meaning of its name. Further, it evokes an incredible sense of import to stroll across a place where so much of Russian history unfolded.

Red Square used to be a market square adjoining the merchants' area in Kitay Gorod. It has always been a place where occupants of the Kremlin chose to congregate, celebrate and castigate for all the people to see. Back in the day, Red Square was the top spot for high-profile executions such as that of the Cossack rebel Stepan Razin in 1671 and the Streltsy (the mutinous palace guard) in 1698. Soviet rulers chose Red Square for their military parades, and nowadays it's the location for concerts, festivals and cultural events.

DON'T MISS...

- St Basil's Cathedral
- Lenin's Tomb
- State History Museum

PRACTICALITIES

- Красная площадь
- Krasnaya pl
- M Ploshchad Revolyutsii or Okhotny Ryad

Red Square is closed to traffic, which means the square is filled with tourists, bridal parties and business people snapping photos and marvelling at their surroundings. From Manezhnaya pl (Okhotny Ryad metro station), enter Red Square through the **Resurrection Gate**, with its twin red towers topped by green tent spires. The first gateway, built in 1680, was destroyed because Stalin thought it an impediment to the parades and demonstrations held in Red Square. This exact replica was built in 1995. Through the gateway is the bright **Chapel of the Iverian Virgin**, originally built in the late 18th century to house the icon of the same name.

St Basil's Cathedral

At the southern end of Red Square, framed by the massive facades of the Kremlin and GUM, stands the icon of Russia: **St Basil's Cathedral** (Собор Василия Блаженного; www.saintbasil.ru; adult/student R250/50; ⏲11am-5pm). This crazy confusion of colours, patterns and shapes is the culmination of a style that is unique to Russian architecture. Before St Basil's, this style of tent roofs and onion domes had been used to design wooden churches.

In 1552 Ivan the Terrible captured the Tatar stronghold of Kazan on the feast of Intercession. He commissioned this landmark church, officially the Intercession Cathedral, to commemorate the victory. From 1555 to 1561 architects Postnik and Barma created this masterpiece, which would become the ultimate symbol of Russia.

The cathedral's apparent anarchy of shapes hides a comprehensible plan of nine main chapels. The tall, tent-roofed tower in the centre houses the namesake Church of the Protecting Veil of the Mother of God. The four biggest domes top four octagonal-towered chapels: the Church of Sts Cyprian & Justina, Church of the Holy Trinity, Church of the Icon of St Nicholas the Miracle Worker, and the Church of the Entry of the Lord into Jerusalem. Finally, there are four smaller chapels in between. Each chapel was consecrated in honour of an event or battle in the struggle against Kazan.

Legend has it that Ivan had the architects blinded so that they could never build anything comparable. This is a myth, however, as records show that they were employed a quarter of a century later (and four years after Ivan's death) to add an additional chapel to the structure.

The interior is open to visitors. Besides a small exhibition on the cathedral itself, it contains lovely frescoed walls and loads of nooks and crannies to explore. A few highlights:

Church of St Vasily the Blessed The northeastern chapel on the first floor contains the colourful crypt of its namesake saint, one of the most revered in Moscow.

Church of the Holy Trinity The 16th-century *Icon of the Old Testament Trinity* in the third tier of the iconostasis is among the oldest and most esteemed pieces of artwork in the cathedral.

Church of St Varlaam of Khutyn The Vision of Acolyte Tarasy is an unusual icon that dates to 16th-century Novgorod.

Church of the Entry of the Lord into Jerusalem Above the northern entrance, you can see the scar left by a shell that hit the wall in October 1917.

Church of St Gregory of Armenia Check out the impressive hanging candelabrum decorated with multicoloured enamel.

Out front of St Basil's is the **statue of Kuzma Minin and Dmitry Pozharsky**, one a butcher and the other a prince, who together raised and led

Red Square is a modern-day misinterpretation of an old name. In old Russian, *krasny* meant 'beautiful'. So the landmark Krasnaya ploshchad was originally called 'beautiful square' not 'red square'.

PHOTO OP

Red Square empties out at night, but this is when the square is most atmospheric. The Kremlin towers and St Basil's domes, illuminated by floodlights and set against the night sky, create a spectacular panorama (even better in person than on a postcard).

The official name of St Basil's Cathedral is the Intercession Cathedral, or Pokrovsky sobor. The misnomer 'St Basil's' actually refers only to the extra northeastern chapel. It was built over the grave of the barefoot holy fool Vasily (Basil) the Blessed, who predicted Ivan's damnation.

the army that ejected occupying Poles from the Kremlin in 1612. Up the slope is the round, walled **Place of Skulls**, where Peter the Great executed the Streltsy.

Lenin's Tomb

Although Vladimir Ilych requested that he be buried beside his mum in St Petersburg, he still lies in state at the foot of the Kremlin wall, receiving visitors who come to pay their respects to the founder of the Soviet Union. The **embalmed leader** (Мавзолей Ленина; www.lenin.ru; admission free; ⏲10am-1pm Tue-Thu, Sat & Sun) has been here since 1924 (apart from a retreat to Siberia during WWII). See the boxed text, p195, to learn how he keeps his waxy demeanour.

After trouping past the embalmed figure, emerge from the mausoleum and inspect the Kremlin wall, where other communist heavy hitters are buried:

Josef Stalin The second general secretary, successor to Lenin.

Leonid Brezhnev The fourth general secretary, successor to Khrushchev.

Felix Dzerzhinsky The founder of the Cheka (forerunner of the KGB).

Yakov Sverdlov A key organiser of the revolution and the first official head of the Soviet state.

Andrei Zhdanov Stalin's cultural chief and the second most powerful person in the USSR immediately after WWII.

Mikhail Frunze The Red Army leader who secured Central Asia for the Soviet Union in the 1920s.

Inessa Armand Lenin's rumoured lover. She was a respected Bolshevik who was the director of Zhenotdel, an organisation fighting for equality for women within the Communist Party.

John Reed The American author of *Ten Days that Shook the World,* a first-hand account of the revolution.

State History Museum

At the northern end of the square, the **State History Museum** (Государственный исторический музей; www.shm.ru; Krasnaya pl 1; adult/student R250/80, audio guide R130; ⏲10am-6pm Wed-Sat & Mon, 11am-8pm Sun) has an enormous collection covering the whole Russian empire from the time of the Stone Age. The first rooms have cases filled with archaeological artefacts from the Paleolithic and Neolithic eras, and the Bronze and Iron ages.

The exhibits about **medieval Rus** are excellent, with two rooms dedicated to the Mongol invasions and the consolidation of the Russian state. The 2nd floor is dedicated to the **Imperial period**, with exhibits featuring personal items of the various tsars, furnishings and decoration from the palace interiors and various artworks and documents from the era. Specific rooms are dedicated to the rule of various tsars. There is an informative exhibit dedicated to the War of 1812 and its after-effects. An unexpected highlight is the exhibit addressing the expansion of the Russian Empire by examining the growing network of roads and how people travelled.

The State History Museum building, dating from the late 19th century, is itself an attraction – each room is in the style of a different period or region, some with highly decorated walls echoing old Russian churches.

Inside GUM department store

GUM

The elaborate 240m facade on the northeastern side of Red Square, **GUM** (ГУМ; www.gum.ru; Krasnaya pl 3; ⏲10am-10pm) is a bright, bustling shopping mall with hundreds of fancy stores and restaurants. With a skylight roof and three-level arcades, the spectacular interior was a revolutionary design when it was built in the 1890s, replacing the Upper Trading Rows that previously occupied this site.

Kazan Cathedral

The original **Kazan Cathedral** (Казанский собор; Nikolskaya ul 3; admission free; ⏲8am-7pm, evening service 8pm Mon) was founded on this site at the northern end of Red Square in 1636 in thanks for the 1612 expulsion of Polish invaders (for two centuries it housed the Virgin of Kazan icon, which supposedly helped to rout the Poles). From here, the archpriest Avvakum Petrov led the opposition against Patriarch Nikon's 17th-century reforms of the Russian Orthodox Church, thus starting the separatist Old Believers' (p141) movement.

Three hundred years later, the cathedral was completely demolished, allegedly because it impeded the flow of celebrating workers in May Day and Revolution Day parades. The little church that occupies the site today is a 1993 replica.

From 1953 to 1961, Lenin shared his tomb with Stalin. In 1961, during the 22nd Party Congress, the esteemed and by then ancient Bolshevik Madame Spiridonova announced that Vladimir Ilych had appeared to her in a dream, insisting that he did not like spending eternity with his successor. With that, Stalin was removed and given a place of honour immediately behind the mausoleum.

LEFT LUGGAGE FOR LENIN

Before joining the queue at the northwestern corner of Red Square, drop your bag at the left-luggage office in the State History Museum, as you will not be allowed to take it with you into Lenin's mausoleum.

Pronounced *goom*, the initials GUM originally stood for the Russian words for 'State Department Store'. When it was privatised in 2005, the name was officially changed to 'Main Department Store'. Fortunately, the words for 'state' and 'main' both start with a Russian 'G', so the acronym remains the same.

SIGHTS

KREMLIN HISTORIC SITE

See p48.

LENIN'S TOMB HISTORIC SITE

See p64.

ST BASIL'S CATHEDRAL CHURCH

See p62.

RED SQUARE HISTORIC SITE

See p62.

STATE HISTORY MUSEUM MUSEUM

See p64.

KAZAN CATHEDRAL CHURCH

See p65.

ARCHAEOLOGICAL MUSEUM MUSEUM

Map p262 (Музей археологии Москвы; www.mosmuseum.ru; Manezhnaya pl 1; admission R60; ⌚10am-5.30pm Tue-Sun; Ⓜ Okhotny Ryad) An excavation of Voskresensky most (Voskresensky Bridge), which used to span the Neglinnaya River and commence the road to Tver, uncovered coins, clothing and other artefacts from old Moscow. The museum displaying these treasures is situated in a 7m-deep underground pavilion that was formed during the excavation itself. The entrance is at the base of the Four Seasons Hotel Moskva.

CENTRAL LENIN MUSEUM NOTABLE BUILDING

Map p262 (Центральный музей В.И. Ленина; pl Revolyutsii 2; Ⓜ Ploshchad Revolyutsii) Part Russian Revival, part neo-Renaissance, this red-brick beauty was built in the 1890s as the Moscow City Hall. It's better known for its later role, the big daddy of all the Lenin museums, which was closed in 1993 after the shootout at the Russian White House (see p196). Nowadays, it is used for special exhibits or communist rabble rousing. More often, it is a backdrop for rows of souvenir kiosks.

MANEZH EXHIBITION CENTRE ART GALLERY

Map p262 (ЦВЗ Манеж; Manezhnaya pl; exhibits R200-300; ⌚11am-8pm Tue-Sun; Ⓜ Biblioteka Imeni Lenina) The long, low building on the southwestern side of the square is the Manezh, housing art exhibitions. This neoclassical landmark was badly damaged by a fire in 2004, sparking much speculation that it was not an accident. It has been newly renovated and reopened, and now has an underground parking garage. Exhibits range from contemporary art and photography to lingerie and lilies.

ZAIKONOSPASSKY MONASTERY MONASTERY

Map p262 (Заиконоспасский монастырь; Nikolskaya ul 7-9; Ⓜ Ploshchad Revolyutsii) This monastery was founded by Boris Godunov in 1600, although the church was built in 1660. The name means 'Behind the Icon Stall', a reference to the busy icon trade that once took place here. On the orders of Tsar Alexey, the Likhud brothers – scholars of Greek – opened the Slavonic Greek and Latin Academy on the monastery premises in 1687. (Mikhail Lomonosov was a student here.) The academy later became a divinity school and was transferred to the Trinity Monastery of St Sergius (p158) in 1814.

MONASTERY OF THE EPIPHANY MONASTERY

Map p262 (Богоявленский монастырь; Bogoyavlensky per 2; Ⓜ Ploshchad Revolyutsii) This monastery is the second-oldest in Moscow; it was founded in 1296 by Prince Daniil, son of Alexander Nevsky. Stefan, one of the first abbots of the monastery, was the brother of Sergei Radonezhsky, who was patron saint of Russia and founder of the Trinity Monastery of St Sergius. The current **Epiphany Cathedral** was constructed in the 1690s in the Moscow baroque style.

SYNOD PRINTING HOUSE HISTORICAL BUILDING

Map p262 (Печатный двор Синод; Nikolskaya ul 15; Ⓜ Ploshchad Revolyutsii) This is where Ivan Fyodorov reputedly produced Russia's first printed book, *The Apostle*, in 1563. (You can see the man himself at Starye Polya.) In 1703 the first Russian newspaper, *Vedomosti*, was also printed here. Up until the early 19th century, Kitay Gorod was something of a printing centre, home at the time to 26 of Moscow's 31 bookshops.

STARYE POLYA HISTORICAL SITE

Map p262 (Старые поля; Teatralny proezd; Ⓜ Teatralnaya) Along Teatralny proezd, archaeologists uncovered the 16th-century fortified wall that used to surround Kitay Gorod, as well as the foundations of the 1493 Trinity Church. Coins, jewellery and tombstones were also excavated here. Besides the remains of the wall and the church, you can now see a statue of Ivan Fyodorov, the 16th-century printer responsible for Russia's first book.

TOWERS OF POWER

The present Kremlin walls were built between 1485 and 1495, replacing the limestone walls from the 14th century. The walls are 6m to 17m tall, depending on the landscape, and 2m to 5m thick. They stretch for 2235m. Originally, a 32m-wide moat encircled the northern end of the Kremlin, connecting the Moscow and Neglinnaya Rivers.

The 20 distinctive towers were built between 1485 and 1500, with tent roofs added in the 17th century. Originally, the towers had lookout posts and were equipped for heavy fighting. Most were designed by Italian masons. Starting at the northern corner and going clockwise, the towers are as follows:

Corner Arsenal Tower (Арсенальная башня) The stronghold of the Kremlin with walls 4m thick. A well built into the basement to provide water during sieges still survives today.

St Nicholas Tower (Никольская башня) Previously a gated defensive tower on the northeastern flank. Through this gate, Dmitry Pozharsky and Kuzma Minin (as depicted in the statue in front of St Basil's Cathedral) led a civilian army and drove out the Polish occupiers.

Senate Tower (Сенатская башня) Originally a nameless, gateless tower, and finally named after the construction of the Senate in the 18th century.

Saviour Gate Tower (Спасская башня) The Kremlin's 'official' exit onto Red Square. This gate – considered sacred – was used for processions in tsarist times. The two white-stone plaques above the gate commemorate the tower's construction. Between the tower's double walls, a staircase links five of its 10 levels. The current clock was installed in the gate tower in the 1850s. Hauling 3m-long hands and weighing 25 tonnes, the clock takes up three of the tower's levels. Its melodic chime sounds every 15 minutes across Red Square and across the country (on the radio).

Tsar Tower (Царская башня) A later addition (1680), which sits on top of the Kremlin wall. Legend has it that Ivan the Terrible watched executions and other Red Square activities from the old wooden tower that previously stood on this site.

Alarm Tower (Набатная башня) Housed the Spassky Alarm Bell, which was used to warn of enemy attacks and to spur popular uprisings. After quashing one uprising, Catherine the Great was so outraged that she had the clapper removed from the bell, so it could sound no more. The bell remained mute in the tower for 30 years before it was finally removed.

Konstantin & Yelena Tower (Константино-Еленинская башня) Built to protect the settlements outside the city, it is complete with firing platforms and a drawbridge over the moat. During the 17th century this tower was used as a prison, earning it the nickname 'torture tower'.

Moskvoretskaya Tower (Москворецкая башня)The round tower at the southeastern corner.

Petrovskaya Tower (Петровская башня) A service entrance used by Kremlin gardeners. Petrovskaya Tower was destroyed first by the Poles in 1612, then again by the French 200 years later, but it was rebuilt each time.

First & Second Nameless Towers Both destroyed in 1771 because they interfered with the construction of the Kremlin Palace, but rebuilt after its completion.

Secret Tower (Тайницкая башня) The first tower built (1485), it is named after a secret passageway leading down to the river.

Annunciation Tower (Благовещенская башня) Named for the miracle-working icon on the facade. In 1633 the so-called Laundry Gate was constructed nearby for Kremlin washerwomen to go down to the Moscow River, but it was later bricked up.

Water Tower (Водовзводная башня) A circular tower erected at the confluence of the Moscow and Neglinnaya Rivers. From 1633 a water lift in the tower pumped water to a reservoir and supplied a system of underground piping for the Kremlin.

The gated walkway of **Tretyakovsky proezd** leads into Kitay Gorod. The archway, built in the 1870s, was financed by the Tretyakov brothers, founders of the namesake gallery (p123). Apparently, the construction of the medieval-style gate and the opening of the passageway were an attempt to relieve traffic on Nikolskaya ul. Since its reopening in 2000, Tretyakovsky proezd is lined with exclusive shops, including Mercury, which financed much of the restoration.

OLD ENGLISH COURT MUSEUM

Map p262 (Палаты старого Английского двора; www.mosmuseum.ru; ul Varvarka 4a; admission R40; ⌚11am-6pm Tue-Sun; Ⓜ Kitay-Gorod) This reconstructed 16th-century house, white with wooden roofs, was the residence of England's first emissaries to Russia (sent by Elizabeth I to Ivan the Terrible). It also served as the base for English merchants, who were allowed to trade duty free in exchange for providing military supplies to Ivan. Today, it houses a small exhibit dedicated to this early international exchange.

ROMANOV CHAMBERS IN ZARYADIE MUSEUM

Map p262 (Палаты Романовых в Зарядье; ul Varvarka 10; admission R150; ⌚10am-5pm Thu-Mon, 11am-6pm Wed; Ⓜ Kitay-Gorod) This small but interesting museum is devoted to the lives of the Romanov family, who were mere boyars (nobles) before they became tsars. The house was built by Nikita Romanov, whose grandson Mikhail later became the first tsar of the 300-year Romanov dynasty. Exhibits (with descriptions in English) show the house as it might have been when the Romanovs lived here in the 16th century. Some of the artistic detail, such as the woodwork in the women's quarters, is amazing. Enter from the rear of the building.

CHURCH OF THE TRINITY IN NIKITNIKI CHURCH

Map p262 (Церковь Троицы в Никитниках; Ipatyevsky per; Ⓜ Kitay-Gorod) This little gem of a church, built in the 1630s, is an exquisite example of Russian baroque. Its onion domes and tiers of red and white spade gables rise from a square tower. Its interior is covered with 1650s gospel frescoes by Simon Ushakov and others. A carved doorway leads into St Nikita the Martyr's Chapel, above the vault of the Nikitnikov merchant family, who were among the patrons who financed the construction of the church.

MOSCOW CITY HISTORY MUSEUM MUSEUM

Map p262 (Музей истории города Москвы; www.mosmuseum.ru; Novaya pl 12; Ⓜ Lubyanka) This elaborate Russian Empire-style building dates from 1825. Formerly the John the Baptist Church, it now houses a small history museum, demonstrating how the city has spread from its starting point at the Kremlin. Exhibits are heavy on artefacts from the 13th and 14th centuries, especially household items, weapons and other representations of medieval Moscow. At the time of research, the museum was closing for renovations.

POLYTECHNICAL MUSEUM MUSEUM

Map p262 (Политехнический музей; www.polymus.ru; Novaya pl 3/4; adult/child R150/70; ⌚10am-6pm Tue-Sun; Ⓜ Lubyanka) Occupying the entire block of Novaya pl, this giant museum covers the history of Russian science, technology and industry. Indeed, the museum claims to be the largest science museum in the world. The permanent exhibits cover just about every aspect of Soviet scientific achievement, from a model of Lomonosov's laboratory to Mendeleev's development of the periodic table to Popov's first radio receiver. It is not as interactive or up to date as you might hope, but there is a hands-on exhibit, *Igroteka,* which allows visitors to conduct their own experiments.

While the museum's focus is scientific, the building is also architecturally interesting and visually appealing. Three different parts of the structure were built at different times and in different styles: the oldest, central section (1877) represents the Russian Byzantine era; the eastern section (1896) is inspired by 17th-century Russian styles; and the western section (1907) is Art Nouveau.

LUBYANKA PRISON NOTABLE BUILDING

Map p262 (Лубянка; Lubyanskaya pl; Ⓜ Lubyanka) In the 1930s Lubyanka Prison was the feared destination of thousands of innocent victims of Stalin's purges. Today the grey building looming on the northeastern side of the square is no longer a prison, but is the headquarters of the newly named Federal Security Service, or *Federalnaya Sluzhba Bezopasnosti*. The FSB keeps a pretty good eye on domestic goings on. The building is not open to the public.

The much humbler **Memorial to the Victims of Totalitarianism** stands in the little garden on the southeastern side of the

START **THEATRE SQ**
END **SLAVYANSKAYA PL**
DISTANCE **3KM**
DURATION **THREE HOURS**

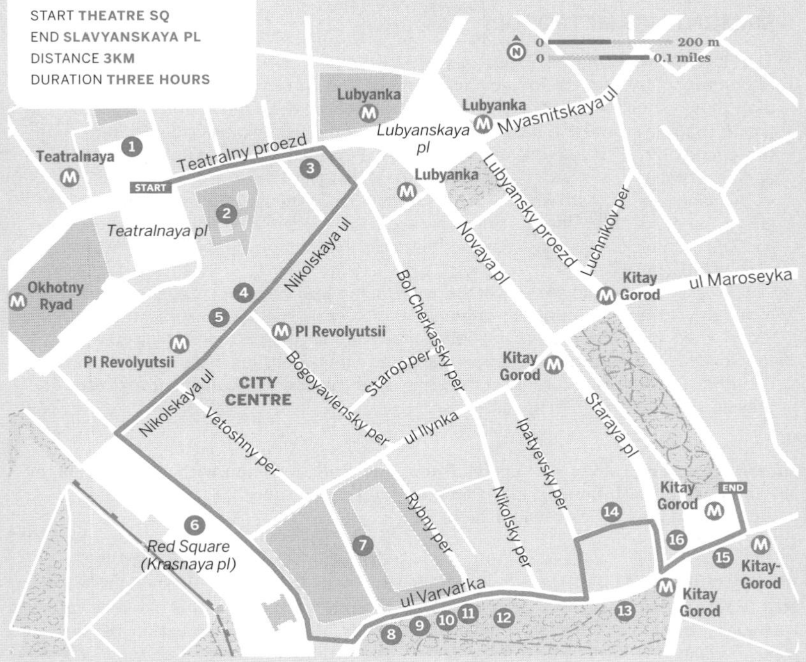

Neighbourhood Walk

Kremlin & Kitay Gorod

Start your tour at Theatre Sq (M Teatralnaya), named for the ring of theatres. The 1 **Bolshoi Theatre** is the impressive pink facade presiding over the territory. The Art Nouveau fantasy on the eastern side is the magnificent 2 **Hotel Metropol**. Stroll up Teatralny proezd to the historical and architectural complex of 3 **Starye Polya**, then walk through Tretyakovsky proezd, doing some window-shopping along the way.

Kitay Gorod's busiest street, Nikolskaya ul was the main road to Vladimir and used to be the centre of a busy icons trade. Admire the 4 **Synod Printing House** and the ancient 5 **Zaikonospassky Monastery**.

At the end of Nikolskaya, you emerge onto the triumphant 6 **Red Square**. With historic buildings all around, this is an awe-inspiring introduction to Moscow. Walk across the expanse of cobblestones and get a good look at the amazing architecture. At the southern end of Red Square, turn left on ul Varvarka. Here 7 **Gostiny Dvor** (Old Merchants' Court) is now partially renovated and filled with shops.

Ul Varvarka has Kitay Gorod's greatest concentration of interesting buildings. They were long dwarfed by the Hotel Rossiya, (demolished in 2006). Walking from west to east, pass the pink-and-white 8 **St Barbara's Church**, dating to 1804; the peak-roofed 9 **Old English Court**, dating to the 16th century; the 17th-century 10 **Church of St Maxim the Blessed**, now housing folk-art; the monks' building and golden-domed cathedral of the 11 **Monastery of the Sign**; the 12 **Romanov Chambers in Zaryadie**; and the 13 **St George's Church** (1658). Tucked down a side street, the enchanting 1630s 14 **Church of the Trinity in Nikitniki** is hidden among surrounding buildings.

Head east from Ipatevsky per out to Staraya pl. On Slavyanskaya pl is 15 **All Saints Cathedral on the Kulishka**, which was built in 1687. Some remains of the 16 **old city wall** can be seen in the underground passage at the corner of ul Varvarka and Staraya pl. This *perekhod* (cross walk) is also the entrance to the Kitay-Gorod metro stop.

MAMONTOV'S METROPOL

The Hotel Metropol, among Moscow's finest examples of Art Nouveau architecture, is another contribution by famed philanthropist and patron of the arts, Savva Mamontov, who hired architects. The decorative panel on the hotel's central facade, facing Teatralny proezd, is based on a sketch by the artist Mikhail Vrubel. It depicts the legend of the Princess of Dreams, in which a troubadour falls in love with a kind and beautiful princess and travels across the seas to find her. He falls ill during the voyage and is near death when he finds his love. The princess embraces him, but he dies in her arms. Naturally, the princess reacts to his death by renouncing her worldly life. The ceramic panels were made at the pottery workshop at Mamontov's Abramtsevo estate (p156).

The ceramic work on the side of the hotel facing Teatralnaya pl is by the artist Alexander Golovin. The script was originally a quote from Nietzsche: 'Again the same story: when you build a house you notice that you have learned something'. During the Soviet era, these wise words were replaced with something more appropriate for the time: 'Only the dictatorship of the proletariat can liberate mankind from the oppression of capitalism'. Lenin, of course.

square. This single stone slab comes from the territory of an infamous 1930s labour camp situated on the Solovetsky Islands in the White Sea.

MAYAKOVSKY MUSEUM — MUSEUM

Map p262 (Музей Маяковского; www.mayakovsky.info; Lubyansky proezd 3/6; admission R180; ⏲1-8pm Thu, 10am-5pm Fri-Tue; MLubyanka) The startling postmodern entrance on this prerevolutionary mansion is appropriate for a museum dedicated to the revolutionary, futurist poet Vladimir Mayakovsky. The building is actually where Mayakovsky lived in a communal apartment during the last years of his life. The room where he worked – and shot himself in 1930 – has been preserved. Run by the poet's granddaughter, the museum contains an eclectic collection of his manuscripts and sketches, as well as the requisite personal items and family photographs.

EATING

LOFT CAFÉ — FUSION $$

Map p262 (www.cafeloft.ru; 6th fl, Nautilus, Nikolskaya ul 25; meals R1000-1500; ⏲9am-midnight; MLubyanka) On the top floor of the Nautilus shopping centre, next door to the luxury spa, you'll find this tiny, trendy cafe. An even smaller terrace gives a fantastic view of Lubyanka pl. Innovative, modern dishes fuse the best of Russian cuisine with Western and Asian influences – for example, grilled salmon with spinach, pine nuts and caviar sauce.

STOLOVAYA 57 — CAFETERIA $

Map p262 (Столовая №57; 3rd fl, GUM, Red Sq; meals R300-400; ⏲10am-10pm; MOkhotny Ryad) Newly minted, this old-style cafeteria offers a nostalgic recreation of dining in post-Stalinist Russia. The food is good – and cheap for such a fancy store. Meat cutlets and cold salads come highly recommended. This is a great place to try 'herring in a fur coat' (herring, beets, carrots and potatoes).

BOSCO CAFE — INTERNATIONAL $$

Map p262 (www.bosco.ru; GUM, Krasnaya pl 3; meals R600-1000; ⏲10am-11pm; MPloshchad Revolyutsii) Sip a cappuccino in view of the Kremlin. Munch on lunch while the crowds line up at Lenin's Mausoleum. Enjoy an afternoon aperitif while admiring St Basil's domes. This café on the 1st floor of GUM is the only place to sit right on Red Square and marvel at its magnificence. Service can be slightly harried, but overall it's a pleasant – and not outrageously overpriced – experience.

SYRNAYA DYRKA — FRENCH $$

Map p262 (Сырная дырка; www.sdyrka.ru; Bolshoi Cherkassky per 15; meals R800-1200; ⏲10am-11pm; MKitay-gorod) Following the success of the original Syrnaya Dyrka in Basmanny, there is now a new, quintessentially quaint location in the heart of Kitay Gorod. Bold paintings and colourful tableware contrast with Victorian-era furniture and greenery, creating a cheerful yet sophisticated atmosphere. This outlet is meant to be French, as opposed to Swiss at the Basmanny restaurant, but that does not result in a dramatically different menu. It still features deliciously aromatic *fromage* in all its forms, including fondue, quiche, sandwiches and cheese plates.

SUSHI VYOSLA — JAPANESE $$

Map p262 (Суши Вёсла; www.sushivesla.by; Nautilus, Nikolskaya ul 25; meals R600-800; noon-1am Sun-Thu, to 3am Fri & Sat; ; Lubyanka) Sushi is all the rage in Moscow these days. To get in on it, head to this hip Japanese cafe in the basement of the Nautilus shopping centre (enter from Teatralnaya proezd). Dishes are colour coded to specify price; at the end of the meal the server clears the empty plates and uses them to calculate the bill.

PELMESHKA — CAFE $

Map p262 (Пельмешка; Nikolskaya ul 8/1; meals R150-200; 10am-midnight; ; Ploshchad Revolyutsii) Pelmeshka is a clean, post-Soviet *stolovaya,* serving many different kinds of *pelmeni,* the most filling of Russian favourites. This place is packed with patrons at lunchtime, a sign that the food is tasty as well as cheap.

DROVA — INTERNATIONAL $

Map p262 (Дрова; www.drova.ru; Nikolskaya ul 5; meals R200-400, all-you-can-eat buffet R630; 24hr; ; Ploshchad Revolyutsii) The self-serve buffet features offerings ranging from *solyanka* (a salty vegetable and meat soup) to sushi and sweet-and-sour pork. It's not the best place to sample any of these items, but the price is right. Hungry student types really take advantage of the all-you-can-eat option: it's not always pretty.

DRINKING & NIGHTLIFE

DISSIDENT VINOTECA — WINE BAR

Map p262 (www.dissident.msk.ru; 5th fl, Nautilus, Nikolskaya 25; 11am-midnight; Lubyanka) Comfortable and classy, this rare Moscow wine bar offers over 200 kinds of wine by the glass, along with appropriate accompaniments such as cheese, paté and other hors d'oeuvres. Certainly wine was considered a bourgeois beverage back in the day, but we're pretty sure that Soviet dissidents were not drinking wines like these. Panoramic views of Lubyanka prison are free.

CUP & CAKE CAFE — CAFE

Map p262 (www.ginzaproject.ru; Nikolskaya ul 10/2; Lubyanka) Fronting a fancy fashion boutique, this tiny cafe is big on style, with plush pillows and rich fabrics strewn about. The menu of sweets, teas and coffee drinks is written with colourful chalk on the slate board, but you might as well just inspect the glass case. This is the perfect place to take a break from your tour of Kitay Gorod.

CLUB CHE — LATIN BAR

Map p262 (www.clubche.ru; Nikolskaya ul 10/2; meals R800-1000; 24hr; ; Lubyanka) The revolution lives on at this popular, divey bar. The walls are covered with revolutionary graffiti and photos of the iconic namesake hero. Patrons groove on the dance floor to salsa and merengue music. The cuisine is more Tex-Mex than Cuban, but nobody is complaining about the huge plates of nachos and the spicy chilli. Bartenders also mix a mean *mojito* (rum drink with lime, sugar and mint) with Havana Club rum.

NEUTRAL TERRITORY — BAR

Map p262 (Нейтральная Территория; www.neutrality.ru; Novaya pl 14; 24hr; Kitay-Gorod) This newish place does not have as much atmosphere as some places, but it's a good option for a business lunch (R210), midday coffee break or late-night drinking. Well-stocked bookshelves warm up the stark B&W atmosphere. The entrance is at the back of the building: enter from the alleyway off ul Ilynka.

ENTERTAINMENT

CHINESE PILOT DZHAO-DA — LIVE MUSIC

Map p262 (Китайский лётчик Джао-да; www.jao-da.ru, in Russian; Lubyansky proezd 25; cover R300-500; concerts 10pm Thu, 11pm Fri & Sat; Kitay-Gorod) A relaxed and relatively inexpensive place to hear live music. This divey basement place hosts lots of different kinds of bands – from around Europe and Russia – so check out the website in advance. Look out for free concerts on Monday nights.

KREMLIN BALLET THEATRE BALLET

Map p262 (Театр "Кремлёвский балет"; www.kremlin-gkd.ru; ul Vozdvizhenka 1; box office noon-8pm; Alexandrovsky Sad) The Bolshoi Theatre doesn't have a monopoly on ballet in Moscow. Leading dancers also appear with the Kremlin Ballet and the Moscow Classical Ballet Theatre, and both companies perform here. The Bolshoi is magical, but seeing a show inside the Kremlin is something special too, and the repertoire is similarly classical. The box office is in the underground passageway, near the entrance to the metro station.

CHINATOWN CAFE LIVE MUSIC

Map p262 (www.chinatown.ru; Lubyansky proezd 25/12; Kitay-Gorod) Right next door to the grungy favourite Chinese Pilot, this is another eastern-themed basement bar that books great live-music acts. The place promises 'all genres' and it delivers jazz, folk, pop-rock, hip-hop, electronica and everything in between. Concerts every night at 9pm with a second concert at 10:30pm on weekends.

SHOPPING

GUS-KHRUSTALNY FACTORY STORE SOUVENIRS

Map p262 (Гусь-Хрустальный заводской магазин; www.ghz.ru; Gostiny Dvor; Ploshchad Revolyutsii) Since the glass production factory was founded there in 1756, the town of Gus-Khrustalny (east of Moscow) has been known for its high-quality glassware. This factory store carries an excellent selection of beautiful and reasonably priced crystal and glassware, especially coloured glass.

VOLOGDA LINEN SOUVENIRS

Map p262 (Вологодский лён; www.linens.ru, in Russian; Gostiny Dvor; Ploshchad Revolyutsii) Russia's cool, moist summers are ideal for producing flax, the fibre used to manufacture linen. This elegant, durable fabric is respectfully known in Russia as 'His Majesty Linen'. High-quality linen products such as tablecloths, napkins, bed covers and even clothing are still manufactured in Russia.

GUM SHOPPING MALL

Map p262 (ГУМ; www.gum.ru, in Russian; Krasnaya pl 3; Ploshchad Revolyutsii) In the elaborate 19th-century building on Red Square, the State Department Store – better known as GUM – is a bright and bustling centre filled with shops and cafés.

ALENA AKHMADULLINA BOUTIQUE CLOTHING & ACCESSORIES

Map p262 (Бутик Алёны Ахмадулиной; www.alenaakhmadullina.ru; Nikolskaya ul 10/2; Lubyanka) Alena Akhmadullina's romantic, flowing fashions have been wowing trendsetters since 2005, when the St Petersburg designer first showed her stuff in Paris. She has received loads of international attention ever since (including an invitation to provide an outfit for Angelina Jolie in the film *Wanted*). The subtly seductive designs are known for offering a new perspective on Russian themes.

OKHOTNY RYAD SHOPPING MALL

Map p262 (Охотный ряд; www.oxotniy.ru, in Russian; Manezhnaya pl; Okhotny Ryad) The best part of this underground mall is the fanciful fountain that splashes the shoppers as they enter and exit from Alexander Garden. Aside from the clothing and electronic stores, there is a big, crowded food court and a 24-hour internet café (p234) on the ground floor.

VLADIMIR MIKHAILOV JEWELLERY

Map p262 (Вдадимир Михаилов; www.vmikhailov.ru; Nikolskaya ul 10; 11am-10pm; Lubyanka) Mikhailov uses precious gems and Orthodox imagery to create religious jewellery that looks like it should be worn by the Patriarch. Think gem-studded crosses and heavy gold rings. The store also carries icons, reliquaries and Easter eggs a la Fabergé, all of which makes interesting and unique (though expensive) souvenirs.

Tverskoy

ULITSA PETROVKA | TVERSKAYA ULITSA | OUTER TVERSKOY

Neighbourhood Top Five

❶ Spending an evening at the **Bolshoi Theatre** (p85), where world-famous opera and ballet companies perform Russian classics.

❷ Inspecting the constructivist architecture and the contemporary works on display at the **Garage Centre for Contemporary Culture** (p78).

❸ Doing the sidewalk scene on **Kamergersky per** (p81).

❹ Sweating away your city stresses amid the luxury of **Sanduny Baths** (p85).

❺ Admiring the fantastical **paintings of Viktor Vasnetsov** (p78) in the studio where he painted them.

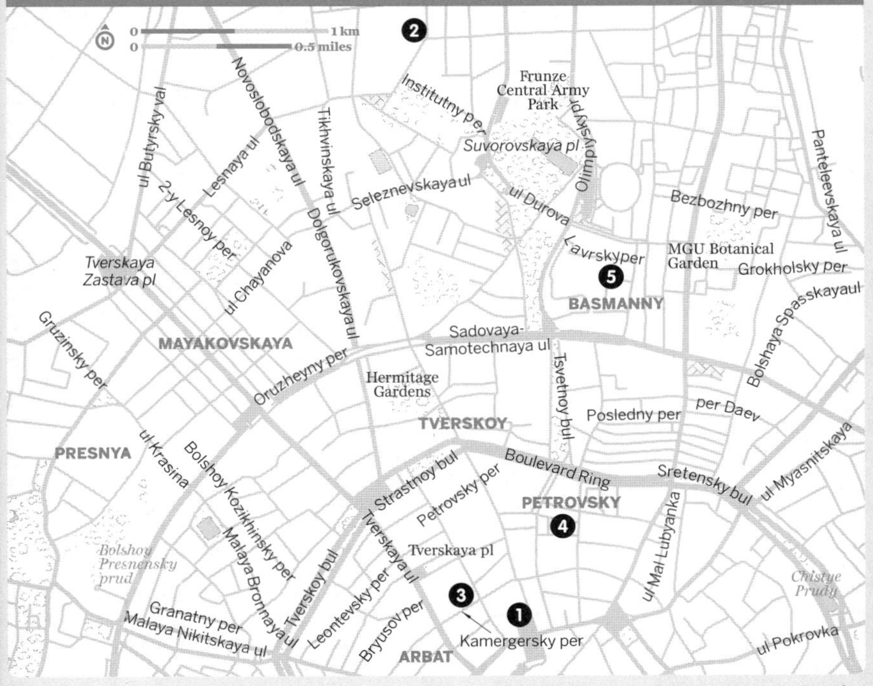

For more details of this area, see Map p260 ➡

Lonely Planet's Top Tip

While the Bolshoi is Russia's most famous theatre, it is not the only one. Several other opera and ballet theatres in Moscow offer the same level of professionalism and panache in their performances at a fraction of the price. If you have your heart set on going to the opera or ballet but can't get tickets to the Bolshoi, consider the Novaya Opera (p86) or the Stanislavsky & Nemirovich-Danchenko Musical Theatre (p86), both gorgeous theatres with highly skilled performers.

Best Places to Eat

- Delicatessen (p79)
- DoDo (p79)
- Barashka (p79)
- Dzhondzholi (p80)

For reviews, see p79

Best Places to Drink

- Cafe Mart (p84)
- Simachyov (p84)

For reviews, see p84

Best Soviet History

- Contemporary History Museum (p76)
- Gulag Museum (p75)
- Central Museum of the Armed Forces (p79)

For reviews, see p75

Explore

If you do nothing else in Tverskoy, pay a visit to majestic Teatralnaya pl (Theatre Sq), home to the world-famous Bolshoi Theatre. Come in the evening if you have managed to snag tickets for a performance. But even by day, this glittering jewel of a theatre is a sight to behold, often attracting tourists and shoppers to the benches and fountains that grace the square.

From here, wander up ul Petrovka for cafe-hopping and window-shopping. There are a few sights to catch your attention, but the stronger draw is the city life. Small lanes such as Kamergersky per and Stoleshnikov per are among Moscow's trendiest places to sip a coffee or a beer and watch the bustle.

Aside from the Bolshoi (and the cafes), the best things to see in Tverskoy are outside the Garden Ring (the area dubbed 'Outer Tverskoy'). If you have a free afternoon, the Garage Centre for Contemporary Culture is a particularly exciting development on the Moscow art and architecture scene, which is worth the time and R28 for a metro ride out of the centre.

Local Life

- **Parks** Hermitage Gardens is the district's popular spot for fresh air and green space, not to mention delightful outdoor drinking and dining at Chaikhona No 1 (p84).
- **Street Scene** See and be seen on Kamergersky per, a pedestrian-only cobblestone street crammed with cafes with outdoor seating.

Getting There & Away

- **Ul Petrovka** To reach ul Petrovka, take the metro to Teatralnaya station on the green Zamoskvoretskaya line.
- **Tverskaya ul** The city's hub at the bottom of Tverskaya ul, at Manezhnaya pl, is accessible by the Okhotny Ryad metro station on the red Sokolnicheskaya line. Heading north, the green Zamoskvoretskaya metro line runs beneath Tverskaya ul, providing easy access to Pushkinskaya pl (at Tverskaya station), Triumfalnaya pl (at Mayakovskaya station), and pl Tverskaya Zastava (at Belorusskaya station).
- **Outer Tverskoy** Tverskaya ul changes name to Tverskaya-Yamskaya ul and, beyond Belorussky vokzal, to Leningradsky pr and eventually to Leningradskoe sh, as this highway heads out of town. The green Zamoskvoretskaya metro line follows this road almost all the way to MKAD, finally terminating at Rechnoy Vokzal. The northeastern corner of Tverskoy district is accessible via the connecting metro stations at Novoslobodskaya or Mendeleevskaya.

SIGHTS

Ulitsa Petrovka

GULAG HISTORY MUSEUM MUSEUM

Map p260 (Государственный музей истории ГУЛАГа; www.museum-gulag.narod.ru; ul Petrovka 16; adult/student R100/20, tour R800; 11am-7pm Tue-Sat; MChekhovskaya) Amid all the swanky shops on ul Petrovka, an archway leads to a courtyard that is strung with barbed wire and hung with portraits of political prisoners. This is the entrance to a unique museum dedicated to the Chief Administration of Corrective Labour Camps and Colonies, better known as the GULAG. Guides dressed like guards describe the vast network of labour camps that once existed in the former Soviet Union and recount the horrors of camp life.

Millions of prisoners spent years in these labour camps, made famous by Alexander Solzhenitsyn's book *The Gulag Archipelago*. More than 18 million people passed through this system during its peak years, from 1929 to 1953, although many camps remained in operation until the end of the 1980s. The gulag became a chilling symbol of political repression, as many of the prisoners were serving time for 'antisocial' or 'counter-revolutionary' behaviour. The museum serves as a history lesson about the system, as well as a memorial to its victims.

MOSCOW MUSEUM OF MODERN ART MUSEUM

Map p260 (MMOMA; Московский музей современного искусства; www.mmoma.ru; ul Petrovka 25; adult/student R150/100; noon-8pm; MChekhovskaya) A pet project of the ubiquitous Zurab Tsereteli (see the boxed text, p112), this museum is housed in a classical 18th-century merchant's home, originally designed by Matvei Kazakov (architect of the Kremlin Senate). It is the perfect light-filled setting for an impressive collection of 20th-century paintings, sculptures and graphics, which includes both Russian and foreign artists. The highlight is the collection of avant-garde art, with works by Chagall, Kandinsky and Malevich. Unique to this museum is its exhibit of 'nonconformist' artists from the 1950s and '60s – those whose work was not acceptable to the Soviet regime. The gallery also hosts temporary

TOP SIGHTS BOLSHOI THEATRE

With its three grand theatres surrounding a wide plaza and flowing fountain, Theatre Sq anchors ul Petrovka. The centrepiece, of course, is the world-renowned Bolshoi Theatre. The present pink-and-white beauty was built in 1824, replacing the Petrovka Theatre that previously stood on this site. This historic theatre saw the premier of Tchaikovsky's *Swan Lake* in 1877 and *The Nutcracker* in 1919. The main stage was closed for much-needed renovations but reopened to much acclaim in November 2011, while the New Stage continues to put on performances (see p85 for details).

The facade of the Bolshoi is famed for the bronze troika that is flying off the front. The **fountain by Vitali** – featuring bronze sculptures of the three muses – is Moscow's oldest existing fountain. It was erected in 1835 as a source for drinking water. The larger 'Theatre Fountain' was erected in honour of the capital's 850th anniversary.

Across and down ul Petrovka from the 'grand' Bolshoi is the 'lesser' **Maly Theatre** (p87), also built in 1824. Back in the day, when there were only two theatres in Moscow, the custom was to label the opera theatre the *bolshoi* and the drama theatre the *maly*. On the west side of the square is the National Youth Theatre.

DON'T MISS

- Petrovsky Fountain
- Bronze Troika
- Ostrovsky Statue

PRACTICALITIES

- Map p260
- 8-800-333 1333
- www.bolshoi.ru
- Teatralnaya pl 1
- MTeatralnaya

exhibits that often feature contemporary artists. Be sure not to bypass the whimsical sculpture garden in the courtyard. There are additional MMOMA outlets, used primarily for temporary exhibits, on Tverskoy bul (p92) and Yermolayevsky per (p92).

UPPER ST PETER MONASTERY MONASTERY

Map p260 (Петровский монастырь; cnr ul Petrovka & Petrovsky bul; ⏲8am-8pm; Ⓜ Chekhovskaya) The Upper St Peter Monastery was founded in the 1380s as part of an early defensive ring around Moscow. The main, onion-domed **Virgin of Bogolyubovo Church** dates from the late 17th century. The loveliest structure is the brick **Cathedral of Metropolitan Pyotr**, restored with a shingle roof. (When Peter the Great ousted the Regent Sofia in 1690, his mother was so pleased she built him this church.)

M'ARS CONTEMPORARY ART CENTRE ART GALLERY

Map p260 (Центр Современного Искусства М'АРС; www.marsgallery.ru; Pushkarev per 5; ⏲gallery noon-8pm Tue-Sun, cafe noon-11pm daily; Ⓜ Tsvetnoy Bulvar or Sukharevskaya) Founded by artists who were banned during the Soviet era, this gallery space includes 10 exhibit halls showing the work of top contemporary artists, as well as a cool club and cafe in the basement.

Tverskaya Ulitsa

HOUSE OF UNIONS & STATE DUMA NOTABLE BUILDINGS

Map p260 (Дом Союзов и Государственная Дума; Okhotny ryad 2/1; Ⓜ Teatralnaya) The buildings lining Okhotny ryad, just north of Tverskaya ul, serve official functions. The glowering State Duma was erected in the 1930s for Gosplan (Soviet State Planning Department), source of the USSR's Five-Year Plans, but it is now the seat of the Russian parliament. The green-columned House of Unions dates from the 1780s. Its ballroom, called the Hall of Columns, is the famous location of one of Stalin's most grotesque show trials, that of Nikolai Bukharin, a leading Communist Party theorist who had been a close associate of Lenin. Both buildings are closed to the public.

TVERSKAYA PLOSHCHAD HISTORIC SITE

Map p260 (Тверская площадь) A statue of the founder of Moscow, **Yury Dolgoruky**, presides over this prominent square near the bottom of Tverskaya ul. So does Mayor Sergei Sobyanin, as the buffed-up five-storey building opposite is the **Moscow mayor's office**. Many ancient churches are hidden in the back streets, including the 17th-century **Church of SS Kosma & Damian**.

CHURCH OF THE NATIVITY OF THE VIRGIN IN PUTINKI CHURCH

Map p260 (Церковь Рождества Богородицы в Путинках; ul Malaya Dmitrovka 4; Ⓜ Pushkinskaya) When this church was completed in 1652, the Patriarch Nikon responded by banning tent roofs like the ones featured here. Apparently, he considered such architecture too Russian, too secular and too far removed from the Church's Byzantine roots. Fortunately, the Church of the Nativity has survived to grace this corner near Pushkinskaya pl.

CONTEMPORARY HISTORY MUSEUM MUSEUM

Map p260 (Музей современной истории России; www.sovr.ru; Tverskaya ul 21; adult/student R100/70; ⏲10am-6pm Tue-Sun; Ⓜ Pushkinskaya) Formerly known as the Revolution Museum, this retro exhibit traces Soviet history from the 1905 and 1917 revolutions up to the 1980s. The highlight is the extensive collection of propaganda posters, in addition to all the Bolshevik paraphernalia. Look for the picture of the giant Palace of Soviets (Дворец Советов) that Stalin was going to build on the site of the blown-up – and now rebuilt – Cathedral of Christ the Saviour. English-language tours are available with advance notice.

Outer Tverskoy

GLINKA MUSEUM OF MUSICAL CULTURE MUSEUM

Map p260 (Музей музыкальной культуры Глинки; www.museum.ru/glinka; ul Fadeeva 4; admission R200; ⏲noon-7pm Tue-Sun; Ⓜ Mayakovskaya) Musicologists will be amazed by this massive collection of musical instruments from all over the world. The museum boasts over 3000 instruments – handcrafted works of art – from the Caucasus to the Far East. Russia is very well represented – a 13th-century *gusli* (traditional instrument similar to a dulcimer) from Novgorod, skin drums from Yakutia, a *balalaika* (triangular instrument) by the master Semyon

STRATEGY-31

On the last day of the month, the 31st, several hundred people gathered in Triumfalnaya Pl. At 6pm, banners were unfurled and voices were raised: 'Support Fair Elections', 'Free Political Prisoners', 'Russia without Putin.' Cameras and microphones were brought out; the police moved in. Special riot-control cops, who outnumbered the protesters, bullied their way through the square. Scores of arrests were made, while the rest of the 31ers were dispersed. By 7pm, a broken barricade was all that was left of the incident.

This act of civil disobedience was not an isolated event. Rather it is a recurring political ritual, held on the last day of each month with 31 days. The significance of the date is from Article 31 of the Russian Constitution, which guarantees the right of free assembly. By such means, the protesters seek to draw attention to what they see as a crackdown on civil liberties in Russia.

The idea for this protest action, dubbed 'Strategy-31', is credited to ex-Soviet political dissident Eduard Limonov, founder and leader of the National Bolshevik Party (NBP), an ultra-nationalist group (banned by the authorities) that was an early advocate of a restored Russian empire. The NBP more recently has joined with liberal politicians, like former chess champion Gary Kasparov and former vice premier Boris Nemtsov, to form Other Russia, a loose coalition of political opponents to the reigning party of power United Russia. The '31' rallies bring together an odd mix of young radicals, workers, intellectuals and grannies.

Organisers have come up against various impediments:

- City-hall officials refuse to issue permits for a public demonstration on Triumfalnaya pl. The now common excuse is that another group – often with a Kremlin affiliation – has already received permission to hold a rally on the 31st.
- The police routinely arrest the organisers and disperse the crowd.
- City officials have allowed the protesters to hold their rallies up the street at Pushkinskaya pl – a compromise that does not satisfy the Strategy-31 organisers. As founder Limonov was quoted by Open Democracy, 'We've never been permitted to hold our protest meeting in Triumfalnaya Square, but other organisations go there. It's not right.'

So far, these obstacles have not deterred the 31ers; on the contrary, on the 31st of the month, protesters now stage rallies in St Petersburg, Ekaterinburg and other Russian cities.

Nalimov – but you can also see such classic pieces as a violin made by Antonio Stradivari. Recordings accompany many of the rarer instruments, allowing visitors to experience their sound.

This incredible collection started with a few instruments that were donated by the Moscow Tchaikovsky Conservatory at the end of the 19th century. The collection grew exponentially during the Soviet period. It was named after Mikhail Glinka in 1945, in honour of the nationalist composer's 150th birthday.

MUSEUM OF DECORATIVE & FOLK ART ART MUSEUM

Map p260 (Всероссийский музей декоративно-прикладного и народного искусства; www.vmdpri.ru; Delegatskaya ul 3 & 5; admission R200; ⏲10am-6pm Wed-Sun; Ⓜ Tsvetnoy Bulvar) Just beyond the Garden Ring, this museum showcases the centuries-old arts-and-crafts traditions from all around Russia and the former Soviet republics. It includes all the goodies you might find in souvenir shops or at the Izmailovo Market (p138), but these antique pieces represent the crafts at their most traditional and authentic. Of the 40,000 pieces in the collection, you might see painted *khokhloma* woodwork from Nizhny Novgorod, including wooden toys and *matryoshka* dolls; baskets and other household items made from birch bark, a traditional Siberian technique; intricate embroidery and lacework from the north, as well as the ubiquitous Pavlov scarves; and playful Dymkovo pottery and Gzhel porcelain. Look also for the so-called 'propaganda porcelain' – fine china decorated with revolutionary themes.

The museum is known for its impressive collection of *palekh* – black lacquer boxes and trays painted with detailed scenes from Russian fairy tales. The collection fills two rooms. It features, among others, pieces by Ivan Golikov and Ivan Markichev, often considered the originators of the *palekh* style.

VASNETSOV HOUSE-MUSEUM ART MUSEUM

Map p260 (Дом-музей Васнецова; www.tretyakovgallery.ru; per Vasnetsova 13; admission R100; ⌚10am-5pm Wed-Sun; Ⓜ Sukharevskaya) Victor Vasnetsov (1848–1926) was a Russian-revivalist painter and architect famous for his historical paintings with mystical and fairy-tale subjects. In 1894 Vasnetsov designed his own house in Moscow, which is now a museum branch of the Tretyakov. Fronted by a colourful gate, it is a charming home in neo-Russian style, still filled with the original wooden furniture, a tiled stove and many of the artist's paintings. The attic studio, where he once painted, is now hung with paintings depicting Baba Yaga and other characters from Russian fairy tales.

Early on, Vasnetsov was scorned for his fantastical style, as it was such a startling contrast to the realism of the Peredvezhniki (Wanderers, 19th-century art movement). Even Pavel Tretyakov, the most prominent patron of the arts at the time, refused to buy his paintings. However, by the turn of the century, he found a source of support in Savva Mamontov, whose financing drove the Russian revivalist movement.

DOSTOEVSKY HOUSE-MUSEUM LITERARY MUSEUM

Map p260 (Дом-музей Достоевского; ul Dostoevskogo 2; admission R50; ⌚11am-6pm Thu, Sat & Sun, 2-7pm Wed & Fri; Ⓜ Novoslobodskaya) While this renowned Russian author is more closely associated with St Petersburg, Fyodor Dostoevsky was actually born in Moscow, where his family lived in a tiny apartment on the grounds of Marinsky Hospital. He lived here until the age of 16, when he went to St Petersburg to enter a military academy. The family's Moscow flat has been re-created according to descriptions written by Fyodor's brother. Visitors can see the family's library, toys and many other personal items, including Fyodor's

TOP SIGHTS GARAGE CENTRE FOR CONTEMPORARY CULTURE

Dasha Zhukova has so many claims to fame: she is the gorgeous girlfriend of Russian billionaire Roman Abramovich, she is a successful fashion designer and she has her own inheritance. Now she is also a proud patron of the Garage Centre for Contemporary Culture (GCCC).

Known affectionately as Dashkin Garazh (Dasha's Garage), it is an old bus depot that has been converted into Moscow's largest exhibition hall. It's an incredible space, originally designed in 1926 by constructivist architect Konstantin Melnikov. The ingenious parallelogram-shaped interior allowed the fleet of 100 buses to enter, park and exit without reversing or turning around.

GCCC opened to much fanfare in 2008, with an exhibit from husband-and-wife team Ilya and Emilia Kabakov (Moscow natives who emigrated to the West in the 1970s). The centre has since hosted a wide variety Russian and international artists, including Francesco Vezzoli, Carsten Höller, Mark Rothko and David Lynch. The GCCC stretches the definition of the word 'exhibit', showcasing interior design, performance art, films and fashion.

Two blocks north and two blocks east from Novoslobodskaya or Mendeleevskaya metro station.

DON'T MISS

- Unique constructivist architecture of the Bakhmetevsky bus garage
- Films, lectures and workshops related to the art exhibits

PRACTICALITIES

- off Map p260
- www.garageccc.com
- ul Obratsova 19a
- admission R200-300
- ⌚11am-9pm Mon-Thu, 11am-10pm Fri-Sun
- Ⓜ Novoslobodskaya

quill pen and an original autograph. From Novoslobodskaya metro station, walk east on Seleznevskaya ul and turn left on per Dostoevskogo.

CENTRAL MUSEUM OF THE ARMED FORCES MUSEUM

Map p260 (Центральный музей Вооружённых Сил; www.cmaf.ru; ul Sovetskoy Armii 2; admission R75; 10am-4.30pm Wed-Sun; M Novoslobodskaya) Covering the history of the Soviet and Russian military since 1917, this massive museum occupies 24 exhibit halls plus open-air exhibits. Over 800,000 military items, including uniforms, medals and weapons, are on display. Among the highlights are remainders of the American U2 spy plane (brought down in the Urals in 1960) and the victory flag raised over Berlin's Reichstag in 1945. Take trolleybus 69 (or walk) 1.3km east from the Novoslobodskaya metro.

EATING

Ulitsa Petrovka

DELICATESSEN INTERNATIONAL $$

Map p260 (495-699 3952; www.newdeli.ru; Savodvaya-Karetnaya ul 20; meals R800-1000; noon-midnight Tue-Sat; M Tsvetnoy Bulvar) 'Thank you for finding us' reads the sign over the door at this casual but classy restaurant bar. It does take some finding, as the place is hidden away in a courtyard with no street-side signage, but it's worth the effort. Although the menu includes burgers, pizza and pasta, you'll also find an eclectic array of offerings like salad Niçoise, shrimp ceviche and beef tartare. It's all very creative and cool.

DODO FUSION $$$

Map p260 (903-105 1010; www.dodoproject.com; ul Petrovka 21/2; meals R1000-1500; 10am-midnight Sun-Thu, 10am-6am Fri & Sat; M Chekhovskaya) Inspired cuisine in a sleek setting at affordable prices: in Moscow this concept is as rare as the dodo itself. You'll want to spend some time perusing the menu, which deftly blends flavors from all corners of the globe, showing off elements of French, Italian, Asian and even Caucasian cuisines. The fresh fish (flown in on Wednesday and Saturday) is a highlight.

BARASHKA AZERI $$$

Map p260 (Барашка; 495-625 2895; www.novikovgroup.ru; ul Petrovka 20/1; meals R1500-2000; M Teatralnaya) Not that we have anything against kitsch, but it's also nice to occasionally dine in as sophisticated a setting as this understated Baku courtyard, adorned with jars of pickled lemons and blooming plants. Barashka offers a menu full of fresh tasty salads, grilled meats and slow-cooked stews, many of which feature the little lamb, for which the restaurant is named. There is another outlet in Presnya (p99).

COURVOISIER CAFE EUROPEAN $$

Map p260 (www.courvoisier-cafe.ru; Malaya Sukharevskaya pl 8; meals R400-800; 24hr; M Sukharevskaya) This informal, French-themed cafe is furnished with picnic tables and park benches, evoking an idyllic outdoor setting. (There is outdoor seating too, but fronting the Garden Ring, it is not so peaceful.) Serving breakfast, soups, pasta and grills, it's a popular spot for breakfast, happy hour (4pm to 7pm) or a late-night snack.

VARVARY RUSSIAN $$$

Map p260 (Варвары; 495-229 2800; www.anatolykomm.com; Strastnoy bul 8A; set menu R8500; M Chekhovskaya) Touted as 'the first Russian haute cuisine restaurant', this is run by molecular chef Anatoly Komm, Russia's only chef with a Michelin star. Komm is an artist who employs scientific processes to break ingredients down to their most basic component and present the flavours in new forms. As you might expect, Vavary is an elegant affair, offering a sophisticated new take on familiar flavours, eg black bread and beet salad in the form of foams and gels. The 'gastronomic spectacle' – aka the set menu – includes no less than 10 courses. Advance booking is essential.

SISTERS GRIMM RUSSIAN $

Map p260 (Сёстры Гримм; www.sgrimm.ru; Stoleshnikov per 11; meals R400-600; M Chekhovskaya) Sabrina and Daphne would be right at home in this cosy country cottage, well stocked with canned fruits and vegetables, books, photos and board games. The menu features 'home-cooking', Russian-style, with an enticing selection of sangria, lemonades and fruity cocktails to complete the fantasy.

KITEZH RUSSIAN $$

Map p260 (Китежъ; 495-650 6685; www.kitezh-town.ru; ul Petrovka 23/10; meals R1000-1500; ; Chekhovskaya) Kitezh is named after a legendary town that, as a defence mechanism, could magically disappear from the sight of an enemy at the sound of a bell. This welcoming eatery re-creates a 17th-century interior in the basement of a building near the Upper St Peter Monastery. The menu specialises in Russian classics, prepared and served as in the days of old.

KORCHMA TARAS BULBA UKRAINIAN $

Map p260 (Корчма Тарас Бульба; www.tarasbulba.ru; ul Petrovka 30/7; meals R400-600; ; Chekhovskaya) Servers at Taras Bulba dress up in traditional embroidered outfits, complemented by Ukrainian tapestries and wood floors, which provide a homey atmosphere. Specialities include black bread with *salo* (lard), and *vareniki* (dumplings) filled with potatoes, cabbage or meat. One of several outlets around town, including one in Zamoskvorechie (p130).

JAGANNATH VEGETARIAN $

Map p260(Kuznetsky most 11; meals R400-600; 10am-11pm; ; Kuznetsky Most) If you are in need of vitamins, this is a funky, vegetarian cafe, restaurant and shop. Its Indian-themed decor is more New Agey than ethnic. Service is slow but sublime, and the food is worth the wait.

YOLKI-PALKI RUSSIAN $

Map p260 (www.elki-palki.ru; Neglinnaya ul 8/10; meals R300-500; 10am-midnight Mon-Fri, 11am-midnight Sat & Sun; Kuznetsky Most;) This Russian chain is beloved for its country-cottage decor and its well-stocked salad bar. Outlets all over the city specialise in traditional dishes and cheap beer. Other Yolki-Palki locations include Zamoskvorechie (p130) and Taganka (p142).

UZBEKISTAN UZBEK $$$

Map p260 (www.uzbek-rest.ru; Neglinnaya ul 29/14; meals R1000-1500; noon-3am; Tsvetnoy Bulvar) One of the city's oldest restaurants, this place opened in 1951 by order of the Ministry of Trade of the Uzbek Soviet Republic. Six decades later, the place has expanded its menu to include Chinese, Arabic and Azeri food, in addition to the Uzbek standards. Make yourself comfortable on the plush cushions, order some spicy *plov* (pilaflike meat and rice) or delicious fried kebabs and enjoy the belly-dancing show.

GALEREYA INTERNATIONAL $$$

Map p260 (495-790 1596; ul Petrovka 27; meals R2000-2500; 24hr; Chekhovskaya) At the end of the night, the best of Moscow's socialites find themselves at this Novikov hot spot. This place is popular around the clock, but it's most crowded in the wee hours, when the beautiful people come to refuel after a night out on the town. And they are beautiful…by the looks of things, high heels and short skirts are part of the dress code. Art on the walls and sushi on the menu complete the trendy picture.

Tverskaya Ulitsa

TOP CHOICE **DZHONDZHOLI** GEORGIAN $$$

Map p260 (Джон Джоли; 495-650 5567; www.ginzaproject.ru; Tverskaya ul 20/1; meals R1000-1500; ; Pushkinskaya) Exposed brick walls, wood and wicker furniture, and muted tones ensure that the focus of the Dzhondzholi dining room is in fact the open kitchen, where the chefs are busy preparing delicious *dolma* (stuffed vine leaves), *khachapuri* (cheese bread), *kharcho* (rice with beef or lamb soup) and other authentic favourites. The food is fabulous, and it comes with none of the kitsch that we've come to expect from Moscow's Georgian restaurants. Fun fact: food connoisseur and cookbook author Darra Goldstein in her book *A Georgian Feast* explains that *dzhondzholi* is 'a garlicky long-stemmed green, usually eaten pickled', that is common in Georgian cuisine. Try it for R190.

AKADEMIYA ITALIAN $$

Map p260 (Академия; www.academiya.ru; Kamergersky per 2; business lunch R280, meals R600-1000; 9am-midnight Mon-Fri, 11am-midnight Sat & Sun; ; Teatralnaya) Somebody at Akademiya knows real estate. That's the only way to explain how this upscale pizzeria is able to find all the sweetest spots. The obvious example is this outlet on Kamergersky per, the pedestrian strip that is the city's prime spot for people-watching. Not surprisingly, you'll also find Akademiya near the Arbat (p115) and in front of the Cathedral of Christ the Saviour (p117).

Neighbourhood Walk

Tverskoy

Start your tour at the stately Teatralnaya plochchad (MTeatralnaya), ringed with eye-goggling architecture. The magnificent **1 Hotel Metropol** is an art nouveau masterpiece. Across the street, the **2 Bolshoi Theatre** is the centrepiece of the square. the Maly Theatre and the National Youth Theatre frame it on either side.

Head up ul Petrovka and turn left onto **3 Kamergersky per**. Lined with restaurants and cafes with outdoor seating, this pleasant pedestrian strip is Moscow's prime people-watching spot. Look out for the **4 Moscow Art Theatre**, founded by Konstantin Stanislavsky in 1898.

From here walk up Tverskaya ul to **5 Tverskaya pl**, home to two Moscow heroes: the centre statue is Yury Dolgoruky, founder of Moscow; across in city hall sits Sergei Sobyanin, mayor of Moscow. East of here, **6 Stoleshnikov per** is another quaint cobblestone strip, lined with fancy boutiques and trendy cafes. The lane terminates at ul Petrovka, where you can pop into the fun-filled **7 Khudozhestvenny Salon** for some souvenir shopping.

Turn left and walk north to pl Petrovskie Vorota, named for the gates that used to guard the city. Here, you can wander around the ancient **8 Upper St Peter Monastery** or the fresh **9 Moscow Museum of Modern Art**.

Cross the Boulevard Ring and walk up ul Karenty Ryad to finish your tour amid the shady greenery of **10 Hermitage Gardens**. Stop for a drink at **11 Chaikhona No 1**, then stroll west on the Boulevard Ring to reach Mayakovskaya metro station.

WORTH A DETOUR

OSTANKINO & AROUND

No other place sums up the rise and fall of the great Soviet dream quite as well as the **All-Russia Exhibition Centre** (Всероссийский Выставочный Центр (ВВЦ); www.vvcentre.ru; ⏲pavilions 10am-7pm, grounds 8am-10pm; ⓂVDNKh). The old initials by which it's still commonly known, VDNKh (ВДНХ), tell half the story – in Russian they stand for Exhibition of Achievements of the National Economy.

Two kilometres long and 1km wide, VDNKh is composed of wide pedestrian avenues and grandiose pavilions glorifying every aspect of socialist construction. The pavilions represent a huge variety of architectural styles, symbolic of the contributions from diverse ethnic and artistic movements to the common goal. Here you will find the kitschiest socialist realism, the most inspiring of socialist optimism and, now, the tackiest of capitalist consumerism.

The soaring 100m titanium obelisk outside the All-Russia Exhibition Centre is a monument 'To the Conquerors of Space', built in 1964 to commemorate the launch of Sputnik. In its base is the **Cosmonautics Museum** (Мемориальный музей космонавтики; www.space-museum.ru; admission R200; ⏲10am-7pm Tue-Sun; ⓂVDNKh), featuring cool space paraphernalia such as the first Soviet rocket engine and the moon-rover Lunokhod. An inspiring collection of space-themed propaganda posters evokes the era of the space race. In 2011, an extensive exhibit opened in honour of the 50th-anniversary of Yury Gagarin's flight. Aside from the historical exhibits, there are some excellent displays about the science of space exploration.

Reach the Cosmonautics Museum from VDNKh metro by promenading along **Cosmonauts' Alley** (аллея Космонавтов), which is lined with the busts of the heroes of the Soviet space program. The entrance to the All-Russia Exhibition Centre is further west, just across Prodolny proezd.

The pink-and-white **Ostankino Palace** (Музей-усадьба Останкино; www.ostankino-museum.ru; admission R80, excursion R150; ⏲10am-6pm Wed-Sun mid-May–Sep; ⓂVDNKh) was built in the 1790s as the summer pad of Count Nikolai Sheremetev. The lavish interior, with hand-painted wallpaper and intricate parquet floors, houses the count's art treasures. Along with the Italian Pavilion and the Egyptian Hall, the centrepiece is the oval theatre-ballroom built for the Sheremetev troupe of 250 serf actors. These days, the theatre hosts a **summer music festival** ('Шереметевские сезоны' музыкальный фестиваль; ☎495-683 4645; tickets R200-750; ⏲Jun-Sep), featuring intimate concerts.

To reach the Ostankino Palace and TV Tower, walk west from VDNKh metro (across the car parks) to pick up tram 7 or 11 or trolleybus 13, 36, 69 or 73 west along ul Akademika Korolyova. Note that the palace is closed on days when it rains or when humidity is high.

When the **Ostankino TV Tower** (Останкинская башня; ☎8-800-100 5553; www.nashabashnya.ru; weekday/weekend R550/850; ⏲10am-8pm Tue-Sun; ⓂVDNKh) was built in 1967, it was the tallest free-standing structure in the world (surpassing the Empire State Building). At 540m, it is now third on the list (though not for too much longer).

The observation deck has recently reopened after a decade-long closure. A super-speedy lift whisks passengers up 337m in less than 60 seconds. From the top, there are 360-degree views. Tours must be booked in advance; bring your passport.

Located at the Hotel Cosmos (opposite the VDNKh metro), the **Kostroma Dance Company** (☎495-234 6373; www.nationalrussianshow.ru; pr Mira 150; tickets R1500; ⏲7.30pm Jun-Sep; ⓂVDNKh) puts on quite a show, with 50 performers, dozens of ensembles and 300 costumes. It amounts to a history of Russian song and dance. Summer months only.

MAKI CAFÉ — ASIAN $

Map p260 (www.makikafe.ru; Glinishchevsky per 3; meals R400-600; ⏲noon-midnight Sun-Thu, noon-5am Fri-Sat; ; ⓂPushkinskaya)

With a menu ranging from its namesake maki rolls to fresh green salads to Italian soft drinks, the theme at the Maki Café is diverse. The cafe is complemented by its minimalist, industrial decor – clunky light fixtures, lots of brick and metal. It appeals to a hip, urban audience, including a regular crowd of gay and lesbian patrons. This is a great place to eat or drink, and the bar gets noisy and fun in the evenings.

SERVICE ENTRANCE CAFETERIA $

Map p260 (Служебный вход; www.svbufet.com; ul Bol Dmitrovka 15; meals 200-400; MPushkinskaya) It doesn't get more 'retro' than the cafeteria of the former Institute of Marxism-Leninism. If you're counting your kopeks, you'll love this throwback, which offers a dozen different salads, several kinds of soup and five or six super-cheap main courses. Fill your tray and take a seat in the dining hall, where you can watch old B&W films on the big screen.

FILIMONOVA & YANKEL FISH HOUSE SEAFOOD $$

Map p260 (Фиш-хаус Филимонова и Янкель; www.fishhouse.ru; Tverskaya ul 23; meals R800-1200; MPushkinskaya) Head to this fish house when you can't stand the sight of another grilled salmon. At Filimonova & Yankel, you can take your pick from 10 varieties of fish – baked, grilled or fried – not to mention other seasonal specialities such as lobster and Kamchatka crab. The fruits of the sea are expertly prepared and efficiently served in an upscale, stylish setting.

PRIME STAR FAST FOOD $

(Map p260; www.prime-star.ru; ul Bolshaya Dmitrovka 7/5; meals R200-300; 7am-11pm; ; MTeatralnaya) Here is a novel concept: a sandwich shop. And not only that, a *healthy* sandwich shop, also serving soups, salads, sushi and other 'natural food'. Everything is preprepared and neatly packaged, so you can eat in or carry out. There are other outlets all over the city, including in Zamoskvorechie (p130) and Arbat (p115).

TRATTORIA VENEZIA ITALIAN $$

Map p260 (www.trattoria-venezia.ru; Strastnoy bul 4/3; meals R600-1000; MChekhovskaya) Pretend that the Boulevard Ring is the Grand Canal. Imagine the cars ensconced in traffic are really gondolas, and the billboard-plastered facade of the Pushkinsky Cinema is actually the Ducal Palace. If you're still reading, then the Trattoria Venezia is for you. The long menu includes more than 25 pasta plates, as well as pizza, risotto, lasagne and Italian-style meat and fish dishes.

BALTISKY KHLEB BAKERY $

Map p260 (Балтийский хлеб; www.baltic-bread.com; ul Malaya Dmitrovka 3/10; meals R200-300, desserts R100-200; 9am-11pm; ; MPushkinskaya) St Petersburg's favourite bakery – 'Baltic Bread' – has made its way to the capital, bringing along its secret recipes for delectable pastries and desserts. This outlet near Pushkinskaya pl, resembling an old-fashioned confectioner, is an excellent place to stop for breakfast, lunch or a late-afternoon coffee.

STARLITE DINER DINER $$

Map p260 (www.starlite.ru; Strastnoy bul 8A;meals R500-700; 24hr; ; MPushkinskaya) Corporate Russia meets vintage America, and the result is a shiny new version of an all-night diner. Sit at the polished chrome counter or sink into a vinyl booth, eat burgers and milkshakes and listen to that old-time rock and roll.

Outer Tverskoy

MI PIACE ITALIAN $$

Map p260 (www.mipiace.ru; 1-ya Tverskaya-Yamskaya 7; meals R600-1000; MMayakovskaya) Outlets of this cool, contemporary pizzeria have spread like wildfire around Moscow. At this outlet near Triumfalnaya pl, big windows allow loads of light into the dining room, and diamond-shaped wine racks are filled with bottles and books. You can sit at a table if you like, but it's much more appealing to hunker down on one of the couches with your pizza pie. There is another outlet at Tverskaya ul 20/1, near Pushkinskaya pl, with outdoor seating.

DRUZHBA CHINESE $$

Map p260 (Дружба; Novoslobodskaya ul 4; meals R600-800; 11am-11pm; ; MNovoslobodskaya) Druzhba earns high marks for authenticity, and as far as Sichuan cuisine goes, that means spicy. Chinese restaurants in Moscow are notorious for turning down their seasoning to appeal to Russian taste buds, but Druzhba is the exception, which goes a long way towards explaining why this place is often packed with Chinese patrons. The chicken with peppers gets red-hot reviews.

DRINKING & NIGHTLIFE

CAFE MART CLUB, CAFE

Map p260 (www.cafemart.ru; ul Petrovka 25; meals R800-1200; ⏲11am-midnight Sun-Wed, 11am-6am Thu-Sat;) Located in the basement of the Moscow Museum of Contemporary Art, this club-cafe is an appropriately artistic place, with warm lighting and mosaic-covered walls. The standard bar menu and decent wine list are accompanied by a selection of enticing exotic teas. Sip your drink while admiring the visual art on display or enjoying a weekly **jazz concert** (⏲9pm Thu). When weather is fine, you can take a seat in the sculpture-filled courtyard.

CHAIKHONA NO 1 CAFE

Map p260 (Чайхона No 1; www.chaihona.com; Hermitage Gardens; ⏲2pm-last guest; MChekhovskaya) Housed in an inviting, exotic tent, laid with oriental rugs and plush pillows, this cool Uzbek lounge and cafe is one of the best chill-out spots in the city. Enjoy fruity drinks and spicy hookahs. If you are hungry, there is *plov* and shashlyk on the menu. There are other outlets around the city, including one near Gorky Park (p132).

SIMACHYOV BAR

Map p260 (www.bar.denissimachev.com; Stoleshnikov per 12/2; ⏲11am-last guest; MChekhovskaya) By day it's a boutique and cafe, owned and operated by the famed fashion designer of the same name. By night, this place becomes a hip-hop-happening nightclub that combines glamour and humour. The eclectic decor includes leopard-skin rugs tossed over tile floors, toilet stools pulled up to a wash-basin bar, Catholic confessionals for private dining, and more. You still have to look sharp to get in here, but at least you can be bohemian about it.

ARTEFAQ CLUB, CAFE

Map p260 (www.artefaq.ru, in Russian; ul Bolshaya Dmitrovka 32; cover R400-600; ⏲24hr, concerts Fri-Sun; MChekhovskaya) It's a club! It's a restaurant! It's a gallery! Set on four levels, ArteFAQ makes use of every inch of space, with music in the basement, a bar and outdoor terrace at ground level and dining upstairs. If you choose to check out the underground, be ready to get your groove on, as the music is heavy on the disco.

GOGOL CLUB, CAFE

Map p260 (Гоголь; www.gogolclubs.ru, in Russian; Stoleshnikov per 11; ⏲24hr, concerts 9pm or 10pm Thu-Sat; MChekhovskaya) Fun, informal and affordable (so surprising on swanky Stoleshnikov), Gogol is great for food, drinks and music. The underground club takes the bunker theme seriously, notifying customers that their food is ready with an air-raid siren. In summer the action moves out to the courtyard, where the gigantic tent is styled like an old-fashioned street scene.

KUKLY PISTOLETY BAR

Map p260 (Куклы Пистолеты; www.kuklypistolety.ru, in Russian; Novoslobodskaya ul 16A; ⏲noon-midnight Sun-Thu, noon-5am Fri & Sat; MMendeleevskaya) Kukly Pistolety is a rarity in Moscow: a friendly bar with good food and reasonable prices that attracts a regular crowd of regular people who like to hang out there on a regular basis. A local. Come to quaff a few cold ones, watch the big screen and enjoy the camaraderie. While you're here, you can ponder the dolls and guns that adorn the walls, thus earning the bar its strange name.

PILSNER BREWERY

Map p260 (Пилзнер; www.pilsner.ru; 1-ya-Yamskaya 1; MMayakovskaya) You don't have to go to Prague to drink delicious freshly drawn Czech beers like Pilsner Urquell and Velkopopovický Kozel. Everything at this place complements the beer, from the wood and leather interior to the *kielbasa* (sausage) on the menu, to the special 'beer infusion', which is recommended after every third mug of beer. There is another outlet in Zamoskvorechie (p132).

12 VOLTS GAY BAR

Map p260 (☎495-933 2815; www.12voltclub.ru, in Russian; Tverskaya ul 12, Bldg 2; meals R400-600; ⏲6pm-6am; MMayakovskaya) The founders of Moscow's lesbian movement opened this cafe-cum-social club, hidden away in a courtyard off Tverskaya ul. Buzz for admission. Once you're in, you'll find both gays and lesbians socialising together in a cosy environment, enjoying great drink specials and listening to pop music.

BAVARIUS PUB

Map p260 (www.bavarius.ru; Sadovaya-Triumfalnaya ul 2/30; MMayakovskaya) German-style brew pubs are popping up all over Moscow, confirming the Russian penchant for salty sausages and thirst-quenching beer. Bavarius competes with the best of them, offering pork chops, sauerkraut and plenty of cold, delicious draughts. It's particularly inviting in summer, when there is seating in the shady beer garden.

ENTERTAINMENT

TOP CHOICE BOLSHOI THEATRE OPERA, BALLET
Map p260 (Большой театр; ☎8-800-333 1333; www.bolshoi.ru; Teatralnaya pl 1; tickets R200-2000; Ⓜ Teatralnaya) An evening at the Bolshoi is still one of Moscow's most romantic and entertaining options for a night on the town. The glittering six-tier auditorium has an electric atmosphere, evoking 235 years of premier music and dance. Both the ballet and opera companies perform a range of Russian and foreign works here. After the collapse of the Soviet Union, the Bolshoi was marred by politics, scandal and frequent turnover. Yet the show must go on – and it will.

The Bolshoi has recently undergone a much-needed renovation. In 2011, the theatre reopened the doors of its main stage after several years of work, revealing expanded theatre space and glittering mouldings. In the meantime, the smaller New Stage (Novaya Stsena), remodelled in 2003, has continued to host performances. See the boxed text, p85, for details on how to purchase tickets.

TOP CHOICE SANDUNY BATHS BANYA
Map p260 (☎private 495-628 4633, general 495-625 4631; www.sanduny.ru; Neglinnaya ul 14; private cabins per 2hr R3000-6000, general admission per 2hr R1000-1800; ⌚8am-midnight; Ⓜ Chekhovskaya) Sanduny is the oldest and most luxurious *banya* (hot bath) in the city. From the moment you disrobe in one of the richly carved wooden dressing stalls to your final plunge in the column-lined swimming pool, you will be surrounded by exoticism and extravagance. Indulge in the 'extra services' such as scrub-down and massage by a professional *parilshchika*. Highly recommended.

MASTERSKAYA LIVE MUSIC
Map p260 (Мастерская; http://mstrsk.livejournal.com, in Russian; Teatralny proezd 3, Bldg 3; cover R300; ⌚noon-6am; Ⓜ Okhotny Ryad) All the best places in Moscow are tucked into far corners of courtyards, and they often have unmarked doors. Such is the case with this super-funky music venue. The eclectic and arty interior makes a cool place to chill out and drink coffee or eat lunch during the day. Evening hours give way to a diverse array of live-music acts or the occasional dance or theatre performance.

MOSCOW ART THEATRE (MKHT) THEATRE
Map p260 (Московский художественный театр (МХАТ); http://art.theatre.ru; Kamergersky per 3; ⌚box office noon-7pm; Ⓜ Teatralnaya) Often called the most influential theatre in Europe, this is where method acting was founded over 100 years ago, by Stanislavsky and Nemirovich-Danchenko (see p86). Besides the theatre itself and an acting studio-school, a small museum about the theatre's history is also on site.

RUSSIAN BALL AT YAR FOLK SHOW
(Ярь; www.sovietsky.ru; Leningradsky pr 32/2, Sovietsky Hotel; tickets R1000, dinner R800-1200; Ⓜ Dinamo) Everything about Yar is over the

TICKETS FOR THE BOLSHOI

Unlike other theatres around Moscow, it is not possible to buy tickets to the Bolshoi at the *teatralnaya kassa* (theatre kiosk). In theory, tickets can be reserved by phone or over the internet up to three months in advance of the performance. It is usually possible to purchase tickets at the Bolshoi's **box office** (☎499-250 7317; ⌚Main Stage 11am-3pm & 4-8pm, New Stage 11am-2pm & 3-7pm), especially if you go several days in advance. Otherwise, you can show up shortly before the show, but you may have to buy tickets from a scalper. Scalpers are easy to find (they will find you); the trick is negotiating a price that is not several times the ticket's face value. Expect to pay upwards of R1000. Most importantly, make sure you examine the ticket and the date of the show (even the year) before money changes hands.

A limited number of reduced-price student tickets (R20) go on sale at the box office one hour before the performance. Go to window number four and bring your student ID.

top, from the vast, gilded interior to the traditional Russian menu to the Moulin Rouge–style dancing girls. The thematic show is infamous for its elaborate costumes. The old-fashioned Russian food is pretty elaborate, too. Buy tickets in advance. Walk 1km southeast from Dinamo metro station.

NOVAYA OPERA OPERA, BALLET

Map p260 (Новая опера; www.novayaopera.ru; ul Karetny Ryad 3; tickets R150-1000; ⏲box office noon-7:30pm; Ⓜ Tsvetnoy Bulvar) This theatre company was founded in 1991 by then-mayor Luzhkov and artistic director Evgeny Kolobov. Maestro Kolobov stated, 'we do not pretend to be innovators in this beautiful and complicated genre of opera'. As such, the 'New Opera' stages the old classics, and does it well. The gorgeous, modern opera house is set amid the Hermitage Gardens.

STANISLAVSKY & NEMIROVICH-DANCHENKO MUSICAL THEATRE OPERA, BALLET

Map p260 (Музыкальный театр Станиславского и Немирович-Данченко; www.stanislavskymusic.ru; ul Bolshaya Dmitrovka 17; tickets R200-1000; ⏲box office 11.30am-7pm; Ⓜ Chekhovskaya) This historic company was founded when two legends of the Moscow theatre scene – Konstantin Stanislavsky and Vladimir Nemirovich-Danchenko – joined forces in 1941. Their newly created theatre became a workshop for applying the innovative dramatic methods of the Moscow Art Theatre to opera and ballet (see the boxed text, p86).

NIKULIN CIRCUS ON TSVETNOY BULVAR CIRCUS

Map p260 (Цирк Никулина; www.circusnikulin.ru; Tsvetnoy bul 13; tickets R400-2500; ⏲box office 11am-2pm & 3-7pm; Ⓜ Tsvetnoy Bulvar) Founded in 1880, this smaller circus is now named after beloved actor and clown Yury Nikulin (1921–97), who performed at the studio here for many years. Unlike performances seen at most traditional circuses, Nikulin's shows centre on a given theme, which serves to add some cohesion to the productions. But the gist is the same – there are lots of trapeze artists, tightrope walkers and performing animals.

OBRAZTSOV PUPPET THEATRE & MUSEUM CHILDREN'S THEATRE

Map p260 (Театр кукол Образцова; www.puppet.ru; Sadovaya-Samotechnaya ul 3; adult R300-1000, child R200-600; ⏲box office 11am-2.30pm & 3.30-7pm; Ⓜ Tsvetnoy Bulvar) The country's largest puppet theatre performs colourful Russian folk tales and adapted classical plays. Kids can get up close and personal with the incredible puppets at the museum, which holds a collection of over 3000.

DOME CINEMA CINEMA

Off Map p260 (www.domecinema.ru; Renaissance Moscow Hotel, Olympiysky pr 18/1; tickets R300; Ⓜ Prospekt Mira) This is one of Moscow's first

STANISLAVSKY'S METHODS

In 1898, over an 18-hour restaurant lunch, actor-director Konstantin Stanislavsky and playwright-director Vladimir Nemirovich-Danchenko founded the Moscow Art Theatre as the forum for method acting. The theatre is known by its Russian initials, MKhT, short for Moskovsky Khudozhestvenny Teatr.

More than just providing another stage, the Art Theatre adopted a 'realist' approach, which stressed truthful portrayal of characters and society, teamwork by the cast (not relying on stars) and respect for the writer. 'We declared war on all the conventionalities of the theatre…in the acting, the properties, the scenery, or the interpretation of the play', Stanislavsky later wrote.

This treatment of *The Seagull* rescued playwright Anton Chekhov from despair after the play had flopped in St Petersburg. *Uncle Vanya, Three Sisters* and *The Cherry Orchard* all premiered in the MKhT. Gorky's *The Lower Depths* was another success. In short, the theatre revolutionised Russian drama.

Method acting's influence in Western theatre has been enormous. In the USA Stanislavsky's theories are, and have been, the primary source of study for many actors, including such greats as Stella Adler, Marlon Brando, Sanford Meisner, Lee Strasberg, Harold Clurman and Gregory Peck.

MKhT (p85), now technically called the Chekhov Moscow Art Theatre, still stages regular performances of Chekhov's work, among other plays.

deluxe American-style theatres. These days films are shown in the original language – usually English – with dubs in Russian on the headphones.

DUROV ANIMAL THEATRE CHILDREN'S THEATRE
Map p260 (Уголок дедушки Дурова; www.ugolokdurova.ru in Russian; ul Durova 4; tickets R150-600; show times vary, 11am-5pm Wed-Sun; Prospekt Mira) Dedushka Durov (Grandpa Durov) founded this zany theatre for kids as a humane alternative to the horrible treatment of animals he saw at the circus. His shows feature mostly domestic animals, including cats and dogs, farm animals and the occasional bear. His most popular show is *Railway for Mice,* and guided tours of the museum give kids a closer look at the railway. Take tram 7 from Prospekt Mira metro station, or walk 1.5km west on ul Durova.

BB KING LIVE MUSIC
Map p260 (www.bbkingclub.ru; Sadovaya-Samotechnaya ul 4/2; noon-midnight, music from 8.30pm; Tsvetnoy Bulvar) This old-style blues club hosts an open jam session on Wednesday night, acoustic blues on Sunday and live performances other nights. The restaurant is open for lunch and dinner, when you can listen to jazz and blues on the old-fashioned jukebox. Enter from the courtyard.

LENKOM THEATRE THEATRE
Map p260 (Ленком театр; www.lenkom.ru, in Russian; ul Malaya Dmitrovka 6; tickets R200-2000; box office noon-3pm & 4-7pm; Pushkinskaya) The Lenkom isn't the most glamorous theatre, but it's widely considered to have the strongest acting troupe in the country. The flashy productions and musicals performed here keep non-Russian speakers entertained.

MALY THEATRE THEATRE
Map p260 (Малый театр; www.maly.ru; Teatralnaya pl 1/6; box office 11am-8pm; Teatralnaya) 'Maly' means small, meaning smaller than the Bolshoi across the street. Actually, these names date back to the time when there were only two theatres in town: the opera theatre was always called the 'Bolshoi' while the drama theatre was the 'Maly'. This elegant theatre, founded in 1824, mainly features performances of 19th-century works by Ostrovsky and the like, many of which premiered here back in the day.

WORTH A DETOUR

KVA-KVA WATER PARK

Calling all kids! This huge **complex** (www.kva-kva.ru; XL Shopping Centre, Yaroslavskoe shosse; adult/child from R830/480; 10am-10pm; VDNKh) features seven long and winding water slides, a terrific tsunami water ride, waterfalls and wave pools. There is something for everyone here: special pools for younger children have shallow waters and warmer temperatures, and adults can relax and feel the soothing pulse of 150 hydromassage jets. Note: children under the age of 18 must be accompanied by an adult. From VDNKh metro station, take bus N333 to the shopping centre, which is about 1km past MKAD.

SATIRIKON THEATRE THEATRE
off Map p260 (Театр Сатирикон; 495-602 6583; www.satirikon.ru, in Russian; Sheremetyevskaya ul 8; tickets R100-1500; box office 11am-8pm; Marina Roshcha) Boasting one of Moscow's most talented theatre producers, Konstantin Raikin, as well as a host of big-name directors, the Satirikon earned a reputation in the early 1990s with its outrageously expensive production of the *Threepenny Opera*. It has since broken its own record for expenditure with *Chantecler,* which featured ducks, cockerels and hens dancing on stage. Located 400m north of Marina Roshcha metro station.

CSKA ARENA SPECTATOR SPORT
off Map p260 (495-225 2600; Leningradsky pr 39A; Aeroport) This 5500-person arena was built in the lead-up to 1980, when it hosted the Olympic basketball tournament. These days it is home to Moscow's most successful basketball and hockey teams. About 1.5km south of Aeroport metro station.

SHOPPING

TOP CHOICE **YEKATERINA** CLOTHING, ACCESSORIES
Map p260 (Екатерина; www.mexa-ekaterina.ru; ul Bolshaya Dmitrovka 11; Teatralnaya) One of Russia's oldest furriers, this place has been manufacturing *shapky* (fur hats) and *shuby* (fur coats) since 1912. While Yekaterina has always maintained a reputation

for high-quality furs and leather, its designs are constantly changing and updating to stay on top of fashion trends.

TOP CHOICE **TRANSYLVANIA** MUSIC

Map p260 (www.transylvania.ru, in Russian; Tverskaya ul 6/1, Bldg 5; 11am-10pm; M Teatralnaya) From the courtyard, look for the black metal door that leads down into this dungeon of a shop, which houses room after room of CDs, in every genre imaginable. If you are curious about the *russky* rock scene, this is where you can sample some songs.

KHUDOZHEZTVENNY SALON ART GALLERY

Map p260 (Художественный салон; 495-628 4593; ul Petrovka 12; 10am-8pm; M Chekhovskaya) Although it has a rather innocuous name, this 'Art Salon' is packed with paintings, sculpture, ceramics, jewellery and handicrafts by local artists. This place is owned by the artists, so you won't have the high gallery mark-ups you might find at some other art centres.

YELISEEV GROCERY FOOD & DRINK

Map p260 (Елисеевский магазин; Tverskaya ul 14; 8am-9pm Mon-Sat, 10am-6pm Sun; M Pushkinskaya) Peek in here for a glimpse of prerevolutionary grandeur, as the store is set in the former mansion of the successful merchant Yeliseev. It now houses an upscale market selling caviar and other delicacies. It's a great place to shop for souvenirs for your foodie friends back home.

RESPUBLIKA BOOKSTORE

Map p260 (Республика; www.respublica.ru; 1-ya Tverskaya Yamskaya 10; 10am-9pm; M Mayakovskaya) It's a bookstore, but it's also a gift shop, a music shop and (of course) a cafe. This is the place to shop for a quirky gift for your friend who (you think) has everything. You will surely be proven wrong. For example, does he have a frog shower cap? Would she like a Swarovki eye mask? For lovers of French toast, how about a toast imprint of the Eiffel Tower?

ATLAS MAP STORE

Map p260 (Атлас; Kuznetsky most 9/10; M Kuznetsky Most) This little shop houses an impressive collection of maps, including city and regional maps covering the whole country. The walls are plastered with most of the maps that are for sale.

SIMACHYOV BOUTIQUE & BAR CLOTHING, ACCESSORIES

Map p260 (www.denissimachev.com; Stoleshnikov per 12/2; M Chekhovskaya) The wild child of Russian fashion, Denis Simachyov has become a household name in Moscow, thanks to his popular nightclub and irreverent clothing. His collections have been inspired by themes as diverse as Russian sailors, Chechen war victims, Siberian peasants, hip hop gangsters and gypsy nomads.

PODIUM CONCEPT STORE CLOTHING, ACCESSORIES

Map p260 (Kuznetsky most 14; noon-midnight; M Kuznetsky Most) This gorgeous 'concept store' offers six storeys of high fashion and fun design. Huge windows framed with heavy drapes, an embossed tin ceiling and plush furniture provide an exquisite setting for edgy and exotic (and expensive) clothing.

BUSTIER LINGERIE

Map p260 (Бюстье; www.bustier.ru; Kuznetsky most 3; M Teatralnaya) Sensational, sexy lingerie is now on sale all over Moscow. Several top-of-the-line stores stock European designer lingerie that is deliciously sensual and devastatingly expensive. Bustier is more moderately priced, but also features classy French and Italian styles, as well as some Russian designs. One of many outlets around town.

TSUM DEPARTMENT STORE

Map p260 (ЦУМ; www.tsum.ru, in Russian; ul Petrovka 2; M Teatralnaya) TsUM stands for Tsentralny Universalny Magazin (Central Department Store). Built in 1909 as the Scottish-owned Muir & Merrilees, it was the first department store aimed at middle-class shoppers. These days it's filled with designer labels and luxury items.

DOM FARFORA HOUSEWARES

Map p260 (Дом Фарфора; www.domfarfora.ru; 1-ya Tverskaya-Yamskaya 17; 10am-9pm; M Belorusskaya) The 'house of china' sells the world's most famous brands of fine china, including Russia's own *Imperatorsky farforovy zavod* (imperial china factory). Designs are tasteful, traditional, whimsical and wonderful, and sometimes all of the above. A Moscow-themed tea set makes a perfect souvenir.

KARPOV CHESS
SOUVENIRS

Map p260 (Шахматы Карпова; www.karpovchess.ru, in Russian; 1-ya Tverskaya-Yamskaya ul 28; ⌚noon-8pm; Ⓜ Belorusskaya) What more apt souvenir from Russia than a handmade chess set with pieces carved from precious hardwoods? And what better promoter than chess master Anatoly Karpov? After half a century of declaring checkmate, Karpov says, he appreciates a chess set where each piece is a thoughtfully crafted work of art. You will too.

RUSSIAN BRONZE
SOUVENIRS

Map p260 (Русская бронза; www.russkayabronza.com, in Russian; ul Kuznetsky most 20; ⌚9am-9pm; Ⓜ Kuznetsky Most) The factory outlet for the Vel metallurgical company is chock-full of bronze sculptures and figurines, as well as office accessories, tableware, teaspoons, candelabras, piggy banks and other potential souvenirs.

K FABERGE
SOUVENIRS

Map p260 (www.moonstone.ru, in Russian; ul Kuznetsky most 20; Ⓜ Kuznetsky Most) Owned by the granddaughter of the famed jeweller to the tsars, this little boutique contains everything that glitters. Besides jewellery, the glass cases are stuffed with crystal and fine china, ornately carved weapons, old-fashioned watches and – of course – the namesake ceramic Easter eggs.

DOM INOSTRANNOY KNIGI
BOOKSTORE

Map p260 (Дом иностранной книги; www.mdk-arbat.ru; Kuznetsky most 18/7; Ⓜ Kuznetsky Most) The House of Foreign Books is a small place with a wide selection of literature in foreign languages. Most books are in English, though there are smaller selections of German, French and other European languages.

MASTERSKAYA ROSEMARIE
SOUVENIRS

Map p260 (Мастерская Розмари; www.m-rosemarie.ru; Kuznetsky most 21/5; ⌚10am-9pm; Ⓜ Lubyanka) Sweet smells greet all comers to Rosemarie's little boutique, much of which is occupied with soaps, creams and lotions. She also sells handmade objects ranging from the very useful to the very useless.

ROOM ARTERIUM
ART GALLERY

Map p260 (www.room.su, in Russian; 1-ya Tverskaya-Yamskaya ul 7; Ⓜ Mayakovskaya) Room is really an interior-design service and showroom, its 1st floor displaying modern furniture and accessories, as well as some on-topic coffee-table books (in English). Downstairs, the 'Arterium' is a sort of gallery with an ever-changing exhibition of contemporary art.

DETSKY MIR
DEPARTMENT STORE

Map p260 (Детский Мир; Teatralny proezd 5; Ⓜ Lubyanka) As of 2008, 'Children's World' is closed for a complex and highly controversial renovation project. Developers have promised not to alter the building's art deco exterior, which is considered a Moscow landmark. But the interior will be completely revamped, with the addition of underground parking, an internal atrium, a multiplex cinema and a family-focused entertainment zone. Stay tuned.

Presnya

INNER PRESNYA | OUTER PRESNYA

Neighbourhood Top Five

❶ Following *The Master and Margarita* from its opening scene at **Patriarch's Ponds** (p93) to its climax at the Central House of Writers, or **CDL** (p96), following up with a visit to the author's **Bulgakov House** (p95).

❷ Stargazing, performing science experiments and braving flight simulation at the **Moscow Planetarium** (p93).

❸ Indulging in an *haute russe* feast at **Café Pushkin** (p96) or a Ukrainian peasant meal at **Shinok** (p98).

❹ Cooling off at the **Ice Sculpture Gallery** (p96).

❺ Attending the **Tchaikovsky Concert Hall** (p100) or **Moscow Tchaikovsky Conservatory** (p101) to listen to a world-class concert (perhaps Tchaikovsky).

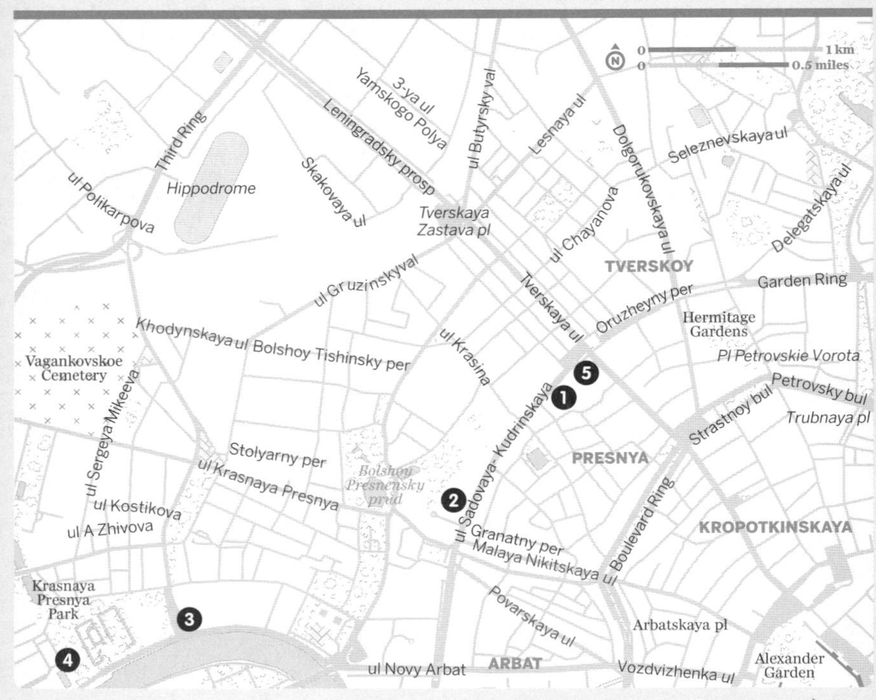

For more detail of this area, see Map p264

Explore: Presnya

Presnya encompasses some of the capital's oldest neighbourhoods as well as its newest development. Start by exploring the lovely residential areas of Inner Presnya, chock-full of evocative architecture, historic parks and fantastic drinking and dining spots. The whole neighbourhood is a wonderful place for a wander, especially with a copy of Bulgakov's *The Master & Margarita* in hand. Come in the late afternoon, then stay for dinner, as the area around Patriarch's Ponds has emerged as a dining hotspot, with restaurants lined up along Spiridonovsky per.

The more traditional sights – the newly reopened planetarium and the huge zoo – are set on the busy Garden Ring (ring road 3km from the Kremlin). Either attraction could entertain you for a few hours.

Further out, the wide roads, heavy traffic and ongoing construction mean that Outer Presnya is not particularly user-friendly. Make the trip only if you have your heart set on a particular destination.

Local Life

➡ **Parks** Packs of teens, grandmothers with wee ones and starry-eyed couples all congregate at Patriarch's Ponds (p93) to sit on the shady benches and feed the ducks.

➡ **Bakery** The queue often runs out the door, as loyal patrons wait their turn for the city's best fresh-baked breads, pastries and pies at Volkonsky (p97).

➡ **Hang-outs** Local faves include Coffee Mania (p99) for the glam crowd, Mayak (p99) for journalists and politiologues, and Kvartira 44 (p99) for the arty intelligentsia.

➡ **Brunch** Weekends at Correa's (p98) are an expat institution.

Getting There & Away

➡ **Inner Presnya** Inner Presnya is most easily accessed from Mayakovskaya station on the green Zamoskvoretskaya line or Pushkinskaya station on the purple Tagansko-Presnenskaya line.

➡ **Outer Presnya** For the more western parts of the district, the most useful metro stations are at Kudrinskaya pl (Barrikadnaya or Krasnopresnenskaya stations) and ul 1905 goda (Ulitsa 1905 Goda station). The new development around Moskva-City has its own minimetro spur branching off from Kievskaya station, with a convenient stop at Vystavochnaya.

Lonely Planet Top Tip

In the back streets around Bolshaya Nikitskaya ul, many old mansions have survived – some renovated, others dilapidated. Most of those on the streets closest to the Kremlin were built by the 18th-century aristocracy, while those further away were built by rising 19th-century industrialists. These days many of these buildings are occupied by embassies and cultural institutions. With little traffic, Bolshaya Nikitskaya ul is excellent for a quiet ramble.

Best Places to Eat

➡ Café Pushkin (p96)

➡ Volkonsky (p97)

➡ Correa's (p98)

For reviews, see p96 ➡

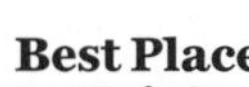

Best Places to Drink

➡ Kvartira 44 (p99)

➡ Mayak (p99)

➡ Coffee Mania (p99)

For reviews, see p99 ➡

Best Kids' Outings

➡ Moscow Planetarium (p93)

➡ Moscow Zoo (p95)

➡ Ice Sculpture Gallery (p96)

➡ Tsereteli Studio-Museum (p95)

For reviews, see p92 ➡

SIGHTS

Inner Presnya

CHURCH OF THE RESURRECTION — CHURCH

Map p264 (Церковь Воскресения; Bryusov per 2; MPushkinskaya) Through the arch off of Tverskaya ul, the unexpected, gold-domed Church of the Resurrection was one of the few churches to remain open throughout the Soviet period. As such, it is full of fine icons and artwork that was rescued from churches torn down during the Soviet era.

ART4.RU — ART GALLERY

Map p264 (www.art4.ru; Khlinovsky tupik 4; adult/student R200/100; ⊙11am-10pm Fri & Sat; MOkhotny Ryad) Anyone can be a museum director, as demonstrated by Moscow businessman-turned-art-collector Igor Markin. His 700-plus piece collection had outgrown his private properties, so he decided to start a museum where he could display his art and share it with the public. And so art4.ru (read 'art for Russia') was born. The small gallery space is used to exhibit not only pieces from Markin's own collection, but also up-and-coming artists that he has 'discovered'. There are also classes and lectures for adults and children.

FREE MATRYOSHKA MUSEUM — MUSEUM

Map p264 (Музей матрёшки; Leontevsky per 7; ⊙10am-6pm Mon-Thu, 10am-5pm Fri; MPushkinskaya) On a quiet side street, this two-room museum – formerly the Museum of Folk Art – showcases designer *matryoshki* (nesting dolls) and different painting techniques. The centrepiece is a 1m-high *matryoshka* with 50 dolls inside. The exhibit demonstrates the history of this favourite Russian souvenir. Don't come looking for modern-day, pop-culture-inspired dolls because the museum takes a traditionalist tack. Downstairs, an excellent souvenir shop offers a wide selection of handicrafts, including hand-painted *matryoshki*.

CHURCHES OF THE GRAND & SMALL ASCENSION — CHURCH

Map p264 (Церковь Большого Вознесения и Церковь Малого Вознесения; Bolshaya Nikitskaya ul; MArbatskaya) In 1831 the poet Alexander Pushkin married Natalya Goncharova in the elegant **Church of the Grand Ascension**, on the western side of pl Nikitskie Vorota. Six years later he died in St Petersburg, defending her honour in a duel. Such passion, such romance... The church is frequently closed, but the celebrated couple is featured in the Rotunda Fountain, erected in 1999 to commemorate the poet's 100th birthday.

Down the street, the festive **Church of the Small Ascension** sits on the corner of Voznesensky per. Built in the early 17th century, it features whitewashed walls and stone embellishments carved in a primitive style.

MOSCOW MUSEUM OF MODERN ART — MUSEUM

Map p264 (Московский музей современного искусства; www.mmoma.ru; Tverskoy bul 9; ⊙noon-8pm; MPushkinskaya) This small exhibition space, known as the 'Zurab' Gallery, was formerly the studio space of sculptor Zurab Tsereteli. As such, the space has seen many talented artists, musicians and writers among its guests. Nowadays it is a branch of the main MMOMA outlet on ul Petrovka (p75), and continues to host exhibits, performances and cultural events. Be sure to check the website to see what's on, as the museum often closes in between shows.

FREE GORKY HOUSE-MUSEUM — MUSEUM

Map p264 (Дом-музей Горького; Malaya Nikitskaya ul 6/2; ⊙11am-6pm Wed-Sun; MPushkinskaya) Also known as the Ryabushinsky house, this fascinating 1906 art nouveau mansion was designed by Fyodor Shekhtel and gifted to celebrated author Maxim Gorky in 1931. The house is a visual fantasy with sculpted doorways, ceiling murals, stained glass, a carved stone staircase and exterior tile work. Besides the fantastic decor it contains many of Gorky's personal items, including his extensive library. A small room in the cupola houses random, rotating exhibits of contemporary or quixotic artwork.

DOM IKONY ON SPIRIDONOVKA — MUSEUM

Map p264 (Дом иконы на Спиридоновке; www.dom-ikony.ru; ul Spiridonovka 4; admission R150; ⊙noon-10pm Tue-Sun; MPushkinskaya) The collection of more than 2000 pieces includes pieces from the 15th to the 20th century, with many countries represented. The prize is perhaps the 15th-century icon of the Mother of God, Odigitria. Other pieces were actually part of the collection of the last Russian tsar Nicholas II.

This unique museum aims to increase the public's appreciation of iconography. In the 'academic hall', interested patrons can learn about the development of Christian art in Europe and Russia, while museum experts also conduct lectures and classes on art history and restoration.

LYUBAVICHESKAYA SYNAGOGUE SYNAGOGUE

Map p264 (Любавическая синагога; Bolshaya Bronnaya ul 6; MPushkinskaya) Converted to a theatre in the 1930s, this building was still used for gatherings by the Jewish community throughout the Soviet period. Today the building serves as a working synagogue, as well as a social centre for the small but growing Jewish community in Moscow.

PATRIARCH'S PONDS PARK

Map p264 (Патриаршие пруды; Bolshoy Patriarshy per; MMayakovskaya) Patriarch's Ponds harks back to Soviet days, when the parks were populated with children and babushky. You'll see grandmothers pushing strollers, and lovers kissing on park benches. In summer children romp on the swings and monkey bars, while winter sees them ice skating on the pond. The small park has a huge statue of 19th-century Russian writer Ivan Krylov, known to Russian children for his didactic tales. Once this area contained several ponds that kept fish for the Patriarch's court (hence the name).

Patriarch's Ponds were immortalised by writer Mikhail Bulgakov, who had the devil appear here in *The Master and Margarita*. The initial paragraph of the novel describes the area to the north of the pond, where the devil enters the scene and predicts the rapid death of Berlioz. Contrary to Bulgakov's tale, a tram line never ran along the pond. Bulgakov's flat, where he wrote the novel and lived up until his death, is around the corner on the Garden Ring.

MOSCOW MUSEUM OF MODERN ART MUSEUM

Map p264 (Московский музей современного искусства; www.mmoma.ru; Yermolayevsky per 17; adult/student R200/100; noon-8pm; MMayakovskaya) This handsome neoclassical building houses a branch of the main MMOMA on ul Petrovka (p75). Formerly the Moscow Union of Artists, it is now utilised for temporary exhibits of paintings, sculpture, photography and multimedia pieces. Be sure to check the website to see what's on, as the museum often closes in between shows.

TOP SIGHTS MOSCOW PLANETARIUM

After a 17-year closure, the Moscow Planetarium has finally reopened its doors to the sky. Dare we say it was worth the wait? The new planetarium shines bigger and brighter than before, expanding in area by more than three times and incorporating all kinds of high-tech gadgetry, interactive exhibits and educational programs.

The centrepiece is the Big Star Hall (the biggest in Europe!), with its 25m silver dome roof. There are two observatories, the larger of which (aka the Big Observatory) employs Moscow's largest telescope. Another favourite attraction is the four-dimensional cinema, which features 3D images plus other special sensual effects like sounds, smells and movement.

The new facility includes the innovative interactive Lunarium, where visitors can perform experiments. Fun hands-on activities include generating electrical energy, riding a cosmic bicycle and determining your weight on another planet. The Space Exploration Hall allows visitors to imagine what it's like to travel in space. When the weather allows, the Sky Park is open for curious minds to investigate astronomical instruments, running the gamut from sun dials to solar panels. Old-school exhibits include the collection of meteorites in the Urania Museum.

DON'T MISS...

- Big Star Hall
- Interactive 'Lunarium' museum
- Sky Park

PRACTICALITIES

- Map p264
- Планетарий Москвы
- www.planetarium-moscow.ru, in Russian
- Sadovaya-Kudrinskaya ul 5
- exhibits R350-500
- museum 10am-9pm, theatre 10am-midnight Wed-Mon
- MBarrikadnaya

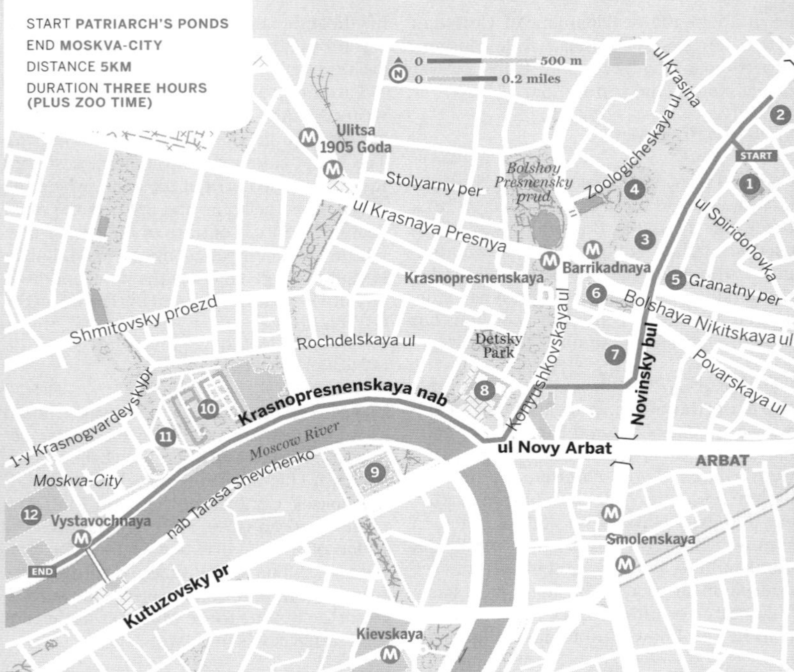

Neighbourhood Walk
Presnya

This tour is like walking from the previous century into the present (and beyond). Start by strolling around 1 **Patriarch's Ponds**. Bring your copy of *The Master and Margarita* and shed a tear for Berlioz, who met his bloody end here, then take a detour to 2 **Bulgakov House**, where the controversial author lived and worked.

Continue along the Garden Ring past the shiny new 3 **Moscow Planetarium** and the 4 **Moscow Zoo**. Each of these sights is a walking tour in itself.

Further south 5 **Chekhov House-Museum** was the playwright's home for four of his most prolific years.

Dominated by the massive skyscraper that is one of 6 **Stalin's Seven Sisters** (see p211), Kudrinskaya pl is a loud, busy square. Just south of here is one of Moscow's last and best examples of modernist architecture, 7 **Narkomfin**.

Continue south to Krasnopresnenskaya nab. On the banks of the Moscow River is the massive facade of the 8 **White House**, home of the Russian parliament. The former 9 **Hotel Ukraine**, another of Stalin's Seven Sisters, stands on the opposite side of the river, almost a tribute to times gone by.

Further west along the embankment, the fountains, flowers and cafes make 10 **Krasnaya Presnya Park** a pleasant place for a pause. Don your woollies and enter the 11 **Ice Sculpture Gallery** to ogle the frozen artwork.

In the distance, the steel and glass structures of the International Business Centre sprout up along the Moscow River. Note the double-pronged 12 **City of Capitals building**. The taller of the two towers is the tallest skyscraper in Europe, looming 302m over the capital. Moskva-City (M Vystavochnaya) will soon be home to legions of bureaucrats, business people and perhaps a few billionaires.

FREE BULGAKOV HOUSE MUSEUM

Map p264 (Дом Булгакова; www.dombulgakova.ru, in Russian; Bolshaya Sadovaya ul 10; ⏲1-11pm Sun-Thu, 1pm-1am Fri & Sat; Ⓜ Mayakovskaya) Author of *The Master and Margarita* and *Heart of a Dog,* Mikhail Bulgakov was a Soviet-era novelist and playwright who was labelled a counter-revolutionary and censored throughout most of his life. His most celebrated novels were published posthumously, earning him a sort of cult following in the late Soviet period. Bulgakov lived with his third wife Yelena Shilovskaya (the inspiration for Margarita) in a flat on the Garden Ring from 1931 until his death in 1940.

Back in the 1990s the empty flat was a hang-out for dissidents and hooligans, who painted graffiti and wrote poetry on the walls. Nowadays, the walls have been whitewashed and the doors locked, but there is a small museum and cafe on the ground floor. The exhibit features some of his personal items, as well as posters and illustrations of his works. More interesting are the readings and concerts that are held here (check the website), as well as the offbeat tours on offer. A black cat hangs out in the courtyard.

CHEKHOV HOUSE-MUSEUM MUSEUM

Map p264 (Дом-музей Чехова; ul Sadovaya-Kudrinskaya 6; admission R100; ⏲11am-6pm Mon, Wed & Sat, 2-8pm Tue & Thu; Ⓜ Barrikadnaya) 'The colour of the house is liberal, ie red', Anton Chekhov wrote of his house on the Garden Ring, where he lived from 1886 to 1890. The red house now contains the Chekhov House-Museum, with bedrooms, drawing room and study all intact. The overall impression is one of a peaceful and cultured family life. The walls are decorated with paintings that were given to Chekhov by Levitan (painter) and Shekhtel (art nouveau architect), who often visited him here. Photographs depict the playwright with literary greats Leo Tolstoy and Maxim Gorky. One room is dedicated to Chekhov's time in Melikhovo, showing photographs and manuscripts from his country estate.

Outer Presnya

MOSCOW ZOO ZOO

Map p264 (Московский зоопарк; www.moscowzoo.ru, in Russian; cnr Barrikadnaya & Bolshaya Gruzinskaya uls; adult/child R200/free; ⏲10am-7pm Tue-Sun May-Sep, 10am-5pm Tue-Sun Oct-Apr; Ⓜ Barrikadnaya) Popular with families, this big zoo is surprisingly well maintained and populated with lots of wildlife, though enclosures are often too small for animal comfort. The highlight is the big cats exhibit, starring several Siberian tigers. Huge flocks of feathered friends populate the central pond, making for a pleasant stroll for bird-watchers. For a new perspective on Moscow's nightlife, check out the nocturnal animal exhibit. At night this interior space is artificially lit so the animals can sleep; by day the black lighting allows visitors to see them prowling around as they would during the darkest hours. For more four-legged fun, follow the footbridge across Barrikadnaya ul to see the exhibits featuring animals from each continent.

TSERETELI STUDIO-MUSEUM MUSEUM

Map p264 (Музея-мастерская Зураба Церетели; www.mmoma.ru; Bolshaya Gruzinskaya ul 15; admission R150; ⏲11am-7pm Fri-Wed, 1-9pm Thu; Ⓜ Belorusskaya) Moscow's most prolific artist is at it again, this time opening up his 'studio' as a space to exhibit his many masterpieces. You can't miss this place – for the whimsical characters that adorn the front lawn. They give just a tiny hint of what's inside: a courtyard crammed with bigger-than-life bronze beauties and elaborate enamel work. The highlight is undoubtedly Putin in his judo costume, although the huge tile Moscow cityscapes are impressive. You'll also recognise some smaller-scale models of monuments that appear around town. Indoors, there are three floors of the master's sketches, paintings and enamel arts.

NARKOMFIN NOTABLE BUILDING

Map p264 (Наркомфин; Novinsky bul 25; Ⓜ Barrikadnaya) The model for Le Corbusier's Unitè D'Habitation design principle, this architectural landmark was an early experiment in semi-communal living. Designed and built between 1928 and 1930 by Moisei Ginzburg and Ignatii Milinis, Narkomfin offered housing for members of the Commissariat of Finances. There was room for 52 families in duplex apartments and a penthouse on the roof for the Commissar of Finances. In line with constructivist ideals, communal space was maximised and individual space was minimised. Apartments had minute kitchens and people were encouraged to eat in the communal dining room in the neighbouring utilities block.

Having been in a semi-ruinous state for many years, a Russian property development group has been trying to buy up apartments in the building with the long-term intention of preserving the constructivist landmark and converting it into a hotel. In the meantime, the dilapidated apartments are being leased to artists for very low rents. Unfortunately, the Moscow city government has not granted the necessary permissions for restoration of the building, so its future remains in limbo.

SHALYAPIN HOUSE-MUSEUM MUSEUM

Map p264 (Дом-музей Шаляпина; Novinsky bul 25; admission R50; ⌚10am-5pm Tue & Sat, 11.30am-6pm Wed & Thu, 10am-3.30pm Sun; Ⓜ Barrikadnaya) The world-famous opera singer Fyodor Shalyapin (also spelt Chaliapin) lived in this quaint cottage from 1910 to 1920 with his Italian wife and five children. In Russian cultural life, the eminent bass stands alongside icons such as Konstantin Stanislavsky and Maxim Gorky. Indeed, his stature is evident from the museum exhibit, which features photographs of the singer in such admirable company, as well as gifts and correspondence that they exchanged. More interesting for theatre buffs are the posters featuring Shalyapin's most celebrated performances, original stage costumes and recordings of his performances. Occasional concerts are held in the museum's white room.

Next door to Shalyapin's house, the small **art gallery** (☎495-255 5787; admission R50; ⌚11am-7pm Wed-Mon) holds temporary exhibits by local artists, most of whom have some historical association with Shalyapin or the surrounding neighbourhood.

WHITE HOUSE NOTABLE BUILDING

Map p264 (Белый дом; Krasnopresnenskaya nab 2; Ⓜ Krasnopresnenskaya) Moscow's White House, scene of two crucial episodes in recent Russian history, stands just north of Novoarbatsky most. It was here that Boris Yeltsin rallied the opposition that confounded the 1991 hard-line coup, then two years later sent in tanks and troops to blast out conservative rivals, some of them the same people who backed him in 1991. The images of Yeltsin climbing on a tank in front of the White House in 1991, and of the same building ablaze after the 1993 assault, are among the most unforgettable from those tumultuous years. These days, things are relatively stable around the White House, where Prime Minister Putin now has his office.

The White House – officially called the House of Government of the Russian Federation (Dom Pravitelstva Rossiyskoy Federatsii) – fronts a stately bend in the Moscow River, with the Stalinist Hotel Ukraina (now the Radisson) rising on the far bank. This corner of Moscow is particularly appealing when these buildings and Novoarbatsky most are lit up at night.

ICE SCULPTURE GALLERY MUSEUM

Map p264 (Галерея лёдовой скульптуры; www.posuda-ice.ru/gallery; Krasnaya Presnya Park; adult/student/child R470/250/250; ⌚11am-8pm; Ⓜ Ulitsa 1905 Goda) Ice sculpture has a long history in Russia, but it's not usually a year-round attraction. Until now. Cool off in the first-ever year-round Ice Sculpture Gallery, which is housed in a refrigerated winter-wonderland tent at the west end of Krasnaya Presnya Park. The changing exhibit is small but spectacular – the frozen masterpieces enhanced by colourful lights and dreamy music. The admission price includes a special down vest and warm fuzzy foot-covers to protect you from the -10°C climate.

EATING

Inner Presnya

CDL RUSSIAN $$$

Map p264 (ЦДЛ; ☎495-691 1515; www.cdlrestaurant.ru; Povarskaya ul 50; meals from R2000; 🚭; Ⓜ Barrikadnaya) The acronym stands for Tsentralny Dom Literatov, or Central House of Writers, which is the historic 19th-century building that houses this fancy restaurant. A glittery chandelier above, plush carpets under foot and rich oak panelling all around create a sumptuous setting for an old-fashioned Russian feast. Reservations recommended.

CAFÉ PUSHKIN RUSSIAN $$$

Map p264 (Кафе Пушкинъ; ☎495-739 0033; www.cafe-pushkin.ru; Tverskoy bul 26a; business lunch R750, meals R1500-2000; ⌚24hr; Ⓜ Pushkinskaya) The tsarina of *haute-russe* dining, with an exquisite blend of Russian and French cuisines – service and food are done to perfection. The lovely 19th-century building has a different atmosphere on each floor, including a richly decorated library and a pleasant rooftop cafe.

VOLKONSKY BAKERY $

Map p264 (Волконский; www.wolkonsky.com; Bolshaya Sadovaya ul 2/46; meals R200-400; ⏲8am-11pm; Ⓜ Mayakovskaya) The queue often runs out the door, as loyal patrons wait their turn for the city's best fresh-baked breads, pastries and pies. It's worth the wait, especially if you decide on a fruit-filled croissant or to-die-for olive bread. Choose something sweet or savoury from the glass case, then head next door to the big wooden tables for large bowls of coffee or tea. There is another outlet in Basmanny (p141).

KHACHAPURI GEORGIAN $$

Map p264 (Хачапури; www.hacha.ru; Bolshoy Gnezdnikovsky per 10; lunch R200-500, meals R500-800; ⏲10am-11pm; Ⓜ Pushkinskaya) Unassuming, affordable and appetising, this urban cafe exemplifies what people love abut Georgian culture: in short, the warm hospitality and the fresh-baked *khachapuri* (cheese bread). Aside from seven types of delicious *khachapuri,* there's also an array of soups, shashlyki (kebabs), *khinkali* (dumplings) and other Georgian favourites.

MARI VANNA RUSSIAN $$

Map p264 (Мари Ванна; ☎495-650 6500; www.marivanna.ru; Spiridonovsky per 10; meals R800-1200; ⏲9am-11pm; Ⓜ Pushkinskaya) Remember when the best Russian food was served in somebody's crowded living room, on tiny mismatched plates, on a table cluttered with dried flowers in vases and framed photographs? Mari Vanna invites you to recall these days – don't look for the sign (there is none), just ring the doorbell at No 10. You will be ushered into these homey environs, complete with overstuffed bookcases and B&W TV showing old Soviet shows. You will be served delicious Russian home cooking and, just when you begin to think it is 1962, you will be handed your bill with the prices of modern-day Moscow. Ouch.

SCANDINAVIA SWEDISH $$$

Map p264 (www.scandinavia.ru; Maly Palashevsky per 7; lunch R600-800, meals R1500-1800; Ⓜ Pushkinskaya) In most parts of the world, Swedish cuisine is not really celebrated; in Moscow, it is. Much beloved of Moscow expats, Scandi offers an enticing interpretation of what happens 'when Sweden meets Russia'. A delightful summer cafe features sandwiches, salads and treats from the grill (including the best burgers in Moscow, by some accounts). Inside, the dining room offers a sophisticated menu of modern European delights.

SULIKO GEORGIAN $$

Map p264 (Yermolayevsky per 7; www.suliko.ru, in Russian; meals R600-1000; ⏲10am-11pm; Ⓜ Mayakovskaya) Suliko further enriches the area around Patriarch's Ponds with delicious Georgian fare. This place foregoes the trends and the tack, serving up tasty, traditional favourites in a tasteful setting.

PAVILION RUSSIAN $$$

Map p264 (Павильон; ☎495-697 5110; www.restsindikat.com; Bolshoy Patriarshy per 7; meals R1200-1800; ⏲24hr; Ⓜ Mayakovskaya) Occupying the old boathouse overlooking Patriarch's Ponds, this place is hard to beat for atmosphere. While the pavilion dates from the 19th century, the interior has gone retro. After a recent renovation, the restaurant reopened with a new 'high Soviet' design and a menu to match. All the old favourites are here, exquisitely prepared, and sometimes with a surprising twist. The *samogon* (home-brewed vodka) is highly recommended!

STOLLE RUSSIAN $

Map p264 (Штолле; www.stolle.ru; Bolshaya Sadovaya ul 8/1; meals R200-600; ⏲8am-10pm; Ⓜ Mayakovskaya) This is one of Moscow's coolest places to come for coffee, although you'd be a fool to leave without sampling one of its magnificent *pirogi* (pies). In fact, the entire menu is excellent, but the pies are irresistible. A 'stolle' is a traditional Saxon Christmas cake: the selection of sweets and savouries sits on the counter, fresh from the oven. It may be difficult to decide (mushroom or meat, apricot or apple?), but you really can't go wrong. There is another outlet in Khamovniki (p117).

CHAGALL JEWISH $$

(Map p264; www.chagall.ru; 47/3 Bolshaya Nikitskaya ul; meals R800-1200; Ⓜ Barrikadnaya) Inside a Jewish community centre, this convivial kosher restaurant serves tasty, freshly made dishes. The sour-sweet beef dish *esik fleish* is delicious as are the *latkes* (potato pancakes).

STARLITE DINER DINER $$

Map p264 (www.starlite.ru; Bolshaya Sadovaya ul 16; meals R500-700; 24hr; ; Mayakovskaya) Outdoor seating and classic diner decor make this a longtime favourite of Moscow expats. The extensive breakfast menu includes all kinds of omelettes, French toast and freshly squeezed juice. Otherwise, you can't go wrong with burgers and milkshakes, any time of day or night. Additional outlets are in Tverskoy (p83) and Zamoskvorechie (p130).

TURANDOT CHINESE $$$

Map p264 (495-739 0011; www.turandotpalace.ru; Tverskoy bul 26/5; meals R1500-2000; Pushkinskaya) If you wanted to go to Disney World, but somehow ended up in Moscow, Turandot should be at the top of your dining wish list. Completely costumed in wigs and gowns, musicians play chamber music and servers scuttle to and fro. The decor is unbelievably extravagant, with hand-painted furniture, gilded light fixtures and frescoed cupola ceiling. It is certainly every bit as elaborate as Cinderella's castle. Turandot is named for a Puccini opera set in old Peking, which is as good a reason as any to serve Chinese and Japanese food in this baroque interior.

Outer Presnya

CORREA'S EUROPEAN $$

Map p264 (495-605 9100; www.correas.ru; Bolshaya Gruzinskaya ul 32; brunch R400-600, sandwiches R200-400, meals R600-1000; 8am-midnight; ; Belorusskaya) It's hard to characterise a place that is so simple. Correa's occupies a tiny space and there are only seven tables. But the existence of large windows and an open kitchen guarantee that it does not feel cramped, just cosy. The menu – sandwiches, pizza and grills – features nothing too fancy, but everything is prepared with the freshest ingredients and the utmost care. There's another outlet near Triumfalnaya pl (p99).

RAGOUT FUSION $$

Map p264 (495-662 6458; www.caferagout.ru; Bolshaya Gruzinskaya ul 69; meals R800-1200; 8am-midnight; ; Belorusskaya) Muscovites are raving about Ragout. The vibe is cool, but not cooler than thou. The food choices are creative, but not crazy. This gastropub is part of a culinary movement to provide fine dining at reasonable prices – a concept that's overdue in Moscow.

BOTANIKA FUSION $$

Map p264 (Ботаника; www.botanika.restoran.ru; Bolshaya Gruzinskaya ul 61; meals R500-700; 11am-midnight; ; Belorusskaya) Rare is the restaurant in Moscow that is both fashionable and affordable. Somehow Botanika manages to be both. It offers light, modern fare, with plenty of soups, salads and grills. Wood furniture and subtle floral prints complement the garden-themed decor, all of which makes for an enjoyable, all-natural eating experience.

BULKA BAKERY $

Map p264 (Булка пекарня; www.bulkabakery.ru; Bolshaya Gruzinskaya ul 69; pastries R100-200; 8am-11pm; ; Belorusskaya) The coffee is good but the pastries are even better. Whether you're hankering for something savoury or sweet, you're sure to find it in the big glass display case. Late in the day, everything goes on sale so they can start afresh the following morning.

TSENTRALNY RESTORANNY DOM CAFETERIA $

Map p264 (Центральный ресторанный дом; Kudrinskaya pl 1; meals R200-300; 10am-11pm; Barrikadnaya) The 'central restaurant house' is in the ground floor of the Stalinist skyscraper at Kudrinskaya pl. That by itself is reason enough to come here, especially since the bombastic Empire-style interior has been preserved, complete with stained-glass windows and magnificent chandeliers. It's an odd setting for a self-service lunch but that's the charm of it. Standard Russian canteen fare for cheap prices.

SHINOK UKRAINIAN $$

Map p264 (Шинок; 495-651 8101; www.shinok.ru; ul 1905 goda 2; meals R1000-1200; 24hr; ; Ulitsa 1905 Goda) In case you didn't think Moscow's themed dining was over the top, this restaurant has re-created a Ukrainian peasant farm in central Moscow. Servers wear colourfully embroidered shirts and speak with Ukrainian accents (probably lost on most tourists). The house speciality is *vareniki* (boiled dumplings). As you dine, you can look out the window at a cheerful babushka while she tends the farmyard animals.

NEDALNY VOSTOK ASIAN FUSION $$$

Map p264 (Недальный восток; ☎495-694 0641; www.novikovgroup.ru; Tverskoy bul 15; meals from R2000; ; MPushkinskaya) Moscow is raving about the 'Not-so-far East'. Foodies love the super fresh seafood prepared in the wok, on the grill or in the oven – all in plain sight of the diners. The Japanese-designed interior also has style-mavens drooling over the juxtaposition of dark woods, granite and glass. Here's one for a splurge.

SOUP CAFE RUSSIAN $

Map p264 (Суп кафе; 1-ya Brestskaya ul 62; meals R300-500; 24hr; ; MBelorusskaya) This aptly named restaurant takes the most appetising element of Russian food to new heights, offering a dozen hot and half as many cold varieties on any given day. The atmosphere is loungey: dim lights, modern furniture and DJs spinning house music from 9pm.

CORNER BURGER BURGERS $$

Map p264 (CBBG76; Bolshaya Gruzinskaya ul 76; meals R800-1200; ; MBelorusskaya) We know you didn't come to Moscow to eat burgers, but just in case you have a hankering, we know where you can get one. These aren't your Whopper burgers, anyway. These babies feature high-quality ground beef, grilled the way you like it and served on an English muffin or on pretzel bread, with a variety of intriguing toppings. There are also turkey burgers, veggie burgers and lots of non-burger items.

UPSIDE DOWN CAKE CO BAKERY $

Map p264 (www.upsidedowncake.ru; Bolshaya Gruzinskaya ul 76; MBelorusskaya) We hope you saved room for dessert. This corner bakery features lots of cupcakes and pastries, delicious sorbet and a great selection of herbal teas by the pot.

CORREA'S EUROPEAN $$

Map p264 (www.correas.ru; ul Gasheka 7; brunch R400-600, sandwiches R200-400, meals R600-1000; 8am-midnight; ; MMayakovskaya) Just because you couldn't get a table at Correa's original location, doesn't mean that you can't enjoy their fabulous fresh food and flawless service. This outlet is bigger and easier to get too – reservations still recommended for brunch.

BARASHKA AZERI $$$

Map p264 (Барашка; ☎495-252 2571; ul 1905 goda 2; meals R1500-2000; ; MUlitsa 1905 goda) Step off a busy Moscow street and into a charming Azeri courtyard, where you can dine on delectable salads, grilled meats and hearty stews.

DRINKING & NIGHTLIFE

Inner Presnya

KVARTIRA 44 BAR

Map p264 (Квартира 44; www.kv44.ru, in Russian; Bolshaya Nikitskaya ul 22/2; noon-2am Sun-Thu, noon-6am Fri & Sat; ; MOkhotny Ryad) Somebody had the brilliant idea to convert an old Moscow apartment into a crowded, cosy bar, with tables and chairs tucked into every nook and cranny. There's jazz and piano music on Friday nights at 10pm, and there is another apartment in **Zamoskvorechie** (p130)

MAYAK CLUB, CAFE

Map p264 (Маяк; Bolshaya Nikitskaya ul 19; meals R600-800; ; MOkhotny Ryad) Named for the Mayakovsky Theatre downstairs, this is a remake of a much beloved club that operated in this spot throughout the 1990s. The reincarnated version is more cafe than club, exuding the air of a welcoming, old-fashioned inn. But it still attracts actors, artists and writers, who come to see friendly faces and eat filling European fare.

ART LEBEDEV CAFE CAFE

Map p264 (Bolshaya Nikitskaya ul 35B; meals R300-600; 9am-11pm; MBarrikadnaya) It's hard to resist the tempting freshly baked cakes and sweet things laid out on the counter at this cool cafe. Owned by design guru Artemy Lebedev, this place attracts an attractive arty crowd.

COFFEE MANIA CAFE

Map p264 (Кофемания; www.coffeemania.ru; Bolshaya Nikitskaya ul 13, Moscow Conservatory; meals R600-800; 24hr; ; MOkhotny Ryad) With all of Moscow's opportunities for high stepping, fine dining and big spending, where is the most popular place for the

WORTH A DETOUR

RUSSIAN GIFT

Still looking for that perfect souvenir? Then it's time to make a trip out to Moscow's enormous handicraft centre, **Russian Gift** (www.russiangifts.ru; ul Zorge 2; ⏲10am-8pm; Ⓜ Polezhaevskaya), dedicated to preserving Russian folk traditions. Interestingly, the centre is housed in a super modern building. In the lobby, you'll likely hear some folk music and sample some *medovukha* (honey ale), before continuing on to peruse the thousands of handicrafts on display. Really crafty folks might be interested in a guided tour, while children can partake of a Russian tea party. There are smaller outlets of this store in GUM and in many of the upscale hotels.

From Polezhaevskaya metro, walk two blocks west and turn right on ul Zorge.

rich and famous to congregate? Can you believe it's somewhere called Coffee Mania? The friendly, informal cafe is beloved for its homemade soups, freshly squeezed juices and steaming (if overpriced) cappuccinos, not to mention its summer terrace overlooking the leafy courtyard of the conservatory.

RYUMOCHNAYA BAR

Map p264 (Рюмочная; Bolshaya Nikitskaya ul 22/2; meals R300-500; ⏲11am-11pm; Ⓜ Okhotny Ryad) This is a hold-over (or a comeback?) from the days when a drinking establishment needed no special name. The *ryumochnaya* was the generic place where comrades stopped on their way to or from work to toss back a shot or two before continuing on their way. This particular Ryumochnaya also offers some tasty food to accompany your *sto grammov* (100 grams).

CAFE MARGARITA CAFE

Map p264 (Кафе Маргарита; Malaya Bronnaya ul 28; meals R400-600; ⏲noon-2am; Ⓜ Mayakovskaya) With walls lined with bookshelves, and a location opposite Patriarch's Ponds, this offbeat cafe is popular with a well-read, young crowd. These bookworms are pretty quiet during the day, but the place livens up in the evening, when it often hosts live acoustic, folk and jazz music.

Outer Presnya

RADIO CITY BAR

Map p264 (www.radiocitybar.ru; Bolshaya Sadovaya ul 5; ⏲24hr; Ⓜ Mayakovskaya) On the ground floor of the Peking Hotel, this is not the most interesting or original bar in Moscow but it has a few things going for it. Twenty-five, to be exact. That's the number of TV screens strewn about the bar (22 plasmas, three big screens), all of which are usually tuned into one sporting match or another. Other than that, the place has seven kinds of beer on tap and a menu of munchies that get mixed reviews.

REAL MCCOY BAR

Map p264 (www.mccoy.ru, in Russian; Kudrinskaya pl 1; meals R500-1000; ⏲24hr; Ⓜ Barrikadnaya) This 'bootlegger's bar' has walls plastered in old newspapers, two-for-one happy-hour specials (5pm to 8pm) and a dance floor crowded with expats. There is live jazz and rock music in the evenings (9pm Wednesday to Sunday) then, after 11pm, the serious drinking begins. The later it gets, the more they drink. The Real McCoy is considered to be the last of Moscow's old-fashioned debauched dive bars, where women are invited to dance on the bar and patrons are practically guaranteed to take home a new friend, if they are not too picky.

RED CAFE

Map p264 (www.redespressobar.com; Bolshaya Gruzinskaya ul 69; 📶🄼; Ⓜ Belorusskaya) In the midst of a strip of trendy restaurants and cafes, Red is a popular spot to look cool while getting a caffeine fix. Delicious coffee roasted in-house.

ENTERTAINMENT

TCHAIKOVSKY CONCERT HALL CLASSICAL MUSIC

Map p264 (Концертный зал им Чайковского; ☎box office 495-232 0400; Triumfalnaya pl 4/31; tickets R100-1000; 👪; Ⓜ Mayakovskaya) Home to the famous State Philharmonic (Moskovsky Gosudarstvenny Akademichesky Filharmonia), the capital's oldest symphony orchestra, the concert hall was established in 1921. It's a huge auditorium, with seating for 1600 people. This is where you can expect to hear the Russian classics such as Stravinsky, Rachmaninov and Shostakovich, as well as other European favourites. Look out for special children's concerts.

SIXTEEN TONS LIVE MUSIC

Map p264 (Шестнадцать тонн; www.16tons.ru; ul Presnensky val 6; cover R300-1000; 11am-6am, concerts 10pm or 11pm Thu-Sat; ; Ulitsa 1905 Goda) Downstairs, the brassy English pub-restaurant has an excellent house-brewed bitter. Upstairs, the club gets some of the best Russian bands that play in Moscow. At the time of research, Sixteen Tons was looking forward to hosting Billy's Band, Mara and Bi-2, among others.

IMPERIA LOUNGE NIGHTCLUB

Map p264 (www.imperia-lounge.livejournal.com; Mantulinskaya ul 5, Bldg 7; 11pm-5am Thu-Sat; Ulitsa 1905 Goda) Owned by the Russian Standard vodka label, Imperia Lounge is the latest in outrageously elaborate and elite Moscow nightclubs. The multiple levels have dance floors packed with patrons, with raised decks for VIPs. Go-go dancers do their thing on pedestals suspended above the crowd, while nonstop music and images make your head spin. Face control is super tight: look sharp.

MOSCOW TCHAIKOVSKY CONSERVATORY CLASSICAL MUSIC

Map p264 (Московская консерватория Чайковского; box office 495-629 8183; www.mosconsv.ru; Bolshaya Nikitskaya ul 13; Okhotny Ryad) The country's largest music school, named for Tchaikovsky of course, has two venues, both of which – the Great Hall (Bolshoy Zal) and the Small Hall (Maly Zal) – are in Moscow. Once every four years, hundreds of musicians gather at the conservatory to compete for the titles of top pianist, singer, cellist and violinist at the prestigious International Tchaikovsky Competition (www.tchaikovsky-competition.com).

KRASNOPRESNENSKY BANI BANYA

Map p264 (Краснопресненские бани; www.baninapresne.ru; Stolyarny per 7; general admission per 2hr R850-1000; 8am-10pm; Ulitsa 1905 Goda) Lacking the old-fashioned, decadent atmosphere of the Sanduny Baths (p85), this modern, clean, efficient place nonetheless provides a first-rate *banya* (hot-bath) experience.

CLUB FORTE LIVE MUSIC

Map p264 (495-694 0881; www.forteclub.com, in Russian; Bolshaya Bronnaya ul 18; cover R300-500; 2pm-midnight, concerts 9pm; Pushkinskaya) Here the nightly concerts range from swing jazz to Latin jazz to golden oldies. The atmosphere is more formal than at some of the other places, attracting a pseudo-intellectual crowd. Be sure to book. The club seems to host the same dozen groups, who rotate nights, so check the website for something you like.

SHOPPING

MINISTERSTVO PODARKOV ART, SOUVENIRS

Map p264 (Министерство подарков; www.buro-nahodok.ru; Maly Gnezdnikovsky per 12/27; 11am-9pm; Pushkinskaya) For quirky, clever souvenirs, stop by this network of artists' cooperatives. Each outlet has a different name, but the goods are more or less the same: uniquely Russian gifts such as artist-designed *tapki* (slippers) and handwoven linens. Most intriguingly, artist Yury Movchan has invented a line of funky, functional fixtures (lights, clocks etc) made from old appliances and other industrial discards.

MOSTOK ART, SOUVENIRS

Map p264 (Мосток; www.mostok-salon.ru, in Russian; Bolshaya Sadovaya 3; Mayakovskaya) Shelves are stacked with trade books and counters are piled high with postcards. The walls are crammed with posters, prints and original artwork, some portraying unusual panoramas and historic Moscow scenes. Part frame store, part graphic-design service, part print shop, you never know what treasures you might find.

PODARKY, DEKOR & PODARKY ART, SOUVENIRS

Map p264 (Подарки, декор и подарки; Malaya Bronnaya ul 28/2; Mayakovskaya) This is another outlet of the artists' cooperative (see Ministerstvo Podarkov, above). Handmade, original and totally impractical, the stuff makes for great gifts or fun souvenirs.

Arbat & Khamovniki

ARBAT | INNER KHAMOVNIKI | OUTER KHAMOVNIKI

Neighbourhood Top Five

❶ Perusing the collections at the **Pushkin Museum of Fine Arts** (p107), especially the incredible array of Impressionist and post-Impressionist art in the Gallery of European & American Art of the 19th & 20th Centuries.

❷ Wandering around **Novodevichy Convent & Cemetery** (p104), soaking up five centuries of artistry and history.

❸ Visiting the **Rerikh Museum** (p111) to uncover the fantastic world of this mystical artist.

❹ Strolling, shopping and doing the cafe scene on the historic **ul Arbat**.

❺ Marvelling at the ostentation and sheer size of the **Cathedral of Christ the Saviour** (p111).

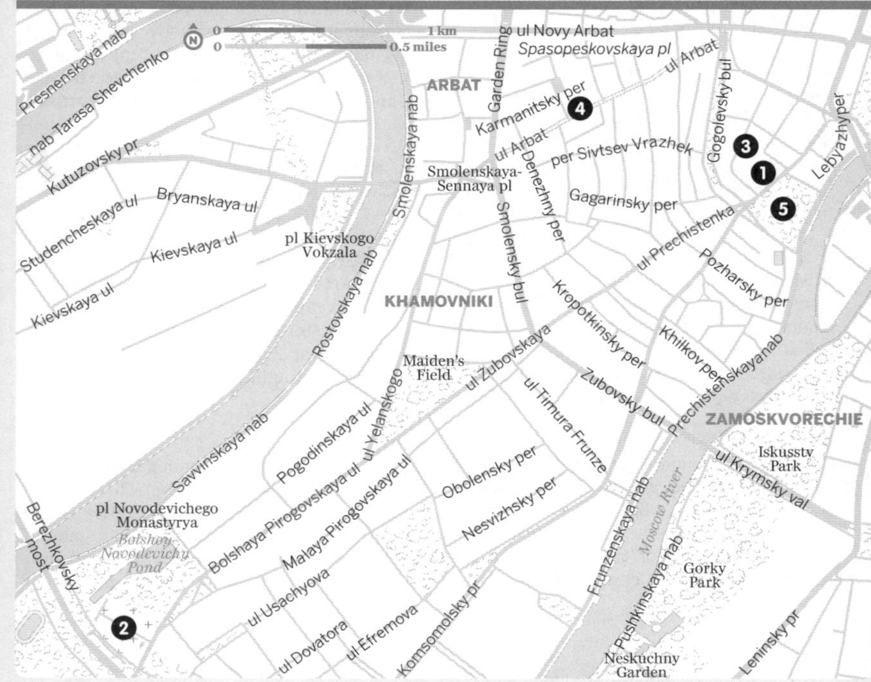

For more detail of this area, see p268 and p270

Explore: Arbat & Khamovniki

These two adjacent districts are an art-lover's dream. Khamovniki is packed with world-class art museums and smaller artist-dedicated galleries, not to mention the elaborate Cathedral of Christ the Saviour. Depending how many stops you make, one might spend the entire day in Inner Khamovniki, starting at the world-class Pushkin Museum of Fine Arts in the morning, then strolling up ul Prechistenka in the afternoon and dropping into sights along the way. The Unesco-recognised Novodevichy Convent & Cemetery is another half-day destination – a welcome break from art-gallery-row.

Evening is the time to wander the storied cobblestones of Arbat, the historic haunt of artists, musicians and street performers. It is undeniable that Arbat today has been taken over by souvenir stands and pavement cafes and it's often packed with tourists; nonetheless, it still evokes the free-thinking artistic spirit of yesteryear. Sights in Arbat are limited to small museums and architectural landmarks – easy to squeeze in here and there when exploring the neighbourhood.

Local Life

➡ **Al fresco** None of Moscow's many summer terraces can beat the pedestrian bridge behind the Cathedral of Christ the Saviour for fabulous Kremlin views. It's also an economical choice: bring your own bottle of *shampanskoe* and pull up a bench.

➡ **Special events** The Pushkin continues to attract local art-lovers with its ambitious and unusual temporary shows. The museum also hosts the prestigious December Nights Festival (p21), which accompanies the artwork with musical performances.

Getting There & Away

➡ **Arbat** The light-blue Filyovskaya line and the dark-blue Arbatsko-Pokrovskaya line run parallel across the Arbat district. They both have stations called Arbatskaya, with the entrance near Arbatskaya pl; and they both have stations called Smolenskaya, with the entrance near Smolenskaya pl. None of these same-named stations are connected to each other, however, so make sure you know which line you are getting on.

➡ **Khamovniki** The red Sokolnicheskaya metro line traverses Khamovniki district, from Kropotkinskaya station at pl Prechistenskie Vorota near the Cathedral of Christ the Saviour; to Park Kultury station along the Garden Ring; to Sportivnaya station in the southwestern corner, near Novodevichy and Luzhniki.

Lonely Planet's Top Tip

Many of the Khamovniki museums stay open in the evening one day per week. On Thursday, for example, the Pushkin Museum of Fine Arts and the Gallery of European & American Art of the 19th & 20th Centuries stay open until 9pm, as does the Tsereteli Gallery. The Shilov Gallery does the same on Wednesday evenings.

Best Places to Eat

➡ Tiflis (p115)

➡ Les Amis de Jean-Jacques (p113)

➡ Moskvich (p117)

For reviews, see p113 ➡

Best Places to Drink

➡ Gogol-Mogol (p118)

➡ Zhiguli Beer Hall (p117)

For reviews, see p117 ➡

Best Art Galleries

➡ Gallery of European & American Art of the 19th & 20th Centuries (p107)

➡ Rerikh Museum (p111)

➡ Pushkin Fine Arts Museum main building (p107)

➡ Multimedia Art Museum (p112)

➡ Burganov House (p111)

For reviews, see p109 ➡

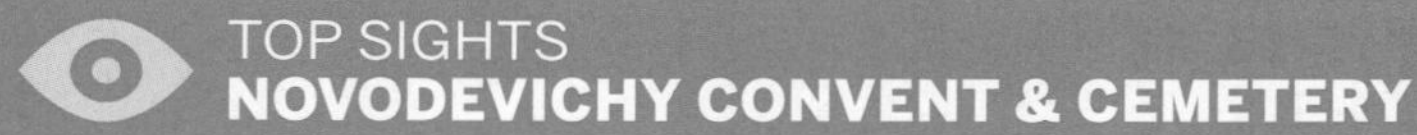

TOP SIGHTS
NOVODEVICHY CONVENT & CEMETERY

In 1524, Grand Prince Vasily III founded the Novodevichy Convent to celebrate the taking of Smolensk from Lithuania, an important step in Moscow's conquest of the old Kyivan Rus lands. Overlooking a strategic bend in the Moscow River, the fortress became an important part of the city's southern defensive line. From early on, the 'New Maidens' Convent' became a place for women from noble families to retire – some more willingly than others. The convent's most famous residents included Irina Godunova (wife of Feodor I and sister of Boris Godunov), Sofia Alexeyevna (half-sister of Peter the Great), and Eudoxia Lopukhina (first wife of Peter the Great).

Over the years, the convent gained territory and power. By the end of the 17th century, it was a major landowner, possessing 36 villages and more than 10,000 serfs around Russia. At various times the convent housed a military hospital, two orphanages and two almshouses. It was a target of Napoleon's retreating army in 1812 but was saved by quick-thinking nuns, who discovered and defused the incendiary bombs before they destroyed the compound.

In 1922 the Soviets shut down the monastery and – always ironic – converted it into a Museum of Women's Emancipation. The nuns were invited to return to the convent in 1994, with services recommencing the following year.

DON'T MISS...

- Smolensk Cathedral frescoes
- Landmark 72m bell tower
- Graves of Nikita Khrushchev and Boris Yeltsin

PRACTICALITIES

- off Map p270
- Новодевичий монастырь и Новодевичье кладбище
- 499-246 8526
- convent & church R250, exhibits R200
- grounds 8am-8pm daily, museums 10am-5pm Wed-Mon
- Sportivnaya

Walls & Towers

You enter the convent through the red-and-white Moscow-baroque **Transfiguration Gate-Church** (Преображенская надвратная церковь), built in the north wall between 1687 and 1689. The striking walls and towers, along with many other buildings on the grounds, were rebuilt in the 1680s under the direction of Sofia Alexeyevna. The elaborate **bell tower** (Колокольня) against the east wall towers 72m over the rest of the monastery. When it was built in 1690 it was one of the tallest towers in Moscow (second only to the Ivan the Great Bell Tower in the Kremlin).

Smolensk Cathedral

The centrepiece of the monastery is the white **Smolensk Cathedral** (Смоленский собор), built in 1524–25 to house the precious *Our Lady of Smolensk* icon. Previously surrounded by four smaller chapels, the floorplan was modelled after the Assumption Cathedral in the Kremlin. The sumptuous interior is covered in 16th-century **frescoes**, which are considered to be among the finest in the city. The huge gilded **iconostasis** – donated by Sofia in 1685 – includes icons that date from the time of Boris Godunov. The icons on the fifth tier are attributed to 17th-century artists Simeon Ushakov and Feodor Zubov. The **tombs** of Sofia, a couple of her sisters and Eudoxia Lopukhina are in the south nave.

Chambers of Sofia Alexeyevna (Pond Tower)

Sofia Alexeyevna used the convent as a residence when she ruled Russia as regent in the 1680s. Fortunately for her, she rebuilt the convent to her liking – since she was later confined here when Peter the Great came of age. In 1698 – after being implicated in the Streltsy rebellion – she was imprisoned here for life, primarily inhabiting the **Pond Tower**

(Напрудная башня). Legend has it that Peter had some of her supporters hanged outside her window to remind her not to meddle.

Chambers of Eudoxia Lopukhina

Sofia was later joined in her enforced retirement by Eudoxia Lopukhina who stayed in the **Chambers of Tsarina Eudoxia Miloslavkaya** (Палаты царевны Евдокии Милославской). Although she bore him a son, Peter detested her conservative and demanding personality, and soon rejected her for the beautiful daughter of a Dutch wine merchant. Eudoxia retired to a monastery in Suzdal, where she further estranged herself by taking her own lover and founding an opposition movement within the church. The tsar responded by executing the bishops involved and banishing his former wife to a more remote location. Upon Peter's death, he was succeeded by Peter II, who recalled his grandmother Eudoxia back to Moscow. She lived out her final years in high style at Novodevichy.

Other Buildings

Other churches on the grounds include the red-and-white **Assumption Church** (Успенская церковь), dating from 1685 to 1687, and the 16th-century **St Ambrose's Church** (Амвросиевская церковь). Boris Godunov's sister, Irina, lived in the building adjoining the latter church. Today, **Irina's Chambers** (Палаты Ирины Годуновой) hold exhibits of religious artwork.

Novodevichy Cemetery

Adjacent to the convent, the **Novodevichy Cemetery** (Новодевичье кладбище; Luzhnetsky proezd; ⏲9am-6pm) is one of Moscow's most prestigious resting places – a veritable who's who of Russian politics and culture. Here you will find the tombs of Rostrovpovich, Bulgakov, Chekhov, Gogol, Mayakovsky, Prokofiev, Stanislavsky and Eisenstein, among many other Russian and Soviet cultural notables.

In Soviet times Novodevichy Cemetery was used for eminent people the authorities judged unsuitable for the Kremlin wall, most notably Khrushchev. The intertwined white-and-black blocks around Khrushchev's bust were intended by sculptor Ernst Neizvestny to represent Khrushchev's good and bad sides.

The tombstone of Nadezhda Alliluyeva, Stalin's second wife, is surrounded by unbreakable glass to prevent vandalism. One of the more recent notable additions to the cemetery is former President Boris Yeltsin, who died of congestive heart failure in 2007. His grave is marked by an enormous Russian flag, which is sculpted out of stone but gives the appearance that it is rippling in the wind.

DISCRETION ADVISED

Novodevichy is a functioning monastery. Women are advised to cover their heads and shoulders when entering the churches, while men should wear long pants.

It is said that Novodevichy was a favourite wintertime destination for Leo Tolstoy, who lived in the neighbourhood and liked to go ice skating on the pond outside the monastery walls. Indeed, one of the main characters of Anna Karenina – Konstantin Levin – meets his future wife Kitty when she is ice skating here.

GRAVE DIGGING

If you want to investigate Novodevichy Cemetery in depth, buy the Russian map (on sale at the kiosk), which pinpoints nearly 200 graves of notable citizens.

NOVODEVICHY CONVENT & CEMETERY

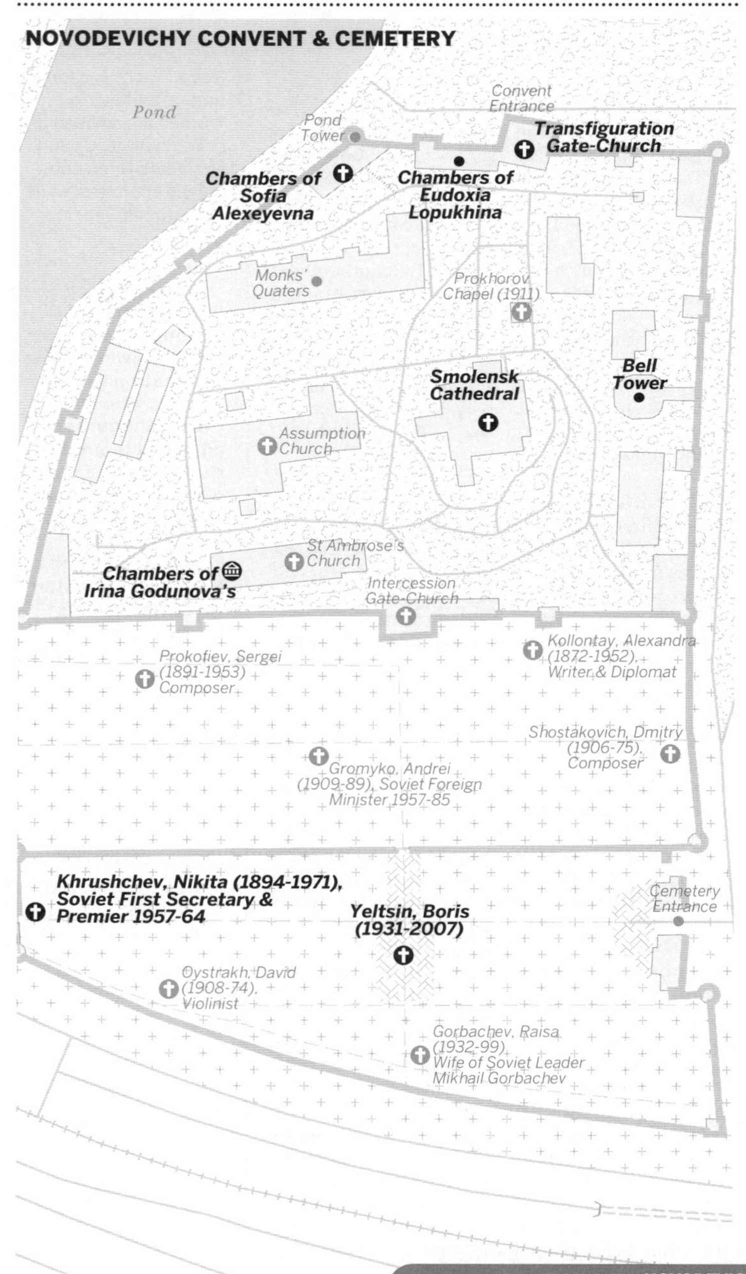
Pond
Convent Entrance
Pond Tower
Transfiguration Gate-Church
Chambers of Sofia Alexeyevna
Chambers of Eudoxia Lopukhina
Monks' Quaters
Prokhorov Chapel (1911)
Bell Tower
Smolensk Cathedral
Assumption Church
St Ambrose's Church
Chambers of Irina Godunova's
Intercession Gate-Church
Prokofiev, Sergei (1891-1953) Composer
Kollontay, Alexandra (1872-1952), Writer & Diplomat
Shostakovich, Dmitry (1906-75), Composer
Gromyko, Andrei (1909-89), Soviet Foreign Minister 1957-85
Khrushchev, Nikita (1894-1971), Soviet First Secretary & Premier 1957-64
Yeltsin, Boris (1931-2007)
Cemetery Entrance
Oystrakh, David (1908-74), Violinist
Gorbachev, Raisa (1932-99) Wife of Soviet Leader Mikhail Gorbachev

TOP SIGHTS PUSHKIN FINE ARTS MUSEUM

Moscow's premier foreign-art museum displays a broad range of European works, mostly appropriated from private collections after the revolution. The Pushkin's collections are located not only in the main building, but also in the Museum of Private Collections and the Gallery of European & American Art of the 19th & 20th Centuries. The museum – celebrating in 2012 its 100-year anniversary – is scheduled to undergo a much-needed renovation and an ambitious expansion of its facilities. While the timetable has not been announced, the museum is likely to close during this construction.

DON'T MISS...

- Treasures of Troy
- Golden Age of Dutch Art
- Impressionist and post-Impressionist collections

PRACTICALITIES

- Map p270
- www.artsmuseum.ru
- Ⓜ Kropotkinskaya

Main Building

The **main building** (Главное здание; ul Volkhonka 12; adult/student R300/150; ⌚10am-6pm Tue-Sun, 10am-9pm Thu; Ⓜ Kropotkinskaya) is the original location of the museum, which opened in 1912 as the museum of Moscow University. It now exhibits the bulk of the holdings that date from antiquity through the 18th century.

Located in rooms 1 and 2, the **Ancient Civilisation** exhibits contain a surprisingly excellent collection, complete with ancient Egyptian weaponry, jewellery, ritual items and tombstones. Most of the items were excavated from burial sites, including two haunting mummies. Room 3 houses the impressive **Treasures of Troy** exhibit, with excavated items dating back to 2500 BC. A German archaeologist donated the collection to the city of Berlin, from where it was appropriated by the Soviets in 1945.

Located in rooms 9 through 11, the highlight of the museum is perhaps the Dutch masterpieces from the 17th century, the so-called **Golden Age of Dutch Art**. Rembrandt is the star of the show, with many paintings on display, including his moving *Portrait of an Old Woman*.

The **Greek and Italian Courts** (rooms 14 and 15) contain examples from the museum's original collection, which was made up almost exclusively of plaster-cast reproductions of the masterpieces from Ancient Greece and Rome, as well as from the Renaissance. You'll find more plaster casts upstairs, including a special room devoted to Michelangelo (room 29).

Otherwise, the 17th and 18th centuries dominate the second floor, with special rooms devoted to various countries. Room 17 contains a diverse collection of Italian paintings, including some formidable large-scale canvases. Rooms 21 through 23 are devoted to France, with a separate gallery for the Rococo period, featuring some appropriately dreamy paintings by Boucher.

Gallery of European & American Art of the 19th & 20th Centuries

The Pushkin's newish **gallery** (Галерея искусства стран Европы и Америки XIX-XX веков; www.newpaintart.ru; ul Volkhonka 14; adult/student R300/150; ⌚10am-6pm Tue-Sun, 10am-9pm Thu) contains a famed assemblage of Impressionist and post-Impressionist works, based on the collection of two well-known Moscow art patrons, Sergei Shchukin and Ivan Morozov. The private collections were nationalised in 1918, thus forming the foundation of the present-day gallery. The collection was further enriched after WWII, when the Red Army seized hundreds of thousands of works from Nazi Germany (most of which were kept secret until 1991). It's a dubious start, but the existing collection is fabulous, with 26 rooms chock-full of treasures, the best of which are on the 2nd and 3rd floors.

The **Impressionists** occupy rooms 8 through 10, with representative paintings by Degas, Manet, Renoir and Pisarro, and an entire room dedicated to Monet. Rodin's sculptures include pieces from the *Gates of Hell* and the *Monument to the Townspeople of Calais*.

MUSEUM TOWN

Museum administration has announced plans for a massive overhaul of the museum buildings and the surrounding area, as designed by UK architect Sir Norman Foster. The idea is to construct several new buildings and to restore and adapt the current museum buildings, along with 12 historic mansions in the surrounding area. The end result will be a cultural quarter called 'Museum Town' with greatly expanded exhibit space, a concert hall and other facilities. The plan will allow the museum to display more art, to receive more visitors and – most importantly – to implement the security and conditions necessary to preserve this incredible collection. At the time of research, there was no construction underway.

Culture vultures flock to the Pushkin Fine Arts Museum in December. Since 1981, the unique December Nights Festival pairs musical performances with accompanying art exhibits, highlighting works from a particular artist, composer, era or theme.

Room 11 is dedicated to **neo-Impressionism**, most notably Van Gogh. The museum contains several of his lesser-known gems, including the scorching *Red Vineyards* and the tragic *Prison Courtyard,* painted in the last year of his life. Room 14 is almost exclusively Cézanne, featuring his sensuous *Bathers*. Room 15 is devoted to works by Gauguin, representing his prime period.

Rooms 19 and 20 display many of the most famous paintings by Matisse, such as *Goldfish*. There are a few exquisite, primitive paintings by Rousseau in room 21, and some lesser-known pieces by Picasso in room 22. The final rooms complete the rich collection of 20th-century art, featuring Miro, Kandinsky, Chagall, Arp and others.

Museum of Private Collections

Across the street from the main building, the smaller **Museum of Private Collections** (Отдел личных коллекций; www.artprivatecollections.ru; ul Volkhonka 10; adult/student R300/150; ⌚noon-7pm Wed-Sun) shows off art collections donated by private individuals, many of whom amassed the works during the Soviet era. Exhibits are organised around the collections, each as a whole, and the details of collectors and donors are displayed alongside the art. The idea is to maintain the integrity of each private collection, even as they are made available to the public.

On the ground floor, the collections in rooms 2 to 5 focus on 20th-century artists. In room 2, the Inna Koretskaya and Boris Mihailovsky Collection includes works by Russians masters like Rerikh, Golovin and Kuznetsov. Rooms 3 and 4 feature paintings, drawings and other pieces from the Alexander Rodchenko and Varvara Stepanova Heritage. In room 5, Svyatoslav Richter's collection adds some Western artists into the mix.

Other highlights are upstairs. Rooms 14 and 15 showcase icons, including an impressive collection of **Old Believer icons** from the 16th to 20th centuries. In rooms 16 to 19, the museum's centrepiece is the **collection of Ilya Silberstein**, the museum's founder and an accomplished historian of Russian literature and art. He had an especially rich collection of pieces by the early-20th-century 'Mir Iskusstva' artists like Benois, Serebryakova, Serov and Kustodiev.

Room 20, also known as the Lemkul room, exhibits some graphic art by Fyodor Lemkul. It also contains the artist's fantastic collection of glassworks from Russia and Europe.

Room 21 showcases the collection of Sergei Solovyov, which includes some excellent representatives from the late 19th century, including paintings by Perov and Repin.

SIGHTS

Arbat

MUSEUM OF ORIENTAL ART MUSEUM

Map p268 (Музей искусства народа востока; www.orientmuseum.ru; Nikitsky bul 12a; admission R300; ⏲11am-7pm Tue-Sun; Ⓜ Arbatskaya) This impressive museum on the Boulevard Ring holds three floors of exhibits, spanning the Asian continent. Of particular interest is the 1st floor, dedicated mostly to the Caucasus, Central Asia and North Asia (meaning the Russian republics of Cukotka, Yakutiya and Priamurie). But the entire continent is pretty well represented, even the countries that were not part of the Russian or Soviet empires. The collection covers an equally vast time period, from ancient times to the 20th century, including painting, sculpture and folk art. One unexpected highlight is a special exhibit on Nikolai Rerikh (p111), the Russian artist and explorer who spent several years travelling and painting in Asia.

FREE **GOGOL HOUSE** MUSEUM

Map p268 (Дом Гоголя; www.domgogolya.ru; Nikitsky bul 7; ⏲noon-7pm Mon & Wed-Fri, noon-5pm Sat & Sun; Ⓜ Arbatskaya) The 19th-century writer Nikolai Gogol spent his final tortured months here. The rooms – now a small but captivating museum – are arranged as they were when Gogol lived here. You can even see the fireplace where he famously threw his manuscript of *Dead Souls*. An additional reading room contains a library of Gogol's work and other reference materials about the author. The quiet courtyard contains a statue of the emaciated, sad author surrounded by some of his better-known characters in bas-relief.

HOUSE OF FRIENDSHIP WITH PEOPLES OF FOREIGN COUNTRIES NOTABLE BUILDING

Map p268 (Дом дружбы с народамн зарубежных стран; Vozdvizhenka ul 16; Ⓜ Arbatskaya) Studded with seashells, this 'Moorish Castle' was built in 1899 for an eccentric merchant, Arseny Morozov, who was inspired by a real Moorish castle in Spain. The inside is sumptuous and equally over the top. Morozov's mother, who lived next door, apparently declared of her son's home, 'Until now, only I knew you were mad; now everyone will'. This place is not normally open to the public, but sometimes exhibitions are held here.

LERMONTOV HOUSE-MUSEUM MUSEUM

Map p268 (Дом-музей Лермонтова; www.goslitmuz.ru, in Russian; ul Malaya Molchanovka 2; Ⓜ Arbatskaya) 'While I live I swear, dear friends, not to cease to love Moscow.' So wrote the 19th-century poet Mikhail Lermontov about his hometown. The celebrated author of *A Hero of Our Time* lived in this little pink house on a small lane off ul Novy Arbat. Here, he was raised by his grandmother, and wrote poetry and prose in the primitive office in the attic. The cosy bungalow evokes the family's everyday life, displaying the poet's books, artwork and hobbies. The museum was closed for renovation at the time of research.

MELNIKOV HOUSE NOTABLE BUILDING

Map p268 (Дом Мельникова; www.melnikovhouse.org; Krivoarbatsky per 10; Ⓜ Smolenskaya) On a side street near ul Arbat, the home of Konstantin Melnikov still stands as testament to the innovation of the Russian avant-garde in the 1920s (see the boxed text, p110). This is the only private house built during the Soviet period, and it's a doozey. This architect created his unusual home from two interlocking cylinders – an ingenious design that employs no internal load-bearing wall and has a self-reinforcing wooden grid floor. It was also experimental in its designation of living space: the whole family slept in one room, painted a golden yellow and divided by narrow wall screens. Melnikov softened the corners in the room, even those on the hexagonal windows, to create a soothing environment for peaceful sleep.

The future of Melnikov House is in jeopardy, due to the corrosion caused by construction in the surrounding area. Family members are working with the Russian Avantgarde Heritage Preservation Foundation to turn the house into a state-run museum (and thus guarantee its preservation), but the process has been tied up in court for years due to ownership disputes.

TOCHKA-G MUSEUM OF EROTIC ART MUSEUM

Map p268 (Музей эротического искусства "Точка-G"; www.tochkag.net; ul Novy Arbat 15; admission R500; ⏲noon-midnight; Ⓜ Arbatskaya) It means g-spot, in case you didn't already guess. Among this gigantic display

LOCAL KNOWLEDGE

INSIDE MELNIKOV HOUSE

Konstantin Melnikov's home is currently inhabited by the architect's granddaughter, Ekaterina Karinskaya. If you knock on the door, you may be lucky and be given a tour (in Russian only). The interior has largely been kept intact since the death of her father, who tried to keep the house exactly as it was when his father lived there, down to the tubes of paint scattered across his desk.

of erotica, you're bound to find something that will titillate yours. Look for 'artistic' interpretations of sex through the ages, from ancient kama-sutra-style carvings to contemporary (and perhaps controversial) sexual-political commentary. Also on site: sex shop and cafe! Look for the Om Cafe and enter from the back.

PUSHKIN HOUSE-MUSEUM MUSEUM

Map p268 (Дом-музей Пушкина; www.pushkinmuseum.ru; ul Arbat 53; admission R80; ⌚noon-9pm Wed, 10am-6pm Thu-Sun; Ⓜ Smolenskaya) After Alexander Pushkin married Natalya Goncharova at the nearby Church of the Grand Ascension, they moved to this charming blue house on the old Arbat. The museum provides some insight into the couple's home life, a source of much Russian romanticism. (The lovebirds are also featured in a statue across the street.) Literary buffs will appreciate the poetry readings and other performances that take place here. This place should not be confused with the Pushkin Literary Museum, which focuses on the poet's literary influences.

Just next door is the **Memorial Apartment of Andrei Bely** (Мемориальная квартира А. Белого; ul Arbat 55; admission R80; ⌚noon-9pm Wed, 10am-6pm Thu-Sun), Silver Age author of the surreal novel *Petersburg*.

Inner Khamovniki

SHILOV GALLERY MUSEUM

Map p270 (Галерея Шилова; www.shilov.su; ul Znamenka 5; adult/student R160/80; ⌚11am-7pm Fri-Wed; Ⓜ Biblioteka imeni Lenina) 'What is a portrait? You have to attain not only an absolute physical likeness…but you need to express the inner world of the particular person you are painting.' So Alexander Shilov described his life work as contemporary Russia's most celebrated portrait painter in an interview posted on the gallery's website. Indeed, Shilov is known for his startling realism. His paintings are so close to the truth that he is sometimes criticised for producing little more than photographs on canvas. But others claim that the artist provides great insight into his subjects, with some high-level political figures among them. (Shilov denies the rumour that he painted all the members of the Politburo during the Soviet period.)

Among Shilov's fans is one Yury Luzhkov, who oversaw the opening of this gallery in 1997. At that time the artist donated 355 paintings to the museum, and he continues to make donations of new paintings – every year on the anniversary of the opening – so the collection continues to grow.

MUSEUM OF PRIVATE COLLECTIONS MUSEUM

See p108.

PUSHKIN FINE ARTS MUSEUM MUSEUM

See p107.

GALLERY OF EUROPEAN & AMERICAN ART OF THE 19TH & 20TH CENTURIES MUSEUM

See p107.

GLAZUNOV GALLERY MUSEUM

Map p270 (Галерея Глазунова; www.glazunov.ru; ul Volkhonka 13; adult/student R160/80; ⌚11am-6pm Tue-Sun; Ⓜ Kropotkinskaya) This elaborate Russian empire-style mansion, opposite the Pushkin Fine Arts Museum, houses a new gallery dedicated to the work of Soviet and post-Soviet artist Ilya Glazunov. Apparently this gallery was a long time coming, due primarily to the artist's own insistence on moulded ceilings, marble staircases and crystal chandeliers. But it was worth the wait, as the interior is impressive: three floors filled with fanciful illustrations of historic events and biblical scenes.

Glazunov is famous for his huge, colourful paintings that depict hundreds of people, places and events from Russian history in one monumental scene. His most famous work is *Eternal Russia (Bechnaya Rossiya),* while more recent examples are *Mystery of the 20th Century* and *Market of*

Our Democracy. Such social commentary is a rather recent development, of course; the artist's earlier work tended to focus on medieval and fairytale themes.

RERIKH MUSEUM MUSEUM

Map p270 (Центр-музей Рериха; www.icr.su; Maly Znamensky per 3/5; adult/student R220/110; ⌚11am-5pm Wed-Sun; Ⓜ Kropotkinskaya) Nikolai Rerikh (known internationally as Nicholas Roerich) was a Russian artist from the late 19th and early 20th centuries, whose fantastical artwork is characterised by rich, bold colours, primitive style and mystical themes. This museum, founded by the artist's son Sergei, includes work by father and son, as well as family heirlooms and personal items. The artwork is intriguing: Rerikh spent a lot of time in Central Asia, India and the Altay Mountains of Siberia, so his paintings feature distinctive landscapes and mythological scenes. The building – the 17th-century Lopukhin manor – is a grand setting in which to admire the artwork.

BURGANOV HOUSE MUSEUM

Map p270 (Дом Бурганова; www.burganov.ru; Bolshoy Afansyevsky per 15; admission R180; ⌚11am-7pm; Ⓜ Kropotkinskaya) Part studio, part museum, the Burganov House is a unique venue in Moscow, where the craft is going on around you, as you peruse the sculptures and other artwork on display. Comprising several interconnected courtyards and houses, the works of sculptor Alexander Burganov are artfully displayed alongside pieces from the artist's private collection. The surrounding streets of the Arbat and Khamovniki districts also contain many examples of the artist's work.

PUSHKIN LITERARY MUSEUM MUSEUM

Map p270 (Литературный музей Пушкина; www.pushkinmuseum.ru, in Russian; ul Prechistenka 12/2; admission R120; ⌚10am-5pm Tue-Sun; Ⓜ Kropotkinskaya) Housed in a beautiful empire-style mansion dating from 1816, this museum is devoted to the life and work of Russia's favourite poet. Personal effects, family portraits, (mostly) reproductions of notes and handwritten poetry provide insight into the work of the beloved bard.

The elegant interior recreates a fancy 19th-century atmosphere, especially the

TOP SIGHTS
CATHEDRAL OF CHRIST THE SAVIOUR

This gargantuan cathedral now dominates the skyline along the Moscow River. It sits on the site of an earlier and similar church of the same name, built between 1839 and 1860, and finally consecrated in 1883. The church commemorates Russia's victory over Napoleon. The original was destroyed during Stalin's orgy of explosive secularism. Stalin planned to replace the church with a 315m-high Palace of Soviets (including a 100m-high statue of Lenin), but the project never got off the ground – literally. Instead, for 50 years the site served an important purpose: the world's largest swimming pool.

This time around, the church was completed in a mere two years, in time for Moscow's 850th birthday in 1997, and at an estimated cost of US$350 million. It is amazingly opulent, garishly grandiose and truly historic. Much of the work was done by former Mayor Luzhkov's favourite architect Zurab Tsereteli (see the boxed text, p112). The cathedral's sheer size and splendour guarantee its role as a love-it-or-hate-it landmark and spark of controversy. Muscovites should at least be grateful they can admire the shiny domes of a church instead of the shiny dome of Lenin's head.

DON'T MISS...

- Tsereteli's controversial bronze reliefs
- Fresco-covered interior dome
- Statues of Alexander II and Nicholas II
- Views from the Patriarshy footbridge

PRACTICALITIES

- Map p270
- ☎495-202 4734
- www.xxc.ru
- admission free
- ⌚10am-5pm
- Ⓜ Kropotkinskaya

grand ballroom, which is decorated with mirrors, sconces, chandeliers and heavy drapes. Several rooms are dedicated to Pushkin's specific works, demonstrating the links between his personal life and the poetry he produced. Perhaps the most interesting exhibit is 'Pushkin & His Time', which puts the poet in a historical context, demonstrating the influence of the Napoleonic Wars, the Decembrists' revolt and other historic events. This literary museum provides much more in-depth insights than the Pushkin House-Museum (p110) on ul Arbat.

TOLSTOY LITERARY MUSEUM MUSEUM

Map p270 (Литературный музей Толстого; www.tolstoymuseum.ru, in Russian; ul Prechistenka 11; adult/student R200/100; 11am-6pm Tue-Sun; Kropotkinskaya) Opposite the Pushkin Literary Museum is the Tolstoy Literary Museum, supposedly the oldest literary memorial museum in the world (founded in 1911). In addition to its impressive reference library, the museum contains exhibits of manuscripts, letters and artwork focusing on Leo Tolstoy's literary influences and output. Family photographs, personal correspondence and artwork from the author's era all provide insight into his work. This museum undoubtedly contains the largest collection of portraits of the great Russian novelist. Entire exhibits are dedicated to his major novels such as *Anna Karenina* and *War and Peace*. The museum does not contain much memorabilia from Tolstoy's personal life, which is on display at the Tolstoy Estate-Museum.

MULTIMEDIA ART MUSEUM ART GALLERY

Map p270 (Мультимедиа Арт Музей; www.mdf.ru; ul Ostozhenka 16; admission R200; Kropotkinskaya) Formerly the Moscow House of Photography (MDF), this slick modern gallery is home to an impressive photographic library and archives of contemporary and historic photography. The facility usually hosts several simultaneous exhibits, often featuring works from prominent photographers from the Soviet period, as well as contemporary artists. The complex also hosts several month-long festivals, Photobiennale and Fashion & Style in Photography (held in alternating years).

TSERETELI GALLERY MUSEUM

Map p268 (Галерея Церетели; www.tsereteli.ru; ul Prechistenka 19; admission R200; noon-7pm Tue-Sat; Kropotkinskaya) Housed in the 18th-century Dolgoruky mansion, this is another endeavour of the tireless Zurab Tsereteli (see the boxed text, p112). The gallery shows how prolific this guy is. The

LEAVING A MARK ON MOSCOW

Zurab Tsereteli is nothing if not controversial. As the chief architect of the Okhotny Ryad shopping mall and the massive Cathedral of Christ the Saviour, he has been criticised for being too ostentatious, too gaudy, too overbearing and just plain too much.

The most despised of Tsereteli's masterpieces is the gargantuan statue of Peter the Great, which now stands in front of the Red October chocolate factory on the Moscow River. At 94.5m, Peter towers over the city (that's twice the size of the Statue of Liberty without her pedestal). Questions of taste aside, Muscovites were sceptical of the whole idea: why pay tribute to Peter the Great, who loathed Moscow, and even moved the capital to St Petersburg? Some radicals even attempted – unsuccessfully – to blow the thing up. After that incident, a 24-hour guard had to stand watch.

Mixed reactions are nothing new to Zurab Tsereteli. An earlier sculpture of Christopher Columbus was apparently rejected by five North American cities for reasons of cost, size and aesthetics. According to recent reports, Chris may finally find his home on the tiny Puerto Rican island of Desecheo.

Despite his critics, who launched a 'Stop Tsereteli' website, this artist does not stop. He launched the Moscow Museum of Modern Art (MMOMA; p75) and took over the Russian Academy of Art. He then opened the aptly named Tsereteli Gallery (p112), which houses room after room of the artist's primitive paintings and elaborate sculptures. Now he has invited the public into his 'studio', which is really another gallery in Presnya (p95). You can't miss the mint-green baroque façade, its front door flanked by crazy clowns, its front yard littered with leftovers – St George killing the dragon and other historical figures.

rooms are filled with his often-over-the-top sculptures and primitive paintings. If you don't want to spend the time or money exploring the gallery, just pop into the Galereya Khudozhnikov cafe, which is an exhibit in itself.

RUSSIAN ACADEMY OF ARTS ART GALLERY

Map p270 (Российская академия художеств; www.rah.ru; ul Prechistenka 21; admission R80; ⏲11am-8pm Tue-Sun; Ⓜ Kropotkinskaya) Next door to the Tsereteli Gallery, the Russian Academy of Arts hosts rotating exhibits in the historic 19th-century mansion of the Morozov estate. Despite the institutional-sounding name, this is part of the Tsereteli empire, but it still puts on inspired and varied shows featuring mostly contemporary Russian and foreign artists.

Outer Khamovniki

TOLSTOY ESTATE-MUSEUM MUSEUM

(Усадьба Толстого 'Хамовники'; www.tolstoymuseum.ru; ul Lva Tolstogo 21; adult/student R200/50; ⏲10am-6pm Wed-Sun, 1-9pm Thu; Ⓜ Park Kultury) Leo Tolstoy's winter home during the 1880s and 1890s now houses an interesting museum dedicated to the writer's home life. While it's not particularly opulent or large, the building is fitting for junior nobility – which Tolstoy was. Exhibits here demonstrate how Tolstoy lived, as opposed to his literary influences, which are explored at the Tolstoy Literary Museum (p112). See the salon where Rachmaninov and Rimsky-Korsakov played piano, and the study where Tolstoy himself wove his epic tales.

CHURCH OF ST NICHOLAS IN KHAMOVNIKI CHURCH

(Церковь Николы в Хамовниках; ul Lva Tolstogo; Ⓜ Park Kultury) This church, commissioned by the weavers' guild in 1676, vies with St Basil's Cathedral for the title of most colourful in Moscow. The ornate green-and-orange-tapestry exterior houses an equally exquisite interior, rich in frescoes and icons. Leo Tolstoy, who lived up the street, was a parishioner at St Nicholas, which is featured in his novel *Resurrection*. Look also for the old white stone house, built in 1689, which housed the office of the **weavers' guild and textile shop** (Бывшая ткацкая гильдия; ul Lva Tolstogo 10).

AUTOVILLE MUSEUM

(Автовиль; www.autoville.ru, in Russian; ul Usachyova 2; admission R300; ⏲10am-10pm; Ⓜ Sportivnaya) This impressive facility brings together under one roof dozens of exquisite automobiles from around the world and different eras. The cars, which are in pristine condition, come from some 50 different private collections. Some date back as far as 1907, while some are from the present day. It's certainly a sort of art exhibit, which presents the vehicles as objects of great beauty as well as functionality.

NOVODEVICHY CONVENT & CEMETERY CONVENT

See p104.

EATING

Arbat

LES AMIS DE JEAN-JACQUES FRENCH $$

Map p268 (Жан-жак; www.jan-jak.com; Nikitsky bul 12; breakfast R150-300, meals R500-800; ⏲7am-midnight Sun-Thu, 7am-1am Fri & Sat; Ⓜ Arbatskaya; wi-fi) In a prime location on the Boulevard Ring, this friendly wine bar welcomes everybody wanting a glass of wine, a bite to eat, some music and a few smiles. The basement setting is cosy but not dark, making it an ideal spot to share a bottle of Bordeaux and nibble on brie. Bottles of wine start at R350, although most are priced around R1000 – still refreshingly reasonable in this town where wine is usually ridiculously overpriced.

GENATSVALE ON ARBAT GEORGIAN $$

Map p268 (Генацвале на Арбате; ☎495-697 9453; www.restoran-genatsvale.ru; ul Novy Arbat 11; meals R600-1000; Ⓜ Arbatskaya) Subtle, it is not. Bedecked with fake trees and flowing fountains, it conjures up the Caucasian countryside, leaving little to the imagination. But what better setting to feast on favourites such as *khachapuri* (cheesy bread) and lamb dishes.

CAFE SINDIBAD LEBANESE $

Map p268 (Кафе Синдбад; Nikitsky bul 14; business lunch R180, meals R300-500; Ⓜ Arbatskaya) The interior of this cosy restaurant resembles a traditional Lebanese village

START ARBATSKAYA PL
END SMOLENSKAYA-SENNAYA PL
DISTANCE 3KM
DURATION TWO HOURS

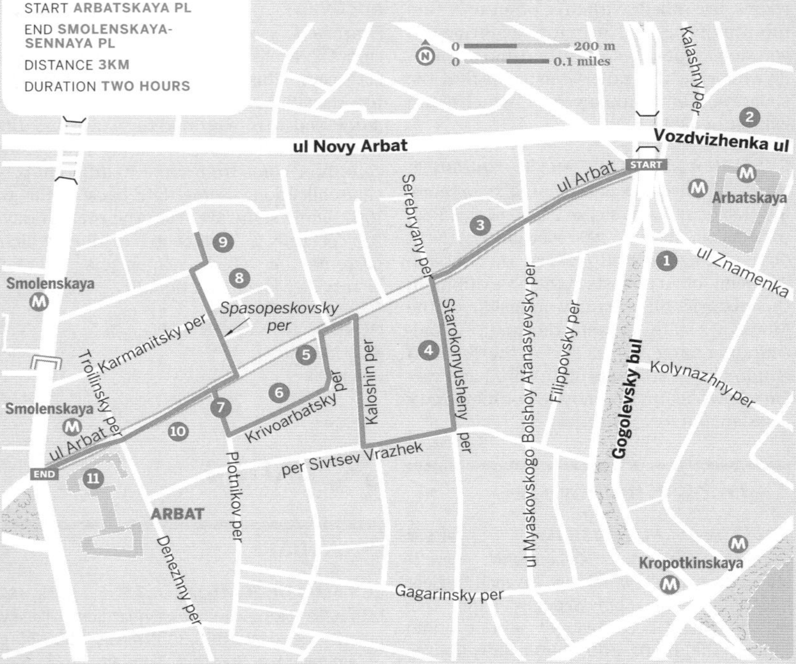

Neighbourhood Walk

A Stroll down the *Stary* Arbat

Your stroll down *stary* Arbat, or 'old' Arbat as it is known, starts at traffic-filled Arbatskaya pl (MArbatskaya), dominated by the 1 **Ministry of Defence building**. Across the street, the whimsical 2 **House of Friendship with Peoples of Foreign Countries** shows off its incongruous Moorish style.

Things slow down alongside of ul Arbat. Besides the sidewalk art and street performers, look for the 3 **Wall of Peace**, composed of individually painted tiles. Look closely to see the whimsy beneath the graffiti.

To escape the feeling that you're caught in a tourist trap, wander down some of the quiet lanes off ul Arbat. 4 **Starokonyushenny per**, for example, contains some exemplary art nouveau architectural details.

Get a glimpse of the counterculture of the old Arbat at the corner of Krivoarbatsky per, where the 5 **Viktor Tsoy memorial wall** is dedicated to the lead singer of the Soviet rock band Kino. Tsoy achieved cult-idol status in 1990, when he died in a car crash at the tragically young age of 28. Further along, the strange cylindrical 6 **Melnikov House** is one of the country's most important architectural sites.

Back on the Arbat, you can't miss the statue of the bard 7 **Bulat Okudzhava** (see p116), who lived nearby. Cross the street and continue north on Spasopeskovsky per. This little lane contains architectural gems such as the lovely 17th-century 8 **Church of the Saviour in Peski.** The handsome neoclassical mansion at No 10 is 9 **Spaso House.** It is now the residence of the US ambassador, but it is most famous as the scene of Satan's ball in Bulgakov's novel *The Master & Margarita*.

Return to the Arbat and the house where Alexander Pushkin and Natalya Goncharova lived after they wed, now holding the 10 **Pushkin House-Museum**. The happy couple is featured in a statue across the street. Continue to the end of the Arbat at Smolenskaya pl (MSmolenskaya). The towering Stalinist skyscraper, 11 **the Ministry of Foreign Affairs**, is one of Stalin's Seven Sisters (p211).

house, complete with Arabian music and the scent of fresh-brewed cardamom coffee. It's the perfect setting to enjoy Lebanese home cooking, including *kefta*, kebabs, *fettoush* and felafel. And hookahs, obviously.

BALKON ASIAN, ITALIAN $$

Map p268 (Балькон; www.ginzaproject.ru; Novinsky bul 8; meals R1000-1500; Smolenskaya) On the 7th floor of the Lotte Plaza, this trendy spot has the requisite outdoor terrace (the largest in the city) and superb city views. But it also gives you something to look at right in the dining area. Little islands of activity are set up around the large hall – each featuring different kinds of food (hot and cold dishes, pizza, sushi, etc). The set-up gives patrons the opportunity to see the preparations and choose their meal. The bar seating and the 'gastronomic show' make this a great place for solo diners.

VOSTOCHNY KVARTAL UZBEK $$

Map p268 (Восточный квартал; ul Arbat 45/24; meals R400-800; Smolenskaya) Vostochny Kvartal used to live up to its name, acting as the 'Eastern Quarter' of the Arbat. Uzbek cooks and plenty of Uzbek patrons are a sign that this is a real-deal place to get your *plov*. The place has since gone the way of the Arbat itself, drawing in more English speakers than anything else. Nonetheless, it still serves some of the best food on the block.

KISHMISH UZBEK $$

Map p268 (Кишмиш; www.novikovgroup.ru; ul Novy Arbat 28; meals R400-800; 11am-1am; Smolenskaya) Besides being a word that rhymes with itself, *kishmish* is a kind of a grape – often a dried grape or raisin – that is common in Central Asian cuisine. This place is decked out like an Uzbek *chaikhona* (teahouse), complete with plush Oriental carpets, staff in national costume and painted ceramic place settings. Everything was imported from Tashkent (except the staff, presumably). It serves simple spicy standards such as shashlyk and *plov* at the cheapest prices you will find. The *dastarkhan* (salad bar) is chock-full of vegies and salads and *kishmish* to fill up the herbivores.

AKADEMIYA ITALIAN $$

Map p268 (Академия; www.academiya.ru; Gogolevsky bul 33/1; meals R600-1000; Arbatskaya) Escape the tourists by wandering one short block away from the Arbat. Here, you'll find delicious pizza, pasta and salad, a decent selection of wines by the glass, and a cool contemporary vibe.

PRIME STAR FAST FOOD $

Map p268 (www.prime-star.ru; ul Arbat 9; meals R200-300; Arbatskaya) Stop in for a quick bite along the old Arbat. Enjoy fresh (and healthy!) salads and sandwiches, premade and ready to take out to the outdoor seating.

SHESH-BESH CAUCASIAN $$

Map p268 (Шеш-беш; www.shesh-besh.rmcom.ru; ul Novy Arbat 24; meals R400-800; Smolenskaya) Following the rhyming restaurant trend, Shesh-Besh is a chain offering hearty Azeri fare. The thick soup is easily a meal in itself, as is the extensive salad bar. The place is not overly atmospheric – this being the TGI Friday's of Azeri cuisine – but the food is still spicy and prices are affordable. There's another rhyming restaurant in Zamoskvorechie (p130).

SHASHLYK MASHLYK CAUCASIAN $$

Map p268 (Шашлык Машлык; www.arbat38.ru; ul Arbat 38/1; meals R400-800; 11am-11pm; Smolenskaya) Can you think of a word that rhymes with shashlyk? Neither can we...but we'll allow a little poetic license when the result is spicy, delicious, affordable grilled meats and vegies. This is a pretty simple place, but the beer is cold and the open-air terrace gives a sweet view of the passers-by on the Arbat.

MOO-MOO CAFETERIA $

Map p268 (Ресторан Му-му; www.moo-moo.ru; ul Arbat 45/24; meals R200-300; 9am-11pm; Smolenskaya) You will recognise this popular cafeteria by its black-and-white Holstein-print decor. The cafeteria-style service offers an easy approach to all the Russian favourites. You'll find other outlets in Basmanny (p141).

Inner Khamovniki

TIFLIS GEORGIAN $$

Map p270 (Тифлис; 499-766 9728; ul Ostozhenka 32; meals R800-1200; Kropotinskaya) 'Guests are a gift from God.' So goes the Georgian saying, and Tiflis will make you believe it. The name of this restaurant comes from the Russian word for the Geor-

ARBAT, MY ARBAT

> Arbat, my Arbat, you are my calling. You are my happiness and my misfortune.
> Bulat Okudzhava

For Moscow's beloved bard Bulat Okudzhava, the Arbat was not only his home, it was his inspiration. Although he spent his university years in Georgia dabbling in harmless verse, it was only upon his return to Moscow – and to his cherished Arbat – that his poetry adopted the free-thinking character for which it is known.

He gradually made the transition from poet to songwriter, stating that, 'Once I had the desire to accompany one of my satirical verses with music. I only knew three chords; now, 27 years later, I know seven chords, then I knew three'. While Bulat and his friends enjoyed his songs, composers, singers and guitarists did not, resenting the fact that somebody with no musical training was writing songs. The ill feeling subsided when a well-known poet announced that '...these are not songs. This is just another way of presenting poetry'.

And so a new form of art was born. The 1960s were heady times, in Moscow as elsewhere, and Okudzhava inspired a whole movement of liberal-thinking poets to take their ideas to the streets. Vladimir Vysotsky and others – some political, others not – followed in Okudzhava's footsteps, their iconoclastic lyrics and simple melodies drawing enthusiastic crowds all around Moscow.

The Arbat today, crowded with tacky souvenir shops and overpriced cafes, bears little resemblance to the hallowed haunt of Okudzhava's youth. But its memory lives on in the bards and buskers, painters and poets who still perform for strolling crowds on summer evenings.

gian capital, Tbilisi, and when you enter this restaurant you might think you are there. Its airy balconies and interior courtyards recall a 19th-century Georgian mansion – a romantic and atmospheric setting.

GALEREYA KHUDOZHNIKOV FUSION **$$**

Map p270 (Галерея художников; ul Prechistenka 19; meals R1000-1500; ; Kropotkinskaya) This fantastical restaurant inside the Tsereteli Gallery is everything you would expect from the over-the-top artist. The gallery's five rooms follow different themes, all of which are equally elaborate and which culminate in a huge, light-filled atrium that is wallpapered with stained glass and primitive paintings. The place certainly lives up to its name, which means Artists' Gallery. The menu is a fusion of European and Asian influences. Though it is secondary to the art, the food is well prepared and, appropriately enough, artistically presented.

GENATSVALE ON OSTOZHENKA GEORGIAN **$$**

Map p270 (495-695 0401; ul Ostozhenka 12/1; meals R600-1000; ; Kropotkinskaya) The well-known Genatsvale on Arbat is three storeys of Georgian kitsch, but this smaller outlet in Khamovniki is quieter and cosier (though Georgian-style ballads are still broadcast throughout in the evenings). The grilled meats, eggplant salads and hot *khachapuri* (cheesy bread) are still reliably delicious.

COLONNA ITALIAN **$$$**

Map p270 (www.restorancolonna.ru; Mansurovsky per 12; meals R1000-2000; noon-10pm; ; Park Kultury) While there has been an Italian restaurant at this location for years, it's only recently that it has transformed into a food and art cafe, complete with live piano and DJ sets, portrait painting, cooking classes and children's events. The maze-like restaurant offers a different atmosphere in every room, from old Italian cinema to modern art. The menu is eclectic modern Italian, with a great selection of fresh seafood and delicious wood-stove pizzas.

VANIL ASIAN **$$$**

Map p270 (Ваниль; 495-637 1082; www.novikovgroup.ru; ul Ostozhenka 1; meals R1500-3000; ; Kropotinskaya) It's hard to say which sight is more grandiose: the glitzy interior of this ultrafancy eating establishment or the Cathedral of Christ the Saviour that looms across the street. Actually, the views of the cathedral through the restaurant's picture windows are a perfect complement to the crystal chandelier and giant gold-framed mirror that hang in the dining room. The modern Asian menu features sushi and other seafood dishes, which are all prepared with delightful innovations. And the service is top notch. Don't be put off by the row of Mercedes parked out the front; you will be treated well here – even if you show up on foot.

AKADEMIYA ITALIAN **$$**

Map p270 (Академия; www.academiya.ru; meals R600-1000; ; Kropotkinskaya) Sip fancy coffee drinks or munch on crispy-crust pizza and watch the world go by. Steps from the Pushkin Fine Arts Museum and the Cathedral of Christ the Saviour, this is the perfect place to recover from a day of art and architecture.

IL PATIO ITALIAN **$**

Map p270 (www.il-patio.rosinter.com; ul Volkhonka 13a; meals R400-800; ; Kropotkinskaya) This ubiquitous chain has a slew of outlets. The most inviting one, near the Cathedral of Christ the Saviour, has a large glass-enclosed seating area, making a perfectly pleasant setting for feasting on wood-oven pizzas and fresh salads.

Outer Khamovniki

MOSKVICH RUSSIAN **$$$**

(Москвич; 495-705 9121; www.moskvich.su; 2/1 ul Usacheva; meals R1500-2000; noon-last guest; Frunzenskaya) Situated atop the stylish classic car gallery Autoville is this retro-chic restaurant named after the sturdy Soviet roadster, one of which is parked in the bar. Both old- and new-style Moscow dishes are on the menu and are very nicely presented.

SKAZKA VOSTOKA CAUCASIAN **$$**

off Map p270 (Сказка востока; www.skazkavostoka1001night.ru; Frunzenskaya nab; meals R400-800; 24hr; ; Frunzenskaya) This boat moored on the Moscow River provides the romantic setting for exotic Eastern fare, just like you heard about in the 'Legend of the East'. Tables are laden with fruits, nuts and salads, while mystical-sounding music drifts through the air. Skazka Vostoka has a huge menu, specialising in spicy Georgian and Azeri delights.

STOLLE RUSSIAN **$**

(Malaya Pirogovskaya ul 16; 9am-9pm; Sportivnaya) After wandering the grounds and examining the graves at Novodevichy, an energy boost is usually in order. The perfect place for this is Stolle, specialising in tasty Saxon pies. Choose from the selection of savoury and sweet pastries sitting on the counter, or order something more substantial from the sit-down menu.

DRINKING & NIGHTLIFE

Arbat

ZHIGULI BEER HALL BREWERY

Map p268 (Пивной зал Жигули; www.zhiguli.net, in Russian; ul Novy Arbat 11; ½ litre beer R100-150; 10am-2am Sun-Thu, 10am-4am Fri & Sat; Arbatskaya) It's hard to classify this old-style *stolovaya* (cafeteria) that happens to brew great beer. The place harks back to the Soviet years, when a popular *pivnoy* bar by the same name was a Novy Arbat institution. The minimalist decor and cafeteria-style service recalls the heyday, although this place has been updated with big-screen TVs and a separate table-service dining room. The overall effect is a nostalgic place without the Soviet memorabilia and other retro kitsch. The namesake Zhiguli beer (not to be confused with the original Zhiguli beer, which comes from Samara) is brewed on site.

MAXIMILIAN'S BRAUEREI BREWERY

Map p268 (ww.maxbrau-moscow.ru; ul Novy Arbat 15; ½ litre beer R150; Arbatskaya) Maximilian's promises live music and 'live beer', both served up in an authentic Bavarian brew-house atmosphere. The place gets rave reviews for its three signature beers, as well as tasty German sausages. Max also books some excellent live-music acts (eg Billy's Band and Leningrad), so it's a win-win-win.

Inner Khamovniki

GOGOL-MOGOL CAFE $

Map p270 (Гоголь-Моголь; Gagarinsky per 6; desserts R100-200; ⌚10am-11pm; ; MKropotkinskaya) The front door is painted with a cake recipe in French, which should give you a pretty good idea of what you are getting into. There are a few lunch items on the menu, but this is really a place to come to indulge in rich French pastries and sweet drinks such as the namesake Gogol-Mogol (which is like egg-nog, but it rhymes).

Outer Khamovniki

SOHO ROOMS NIGHTCLUB

off Map p270 (www.sohorooms.ru; Savvinskaya nab 12; ⌚club 11pm-last guest, restaurant 24hr; MSportivnaya) At the time of research, one of the hottest clubs in Moscow is this uberexclusive nightclub with scantily clad women, cool music and expensive cocktails. Of course, many clubs in Moscow can boast such things, but only Soho Rooms has a swimming pool and a poolside terrace, too. Face control.

ENTERTAINMENT

RHYTHM BLUES CAFE LIVE MUSIC

Map p268 (Ритм Блюз Кафе; ☎499-245 5543; www.blueshouse.ru, in Russian; Starovagankovsky per; ⌚noon-midnight Sun-Thu, noon-5am Fri & Sat; MAleksandrovsky Sad) If your dog got run over by a pick-up truck, you could find some comfort at the Rhythm Blues Cafe, with down-and-out live music every night, plus cold beer and a whole menu of salty cured meats. Great fun and a friendly vibe, with people actually listening to the music. Book a table if you want to sit down.

GELIKON OPERA OPERA

Map p268 (Геликон опера; www.helikon.ru; ul Novy Arbat 11; tickets R200-2000; ⌚box office noon-2pm & 2.30-7pm; MArbatskaya) Named after famous Mt Helicon, home to the muses and inspiration for musicians, this early-1990s opera company is unique in Moscow for its innovative, even experimental, opera performances. Director Dmitry Bertman is known for 'combining musical excellence with artistic risk', according to one local dramaturge. The Gelikon's 250-seat theatre provides an intimate setting that allows for some interaction between the performers and the audience.

CHAIKA SPORTS COMPLEX SWIMMING POOL

off Map p270 (Чайка спортивный комплекс; www.chayka-sport.ru; Turchaninov per 1/3; admission R400-600; ⌚7am-10.30pm Mon-Sat, 8.30am-7.30pm Sun; MPark Kultury) Boasting eight lanes and heated to a pleasant 29°C, this 50m open-air pool is an ideal place for swimming laps year-round. It is attached to a training room, so the price of admission also allows access to cardiovascular equipment and weights on site. Kids under 16 are only welcome at designated times, so phone before bringing the little ones along.

LUZHNIKI SPORTS PALACE SPORTS

(www.luzhniki.ru; Luzhnetskaya nab 24; MSportivnaya) Moscow's largest stadium seats up to 80,000 people and gleams after its recent reconstruction. Luzhniki is home to Torpedo and Spartak, both of which are teams in Russia's premier football league. This stadium is part of a larger complex, which was the main venue for the 1980 Olympics. Besides the giant stadium, Luzhniki includes a collection of swimming pools: two outdoor, two indoor and a kiddie pool. The pools are open year-round and the water is heated to between 27°C and 29°C. The complex also includes a training room, a sauna and tennis courts.

SHOPPING

Arbat

BUKLE CLOTHING & ACCESSORIES

Map p268 (www.vereteno.com, in Russian; ul Arbat 27/47; MArbatskaya) The collection of Liudmila Mezentseva, called Vereteno, is on display at this little cafe-cum-boutique. It's not as outrageous as some other Russian fashion, but it's no less creative. On sale is mostly casual wear, including T-shirts, skirts, sweaters, scarves, handbags and watches, all with an innovative twist. For shoppers who are not worried about squeezing into a miniskirt, there is a cafe on site.

LOCAL KNOWLEDGE

EATING IN MOSCOW

Laura Bridge is the executive chef at Soho Rooms and was recently named by Haute Living one of the top five celebrity chefs in Moscow.

Best dinner in Moscow?
I like Nedalny Vostok (p99), where my friend Glen Ballis is the chef. It's Asian-influenced cuisine but it's so unique – his menu and preparations are different than any place in the city.

Best Russian cuisine?
Pushkin Cafe (p96) is the best Russian restaurant with amazing service and attention to detail.

Best Russian foods to try?
Try delicious dishes such as beluga caviar on homemade bliny; borsch, the traditional beetroot soup; and shashlyk, which is grilled barbecued meat. These dishes shatter the myth that Russian cuisine is bland, heavy and tasteless.

Best budget dining?
Some of the local canteens have good food for cheap prices, especially if you stick to the Russian basics like *solyanka* (salty meat soup) and *plov* (rice dish with meat and vegetables).

Best night out?
Soho Rooms (p118) is so big that you can go bar-hopping from room to room, level to level, and never leave the club.

Where do you go on your day off?
In summer I like to go to Swan Lake (Lebedinoe Ozero, p130). Last weekend we went there at noon and stayed until 2am!

DOM KNIGI BOOKS
Map p268 (Дом книги; www.mosdomknigi.ru, in Russian; ul Novy Arbat 8; ⏲9am-11pm Mon-Fri, 10am-11pm Sat & Sun; Ⓜ Arbatskaya) Among the largest bookstores in Moscow, Dom Knigi has a selection of foreign-language books to rival any other shop in the city, not to mention travel guidebooks, maps, and reference and souvenir books. This huge, crowded place holds regularly scheduled readings, children's programs and other bibliophilic activities.

CHOCOLATE SALO=N FOOD & DRINK
Map p268 (Шоколадный салон; Povarskaya ul 29/36; ⏲10am-9pm; Ⓜ Barrikadnaya) This bustling store is the factory outlet for several local candy makers, including the most famous, Krasny Oktyabr (Red October). The display case is filled with tempting filled candies and chocolate sculptures in all forms. We can't resist the old-fashioned Alyonka candybar.

RUSSIAN EMBROIDERY & LACE SOUVENIRS
Map p268 (Русская вышивка и кружево; ul Arbat 31; Ⓜ Smolenskaya) Considering the lack of flashy signs and kitsch it would be easy to miss this plain storefront on the Arbat. But inside there are treasures galore, from elegant tablecloths and napkins to delicate handmade sweaters and embroidered shirts.

ARTEFACT GALLERY CENTRE ART GALLERY
Map p270 (ul Prechistenka 30; Ⓜ Kropotkinskaya) Near the Russian Academy of Art, this is a sort of art mall, housing a few dozen galleries under one roof. Look for paintings, sculptures, dolls, pottery and other kinds of art that people actually buy, as opposed to the more avant-garde exhibits at other art centres.

BURO NAHODOK ART GALLERY
Map p270 (Бюро находок; www.buro-nahodok.ru, in Russian; Smolensky bul 7/9; Ⓜ Park Kultury) In 2003 three Moscow artists opened this shop to sell their fun and funky gifts and souvenirs. It was the first of what would

become a network of artists' cooperatives around the city. See Ministerstvo Podarkov, p101, for a full review.

VASSA & CO CLOTHING & ACCESSORIES

Map p268 (www.vassatrend.com; ul Novy Arbat 2/5; Ⓜ Arbatskaya) Vassa is a Russian designer but was trained in New York City. Her designs reflect a classical and classy sense of style. Catering to modern Moscow men and women, Vassa offers suits, shirts, skirts, dresses and other professional clothing that stylish folks might wear at the office or out on the town.

CHAPURIN BOUTIQUE CLOTHING & ACCESSORIES

off Map p270 (www.chapurin.com; Savvinskaya nab 21; Ⓜ Sportivnaya) Fashion maven Igor Chapurin got his start designing theatre costumes, but his creativity knows no bounds: in addition to men's and women's clothing, he has lines of children's clothing and sportswear. Rich fabrics, playful textures and solid colours.

CONFAEL CHOCOLATE FOOD & DRINK

Map p268 (http://confael.ru; Nikitsky bul 12; Ⓜ Arbatskaya) This upmarket boutique and cafe is chock-full of mouth-watering chocolates, in every shape and size imaginable. Besides the boxes of truffles and chocolate-covered cherries, Confael also stocks themed chocolates relating to holidays, hobbies and national events. Sample the goods in the cafe.

RUSSKIE CHASOVYE TRADITSII JEWELLERY & WATCHES

Map p268 (Русские часовые традиции; ul Arbat 11 & 25; Ⓜ Arbatskaya) If you are in the market for a fancy timepiece, pop into one of the Arbat outlets of 'Russian Watch Traditions'. On this touristy drag, these small shops cater primarily to tourists, meaning they carry exclusively Russian brands, including Aviator, Buran, Vostok, Poljot, Romanoff and Denissov.

SKAZKA ARTS & CRAFTS

Map p268 (Сказка; www.skazka-shop.com; ul Arbat 51; ⌚9am-11pm; Ⓜ Smolenskaya) The Arbat is lined with souvenir shops, not to mention the hawkers with their stalls set up on the street. You won't find any deals here, but you might find a fun souvenir that's worth the price. Skazka is one of the largest shops on Arbat, with loads of excellent hand-painted crafts, dolls and toys, plus Pavlov Posad scarves, Russian watches and more.

ARMY STORE MILITARY STORE

Map p268 (www.armystore.ru; ul Arbat 49; ⌚10am-8pm; Ⓜ Smolenskaya) Boots and binoculars and camouflage bags, army knives, flasks and loads of other gear to help you survive your next battle, whatever it may be. Some of the stuff here is a little whacky, but you never know when you're going to need it. Enter the Army Store from the courtyard.

Zamoskvorechie

Neighbourhood Top Five

❶ Spending a half-day at the **Tretyakov Gallery** (p123), admiring the superb collection of Russian icons, the cutting social commentary of the Peredvizhniki ('Wanderers'), the whimsy of the Symbolists, and other prerevolutionary art.

❷ Catching a concert, film or event at the **Strelka Institute** (p132) in the former Red October chocolate factory.

❸ Seeing the fallen heroes of the Soviet era at **Art Muzeon Sculpture Park** (p126).

❹ Visiting the **Danilov Monastery** (p125), the spiritual and administrative centre of the Orthodox Church.

❺ Wiling away a summer afternoon at **Lebedinoe Ozero** (p130), the city's most enticing terrace restaurant.

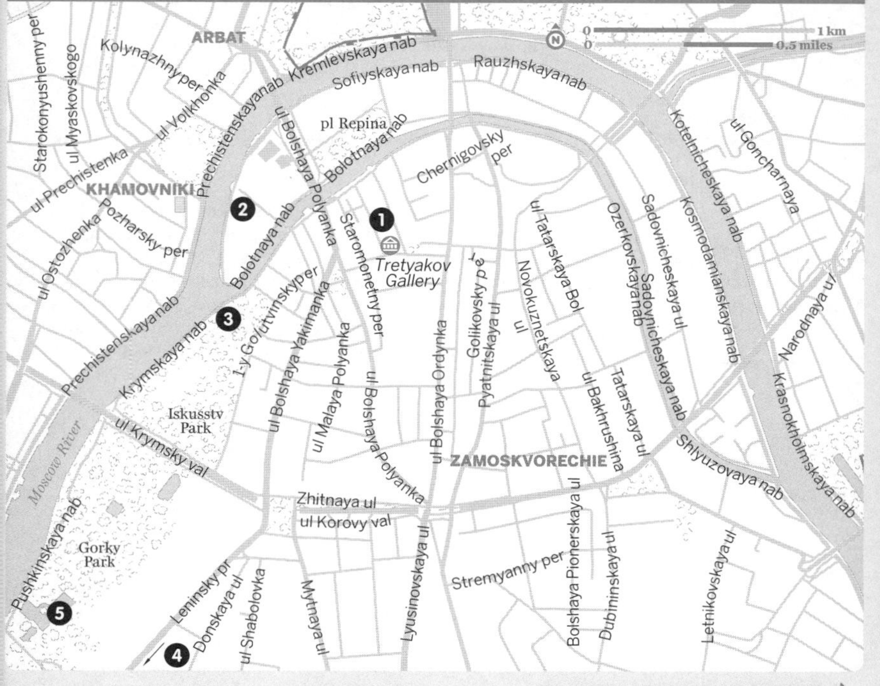

For more detail of this area, see p276

Lonely Planet's Top Tip

The northern part of Zamoskvorechie – including the Red October complex on Bolotny Island – is easiest to access by walking over the Bolshoy Moskvoretsky most from the Kremlin or walking over the Patriarshy most from the Cathedral of Christ the Saviour.

Best Places to Eat

- Bar Strelka (p130)
- Correa's (p129)
- Suliko (p129)

For reviews, see p129

Best Places to Drink

- Bar Strelka (p130)
- Lebedinoe Ozero (p130)
- Art Akademiya (p131)

For reviews, see p130

Best Art Venues

- Tretyakov Gallery (p123)
- Art Muzeon Sculpture Park (p126)
- Red October chocolate factory (p126)
- Central House of Artists (p133)

For reviews, see p126

Explore: Zamoskvorechie

The atmosphere of 19th-century Moscow lives on in the low buildings, old courtyards and clusters of onion domes in Zamoskvorechie. The many churches in the area make up a wonderful scrapbook of Muscovite architectural styles. It's worth taking a few hours to wander the neighbourhood before or after your visit to the Tretyakov.

Zamoskvorechie has long been a thriving art district, thanks to the proliferation of galleries at the Central House of Artists, not to mention both branches of the Tretyakov Gallery. With the recent conversion of the Red October chocolate factory into galleries, clubs and cafes, this has become Moscow's hottest spot for art and entertainment. Plan to spend at least one evening exploring Bolotny Island: come early to eat dinner and browse the galleries; stay late to drink and dance the night away.

Local Life

- **Markets** The Danilovsky Market (p130) is a trek from the centre but it's worth it for fresh meat and produce and cheap prices.
- **Outdoor Activities** A string of peaceful parks lines the Moscow River, offering respite from the city. Traverse Gorky Park (p126), continue along the river to the wilder Neskuchny Garden, and find your way all the way to Vorobyovy Gory Nature Preserve (see p150). It's a lovely (long) walk, perhaps even better for in-line skating or cycling.

Getting There & Away

- **Metro** Three different metro lines cut through Zamoskvorechie in a north–south direction. The green Zamoskvoretskaya line has stops at Novokuznetskaya and Paveletskaya. The orange Kaluzhsko-Rizhskaya line also has a stop at Novokuznetskaya, as well as at Oktyabrskaya. The grey Serpukhovsko-Timiryazevskaya line has stations at Polyanka and Serpukhovskaya.

TOP SIGHTS
TRETYAKOV GALLERY

The Tretyakov Gallery started as the private collection of the 19th-century industrialist brothers Pavel and Sergei Tretyakov. Pavel was a patron of the Peredvizhniki, or 'Wanderers', a group of 19th-century painters who broke away from the conservative Academy of Arts and started depicting common people and social problems. Nowadays, these are among Russia's most celebrated painters, and the Tretyakov boasts some of the most exquisite examples of their work.

Main Building

The exotic boyar (high-ranking noble) castle on a little lane in Zamoskvorechie contains the **main branch** (Lavrushinsky per 10; MTretyakovskaya) of the State Tretyakov Gallery, housing the world's best collection of Russian icons and an outstanding collection of other prerevolutionary Russian art. The building was designed by the Russian revivalist artist Viktor Vasnetsov between 1900 and 1905.

The rooms are numbered and progress in chronological order, starting on the 2nd floor.

Second Floor

Rooms 1 through 7 display painting and sculpture from the 18th century, with many portraits and official-looking commissioned paintings. Things get more interesting in rooms 8 through 15, which display landscapes, character paintings and more portraits from the 19th century.

The real gems of the collection, however, start with room 16. In the 1870s daring artists started to use their medium to address social issues, thus founding the **Peredvizhniki** (Wanderers).

Room 17 is dedicated to Vasily Perov, one of the original founders of the movement. Look for his famous portrait of Dostoevsky and the moving painting *Troika,* with its stark depiction of child labour. Ivan Kramskoi (room 20) was another of the original Wanderers, and Ivan Shishkin (room 25) was a landscape painter closely associated with the same movement.

Viktor Vasnetsov (room 26) paints fantastical depictions of fairy tales and historical figures. His painting *Bogatery* (Heroes) is perhaps the best example from the revivalist movement, although *A Knight at the Crossroads* is more dramatic. By contrast, Vasily Vereshchagin (room 27) is known for his harsh realism, especially in battle scenes. *The Apotheosis of War,* for example, is not subtle.

Vasily Surikov (room 28) excels at large-scale historical scenes. Most famously, *Boyarina Morozova* captures the history of the schism in the Orthodox Church and how it tragically played out for one family.

Ilya Repin (rooms 29 and 30) is perhaps the most beloved Russian realist painter. *Ivan the Terrible and his Son Ivan* is downright chilling. Room 31 has a few masterpieces by Nicholas Ge, another founder of the Peredvizhniki movement.

Mikhail Vrubel (rooms 32 to 34) was a Symbolist-era artist who defies classification. One entire wall is covered with his fantastic **art nouveau mural** *The Princess of the Dream.* The melancholy *Demon Seated* is also provocative.

DON'T MISS...

- *Vladimir Icon of the Mother of God* in the Church of St Nicholas in Tolmachi
- Mikhail Vrubel's mural *The Princess of the Dream*
- *A Knight at the Crossroads* by Viktor Vasnetsov
- *Ivan the Terrible and his Son Ivan* by Ilya Repin

PRACTICALITIES

- Map p276
- www.tretyakovgallery.ru, in Russian
- adult/student R360/220
- 10am-7.30pm Tue-Sun

SPECIAL EXHIBITS

The Tretyakov hosts exciting temporary exhibits in the **Engineer's Building** (Lavrushinsky per 12), next door to the main building.

The Church of St Nicholas in Tolmachi is where Pavel Tretyakov regularly attended church. He is now buried in Novodevichy Cemetery.

CENTRAL HOUSE OF ARTISTS

In the same building as the New Tretyakov, the **Central House of Artists** (Центральный дом художника; www.cha.ru; admission R200; ⌚11am-7pm Tue-Sun) is a huge exhibit space used for contemporary-art shows. The surrounding grounds contain the Art Muzeon Sculpture Park (p126).

First Floor

A selection of Isaac Levitan's landscapes is in room 37. Mikhail Nesterov – in room 39 – combines **Symbolism** with religious themes. *The Vision of the Youth Bartholomew* depicts an episode from the childhood of St Sergius of Radonezh (patron saint of Russia). In rooms 41 and 42, Valentin Serov was the most celebrated portraitist of his time.

Moving into the 20th century, artists began to reject the rules of realism. Room 43 displays Konstantin Korovin's foray into Impressionism. Alexander Golovin and Boris Kustodiev represent the 'World of Art' art nouveau movement in room 44. In room 46, Pavel Kuznetsov was the founder of the Blue Rose, the Moscow group of Symbolist artists. Sergei Sudeykin and Nikolai Sapunov were known for their set and costume designs. Nicholas Rerikh (Roerich) shows off his fantastical storytelling style in room 47. In room 48, Martiros Saryan is also a Symbolist, although his work was influenced by his Armenian heritage.

Rooms 49 to 54 contain drawings, watercolours, pastels and prints, with rotating exhibits of works from the museum's permanent collection. Room 55 houses the **Treasury**, with its collection of metals, jewellery, embroidery and precious knick-knacks.

Icons are found on the ground floor in rooms 56 to 62. Andrei Rublyov's *Holy Trinity* (1420s) from Sergiev Posad, regarded as Russia's greatest icon, is in room 60. Within the museum grounds is the **Church of St Nicholas in Tolmachi** (⌚noon-4pm Tue-Sun), which was transferred to this site and restored in 1997. The centrepiece is the revered 12th-century *Vladimir Icon of the Mother of God,* protector of all Russia, which was transferred here from the Assumption Cathedral in the Kremlin.

New Tretyakov Gallery

The premier venue for 20th-century Russian art is the State Tretyakov Gallery on Krymsky val, better known as the **New Tretyakov Gallery** (Map p276; ul Krymsky val 10; Ⓜ Park Kultury). The exhibits showcase the Russian avant-garde – noteworthy since many of these artists were censored at the time they painted.

The primitive works of Natalia Goncharova are on display in rooms 1 and 2, as are some abstract paintings by her partner Mikhail Larianov. Kazimir Malevich is in room 6, including one version of his Black Square. Room 9 contains pieces by Vasily Kandinsky, especially his futuristic urban landscape of Moscow, and a few fanciful paintings by Marc Chagall. In room 10, look for the Cubist pieces by Lyubov Popova.

In rooms 39 to 42, there is a small collection of contemporary paintings from the 1990s and 2000s, with a few 'art-object' pieces by Ilya Kabakov.

TOP SIGHTS
DANILOV MONASTERY

The headquarters of the Russian Orthodox Church stand behind the whitewashed walls of the Danilov Monastery. The monastery holds a special status as the administrative centre of the Russian Orthodox Church, and it radiates an air of purpose befitting the Church's role in modern Russia. More important to believers, however, is its foundation and continued protection by its namesake, St Daniil. As such the place seethes with devotion, as worshippers murmur prayers, light candles and ladle holy water into jugs.

In the late 13th century, this fortress was built as an outer city defence by Daniil, the youngest son of Alexander Nevsky and the first Prince of Moscow. It was in fact Moscow's first monastery, and Prince Daniil was buried on the grounds when he died.

Over the centuries, the fortress was greatly altered, due to neglect, war, fire and subsequent rebuilding. The cemetery became a prestigious final resting place for cultural dignitaries, including the writer Nikolai Gogol, the painter Vasily Perov, the pianist Nikolai Rubinstein and others (most of whom were eventually moved to Novodevichy Cemetery).

DON'T MISS...

- Church of the Holy Fathers of the Seven Ecumenical Councils
- Historic Danilov bells
- 13th-century *khachkar*

PRACTICALITIES

- off Map p276
- www.msdm.ru
- Danilovsky val
- admission free
- 7am-7pm
- Tulskaya

The monastery was closed during the Soviet period, when the facility served as a factory and a detention centre, but it was returned to the Orthodox Church in 1983. Five years later, during the Russian Orthodoxy's millennium celebrations, the Danilov Monastery replaced Sergiev Posad as the Church's spiritual and administrative centre, becoming the official residence of the Patriarch.

Enter beneath the pink **St Simeon Stylite Gate-Church** (1732) on the north wall. The monastery's oldest and busiest church is the 17th-century **Church of the Holy Fathers of the Seven Ecumenical Councils**, where worship is held continuously from 10am to 5pm daily. The main chapel upstairs contains a 17th-century iconostasis from the Kostroma school. It is flanked by side chapels to St Daniil (on the northern side) and SS Boris and Gleb (south). On the ground level, the small main chapel is dedicated to the Protecting Veil, and the northern one to the prophet Daniil. The tabernacle contains the holy relics of St Daniil.

The **belfry** contains 17 of the original Danilov bells, which had been removed during the Soviet period. Apparently the local militia complained that the ringing of the bells was disruptive; the faithful were concerned that the bells would be melted down and destroyed forever. As such, the bells were sold to an American capitalist who made a gift of them to Harvard University. For 75 years, the bells hung in a New England belfry, summoning students to class. Thanks to a patriotic Russian financier, the 24 tonnes of bells were returned to their original location in 2008.

The yellow and neoclassical **Trinity Cathedral**, built in the 1830s, is an austere counterpart to the other buildings. The *Three-handed Mother of God* icon is said to be miraculous.

West of the cathedral are the patriarchate's External Affairs Department and, at the far end of the grounds, the **Patriarch's Official Residence**. Against the north wall, to the east of the residence, there's a 13th-century Armenian carved-stone cross, or *khachkar,* a gift from the Armenian Church.

The church guesthouse, in the southern part of the monastery grounds, has been turned into the elegant Danilovskaya Hotel (p176).

SIGHTS

FREE RED OCTOBER — ART CENTRE

Map p276 (Красный Октябрь завод; Bersenevskaya nab; M Kropotkinskaya) After more than a century of producing chocolates and other sweets, the famed Krasny Oktyabr factory, opposite the Church of Christ the Saviour, was finally forced to close as part of an effort to remove industry from the historic centre of the capital. In a rare and enlightened move, the historic industrial building has been preserved and converted into Moscow's hottest spot for art and entertainment. The red-brick buildings of this former chocolate factory now host **Pobeda Gallery** (pobedagallery.com; Bolotnaya nab 3, Bldg 4; 1-8pm), **Lumiere Brothers Photography Centre** (www.lumiere.ru; Bolotnaya nab 3, Bldg 1; noon-9pm Tue-Sun) and **Igor Kormyshev** (www.kormyshev.rul; Bersenevsky per 2, Bldg 1), plus the centrepiece Strelka Institute (p132).

FREE DOM NA NABEREZHNOY — NOTABLE BUILDING

Map p276 (Дом на набережной; www.museum-dom.narod.ru, in Russian; ul Serafimovicha 2; 5-8pm Wed, 2-6pm Sat; M Kropotkinskaya) It isn't much to look at, but this big 'House on the Embankment' on Bolotny Island is a historic building, once home to many old Bolsheviks and Civil War heroes, as well as artists, writers and scientists. The small museum on-site recounts the life histories of its noteworthy residents, many of whom were eventually persecuted for their accomplishments. As such, the exhibit is sometimes called the Museum of Repression. Unfortunately, hours are sporadic and information is only in Russian.

TRETYAKOV GALLERY — ART MUSEUM

See p123.

NEW TRETYAKOV GALLERY — ART MUSEUM

See p124.

ART MUZEON SCULPTURE PARK — PARK

Map p276 (Парк искусств Арт-Музеон; www.muzeon.ru, in Russian; ul Krymsky val 10; admission R100; 10am-9pm; M Park Kultury or Oktyabrskaya) The wonderful, moody sculpture park, behind and beside the New Tretyakov, is Moscow's most atmospheric spot to indulge in some Soviet nostalgia. Formerly called the Park of the Fallen Heroes, it started as a collection of Soviet statues (Stalin, Dzerzhinsky, Sverdlov, a selection of Lenins and Brezhnevs) put out to pasture after they were ripped from their pedestals in the post-1991 wave of anti-Soviet feeling.

These discredited icons have now been joined by contemporary works, ranging from the playful to the provocative. Tsereteli's **Peter the Great** (see the boxed text, p112) surveys the scene from his post on the embankment of the Moscow River.

GORKY PARK — HISTORIC PARK

Map p276 (Парк Горького; www.propark.ru, in Russian; ul Krymsky val; 10am-10pm; M Park Kultury) Amusement park no longer, Gorky Park is still one of the most festive places in Moscow – a perfect way to escape the hubbub of the city. Officially the Park Kultury (Park of Culture), it's named after Maxim Gorky. The park stretches almost 3km along the river, upstream of Krymsky most. This place is undergoing a major overhaul: the rides, games and beer tents have been cleared out, leaving a pleasant and peaceful green space to rent bikes or have a picnic. Apparently Gorky Park has been bought out by Roman Abramovich, who is working with the city of Moscow to revamp the whole place.

OSTROVSKY ESTATE-MUSEUM 'SCHELYKOVO' — MUSEUM

Map p276 (Музей-заповедник Островского 'Щелыково';www.museum.ru/m308, in Russian; ul Malaya Ordynka 9; admission R100; 9am-4pm Tue-Sun; M Tretyakovskaya) Alexander Ostrovsky is the 19th-century playwright who is often considered to be Russia's greatest realist writer. This museum is devoted to his life and work. It is a tribute to Ostrovsky's work for the Maly Theatre, which he founded, and also covers the area of Zamoskvorechie, where he lived and loved. Some of the writer's personal effects are on display here. More intriguing are the paintings and engravings of old Moscow, which featured so prominently in Ostrovsky's work.

CHURCH OF ST JOHN THE WARRIOR — CHURCH

Map p276 (Церковь Иоанна Воина; ul Bolshaya Yakimanka 48; M Oktyabrskaya) The finest of all Zamoskvorechie's churches mixes Moscow and European baroque styles, resulting in a melange of shapes and colours. It was commissioned by Peter the Great in thanks for his 1709 victory over Sweden at Poltava. Inside, the gilt, wood-carved iconostasis was

WORTH A DETOUR

KOLOMENSKOE MUSEUM-RESERVE

Set amid 4 sq km of picturesque parkland, on a bluff above a bend in the Moscow River, **Kolomenskoe** (Музей-заповедник "Коломенское"; www.mgomz.ru; grounds admission free; ⌚grounds 8am-9pm; Ⓜ Kolomenskaya or Kashirskaya) is an ancient royal country seat and Unesco World Heritage Site. Shortly after its founding in the 14th century, the village became a favourite destination for the princes of Moscow. The royal estate is now an eclectic mix of churches and gates and other buildings that were added to the complex over the years.

Ethnographic Centre

Located on one of the original roads from Kolomenskoe village, the **ethnographic centre** (Bolshaya ul; Ⓜ Kolomenskoe) is a work in progress. For starters, historians have reconstructed a peasant's farm and a blacksmith's compound, as well as a three-domed wooden church. Further south, there is a working stable yard and apiary. The idea is to make this a living museum, where visitors can witness 17th-century village life firsthand.

Churches & Gates

From Bolshaya ul, enter the grounds of the museum-reserve through the 17th-century **Saviour Gate** to the star-spangled **Our Lady of Kazan Church**. Ahead, the whitewashed, tent-roofed 17th-century **Front Gate** – guarded by two stone lions – was the main entrance to the royal palace.

Wooden Buildings

Among the old wooden buildings on the grounds is the **cabin** where Peter the Great lived while supervising ship- and fort-building at Arkhangelsk. The cabin is surrounded by a re-creation of the tsar's orchards and gardens. There are also a few handsome structures that were brought here from other regions, specifically the **Bratsk fortress tower** and the **gate-tower of St Nicholas Monastery** from Karelia.

Ascension Church

Outside the front gate, overlooking the river, rises Kolomenskoe's loveliest structure, the **Ascension Church**, sometimes called the 'white column'. Built between 1530 and 1532 for Grand Prince Vasily III, it probably celebrated the birth of his heir, Ivan the Terrible. As the first brick church with a tent-shape roof (previously found only on wooden churches), it represents an important development in Russian architecture. This break with the Byzantine tradition would pave the way for St Basil's Cathedral, which was built 25 years later.

There is an exhibit on **Milestones in Kolomenskoye History** in the tent-roofed gatehouse nearby.

Great Wooden Palace

In the mid-17th century, Tsar Alexey built a palace so fab it was dubbed 'the eighth wonder of the world'. This whimsical building was famous for its mishmash of tent-roofed towers and onion-shaped eaves, all crafted from wood and structured without a single nail. Unfortunately, this legendary building had fallen into disrepair and was demolished in 1768 by Catherine the Great.

Some 230 years later, architects and builders managed to construct a replica of the palace based on an existent model of the original. Now, the **wooden palace of Tsar Alexey** (Дворец царя Алексея Михайловича; ⌚10am-6pm; Ⓜ Kashirskaya) stands about 1km south of its original location. This lack of historical accuracy has raised some eyebrows, but the masterpiece is open for visitors to admire its exquisite 17th-century interiors. In total, 24 rooms have been replicated, based on the records of the original architects and decorators.

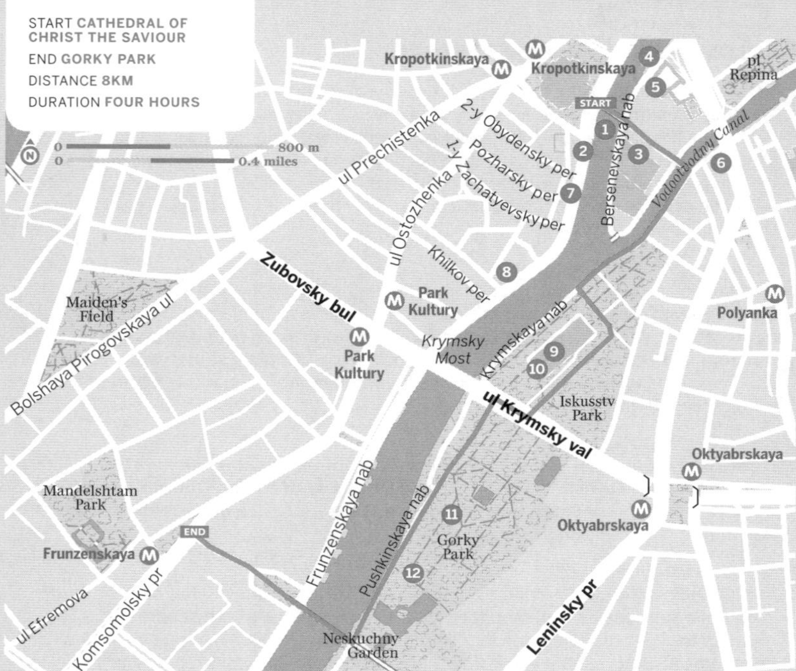

Neighbourhood Walk
Zamoskvorechie

From the Cathedral of Christ the Saviour (MKropotkinskaya) a pedestrian bridge leads across the Moscow River to Bolotny Island, the small slice of land south of the Kremlin. The 1 **Patriarshy most** offers a fantastic panorama of the Kremlin towers and of the cathedral itself.

South of the bridge on Bolotny Island is the old 2 **Red October chocolate factory**, now housing a cluster of galleries, shops, clubs and cafes, as well as the centrepiece 3 **Strelka Institute**. This is Moscow's hottest spot for art and entertainment.

Detour north along Sofiyskaya nab to 4 **Dom na Naberezhnoy**, which was a prestigious residential building during Soviet times. The little park 5 **Bolotnaya Ploshchad** contains an intriguing sculpture by Mikhail Shemyakin, *Children are Victims of Adults' Vices* (with all the vices depicted in delightful detail).

Walk across the Maly Kamenny most. The 6 **Tretyakov Gallery** is a few blocks to the east, but if you don't want to be sidetracked for the rest of the day, head south along Yakimanskaya nab, passing Zurab Tsereteli's sculpture of 7 **Peter the Great**, or 'Peter the Ugly' according to some sources.

From the embankment, along Krymskaya nab, enter the 8 **Art Muzeon Sculpture Park**, an art museum and history lesson all in one. From here, you can enter the 9 **New Tretyakov**, dedicated to 20th-century art, and the 10 **Central House of Artists**, filled with galleries and exhibitions.

Cross ul Krymsky val using the underground passageway. You will reappear at the entrance to 11 **Gorky Park**, marked by colourful flags and an old-fashioned carousel. Stroll across the fun-filled theme park, stopping to eat an ice cream or ride the Ferris wheel. At the southern end, you can have a drink at 12 **Chaikhona No 1** or stroll across the pedestrian bridge to Frunzenskaya metro station.

originally installed in the nearby **Church of the Resurrection at Kadashi** (Церковь Воскрессения на Кадашах; 2-y Kadashevsky per 7). The iconostasis was moved when the latter church was closed (it now houses a restoration centre).

BAKHRUSHIN THEATRE MUSEUM MUSEUM
Map p276 (Театральный музей Бахрушина; www.gctm.ru, in Russian; ul Bakhrushina 31/12; admission R150; ⌚noon-6pm Wed-Sun; Ⓜ Paveletskaya) Russia's foremost stage museum, founded in 1894, is in the neo-Gothic mansion on the north side of Paveletskaya pl. The museum exhibits all things theatrical – stage sets, costumes, scripts and personal items belonging to some of Russia's stage greats. The exhibits are not limited only to drama, also tracing the development of opera, ballet and puppetry. Highlights include the costumes and stage set from *Boris Godunov* (starring the famous bass, Fyodor Shalyapin) and the ballet shoes worn by Vaslav Nijinsky.

DANILOV MONASTERY MONASTERY
See p125.

DONSKOY MONASTERY MONASTERY
off Map p276 (Донской монастырь; www.donskoi.org, in Russian; Donskaya ul; Ⓜ Shabolovskaya) The youngest of Moscow's fortified monasteries, Donskoy was founded in 1591 and built to house the *Virgin of the Don* icon (now in the Tretyakov Gallery). This revered icon is credited with the victory in the 1380 battle of Kulikovo; it's also said that, in 1591, the Tatar Khan Giri retreated without a fight after the icon showered him with burning arrows in a dream.

Most of the monastery, surrounded by a brick wall with 12 towers, was built between 1684 and 1733 under Regent Sofia and Peter the Great. The **Virgin of Tikhvin Church** over the north gate, built in 1713 and 1714, is one of the last examples of Moscow baroque. In the centre of the grounds is the large brick **New Cathedral**, built between 1684 and 1693. Just to its south is the smaller **Old Cathedral**, dating from 1591 to 1593.

When burials in central Moscow were banned after the 1771 plague, the Donskoy Monastery became a graveyard for the nobility, and it is littered with elaborate tombs and chapels.

Donskoy Monastery is a five-minute walk from Shabolovskaya metro. Go south along ul Shabolovka, then take the first street west, 1-y Donskoy proezd.

EATING

CORREA'S EUROPEAN $$
Map p276 (www.correas.ru; ul Bolshaya Ordynka 40/2; brunch R400-600, sandwiches R200-400, meals R600-1000; ⌚8am-midnight; Ⓜ Polyanka) Correa's now has outlets all over the city. Though none are quite as cosy and quaint as the original in Presnya (p98), a restaurant with a bit more space has its advantages. This one is oddly located in a cement courtyard, but it does mean there is outdoor seating; and the spacious light-filled interior is inviting too. The same fresh ingredients and simple preparations mean that the food is impeccable.

SULIKO CAUCASIAN $$
Map p276 (Сулико; www.suliko.ru, in Russian; ul Bolshaya Polyanka 42/2; meals R600-1000; Ⓜ Polyanka) Often cited as the city's most authentic Georgian restaurant, this place has fantastic Caucasian dishes, especially the *khachapuri* (cheese bread) topped with a fried egg. The dining room evokes the Caucasian countryside, with grape vines hanging from the ceiling and a huge stone fireplace. If you're short of time (or cash), the same food is available ready-made at the cafe just around the corner – at a fraction of the cost. There is another outlet in Presnya (p97).

GRABLY CAFETERIA $
Map p276 (Грабли; www.grably.ru, in Russian; Pyatnitskaya ul 27; meals R200-300; ⌚10am-11pm; Ⓜ Novokuznetskaya) The big buffet features an amazing array of fish, poultry and meat, plus breakfast items, salads, soups and desserts. After you run the gauntlet and pay the bill, take a seat in the elaborate winter-garden seating area. This Zamoskvorechie outlet is particularly impressive, with two levels of tiled floors, vines draped over wrought-iron rails, and chandeliers suspended from the high ceilings. Beer and wine are available at the bar upstairs.

SOK VEGETARIAN $$
Map p276 (Сок; www.cafe-cok.ru, in Russian; Lavrushinsky per 15; meals R500-800; ⌚11am-11pm; Ⓜ Tretyakovskaya) Citrus-coloured walls and delicious fresh-squeezed juices are guaranteed to brighten your day. All the soups, salads, pasta and fabulous desserts are vegetarian, with many vegan options too. The menu even features a few Russian classics like beef stroganoff, made with seitan (a wheat-based meat substitute).

PRODUKTY — ITALIAN $$

Map p276 (Продукты; ☎903-789 3474; www.productscafebar.ru; Bersenevsky per 5, Bldg 1; meals R600-1000; ; MKropotkinskaya) The cool, post-industrial decor, simple Italian food and affordable prices make this place a welcome addition to Moscow's restaurant scene. The location inside the Red October complex doesn't hurt either.

PANCHO VILLA — MEXICAN $

Map p276 (www.panchovilla.ru; ul Bolshaya Yakimanka 52; meals R300-600; 24hr; ; MOktyabrskaya) Near Oktyabrskaya pl, this is still Moscow's top choice for 'Meksikansky' food. If the fajitas and margaritas aren't enough of a draw, come for breakfast burritos, happy-hour specials or live Latin music nightly (from 8pm).

DANILOVSKY MARKET — MARKET

off Map p276 (Mytnaya ul 74; 8am-6pm; MTulskaya) The Russian market *(rinok)* is a busy, bustling place, full of activity and colour. Even if you're not shopping, it's entertaining to peruse the tables piled high with multicoloured produce: homemade cheese and jam; golden honey straight from the hive; vibrantly coloured spices pouring out of plastic bags; slippery silver fish posing on beds of ice; and huge slabs of meat hanging from the ceiling.

KORCHMA TARAS BULBA — UKRAINIAN $

Map p276 (Корчма Тарас Бульба; ☎495-953 7153; Pyatnitskaya ul 14; noon-2am; meals R400-600; ; MTretyakovskaya) Food fit for a Cossack, meaning the heartiest of Ukrainian specialties at affordable prices. One of many outlets around town.

STARLITE DINER — DINER $$

Map p276 (www.starlite.ru; Bolotnaya pl 16/5; meals R500-700; 24hr; ; MTretyakovskaya) You're never far from a burger and a beer. Or breakfast any time of day or night. Bring on the nostalgia with classic diner decor and no-frills filling food.

YOLKI-PALKI — RUSSIAN $

Map p276 (☎495-953 9130; www.elki-palki.ru; Klimentovsky per 14; meals R300-500; 10am-9pm; MTretyakovskaya) The Russian chains are well-represented in this restaurant-rich neighbourhood. This outlet is a favourite among student-types for cheap and tasty Russian specialities.

SHESH-BESH — CAUCASIAN $$

Map p276 (Шеш-беш; www.shesh-besh.rmcom.ru; Pyatnitskaya ul 24/1; meals R400-800; ; MNovokuznetskaya) One of Moscow's many kitschy, rhyming chain restaurants, this one serving up decent Caucasian dishes at affordable prices.

PRIME STAR — FAST FOOD $

Map p268 (www.prime-star.ru; Pyatnitskaya ul 5; meals R200-300; ; MNovokuznetskaya) Fast and fresh, Prime Star serves pre-made sandwiches and salads to hungry folks on the go.

DRINKING & NIGHTLIFE

BAR STRELKA — BAR

Map p276 (www.barstrelka.com; Bersenevskaya nab 5, Bldg 14; 9am-midnight Mon-Thu, noon-5am Fri & Sat, noon-midnight Sun; MKropotkinskaya) Located just below the Patriarshy most, the bar-restaurant at the Strelka Institute is the ideal starting point for an evening in the Red October complex. The rooftop terrace is unbeatable for its Moscow River views, but the interior is equally cool in a shabby-chic sort of way. The bar menu is excellent and there is usually somebody tinkling the ivories.

LEBEDINOE OZERO — CAFE

Map p276 (Лебединое озеро; http://s-11.ru/lebedinoe-ozero; Neskuchny Garden; noon-2am May-Sep; MFrunzenskaya) The name means 'Swan Lake' and, yes, it overlooks a little pond where resident swans float contentedly. Aside from the idyllic setting at the southern end of Gorky Park, this place is a happening summertime haunt thanks to lounge chairs in the sun, (expensive) fruity cocktails and a small swimming pool for cooling dips or late-night aquatic dancing. To really cure the summertime blues, book some time in the massage hut (per hour R1400 to R1600).

KVARTIRA 44 — BAR

Map p276 (Квартира 44; www.kv44.ru, in Russian; ul Malaya Yakimanka 24/8; noon-2am Sun-Thu, noon-6am Fri & Sat; ; MPolyanka) Back in the olden days, the best place to go for a drink was your neighbour's flat, which would be crowded with mismatched furniture and

WORTH A DETOUR

TSARITSYNO

On a wooded hill in far southeast Moscow, **Tsaritsyno Palace** (Музей-заповедник Царицыно; www.tsaritsyno-museum.ru, in Russian; grounds admission free; ⏰grounds 6am-midnight, exhibits 11am-6pm Tue-Fri, 11am-8pm Sat & Sun; Ⓜ Tsaritsino) is a modern-day manifestation of the exotic summer home that Catherine the Great began in 1775 but never finished. Architect Vasily Bazhenov worked on the project for 10 years before he was sacked. She hired another architect, Matvey Kazakov, but the project was eventually forgotten as she ran out of money. For hundreds of years, the palace was little more than a shell, until the Russian government finally decided to finish it in 2007.

Nowadays, the **Great Palace** (Большой дворец; admission R150) is a fantastical building that combines old Russian, Gothic, classical and Arabic styles. Inside, exhibits are dedicated to the history of Tsaritsyno, as well as the life of Catherine the Great. The nearby kitchen building, or **khlebny dom** (Хлебный дом; admission R100), also hosts rotating exhibits, sometimes culinary and sometimes on less-tantalising topics such as icons and art. The *khlebny dom* is a pleasant place to hear classical **concerts** (☎499-725 7291; tickets R150-300; ⏰5pm Sat & Sun) in summer.

The extensive grounds include some other lovely buildings, including the **Small Palace**, the working **Church of Our Lady Lifegiving Spring**, the cavalier buildings and some interesting bridges. A pond is bedecked by a fantastic fountain set to music. The English-style wooded park stretches all the way south to the **Upper Tsaritsynsky Pond**, which has rowing boats available for hire in summer, and west to the Tsaritsyno Palace complex.

Tsaritsyno is easy to find: just follow the signs from the eponymous metro station.

personal memorabilia. This is the atmosphere evoked at 'Apartment 44', where the drinks flow, the music plays and life is merry.

ART AKADEMIYA — CLUB, CAFE

Map p276 (Арт-академия; www.academiya.ru; 6/3 Bersenevskaya nab 6/3; ⏰noon-midnight Sun-Thu, to 6am Fri & Sat; 🚭📶🍸📋👪; Ⓜ Kropotkinskaya) The pizza chain with all the best locations has nabbed a massive space in the Red October factory complex for this super stylish, contemporary-art-packed lounge bar. Relax on caramel leather sofas or perch at the long central bar (supposedly the longest in Moscow). Besides the pizza, there is a summer terrace, a bookstore, video and art exhibits, film screenings and DJs spinning tunes until the wee hours.

PROGRESSIVE DADDY & DADDY'S TERRACE — BAR

Map p276 (www.progressivedaddy.ru; Bersenevskaya nab 6/2; Ⓜ Kropotkinskaya) Daddy managed to snag the prime location in the Red October complex: at the tip of the island, on the top floor of the factory, the restaurant-bar-club has the best views in the joint (if not the city). Sit on the terrace and sip a bellini while you admire the Cathedral of Christ the Saviour in the distance. It's very modern Moscow.

ROLLING STONE — BAR

Map p276 (Bolotnaya nab 3; ⏰noon-midnight Sun-Thu, noon-6am Fri & Sat; Ⓜ Kropotkinskaya) Plastered with covers of the namesake magazine and lit by naked bulbs, this place has the feel of an upscale dive bar. What makes it upscale is the location – the ultratrendy Red October complex – and the clientele – they might be dressed in casual gear but they still have to look impeccable to get past the face control. The music spans all genres and there is a small dance floor if you are so inspired.

COFFEE BEAN — CAFE

Map p276 (www.coffeebean.ru; Pyatnitskaya ul 5; ⏰8am-11pm; Ⓜ Tretyakovskaya) One could claim that Coffee Bean started the coffee thing in Moscow. While the original location on Tverskaya is no longer open, there are a few of these excellent affordable cafes around town, including one in Basmanny (p143).

GQ BAR — BAR

Map p276 (http://bar.gq.ru; ul Balchug 5; ⏰24hr; Ⓜ Novokuznetskaya) Anything that Arkady Novikov touches seems to turn to gold. Which may explain why this joint project with Condé Nast is one of Moscow's hip destinations for drinks, dinner and other early evening socialising. The contemporary decor features an open kitchen and a subtle Asian theme, which is echoed in the menu. If you actually intend to sit down and eat, be sure to reserve a table and bring a bucket of money.

CHAIKHONA NO 1 CAFE

Map p276 (www.chaihona.com; Gorky Park; ⏲noon-6am; Ⓜ Frunzenskaya) Although there are many outlets of this Uzbek lounge around town, the one at Gorky Park is among the most enticing. The riverside setting and surrounding greenery complement the oriental rugs and plush pillows, offering an exotic place for drinks.

PILSNER BREWERY

Map p276 (Bolshaya Polyanka 44/2; Ⓜ Polyanka) In recent years, beer has replaced vodka as Russia's alcohol of choice. This is no doubt thanks – in part – to the availability of delicious Czech brews. As a complement to the beer, you'll enjoy spicy sausages and other salty snacks.

ENTERTAINMENT

STRELKA INSTITUTE FOR ARCHITECTURE, MEDIA & DESIGN ART CENTRE

Map p276 (www.strelkainstitute.ru; Bersenevskaya nab 14/5; Ⓜ Kropotkinskaya) This Institute for Media, Architecture and Design is the focal point of the new development at the Red October chocolate factory. Aside from the course offerings and the popular bar, Strelka promises to give Moscow a healthy dose of contemporary culture, hosting lectures, workshops, film screenings and concerts.

MOSCOW INTERNATIONAL HOUSE OF MUSIC CLASSICAL MUSIC

Map p276 (Московский международный дом музыки; ☎495-730 1011; www.mmdm.ru; Kosmodamianskaya nab 52/8; tickets R200-2000; Ⓜ Paveletskaya) This graceful, modern, glass building has three halls, including Svetlanov Hall, which holds the largest organ in Russia. Needless to say, organ concerts held here are impressive. This is the usual venue for performances by the **National Philharmonic of Russia** (☎495-730 3778; www.nfor.ru, in Russian), a privately financed and highly lauded classical-music organisation. Founded in 1991, the symphony is directed and conducted by the esteemed Vladimir Spivakov.

DOME CINEMA

Map p276 (www.domebar.com; Bersenevsky per 3/10; ⏲noon-midnight Sun-Thu, noon-6am Fri & Sat; Ⓜ Kropotkinskaya) This place is just as arty and hip as any other place in the Red October complex, offering reasonably priced, creative food and cool-vibe music. What makes it stand out is the 'cinema-lounge' – a 60-seat screening room, where art flicks and foreign films are shown in the evenings (free with your order).

GARAGE CLUB NIGHTCLUB

Map p276 (Клуб Гараж; www.garageclub.ru; Brodnikov per 8; ⏲24hr; Ⓜ Polyanka) Not to be confused with the art gallery, this is the reincarnation of a Yeltsin-era nightclub. Nowadays, it's the place to be on Wednesday and Sunday nights, if you want to strut your R&B stuff on the dance floor. It also gets packed in the early morning hours of the weekend (technically Saturday and Sunday), when the clubbing crowd comes for the famous 'after party'. At other times, it's just a cool place to get comfortable in a car seat and have a few drinks. This is the only place in Moscow you can drink and drive.

OLIVER BIKES CYCLING

Map p276 (Оливер Байкс; www.bikerentalmoscow.com; Pyatnitskaya ul 2; 1hr/24hr R200/700; ⏲noon-10pm Mon-Fri, 10am-10pm Sat & Sun; Ⓜ Novokuznetskaya) Oliver rents all kinds of two-wheeled vehicles, including cruisers, mountain bikes, folding bikes and tandem bikes, all of which are in excellent condition. The place is conveniently located for bike rides along the Moscow River, in Gorky Park, Neskuchny Garden and Vorobyovy Gory Nature Preserve. Ride carefully!

GORKY PARK SKATING RINK ICE SKATING

Map p276 (Парк Горького; ul Krymsky val; adult/child R80/20; ⏲10am-10pm; Ⓜ Park Kultury) When the temperatures drop, Gorky Park becomes a winter wonderland. The ponds are flooded, turning the park into the city's biggest ice-skating rink. Tracks are created for cross-country skiers to circumnavigate the park. Ice skates and cross-country skis are available to rent (R100 to R200 per hour). Bring your passport.

LOCAL KNOWLEDGE

MOSCOW NIGHTLIFE

In his five years living in the capital, Campbell Bethwaite has created a popular nightlife blog and promoted various Moscow nightclubs. He is now a co-owner of Garage Club.

What do you love about Moscow nightlife?
The fast pace, the glamour, the freshness, the show.

Best for drinking?
Art Akademiya (p131) is a nice place to go for a drink. Sky Lounge (p152) has good cocktails and gorgeous views.

Best for dancing?
The best glamour scene is currently at Imperia Lounge (p101). Other places with a fun atmosphere include Garage (p132) and Solyanka (p143). There are a few excellent places in Red October – Rolling Stone (p131) and Progressive Daddy's (p131).

Best for meeting people?
Rolling Stone is good for English speakers. Art Akademiya and Simachyov (p84) are good meet-up spots.

Any tricks for getting past face control?
Dress up and put a smile on your face. It also helps to arrive early, say between midnight and 1am.

Best for late-night munchies or early morning breakfast?
Starlite Diner (p98). The glam crowd goes to Café Pushkin (p96).

Best budget nightlife?
Fun places with (relatively) cheap drinks include Garage and Propaganda (p142).

Where do you go on your night off?
Soho Rooms (p118) or Rolling Stone.

SHOPPING

RUSSKAYA ULITSA CLOTHING, ACCESSORIES

Map p276 (Русская улица; www.russian-street.ru; Bersenevskaya nab 8/1; ⓜKropotkinskaya) Showcasing Moscow's burgeoning fashion industry, this little boutique 'Russian street' is crammed with cool clothes and accessories from more than 60 different Russian designers. Items run the gamut from trendy tees to sophisticated dresses.

CENTRAL HOUSE OF ARTISTS (TSDKH) ART, SOUVENIRS

Map p276 (Центральный дом художника; www.cha.ru; admission R200; ⏲11am-7pm Tue-Sun; ⓜPark Kultury) Sometimes called by its initials (ЦДХ), this huge building attached to the New Tretyakov contains studios and galleries, as well as exhibition space for rotating collections. This is a great place to browse if you're in the market to acquire a painting or print from Moscow's red-hot contemporary art scene. Artists also set up a more informal art market on ul Krymsky val, opposite the entrance to Gorky Park.

PORADKY ART, SOUVENIRS

Map p276 (Порадки; www.magsnov.ru; ul Bolshaya Ordynka 68; ⏲11am-9pm Mon-Sat, 11am-8pm Sun; ⓜSerpukhovskaya) Perhaps a little creative whimsy is just what the doctor ordered. If so, this is just the place for you. This is a boutique of creative gifts and souvenirs – one in a network of artists' cooperatives around Moscow.

ZAZKI-PETSKI SOUVENIRS

Map p276 (Цацки-пецки; www.zazki.ru; Bolotnaya nab 3/4; ⏲1-8.30pm; ⓜKropotkinskaya) This 'store of unusual things' is hidden away on the 2nd floor of one of the outer buildings of the Red October complex. The tiny place is packed with funny, funky handmade knickknacks – some of which are bound to make you smile.

Basmanny & Taganka

Neighbourhood Top Five

❶ Contemplating Moscow's hot contemporary art scene at any one of the city's post-industrial art complexes, such as **Winzavod** (p137), **ArtPlay** (p137) and **Proekt_Fabrika** (boxed text, p137).

❷ Descending 60m underground to explore the Cold War communications centre at **Bunker-42** (p136).

❸ Finding your way to **Petrovich** (p142) to reminisce about the good ol' days.

❹ Absorbing the atmosphere and admiring the devotion at the **Old Believers' Community** (boxed text, p141).

❺ Whiling away some hours at **Art Garbage** (p144), with food, music and art.

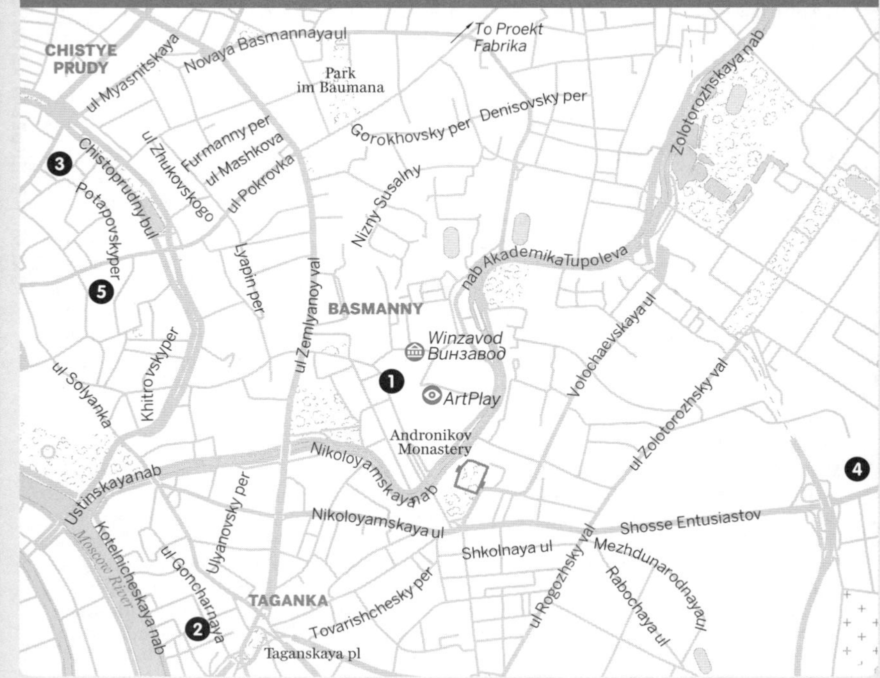

For more detail of this area, see Map p272 and Map p271

Explore: Basmanny & Taganka

Together, Basmanny and Taganka comprise a huge eastern section of Moscow. Even so, travellers could easily bypass them unless they are arriving at one of the train stations at Komsomolskaya pl. That's because there are vast swathes of territory that are mostly industrial. At least, they *were* mostly industrial. Nowadays, many of these defunct factories are being repurposed for art centres, design institutes and music and nightclubs. And that's exactly why most people come to Basmanny.

Within the Garden Ring, Basmanny is a pleasant residential area that is an extension of Kitay Gorod – packed with prerevolutionary architecture, interesting boutiques and inviting restaurants. Despite a lack of traditional tourist sights, the neighbourhood is a very pleasant and convenient place to stay.

South of the Yauza River, Taganka centres on the eponymous city square, which is loud, dusty and crowded. The chaotic square is something of an entertainment district, with several noteworthy theatres and clubs.

Local Life

➡ **Hidden Haunts** If you can find them, clubs Petrovich (p142) and Vysotsky (p143) offer warm camaraderie and retro reminiscence.

➡ **Budget Joint** Students and other thrifty folks spend lots of time (but not lots of money) at the friendly cafe Liudi kak Liudi (p140).

➡ **Outdoors** Whatever the weather, locals stroll and socialise around Chistye Prudy.

Getting There & Away

➡ **Basmanny** Several metro lines pass through Basmanny. Both the purple Tagansko-Krasnopresnenskaya line and the orange Kaluzhsko-Rizhakaya line have stops at Kitay-Gorod. Along the Boulevard Ring, Chistye Prudy is on the red Sokolnicheskaya line; Turgenevskaya is on the orange Kaluzhsko-Rizhskaya line; and Sretensky Bulvar is on the light green Lyublinskaya line. Further out along the Garden Ring, take the dark blue Arbatsko-Pokrovskaya line or the ring Koltsevaya line to Kurskaya; or take the light green Lyublinskaya line to Chkalovskaya station.

➡ **Taganka** The metro stations that serve Taganka are Marksistskaya on the yellow Kalininskaya line, Taganskaya on the ring line and the purple Tagansko-Krasnoprenskaya line.

Best Places to Eat

➡ Madam Galife (p144)

➡ Art Clumba (p139)

➡ Liudi kak Liudi (p140)

For reviews, see p139 ➡

Best Places to Drink

➡ Petrovich (p142)

➡ Art Garbage (p144)

➡ Solyanka (p143)

➡ Propaganda (p142)

For reviews, see p142 ➡

Best Art Centres

➡ Winzavod (p137)

➡ Proekt_Fabrika (boxed text, p137)

➡ ArtPlay (p137)

For reviews, see p136 ➡

SIGHTS

Basmanny

CHOLAR SYNAGOGUE NOTABLE BUILDING

Map p272 (Московская Хоральная Синагога; Bolshoy Spasoglinishchevsky per 10; ⌚9am-6pm; Ⓜ Kitay-Gorod) Construction of a synagogue was banned inside Kitay Gorod, so Moscow's oldest and most prominent synagogue was built just outside the city walls, not far from the Jewish settlement of Zaryadye. Construction started in 1881 but dragged on due to roadblocks by the anti-Semitic tsarist government. It was completed in 1906 and was the only synagogue that continued to operate throughout the Soviet period, in spite of Bolshevik demands to convert it into a workers' club. Apparently, Golda Meir shocked the authorities when she paid an unexpected visit here in 1948. The building hosts the **International Jewish Social Club** (⌚2-5pm Sun).

MENSHIKOV TOWER HISTORICAL BUILDING

Map p272 (Башня Меншыкова; Arkhangelsky per; Ⓜ Chistye Prudy) In the late 17th century Peter the Great gifted much of the land in Basmanny to his pal Alexander Menshikov. Hidden behind the post office, this famous tower was built between 1704 and 1706 on the order of Menshikov. The tower – one of Moscow's first baroque buildings – was originally 3m taller than the Ivan the Great Bell Tower. A thunderstorm in 1723 saw it hit by lightning and seriously damaged by fire. Trouble plagued the owner as well. Menshikov fell from grace after the death of Peter the Great, and he was exiled to Siberia. The tower was neglected. When finally repaired in the 1780s, it lost much of its height and elegance. Today, it houses the working Church of Archangel Gabriel.

CHISTYE PRUDY PARK

Map p272 (Чистие пруды; Chistoprudny bul; Ⓜ Chistye Prudy) Chistye Prudy (Clean Ponds) refers to the lovely little pond that graces the Boulevard Ring at the ul Pokrovka intersection. The Boulevard Ring is always a prime location for strolling, but the quaint pond makes this a desirable address indeed. Paddleboats in summer and ice skating in winter are essential parts of the ambience. Pick a cafe and sip a beer or a coffee while watching strollers or skaters go by.

TOP SIGHTS BUNKER-42

On a quiet side street near Taganskaya pl sits a nondescript neoclassical building. This is the gateway to the secret Cold War–era communications centre, Bunker-42 on Taganka. Operated during the Cold War by Central Telephone and Telegraph, the facility was meant to serve as the communications headquarters in the event of a nuclear attack. As such, the building was just a shell and served as entry into the 7000-sq-metre space that is 60m underground.

Visitors are herded into a small elevator and whisked downwards for 18 storeys to the museum. A 20-minute film about the history of the Cold War is followed by a guided tour of the four underground 'blocks', which are dark, dank and more than a little bit creepy. Through a locked door, visitors can hear the rumble of trains ploughing by – this facility is at the same depth underground as the Taganskaya metro station.

This museum has the potential to provide a unique perspective on a secret and sexy subject. So far there is not a whole lot to see, however, especially considering the admission price. That said, this may be your only opportunity to explore a secret underground Cold War command centre.

DON'T MISS

- Express elevator descending 60m in a few seconds flat
- Air-tight doors and metre-thick walls protecting the secret command post
- Simulated air raid

PRACTICALITIES

- Map p271
- ☎495-500 0554
- www.bunker42.ru
- 5-y Kotelnichesky per 11
- admission R1300
- ⌚by appointment
- Ⓜ Taganskaya

FREE **SAKHAROV MUSEUM** MUSEUM

Map p272 (www.sakharov-center.ru; Zemlyanoy val 57; ⏲11am-7pm Tue-Sun; Ⓜ Chkalovskaya) South of Kursky vokzal, by the Yauza River, is a small park with a two-storey house containing the Andrei Sakharov Museum. The park is dotted with unusual sculptures, most built from weapons and other military-industrial waste. Look out for a piece of the Berlin Wall that has been repurposed in a poignant display. The exhibits recount the life of Sakharov, the nuclear-physicist-turned-human-rights-advocate, detailing the years of repression in Russia and providing a history of the courage shown by the dissident movement. Temporary expositions cover current human-rights issues and contemporary art. Curators at the Sakharov are frequently in the news for the controversy surrounding their exhibits.

FREE **WINZAVOD** ART GALLERY

Map p272 (Винзавод; ☎495-917 4646; www.winzavod.ru; 4-y Syromyatnichesky per 1; exhibits free-R200; ⏲noon-8pm Tue-Sun; Ⓜ Chkalovskaya) Formerly a wine-bottling factory, this facility was converted into exhibit and studio space for Moscow artists in 2007. The post-industrial complex is now home to Moscow's most prestigious art galleries, including M&J Guelman, Aidan and XL. The complex also contains several photo galleries, a design studio and furniture showroom and a concept clothing store, as well as a few funky gift shops and boutiques. Even if you're not in the market for the next Black Square, you can lounge with the cool cats at the cafe or catch a flick or a lecture at one of the entertainment venues.

FREE **ARTPLAY ON YAUZA** ART GALLERY

Map p272 (☎495-620 0882; www.artplay.ru; Nizhnaya Syromyatnichesky ul 10; ⏲noon-8pm Tue-Sun; Ⓜ Chkalovskaya) Following on the successes of Winzavod, ArtPlay operates according to a similar concept, occupying the buildings of the former Manometer factory. The 'design centre' is home to firms specialising in urban planning and architectural design, as well as furniture showrooms and antique stores. Considering the architectural emphasis, there is perhaps less for the casual caller to see, although there are always diverse and dynamic rotating exhibits in the various display spaces. Come for the art; stay for dinner (see p139) or music.

WORTH A DETOUR

PROEKT_FABRIKA

Since 2004, the functioning October glass factory has shared its space with this innovative **art venue** (Factory Project; www.proektfabrika.ru; Perevedonovsky per 18; ⏲noon-8pm Tue-Sun; Ⓜ Baumanskaya). Fabrika was actually the first independent, nonprofit contemporary art organisation in Moscow, opening in 2004. Nowadays it is home to architectural firms, a publishing house and a film studio, in addition to the 'interdisciplinary' exhibition space. As such, Fabrika hosts dance, theatre and other interactive exhibits, plus visual art displays. The most active space is (appropriately enough) the **Aktovy Zal** (☎499-265 4935; www.aktzal.ru; tickets R250-300), a black box theatre that was formerly used by factory workers for amateur theatre and worker meetings. Contemporary dance, theatre and music are performed every evening.

MGU BOTANICAL GARDEN GARDEN

off Map p272 (Ботанический сад МГУ; www.hortus.ru, in Russian; pr Mira 26; day/evening admission R100/150; ⏲10am-10pm May-Sep, 10am-5pm Oct-Apr; Ⓜ Prospekt Mira) When you need an escape from the city's hustle and bustle, the MGU Botanical Garden offers a wonderful retreat. Established in 1706, the garden was originally owned by the Moscow general hospital to grow herbs and other medicinal plants. These days it is operated by Moscow State University (MGU) for research and recreation. Visitors can wander along the trails, enjoy an exhibition of ornamental plants and explore three greenhouses containing plants from various climate zones.

YELOKHOVSKY CATHEDRAL CHURCH

off Map p272 (www.mospat.ru; Spartakovskaya ul 15; Ⓜ Baumanskaya) The Church of the Epiphany in Yelokhovo has been Moscow's senior Orthodox cathedral since 1943. Built between 1837 and 1845 with five domes in a Russian eclectic style, the cathedral is full of gilt and icons, not to mention old women kneeling, polishing, lighting candles, crossing themselves and kissing the floor. In the northern part is the **tomb of St Nicholas the Miracle**

WORTH A DETOUR

IZMAILOVO

Kremlin in Izmailovo

Izmailovo has undergone a remarkable transformation, as the city has finally made good on promises to clean the place up. Now the flea market is only part of a big **theme park** (Кремль в Измайлово; www.kremlin-izmailovo.com; Izmaylovskoe sh 73; ⏱10am-8pm; Ⓜ Partizanskaya), which includes shops, restaurants, museums and monuments, all contained within a mock 'kremlin' (complete with walls and towers which make a great photo op).

Enter through a whitewashed tower that evokes medieval Rus, even though it was built in the last few years. Within the walls, the place re-creates the workshops and trade rows of an old settlement. Named for the patron saint of merchants and craftsmen, the **Church of the Sanctifier of St Nicholas** (Храм Святителя Николая) is the tallest wooden church in Russia (46m).

A concept long overdue, the **Vodka History Museum** (www.vodkamuseum.ru; ⏱10am-6pm) is just three rooms, with the all-important *traktir* (tavern) attached. The historical exhibits start with the early consumption and production of vodka, including demonstrations of the early distilling process. The Soviet period – especially WWII – is fascinating. Other museums in the complex include the **Russian Costume & Culture Museum** and a small **Toy Museum**.

The centrepiece of Izmailovo is still the **Vernisage market**, packed with art, handmade crafts, antiques, Soviet paraphernalia and just about anything you might want for a souvenir. Various 'trade rows' are dedicated to icons, carpets, textiles, antiques, paintings and more. There is also a functioning **blacksmith workshop**, where you can watch the smithies doing their thing. Feel free to negotiate, but don't expect vendors to come down much more than 10%.

Izmailovsky Park & Royal Estate

A former royal hunting reserve east of the Kremlin, **Izmailovsky Park** (www.izmailovsky-park.ru, in Russian; Izmaylovskoe sh; admission free; ⏱11am-9pm; Ⓜ Partizanskaya) is the nearest large tract of undeveloped land to central Moscow. Its 15 sq km contain a **recreation park** and a much larger expanse of **woodland** (Izmailovsky Lesopark) east of Glavnaya alleya, the road that cuts north–south across the park. Trails wind around this park, making it a good place to escape the city for hiking or biking. From Partizanskaya metro station, take bus 7 or 131 and get off at the third stop.

The **royal estate** is on a small, moated island to the northwest of the eponymous park. Tsar Alexey had an experimental farm here in the 17th century, where Western farming methods and cottage industries were sampled. It was on the farm ponds that his son Peter learned to sail in a little boat; he came to be called the 'Grandfather of the Russian Navy'.

Past an extensive 18th-century barracks (now partly occupied by the police) is the beautiful five-domed 1679 **Intercession Cathedral**, an early example of Moscow baroque. The nearby triple-arched, tent-roofed **Ceremonial Gates** (1682) and the squat brick **bridge tower** (1671) are the only other original buildings remaining.

This place comes alive on summer weekends, with children's programs by day and live music by night. Kids will have a blast with rowboats on the pond, a Ferris wheel and other rides. There is also bike rental for rides in the park.

Stalin's Bunker

A branch of the Central Museum of Armed Forces, this **secret bunker** (Бункер Сталина; www.cmaf.ru; Sovietskaya ul 80; Ⓜ Partizanskaya) was built under a sports stadium in the late 1930s in anticipation of the conflict with Germany. It would later be designated the 'command centre of the Supreme commander-in-chief of Red Army'. You must make advance arrangements for a group tour of this facility, which includes the command room, dining room, an elegant marble meeting hall, and Stalin's office and living area. Tours are in Russian, but tour companies occasionally bring groups here for English tours.

Worker. A shrine in front of the right side of the iconostasis contains the remains of St Alexey, a 14th-century metropolitan.

Taganka

VYSOTSKY CULTURAL CENTRE MUSEUM

Map p271 (Дом Высоцкого; www.vysotsky.ru; Nizhny Tagansky tupik 3; admission R100; ⊙11am-6pm Thu-Sat; Ⓜ Taganskaya) Part museum, part performance space, part art exhibit, this cultural centre tributes the local legend Vladimir Vysotsky. Singer and songwriter, poet and actor, Vysotsky was one of the Soviet Union's most influential pop-culture figures, thanks mostly to the witty lyrics and social commentary in his songs. The permanent exhibit features a slew of photos and documents, as well as personal items like the bard's guitar. Theatre, dance and musical performances take place every night in the performance hall.

FREE **MUSEUM OF THE RUSSIAN ICON** ART MUSEUM

Map p271 (Частный музей русской иконы; www.russikona.ru, in Russian; ul Goncharnaya 3; ⊙11am-7pm Thu-Tue; Ⓜ Taganskaya) Now located in new permanent digs, this museum houses the private collection of Russian businessman and art patron Mikhail Abramov. He has personally amassed a collection of more than 4000 pieces of Russian and Eastern Christian art, including some 600 icons. The collection is unique in that it represents nearly all schools of Russian iconography. Highlights include Simon Ushakov's 14th-century depiction of the Virgin Odigitria and an icon of St Nikolai Mirlikiisky from the same era.

RUBLYOV MUSEUM OF EARLY RUSSIAN CULTURE & ART ART MUSEUM

Map p271 (Музей Андрея Рублёва; Andronevskaya pl 10; adult/student R200/100; ⊙11am-5.30pm Thu-Tue; Ⓜ Ploshchad Ilycha) On the grounds of the former Andronikov Monastery, the Rublyov Museum exhibits icons from days of yore and from the present. Unfortunately, it does not include any work by its acclaimed namesake artist. It is still worth visiting though, not least for its romantic location. Andrei Rublyov, the master of icon painting, was a monk here in the 15th century. He is buried in the grounds, but no one knows quite where.

In the centre of the monastery grounds is the compact **Saviour's Cathedral**, built in 1427, the oldest stone building in Moscow. The cluster of *kokoshniki,* or gables of colourful tiles and brick patterns, is typical of Russian architecture from the era. To the left is the combined rectory and 17th-century Moscow-baroque **Church of the Archangel Michael**; to the right, the old monks' quarters house the museum.

NOVOSPASSKY MONASTERY MONASTERY

Map p271 (www.spasnanovom.ru, in Russian; Verkhny Novospassky pro; ⊙7am-7pm; Ⓜ Proletarskaya) Novospassky Monastery is a 15th-century fort-monastery, about 1km south of Taganskaya pl. The centrepiece of the monastery, the **Transfiguration Cathedral**, was built by the imperial Romanov family in the 1640s in imitation of the Kremlin's Assumption Cathedral. Frescoes depict the history of Christianity in Russia, while the Romanov family tree, which goes as far back as the Viking Prince Rurik, climbs one wall. The other church is the 1675 **Intercession Church**.

Under the river bank, beneath one of the towers of the monastery, is the site of a mass grave for thousands of Stalin's victims. At the northern end of the monastery's grounds are the brick **Assumption Cathedral** and an extraordinary Moscow-baroque **gate tower**.

ECCLESIASTIC RESIDENCE HISTORICAL BUILDING

Map p271 (Крутицкое подворье; 1-y Krutitsky per; admission free; ⊙10am-6pm Wed-Mon; Ⓜ Proletarskaya) Across the road that runs south of Novospassky Monastery is the sumptuous Ecclesiastic Residence. It was the home of the Moscow metropolitans after the founding of the Russian patriarchate in the 16th century, when they lost their place in the Kremlin.

EATING

Basmanny

ART CLUMBA INTERNATIONAL $$

Map p272 (www.art-clumba.ru; Nizhnyaya Syromyatnicheskaya ul 5/7, bldg 10; meals R1000-1200; Ⓜ Chkalovskaya) On the grounds of ArtPlay on Yauza, this is an appropriately artistic venue, where creative types come to socialise or poke away on their MacBooks. The excellent menu is accurately described as 'eclectic with a strong accent of Russian home-cooking'. You'll find the traditional Russian favourites, done up with delightfully unexpected accompaniments. Even the basics (soups, *pelmeni* – Russian-style ravioli) are expertly prepared with subtle seasoning and impeccable ingredients.

DACHA ON POKROVKA RUSSIAN $$

Map p272 (www.dacha-napokrovke.ru; Pokrovsky bul 18/15; meals R500-800; Ⓜ Kitay-Gorod) Typical of many dachas, this one contains an odd assortment of mismatched furniture, antique appliances and random household objects that nobody really uses anymore. Strewn about three rooms of a ramshackle old mansion, it creates a welcoming and familiar atmosphere – the perfect place to enjoy delicious and affordable Russian home-cooking.

LIUDI KAK LIUDI FAST FOOD $

Map p272 (Люди как люди; www.ludikakludi.ru; Solyansky tupik 1/4; meals R300; 11am-10pm Mon-Sat, 11am-8pm Sun; ; Ⓜ Kitay-Gorod) This cute cafe has a few things going for it: its location makes it the perfect lunch stop for anyone strolling around Kitay Gorod; its warm welcome and tasty food make it a perfect lunch stop for anyone who is tired or hungry; and its prices make it the perfect lunch stop for anyone who is not made of money. That makes it the perfect lunch stop for pretty much anyone, which explains why this is such a popular place.

GLAVPIVTORG RUSSIAN $$

Map p272 (www.glavpivtorg.ru; ul Bolshaya Lubyanka 5; business lunch R200, meals R800-1200; Ⓜ Lubyanka) At the 'central beer restaurant No 5' every effort is made to re-create an upscale apparatchik drinking and dining experience. The Soviet fare is authentic, as is the *russky* crooner music (maybe too authentic for some tastes). But the three varieties of beer brewed on-site are decidedly New Russia.

KAVKAZSKAYA PLENNITSA GEORGIAN $$$

off Map p272 (Кавказская Пленница; 495-280 5111; http://novikovgroup.ru; pr Mira 36; meals R1200-1500; ; Ⓜ Prospekt Mira) Moscow's long-standing favourite Georgian restaurant is named after a popular Soviet film (and a Tolstoy novella), *Prisoner of the Caucasus*. Feast on *lavash* (flat bread) straight from the oven, cheeses from the restaurant's own dairy, and shashlyk from seemingly every animal. Come with a group and enjoy the classically cheesy Georgian music and the over-the-mountain-top decor.

NOEV KOVCHEG ARMENIAN $$

Map p272 (www.noevkovcheg.ru; 495-917 0717; Maly Ivanovsky per 9; meals R1000-1500; ; Ⓜ Kitay-Gorod) This Armenian grill – Noah's Ark – features many varieties of shashlyk, many more varieties of *konyak* (brandy) and an Armenian orchestra every night. The vast dining hall is aromatic and atmospheric, thanks to the meat roasting over charcoal in the central brazier.

PASTA & BASTA ITALIAN $$

Map p272 (495-624 5252; www.pastaandbasta.ru; Sretensky bul 4; meals R800-1200; ; Ⓜ Turgenevskaya) The faux classical facade on Sretensky bul hides a popular little pasta house that really capitalises on a theme. With funky spaghetti-shaped lamps hanging from the high ceiling and noodle art on the walls, it's no secret what this place is all about. Also on the menu: pizza, soups, salads and other fresh and tasty Italian fare.

SHERBET UZBEK $$

Map p272 (www.scherbet.ru; ul Sretenka 32; business lunch R300, meals R400-800; 24hr; Ⓜ Sukharevskaya) Sitting amid plush pillows and woven tapestries, you'll feel like a sheik in this extravagantly decorated eatery. Feast on *plov* (rice mixed with lamb and vegetables), shashlyk and other Uzbek specialities. And of course, it wouldn't be Moscow if they didn't also offer hookahs and an evening belly-dance show.

SYRNAYA DYRKA EUROPEAN $$

Map p272 (Сырная дырка; www.sdyrka.ru; Pokrovsky bul 6/20; meals R800-1200; ; Ⓜ Kitay-Gorod) Fondue, *fromage* plates and other cheesy specialities are the highlights of the menu at this 'Cheese Hole' in the wall. Besides the warm basement with windows looking on to the Boulevard Ring, there is also a summer terrace out the back. Both are perfectly delightful settings for a romantic date or even a solo meal. The place is Swiss-owned, which means French, Italian and German fare all show up on the menu.

WORTH A DETOUR

OLD BELIEVERS' COMMUNITY

One of Russia's most atmospheric religious centres is the **Old Believers' Community** (Старообрядческая Община; 9am-6pm Tue-Sun; M Ploshchad Ilycha), at Rogozhskoe, 3km east of Taganskaya pl. The Old Believers split from the main Russian Orthodox Church in 1653, when they refused to accept certain reforms. They have maintained the old forms of worship and customs ever since. In the late 18th century, during a brief period free of persecution, rich Old Believer merchants founded this community, which is among the most important in the country.

The yellow, classical-style **Intercession Church** contains one of Moscow's finest collections of icons, all dating from before 1653, with the oldest being the 14th-century *Saviour with the Angry Eye* (Spas yaroe oko), protected under glass near the south door. The icons in the Deesis row (the biggest row) of the iconostasis are supposedly by the Rublyov school, while the seventh, *The Saviour*, is attributed to Rublyov himself. North of the church is the **Rogozhskoe Cemetery**.

Visitors are welcome at the church, but women should take care to wear long skirts (no trousers) and headscarves. The community is a 30-minute walk from pl Ilycha. Otherwise, take trolleybus 16 or 26, or bus 51, east from Taganskaya pl and get off after crossing a railway.

MAHARAJA — INDIAN $$

Map p272 (www.maharaja.ru; Starosadsky per 1; meals R600-1000; 11am-11pm; M Kitay-Gorod) Moscow's oldest Indian restaurant features lots of spicy tandoori specialities, including several variations of kebabs and roti hot from the tandoor. The decor of the lower-level restaurant is understated which is a welcome change from the over-the-top theme restaurants common in Moscow's dining scene.

AVOCADO — VEGETARIAN $

Map p272 (Chistoprudny bul 12/2; meals R200-400; 10am-11pm; M Chistye Prudy) Less atmospheric than Jagannath (p80), Avocado has a more diverse menu, drawing on cuisines from around the world. Meatless versions of soups and salads, pasta and *pelmeni* are all featured (there is no English-language menu, so bring a phrasebook). Grab a seat near the window to watch the passers-by on the boulevard, because the place is otherwise rather austere.

EXPEDITION — RUSSIAN $$$

Map p272 (Экспедиция; 495-775 6075; www.expedicia.ru; Pevchesky per 6; meals R1500-2000; M Kitay-Gorod) This outrageous themed restaurant takes diners on an expedition to the great white north, capturing the adventure and excitement of Siberia. You can imagine you arrived by helicopter, as the vehicle is the centrepiece of the dining room. Feast on some typical 'northern cuisine' – famous Baikal fish soup *(ukha)*; *pelmeni* stuffed with wild boar or Kamchatka crab; and venison stroganoff. There is also an expensive but authentic Siberian *banya* (hot bath) on the premises.

VOLKONSKY — BAKERY $

Map p272 (Волконский; www.wolkonsky.com; ul Maroseyka 4/2; meals R200-400; 8am-11pm; M Kitay-Gorod) The original location in Presnya is quaint and crowded, but this one is spacious and stylish. You can still buy your pastries to go – or take a seat and order from the menu of soups, sandwiches and snacks.

SHATYOR — ARABIAN $$$

Map p272 (Шатёр; 495-916 9486; Chistoprudny bul 12A; meals R1000; 24hr; M Chistye Prudy) Step into this 'Tent' and step inside a Bedouin camp, right on the shores of Chistye Prudy. Lounge on comfy cushions and feast on grilled meats, à la the *Thousand and One Nights*.

MOO-MOO — CAFETERIA $

Map p272 (Ресторан Му-му; www.moo-moo.ru; Myasnitskaya ul 14; meals R200-300; M Lubyanka) This chain of cow-themed cafeterias is ubiquitous in Moscow. The decor is hokey, but the food is filling and cheap.

Taganka

AMERICAN BAR & GRILL — AMERICAN $$

Map p271 (http://ambar.rosinter.com; ul Zemlyanoy val 59; meals R600-800; noon-2am; M Taganskaya) One of Moscow's oldest expat hang-outs, this place still attracts a regular crowd for its enormous portions, its outdoor terrace and its Wild West interior. With classic fare such as big burgers and spicy chicken wings, it's always a pleasant place for cold beers. You're bound to meet some other *innostrantsy* (foreigners) who are quaffing them, too.

BERYOZKA RUSSIAN $

Map p271 (Берёзка; Nikoloyamskaya ul 29; meals R400-600; ; Taganskaya) At first glance this little place appears to be your typical kitschy *pelmeni* bar, decorated with faux birch trees and serving up the Siberian speciality. Indeed, you'll find more kinds of *pelmeni* on the menu than in any other restaurant. But you'll also find freshly brewed *pivo* (beer), sometimes available for self-service from the table-side taps. Each table is also equipped with a mini-TV, often showing cartoons, old movies and other nostalgia. *Pelmeni, pivo* and moving pictures: what more can you ask for?

YOLKI-PALKI RUSSIAN $

Map p271 (www.elki-palki.ru; 495-912 9187; Taganskaya pl 2; meals R300-500; 9am-11pm Mon-Fri, 10am-11am Sat & Sun; Taganskaya) Retreat from Taganka's traffic-filled streets to the pastoral countryside and enjoy the bounty from the famous Yolki-Palki salad bar.

DRINKING & NIGHTLIFE

Basmanny

PETROVICH BAR

Map p272 (495-923 0082; www.club-petrovich.ru; Myasnitskaya ul 24/1; meals R800-1000; Chistye Prudy) Soviet times may not have been happier; they may not have been simpler. But they were definitely funnier, according to local cartoonist and restaurateur Andrei Bilzh. See his eponymous masterpieces at this popular retro restaurant, which reminisces with Soviet propaganda and pop music. The menu is riddled with inside jokes about the good ol' days. This doesn't seem like the kind of place that would have face control, but it is, so book a table in advance to play it safe. Enter through an unmarked door in the courtyard.

BILINGUA CAFE/BAR

Map p272 (www.bilinguaclub.ru; Krivokolenny per 10/5; cover R200-300; noon-midnight, concerts 9pm or 10pm Tue-Sun; ; Chistye Prudy) Crowded with grungy, artsy, student types, this cafe also sells books and funky clothing. If you can stand the smoke, it's a cool place to grab a bite to eat and listen to some music or peruse the literary offerings. Despite the name, there's not much in the way of foreign-language literature.

RED CAFE

Map p272 (www.redespressobar.com; Myasnitskaya 24/7, Bldg 8; ; Chistye Prudy) The latest place for good-looking, laptop-toting busy bees to sip strong coffee drinks and do their thing. There are a few pastries and sandwiches on the menu, but Red's selling point is the java, which is freshly roasted in-house every day. Wake up and smell it! There is another outlet in Presnya (p144).

KRIZIS ZHANRA NIGHTCLUB

Map p272 (www.kriziszhanra.ru; ul Pokrovka 16/16; concerts 9pm Sun-Thu, 11pm Fri & Sat; ; Chistye Prudy) Everybody has something good to say about Krizis: expats and locals, old-timers and newcomers, young and old. What's not to love? Good cheap food, copious drinks and rockin' music every night, all of which inspires the gathered to get their groove on.

PROPAGANDA NIGHTCLUB

Map p272 (www.propagandamoscow.com; Bolshoy Zlatoustinsky per 7; meals R500-700; noon-6am; Kitay-Gorod) This long-time favourite looks to be straight from the warehouse district, with exposed brick walls and pipe ceilings. It's a cafe by day, but at night they clear the dance floor and let the DJ do his stuff. This is a gay-friendly place, especially on Sunday nights.

TEMA BAR BAR

Map p272 (www.temabar.ru; Potapovsky per 5; 24hr; Chistye Prudy) There are too many cocktails to count…but we know that Tema serves more than 20 different martinis, so that should give you an idea of the extent of the drinks menu. The talented bar staff are sure to serve up something that you like. Popular among both expats and locals, Tema has a fun, friendly and sometimes raucous vibe.

SOLYANKA BAR

Map p272 (http://s-11.ru; ul Solyanka 11; cover R300-500; ⌚noon-midnight Sun-Wed, noon-5am Thu-Sat; @; MKitay-Gorod) Solyanka No 11 is a historic 18th-century merchant's mansion that has been revamped into an edgy, arty club. Wide plank-wood floors, exposed brick walls, leather furniture and funky light fixtures transform the space. By day it's an excellent restaurant, serving contemporary, creative Russian and European food. On Thursday, Friday and Saturday nights, the big bar room gets cleared of tables and the DJ spins hip-hop, techno and rave. The music usually starts at 11pm (and so does the face control).

LIGA PAP SPORTS BAR

Map p272 (www.ligapap.ru; ul Bolshaya Lubyanka 24; meals R500-1000; MLubyanka) It's a sports bar, but it sure is a snazzy one. The gorgeous interior features big windows, tiled floors and Gothic arched ceilings, in addition to the 20-plus flat-screen TVs. The centrepiece of the main hall is the huge screen, complete with projector as well as dramatic auditorium-style seating.

CAFE DIDU BAR

Map p272 (☎495-624 1320; www.cafe-didu.ru; Myasnitskaya ul 24; lunch R190-320, meals R1000; ; MChistye Prudy) This playful club-cafe invites relaxation and fun with lounge furniture, tantalising cocktails and colourful modelling clay. Containers of pliable playdough are found on each table (right next to the condiments) and the sculpted results are on display all around the restaurant. If that is not enough to keep you entertained, there are also late-night movies (midnight Sunday to Thursday) and weekend dance parties (11pm Friday and Saturday).

ART LEBEDEV CAFE CAFE

Map p272 (http://store.artlebedev.com/offline/lik; 22/1 Myasnitskaya ul; meals R300-600; ⌚9am-11pm; MChistye Prudy) Artemy Lebedev is a minor celebrity around Moscow, famed for his crafty creations and innovative designs. Check out the shop, then join his beautiful bohemian entourage for coffee and sweets at the cosy cafe upstairs. When weather is fine, the courtyard is a delightful place to see and be seen.

CENTRAL STATION MSK NIGHTCLUB

Map p272 (Центральная Станция МСК; www.centralclub.ru; Yuzhny pro 4; ⌚restaurant from 7pm, club from 9pm; MKomsomolskaya) The Moscow branch of St Petersburg's biggest gay club. The downstairs lounge holds a gay cabaret featuring some of Moscow's loveliest ladies, while the masses get their groove on upstairs on the main dance floor. Check the website for the weekly schedule of parties, karaoke and other events. Enter through the yellow gate.

DISCOTEQUE NIGHTCLUB

Map p272 (www.discoteque.ru; Nizhny Susalny per 5, Bldg 5; cover R500; MKurskaya) The industrial area behind Kursky vokzal has become a clubbing hot spot, and Discoteque is just one of several former-factory clubs that are pumping until early morning. DJs play house music; barely dressed girls dance in cages; and the crowd lets loose down below on the dance floor.

SECRET NIGHTCLUB

Map p272 (Nizhny Susalny per 7, Bldg 8; cover free-R250; MKurskaya) The 'sliding scale' cover charge and cheap drinks attract a young, student crowd to this gay nightclub. The earlier you arrive, the cheaper the admission, but if you're a male aged 18 to 22 it's free any time. Two dance floors, plus live music or drag shows on weekends.

COFFEE BEAN CAFE

Map p272 (www.coffeebean.ru; ul Pokrovka 21; ⌚8am-11pm; MChistye Prudy) Beating out Red, Coffee Mania and even Starbucks, Coffee Bean is Moscow's original coffee chain (since 1996). Some argue that it's still the capital's best coffee.

Taganka

VYSOTSKY BAR

Map p271 (☎495-915 0434; www.club-vysotsky.ru; Nyzhny Tagansky tupik 3; meals R800-1000; ⌚noon-5am; MTaganskaya) Imagine what it was like when there was no place to go out except your friends' flats, where you would sit around and drink cheap champagne and argue about politics and sing along while somebody played the guitar. This is the atmosphere that is evoked at Club Vysotsky, named for the iconic Soviet film star, poet and music maker. The place resembles a worn but comfortable apartment, with mismatched furniture and black-and-white Vysotsky films playing in the background. Live or piano music nightly.

ENTERTAINMENT

ART GARBAGE LIVE MUSIC

Map p272 (www.art-garbage.ru; Starosadsky per 5; noon-6am; ; Kitay-Gorod) Enter this funky club-cafe through the courtyard littered with sculpture. Inside, the walls are crammed with paintings of all genres, and there are DJs spinning or live music playing every night. The restaurant is relatively minimalist in terms of decor, but the menu is creative. Is it art or is it garbage? We'll let you decide.

MADAM GALIFE LIVE MUSIC

off Map p272 (www.madamgalife.ru; Prospect Mira 26/1; ; Prospekt Mira) We can't decide what we like best about this funky art cafe that was opened by a local director and playwright. It could be the glass wall looking out to the MGU Botanical Garden, which makes it like an outdoor cafe where you don't have to think about the weather. Or it might be the eclectic assortment of art and artefacts – the owner's personal collection – that decorates the place. Also adding to the awesome atmosphere is the live music – mostly piano and some other jazzy ensembles – that plays every night.

MUSIC TOWN LIVE MUSIC

Map p272 (www.musictownclub.ru, in Russian; Sadovaya-Chernogryazskaya 8/2; cover R500-1000; 24hr, concerts 9pm or 10pm; Krasnye Vorota) True to its name, Music Town books live acts seven nights a week. The bands run the gamut, from true blues to exotic ethno-jazz to raw rock and roll, with the occasional big name like Boris Grebenshikov or Mashina Vremeny. You never know what you're getting, but you're sure to get your groove on.

PIROGI ON MAROSEYKA LIVE MUSIC, CINEMA

Map p272 (www.ogipirogi.ru; ul Maroseyka 9/2; 24hr; ; Kitay-Gorod) If you have ever visited PirOGI's earlier incarnations, you might be surprised by the club's slick storefront. Inside, it's not dark, it's not smoky and it's not grungy. Do not fear, however, as the crucial elements have not changed: decent food, affordable beer and movies and music every night, all of which draw the young, broke and beautiful.

TAGANKA THEATRE THEATRE

Map p271 (www.taganka.org, in Russian; ul Zemlyanoy val 76; Taganskaya) This legendary theatre is famous for its rebellious director, Yury Lyubimov, and the unruly actor Vladimir Vysotsky. The Taganka received attention for its exploration of 'epic theatre' – a reaction against the method acting that was pioneered across town by Stanislavsky. After Lyubimov's sudden retirement in 2011, the theatre is in limbo.

ROLAN CINEMA CINEMA

Map p272 (495-916 9190; Chistoprudny bul 12; tickets R200-600; Chistye Prudy) The two theatres – one large and one small – show arthouse films and host interesting festivals, usually featuring contemporary Russian cinema. This place is popular with Moscow's bohemian crowd.

NEW BALLET DANCE

Map p272 (www.newballet.ru, in Russian; Novaya Basmannaya ul 25/2; box office 11am-7pm; Krasnye Vorota) If you can't stand to see another *Swan Lake,* you will be pleased to know that the New Ballet performs innovative contemporary dance. This performance art, called 'plastic ballet', incorporates elements of classical and modern dance, as well as pantomime and drama. The theatre is tiny, providing an up-close look at original, cutting-edge choreography.

ILLUZION CINEMA CINEMA

Map p271 (www.gosfilmofond.ru; Kotelnicheskaya nab 1/15; tickets R60-200; Taganskaya) The location inside one of Stalin's Seven Sisters (see p211) is appropriate for the repertoire, which focuses on old-school Soviet films, including some that were stolen by the Nazis.

SHOPPING

BOOKHUNTER BOOKSTORE

Map p272 (www.bookhunter.ru; Krivokolenny per 9; 9am-9pm; Chistye Prudy) It's a tiny little shop, but it's stuffed with fiction and nonfiction books in English (not to mention German, French and Spanish). You'll find all sorts of art, academic and other reference books (including a good selection of travel guides) as well as Russian and foreign literature.

TRICOTAGE CLUB CLOTHING, ACCESSORIES

Map p272 (Трикотаж-клуб; www.sviterok.ru; ul Pokrovka 4; 10am-10pm Mon-Fri, 11am-10pm Sat & Sun; Kitay-Gorod) Hand-knit sweaters,

THE LOVE OF LYUBIMOV'S LIFE

In 1963, Yury Lyubimov founded the Taganka Theatre, to which he dedicated the next 40-plus years of his life. Thanks to Lyubimov – as well as popular actors Vladimir Vysotsky and Alla Demidova – the theatre became one of the most beloved in Moscow, especially after bringing to the stage the underground cult classic *The Master and Margarita*. In the 1980s the Soviet authorities decided they had finally had enough of this provocation. Vysotsky had died and Lyubimov was blacklisted. He eventually had his citizenship revoked and was exiled to London.

Lyubimov returned to Moscow in 1989. With much fanfare, he celebrated his 85th birthday with a premier of *Evgeny Onegin* at his beloved theatre. For the next 20-plus years, Lyubimov continued to direct award-winning theatre.

In 2011, Lyubimov did the unthinkable. He quit the Taganka in a huff, when a group of actors refused to rehearse without first getting paid. He had – no doubt – given the theatre his best, and was frustrated by his perception that others were not willing to do the same. He was 94 years old.

socks and mittens in all shapes and sizes. But that's not all. You'll find a fun selection of toys and homemade souvenirs, as well as sleek and sexy styles of men's and women's clothing. This is not your grandmother's knitwear.

ODENSYA DLYA SCHASTYA CLOTHING

Map p272 (Оденься для счастья; ul Pokrovka 31; ⌚11am-9pm; Ⓜ Kurskaya) This sweet boutique – encouraging shoppers to 'dress for happiness' – carries unique clothing by a few distinctive designers, including Moscow native Oleg Biryukov. The designer's eponymous label features refined styles with long, flowing lines and subdued, solid colours. The tastefulness and elegance exemplify the new direction of Russian fashion.

SALON PODARKOV SOUVENIRS

Map p272 (Салоны Подарков; Myasnitskaya ul 5; ⌚11am-7pm Mon-Sat; Ⓜ Lubyanka) This 'gift salon' is a sort of indoor souvenir market, with dozens of individual stalls selling all kinds of arts and crafts and more. Look for sellers dedicated to watches, glass, china, knitwear, linen, jewellery, bronze, stonework, painted folk toys and more. If you don't have the time or inclination to go out to Izmailovo this is the place to come.

BIBLIO-GLOBUS BOOKSTORE

Map p272 (www.biblio-globus.ru; Myasnitskaya ul 6; ⌚9am-10pm Mon-Fri, 10am-9pm Sat & Sun; Ⓜ Lubyanka) Moscow's favourite bookshop is huge, with lots of reference and souvenir books on language, art and history, and a good selection of maps and travel guides. A user-friendly computerised catalogue will help you find what you're looking for. Just to prove that Russia's consumer culture can keep up with the best of them, this old-school bookshop now has a coffee shop on the ground floor.

MASHA TSIGAL SHOWROOM CLOTHING

Map p272 (www.mashatsigal.com; Yauzskaya ul 1; ⌚11am-7pm Mon-Fri; Ⓜ Kitay-Gorod) Masha Tsigal sells mostly casual clothes in skimpy styles, bright colours and bold designs – very playful and a little trampy. She also has a line of men's sweatsuits and T-shirts and (new in 2011) a cute little girl's collection. Masha has outfitted Russian pop stars tATu, among others.

SHALTAI-BOLTAI SOUVENIRS

Map p272 (Шалтай-болтай; www.shaltai-boltai.ru; 4-y Syromyatnichesky per 1, Guelmann Gallery; ⌚noon-10pm; Ⓜ Chkalovskaya) Named for the famous egg who had a great fall, this fun and funky store is filled with unexpected, arty clothes, household items and objets d'art. These contemporary handicrafts were all designed and created by artists, so it's appropriate that the place is located on the grounds of Winzavod art centre.

BEL POSTEL HOMEWARES

Map p272 (www.belpostel.com; ul Sretenka 27/29; Ⓜ Sukharevskaya) This lovely linens store carries a sumptuous selection of bathrobes, blankets, sheets and towels. Take home a set of richly coloured tablecloths and napkins made from Russian linen. You will find some international designers, but most of the product line is soft Russian fabrics and Eastern prints.

A KORKUNOV FOOD & DRINK

Map p272 (www.korkunov.ru; ul Bolshaya Lubyanka 13/16; ⌚10am-8pm; Ⓜ Lubyanka) That this candy company was founded in 1997 may come as a surprise, as the shop's interior feels like an old-fashioned confectioner. The seductive handmade chocolates – 14 kinds of filled candies and three types of bars – are lined up in a glass case, defying your willpower. There are also a few tables, in case you care to indulge in a hot chocolate (R75 to R120).

MAGAZIN CHAI-KOFE FOOD & DRINK

Map p272 (Магазин Чай-Кофе; Myasnitskaya ul 19; ⌚9am-9pm Mon-Fri, 10am-7pm Sat & Sun; Ⓜ Turgenevskaya) In 1894 the old Perlov Tea House was redecorated in the style of a Chinese pagoda. Today this fantastical facade contains the Tea-Coffee Store – a simple name for a place that is filled with coffee beans from Italy, Brazil, Costa Rica and Kenya, and tea leaves from China, India and South Africa.

ART SALON ON MAROSEYKA SOUVENIRS

Map p272 (ul Maroseyka 4; ⌚10am-9pm) It's a bit of a stretch to call it an 'art salon' as it's stocked mostly with dolls and knick-knacks and other kitschy-coo. But there is a selection of appealing paintings, lovely interesting jewellery and some other fun and funky gift items.

IKONY-PODARKY SOUVENIRS

Map p272 (Иконы-Подарки; ul Bolshaya Lubyanka 17; Ⓜ Lubyanka) Not much remains of the 14th-century Sretensky Monastery, only the main church, Vladimirsky Cathedral, and, as it turns out, the gift shop. Get your icons – hanging icons, tabletop icons, triptych icons – and other souvenirs to soothe the spirit.

FACTORY-EXPEDITION OUTDOORS

Map p272 (Фактория-Экспедиция; www.expedicia.ru; Pevchesky per 6; Ⓜ Kitay-Gorod) For all your hunting expedition needs, find this tiny shop below the restaurant of the same name. As well as guns, knives, camping equipment and outdoor expedition gear, you'll also find some strange and scary souvenir items from the great Russian countryside.

Dorogomilovo & Sparrow Hills

Neighbourhood Top Five

❶ Recalling Russia's greatest tragedy and triumph of the 20th century at the Museum of the Great Patriotic War and the monuments at **Park Pobedy** (p149).

❷ Hiking through **Vorobyovy Gory Nature Preserve** (p150) and emerging at the top for fabulous views from **Universitetskaya pl** (p150).

❸ Watching the frolicking **Kuklachev cats** (p152) at this unique animal theatre.

❹ Catching the sunrise from the summer terrace at the **Sky Lounge** (p152) at the tippety-top of 'the Brains'.

❺ Cruising the **Moscow River** (p231) on board the Radisson's river boats or Capital Shipping Co ferries.

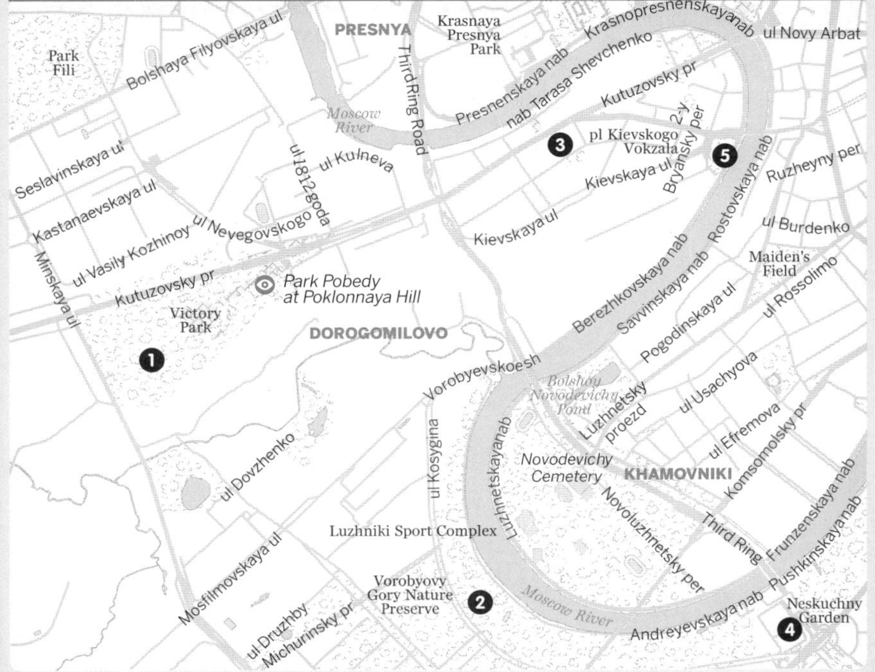

For more detail of this area, see p278 ➡

Best Places to Eat

- Darbar (p152)
- Dorogomilovsky Market (p151)
- Pinocchio on Kutuzovsky (p151)

For reviews, see p151

Best Places to Drink

- Sky Lounge (p152)
- Probka (p152)

For reviews, see p152

Best Viewpoints

- Universitetskaya pl (p150)
- Sky Lounge (p152)
- Krysha Mira (p152)
- Evropeysky Skating Rink (p152)

For reviews, see p150, p152 and p152

Explore: Dorogomilovo & Sparrow Hills

Further away from the city centre, the roads become wider, the traffic faster and the distances greater. As such, these overlapping districts are not great for wandering. But it's worth making a special trip for a few choice destinations. In particular, the monuments and museums at Park Pobedy (Victory Park) are an inspiring way to spend an afternoon. If you're feeling hemmed in by city life, you can explore the forested hillsides of Vorobyovy Gory Nature Preserve by walking, biking or riding the eco-train. You might even come just for dinner (or drinks), as the elevation of Sparrow Hills promises wonderful vistas over the otherwise flat city.

Local Life

- **Markets** Those in the know get the best fresh foods and produce at Dorogomilovsky (p151) and the best deals on music, movies and electronics at Gorbushka (p153).
- **Hang-outs** Fresh-brewed beer, hearty portions and reasonable prices make Probka (p152) a perennial local favourite.

Getting There & Away

- **Dorogomilovo** From Kievskaya station, two metro lines run west across Dorogomilovo. The light-blue Filevskaya line goes to Studencheskaya and Kutuzovskaya stations before turning north to Fili and Bagrationovskaya. The newer dark-blue Arbatsko-Pokrovskaya line goes to Park Pobedy (at 84m the deepest metro station in Moscow) and beyond.
- **Sparrow Hills** On the red Sokolnicheskaya line, the most useful stations are Vorobyovy Gory (use the entrance on the south side of the Moscow River) and Universitet. Alternatively, use Leninsky Prospekt station on the orange Kaluzhsko-Rizhskaya line.

TOP SIGHTS
PARK POEBEDY AT POKLONNAYA HILL

The Great Patriotic War – as WWII is known in Russia – was a momentous event that is still vivid in the hearts, minds and memories of many Russian citizens. Magnificent Park Pobedy (Victory Park) at Poklonnaya Hill is a huge memorial complex commemorating the sacrifice and celebrating the triumph of the war. Unveiled on the 50th anniversary of the victory, the park includes endless fountains and monuments, as well as the memorial church, synagogue and mosque.

The dominant monument is an enormous **obelisk**, topped with a sculpture of St George slaying the dragon (the work of Zurab Tsereteli). The height of the obelisk is exactly 141.8m, with every 10cm representing one day of the war. The obelisk is surrounded by fountains and benches, as well as the sweet memorial Church of St George. Facing the obelisk, the **Museum of the Great Patriotic War** (Центральный музей Великой Отечественной Войны; www.poklonnayagora.ru, in Russian; ul Bratiev Fonchenko 10; adult/child R100/40; ⏲10am-5pm Tue-Sun Nov-Mar, to 7pm Apr-Oct) has two impressive memorial rooms: the **Hall of Glory** honours the many heroes of the Soviet Union, while the moving **Hall of Remembrance and Sorrow** is hung with strings of glass-bead 'teardrops' in memory of the fallen. The huge museum has hundreds of exhibits, including dioramas of every major WWII battle the Russians fought in, as well as weapons, photographs, documentary films, letters and many other authentic wartime memorabilia.

The **Memorial Synagogue at Poklonnaya Hill** (Мемориальная синагога; ☎495-148 1907; www.poklonnaya.ru; Minskaya ul; admission free; ⏲10am-6pm Tue-Thu, noon-7pm Sun) opened in 1998 as a memorial to Holocaust victims, as well as a museum of the Russian Jewry. Admission is with a guide only, so you must make arrangements in advance, especially if you want a tour in English. Otherwise, you might be able to join an existing group. Not far from the synagogue, a moving sculpture commemorates the victims of the Holocaust.

Park Pobedy is a monument to the Great Patriotic War, but historians recognise many parallels with the War of 1812, not the least of which is the route taken by attacking and retreating armies. Following the vicious but inconclusive battle at Borodino (see p167) in August 1812, Moscow's defenders retreated along what are now Kutuzovsky pr and ul Arbat, pursued by Napoleon's Grand Army. Today, less than 1km east of Park Pobedy is the **Borodino Panorama** (Музей-панорама "Бородинская битва"; Kutuzovsky pr 38; adult/student R150/50; ⏲10am-5pm Sat-Thu), a pavilion with a giant 360-degree painting of the Borodino battle. Standing inside this tableau of bloodshed – complete with sound effects – is a powerful way to visualise the event. The museum also contains other artefacts and artwork related to the battle.

The nearby **Triumphal Arch** celebrates the eventual defeat of Napoleon in 1812. The original arch was demolished at its original site in front of the Belorusskaya metro station during the 1930s and reconstructed here in a fit of post-WWII public spirit.

On your way back to the centre, check out the **artwork** in Park Pobedy metro station. Created by the tireless Zurab Tsereteli, the two mosaics depict events from the War of 1812 and the Great Patriotic War, respectively. This newish station rivals the more central stations for artistry – and it is also the deepest metro station in the city.

DON'T MISS...

- Hall of Remembrance and Sorrow
- Memorial Synagogue at Poklonnaya Hill

PRACTICALITIES

- Map p278
- Kutuzovsky prospekt
- Admission free
- ⏲dawn-dusk
- Ⓜ Park Pobedy

SIGHTS

Dorogomilovo

BORODINO PANORAMA MUSEUM
See p150.

PARK POBEDY PARK
See p149.

MUSEUM OF THE GREAT PATRIOTIC WAR MUSEUM
See p150.

MEMORIAL SYNAGOGUE AT POKLONNAYA HILL SYNAGOGUE
See p149

CHURCH OF THE INTERCESSION AT FILI CHURCH
Map p278 (Церковь в Филях; Novozavodskaya ul 6; MFili) North of Kutuzovsky pr is Fili, a neighbourhood that was once the estate of Lev Naryshkin (brother-in-law to Tsar Alexey Mikhailovich and uncle to Peter the Great). The story goes that Naryshkin's brothers were killed in the Moscow uprising of 1682. In their honour, he constructed the Church of the Intercession at Fili in the 1690s. All church records were destroyed in a fire, so the name of the architect and exact date of construction are not known.

Fili is most famous for the events that unfolded here after the Battle of Borodino. While the Russian Army was camped nearby, a meeting took place in Fili. Here, General Kutuzov insisted that the army abandon Moscow without fighting, allowing the city to burn to the ground.

Sparrow Hills

FREE **VOROBYOVY GORY NATURE PRESERVE** NATURE RESERVE
Map p278 (Воробёвы горы; 499-739 2708; www.vorobyovy-gory.ru, in Russian; MVorobyovy Gory) Vorobyovy Gory, or Sparrow Hills, is the green hilly area south of the Moscow River, opposite the tip of the Khamovniki peninsula. This wooded hillside is a pleasant surprise, especially since it has been converted into an ecological park. Following the south shore of the Moscow River, the narrow strip of land contains a network of wooded trails and a sandy beach. An eco-train runs along the bank of the river. Free guided tours are available (in Russian) with advanced arrangements.

If you prefer to go it alone, you can follow the walking trails from the river bank up to Universitetskaya pl. Alternatively, bikes and skates are available to rent at the eastern entrance of the eco-park. The paved path that originates in Neskuchny Garden continues along the river for several kilometres. Brave souls can try riding inland from the river, where the trails are not paved, nor are they flat.

MOSCOW STATE UNIVERSITY (MGU) NOTABLE BUILDING
Map p278 (Московский Государственный Университет; Universitetskaya pl; MUniversitet) The best view over Moscow is from Universitetskaya pl, at the top of the hill. From here, most of the city spreads out before you. It is also an excellent vantage point to see Luzhniki, the huge stadium complex built across the river for the 1980 Olympics, as well as Novodevichy Convent and the Cathedral of Christ the Saviour.

Behind Universitetskaya pl is the Stalinist spire of Moscow State University, one of the 'Seven Sisters' (see p211). The building is the result of four years of hard labour by convicts between 1949 and 1953. It boasts an amazing 36 storeys and 33km of corridors. The shining star that sits atop the spire is supposed to weigh 12 tonnes. Among other socialist realist frills on the facade, look for the eager students looking forward to communism. The building is not open to the public, which is a shame, because the lobby is equally elaborate, featuring bronze statues of distinguished Soviet scientists.

MOSFILM FILM STUDIO
Map p278 (Мосфильм; 499-143 9599; www.mosfilm.ru; Mosfilmovskaya ul 1; adult/student R140/85; tours 3pm Tue-Thu; MKievskaya) It's not exactly Universal Studios, but it is the oldest and most established film studio in Russia, responsible for films such as *Alexander Nevsky, War & Peace, White Sun of the Desert* and *Irony of Fate* (see p216). Make a reservation to book your spot on a 90-minute tour (some tours are in English, so be sure to inquire).

The highlight of the tour is the opportunity to stroll around some of the sets. There is also an impressive display of old cars, tanks, Rolls Royces and fire engines

WORTH A DETOUR

ROUBLE ROAD

West of Moscow, just outside MKAD (the outer ring road), the swanky street called 'Rublyovka' is the residence of choice for the movers, the shakers, the big money-makers...Moscow's mega-rich.

In Soviet times, high-level political officials and cultural figures were awarded modest cottages in this ecologically pure district. These days, the Moscow River provides a picturesque backdrop for multimillion-dollar mansions. The average cost of a house in this high-rolling 'hood is upwards of 100 million roubles, and prices are climbing. Home to Vladimir Putin and Dmitry Medvedev, Rublyovka is the pinnacle of prestige in Moscow.

But it's not only Russians that are here: Armani, Dolce & Gabana, Ferrari, Gucci and Lamborghini all have outlets along this strip, as do Ralph Lauren and Harley Davidson. For a spot of shopping, stop in at **Barvikha Luxury Village**. This is where local folk might pop in to pick up a Prada handbag, an Armani suit or – why not – a Ferrari Testarossa. There is also a hotel in this swanky shopping centre.

About 17km further west, the village of Nikolina Gora is Moscow's original *elitny* district, where you can actually see the Soviet-era dachas that were so sought-after back in the day. It is no longer so exclusive, and you can wander down to the banks of the Moscow River, where you will find the beach that was prominently featured in the Oscar-winning film, *Burnt by the Sun*. Apparently, director Nikita Mikhalkov has a place around here, and is sometimes spotted swimming in the river.

that are all in working order for use in the films. A costume exhibit features some of the outfits from famous films such as *Ruslan & Ludmila* and *Andrei Rublyov*. Otherwise, the display of costumes, masks and make-up is rather half-hearted. Of course, it wouldn't be Russia without the obligatory exhibit of old equipment, which is mildly amusing. Film buffs should look out for the camera used by Sergei Eisenstein to shoot *The Battleship Potemkin*.

To reach Mosfilm take trolleybus 7, 17 or 34 from Kievskaya metro station.

EATING

Dorogomilovo

DOROGOMILOVSKY MARKET MARKET

Map p278 (Дорогомиловский рынок; ul Mozhaysky val 10; ⌚8am-10pm; Ⓜ Kievskaya) This is one of Moscow's largest markets, with overflow spreading along Kievskaya ul as far as the train station. You'll find amazing fresh produce, meats, fish and dairy products, as well as some prepared foods. Stay alert for pickpockets and hustlers, especially in the streets surrounding the main building.

PINOCCHIO ON KUTUZOVSKY ITALIAN $$$

Map p278 (☎495-545 0171; www.pinocchio-rest.ru; Kutuzovsky pr 4/2; meals R1000-2000; Ⓜ Kievskaya) This classy trattoria evokes 1930s Italy, with its black-and-white tiled floors, comfy leather armchairs and sky-high ceilings. Music from the era imbues the neoclassical dining room, creating a luxury setting to sip wine and feast on pasta and grills.

PINOCCHIO BAR & CAFE ITALIAN $

Map p278 (☎495-730 0818; www.pinocchio-rest.ru; nab Tarasa Shevchenko 23a; meals R300-500, desserts R100-200; Ⓜ Vystavochnaya) Strolling across the pedestrian bridge over the Moscow River, you'll run smack into this little bakery and cafe, which is in the tall tower on the embankment. It's not just for sweets and snacks, as it also serves soups, salads and pastas. Snag a table on the balcony for a windy view of Moskva-City.

EVROPEYSKY SHOPPING CENTRE SHOPPING MALL $

Map p278 (ТД Европейский; www.europe-trade.ru, in Russian; Kievskaya pl 1; Ⓜ Kievskaya) This oversized shopping mall is filled with restaurants of every shape and size, including branches of some of Moscow's most popular chain restaurants. Many options for the budget conscious.

Sparrow Hills

DARBAR INDIAN $$

Map p278 (www.darbar.ru; Leninsky pr 38; meals R600-1000; ⏲noon-midnight; Ⓜ Leninsky Prospekt) This is a long-standing favourite of spice-loving Muscovites, who are willing to make the trek south of the centre to feast on samosas, dhal and curries. The restaurant has fancy new digs on the 16th floor, which offers wonderful panoramic views. Still a favourite destination for Indian families.

DRINKING & NIGHTLIFE

Dorogomilovo

PROBKA BREWERY

Map p278 (Ukrainsky bul 15; beer R185-290, meals R500-800; Ⓜ Kievskaya) With exposed brick walls, copper ceiling and dark stained-wood bar, this is a classy brewpub. Join the crowds who come to quench their thirst on one of 15 beers on tap. Whether you want to watch sports on the big screen or enjoy the Russian version of pub grub, this is one of the more atmospheric places in the neighbourhood.

Sparrow Hills

SKY LOUNGE BAR

Map p278 (www.skylounge.ru; Leninsky prospekt 29, fl 22; ⏲1pm-last guest; Ⓜ Leninsky Prospekt) High up on the top floor of the Russian Academy of Sciences building (fondly known as 'the Brains') this chic Japanese restaurant is a sweet spot to go for a sundown drink. The party picks up after dark, when a DJ spins tunes and the Moscow lights twinkle in the distance.

ENTERTAINMENT

KUKLACHEV CAT THEATRE THEATRE

Map p278 (Театр кошек Куклачёва; www.kuklachev.ru; Kutuzovsky pr 25; tickets R200-800; ⏲noon, 2pm or 4pm Thu-Sun; Ⓜ Kutuzovskaya) At this unusual theatre, acrobatic cats do all kinds of stunts for the audience's delight. Director Yury Kuklachev says: 'We do not use the word "train" here because it implies forcing an animal to do something, and you cannot force cats to do anything they don't want to. We *play* with the cats.'

FOMENKO STUDIO THEATRE THEATRE

Map p278 (Московский театр Мастерская Фоменко; ☎499-249 1740; www.fomenko.theatre.ru; Tarasa Shevchenko nab 29; tickets R100-5000; Ⓜ Kutuzovskaya) The theatre world is talking about Pyotr Fomenko. Ever since the founding of his theatre in 1988, he has been known for his experimental productions, which used to take place in a rundown old cinema house. In 2008, Fomenko moved his troupe into fancy new digs overlooking the Moscow River – a marble-and-glass beauty built by architect Sergei Gnedovsky.

KRYSHA MIRA NIGHTCLUB

Map p278 (Крыша мира; www.kryshamira.ru; Tarasa Shevchenko nab; drinks R500-1000; ⏲midnight-last guest Fri & Sat; Ⓜ Kievskaya) The legendary 'roof of the world' is hidden away in the old Badaevsky brewery. With an unmarked entrance and ultratight face control, it is among Moscow's most exclusive places to party in the wee hours of the morning. The rooftop terrace, which earns the place its name, is apparently an amazing place to watch the sunrise over the city. If you think you have the look (or the connections) to get into this place, walk along the embankment about 500m past the Hotel Ukraine (the Radisson) and look for the cars parked in front of a rickety metal staircase leading into an unmarked entrance.

EVROPEYSKY SKATING RINK ICE SKATING

Map p278 (ТД Европейский; www.europe-trade.ru, in Russian; Evropeysky Shopping Centre, Kievskaya pl 1; per hr R240-300; ⏲10am-1.30pm Sun-Thu, 11.30pm-6am Fri & Sat; Ⓜ Kievskaya) The top floor of the Evropeysky Shopping Centre contains an indoor ice rink, with big windows looking out at the Moscow city skyline. You'll often see young figure-skaters-in-training, practising their spins and twirls. On weekends, come late at night for a party on the ice.

BOLSHOI CIRCUS ON VERNADSKOGO CIRCUS

Map p278 (www.bolshoicircus.ru, in Russian; pr Vernadskogo 7; tickets R100-1000; ⏲shows 7pm

THE COMMUTE'S A BRUTE

Like most medieval fortress towns, Moscow was not built to accommodate the modern automobile age. Its main roads consisted of concentric rings, where old defensive walls once stood, containing a labyrinth of narrowly twisting lanes and abruptly ending alleys. In the 1930s, Stalin added a spoke system of long boulevards, sprayed outward from the Kremlin. Traffic was not a major problem in communist times because there were not many cars. Even if you could save enough roubles, the waiting list to purchase an automobile was five years long. Today, it is not the waiting list but the commute that seems like five years.

Moscow's eternal combustion congestion has thrust the capital into contention for world's worst driving cities. The number of car-owning Muscovites rose exponentially from roughly a quarter million in 1990 to 3.5 million in 2010. Traffic jams are especially bad during summer holiday dacha drives and winter workday snowstorms. Moreover, all these cars need somewhere to park, which could be any free space in which you can squeeze one-tenth of your vehicle. The city's reliably car-clogged streets provide material for political theatre (traffic was cited as one of the main reasons for Mayor Yury Luzhkov's dismissal) as well as for popular entertainment (a top-rated TV program had driver contestants try to elude traffic police for 35 minutes in a rambling chase around town).

Authorities have not simply been idling. The city's 'third' suburban-ring-road was completed in 2004, enabling drivers to go around the crowded centre; and the 'fourth' outer-ring-road – better known as MKAD – was widened from four to 10 lanes. Construction of a new Moscow–St Petersburg motorway, however, brought urban planners into conflict with environmental protesters over the proposed destruction of Khimki forest land. The project was eventually halted to find a more eco-friendly route.

Other official actions have included encouraging more public transport, building more parking garages and imposing more automobile taxes. Still, Moscow's notorious street snarls continue. One notable improvement is in driver–pedestrian relations. Not so long ago, cars possessed an unquestionable right-of-way over pedestrians, even on the sidewalk. But a tough police campaign successfully impressed upon drivers that pedestrians are not fair game – as long as they keep to the crosswalk.

Wed, 1pm & 5pm Sat & Sun; MUniversitet) This huge circus has five rings and holds 3400 spectators. The company includes hundreds of performers, from acrobats to animals. It is a great spectacle that is certain to entertain and amaze.

MOSCOW CHILDREN'S MUSICAL THEATRE THEATRE

Map p278 (Театр им НИ Сац; www.teatr-sats.ru, in Russian; pr Vernadskogo 5; tickets R50-500; times vary Wed, Fri & Sun Sep-Jun; MUniversitet) Founded by theatre legend Natalya Sats (the official name of the theatre is the Natalya Sats Moscow Children's Theatre) in 1965, this was the country's first children's theatre. Sats, apparently, was said to be the inspiration for Prokofiev's famous rendition of *Peter and the Wolf*, which is still among the best and most popular performances at the children's theatre. All performances staged here are highly entertaining and educational, as actors appear in costume before the show and talk with the children.

SHOPPING

GORBUSHKA SHOPPING CENTRE ELECTRONICS

Map p278 (ТЦ Горбушка; www.gorbushka.ru, in Russian; ul Barklaya 8; 10am-9pm Mon-Fri; MBagrationovskaya) Now located in the former Rubin furniture factory, this is the reincarnation of the famous black market for CDs and DVDs from the 1990s. The place carries electronics on the 1st floor, and music and movies on the 2nd floor, all for sale for cheap, cheap, cheap. Police raids are still a regular occurrence here, which may have the effect of making the pirated goods slightly less visible, but they are still here.

VALENTIN YUDASHKIN BOUTIQUE CLOTHING, ACCESSORIES

Map p278 (www.yudashkin.com; Kutuzovsky pr 19; MKievskaya) The best-known Russian fashion designer is Valentin Yudashkin, whose classy clothes are on display at the Louvre and the Met, as well as the State History Museum in Moscow (look but don't touch!). If you wish to try something on, head to this swanky boutique, which seems like a museum but has many things that you can, in fact, buy.

EVROPEYSKY SHOPPING CENTRE SHOPPING MALL

Map p278 (ТД Европейский; www.europe-trade.ru, in Russian; Kievskaya pl 1; MKievskaya) At the time of construction this was the largest urban shopping centre in the world. It does not compare to the megamalls on the city outskirts, but it is big. Besides the hundreds of shops and restaurants, highlights include an ice-skating rink, a movie theatre and a supermarket.

Day Trips from Moscow

Abramtsevo p156

Artists colony and country estate, Abramtsevo was a font of artistic inspiration for the renaissance of traditional Russian painting, sculpture, architecture and arts in the 19th century.

Sergiev Posad p157

Site of the Trinity Monastery of St Sergei, Sergiev Posad is the most visited destination in the Golden Ring (series of ancient towns northeast of Moscow), because of its accessibility from Moscow and its atmosphere of history and holiness.

Vladimir p159

The ancient town of Vladimir – 12th-century capital of medieval Rus – was formative in establishing a distinctively Russian architectural style. The city still shows off several remarkable structures that date back to this heyday.

Suzdal p163

Dating to the 11th century, Suzdal was a medieval capital and a spiritual centre in later years. The village is still ringed with monasteries and peppered with merchant churches, making for an ideal fairy-tale setting.

Borodino p167

Site of turning-point battles in the Napoleonic War of 1812 as well as the Great Patriotic War (WWII), Borodino Battlefield is also an idyllic destination that's far from any crowds, traffic or smog.

Abramtsevo

Explore

An entire generation of artists considered Savva Mamontov's country estate (Абрамцево) to be an ideal retreat from Moscow, and you will too. The buildings and grounds remain largely as they were when the great Russian revivalist artists worked here, so you can spend a half-day exploring the manor house and outbuildings, walking the trails and admiring the artwork that they left behind. Many of the buildings house interesting temporary exhibits.

There is a cafe on the museum grounds, but selection is limited so you might want to bring your own picnic lunch.

If you can't get enough of the Russian revivalists, continue on to the nearby village of Khotkovo to see the woodworking exhibit at the Arts & Crafts Department.

The Best

➡ **Sight** Saviour Church 'Not Made by Hand'

Top Tip

While wandering the grounds, don't miss Viktor Vasnetsov's rendition of the *Hut on Chicken Legs,* the house of Baba Yaga, witch of fairy-tale fame.

Getting There & Away

Train Suburban trains run every half-hour from Yaroslavsky station (R150, 1½ hours). Most – but not all – trains to Sergiev Posad or Alexandrov stop at Abramtsevo. For the Arts & Crafts Department take the same train to Khotkovo station.

Car Turn west off the M8 Moscow-Yaroslavl highway just north of the 61km post (signs to Khotkovo and Abramtsevo mark the turn-off) and continue over the railroad tracks.

Need to Know

➡ **Area Code** ☎254

➡ **Location** Abramtsevo is 60km north of Moscow.

RIDING THAT TRAIN

When taking trains from Moscow, note the difference between long-distance and 'suburban' trains. Long-distance trains run to places at least three or four hours out of Moscow (such as Vladimir), with limited stops and a range of classes. Suburban trains, known as *prigorodny poezdy* or *elektrichki,* run to within 100km or 200km of Moscow (such as Abramtsevo, Sergiev Posad and Borodino).

Long-distance Trains

The regular long-distance service is a fast train *(skory poezd),* which is really a relative term. Foreigners booking rail tickets through agencies are usually put on a *skory* train. The best *(firmenny)* have cleaner cars, more polite attendants and much more convenient arrival and departure hours.

On long-distance trains, your ticket will normally give the numbers of your carriage *(vagon)* and seat *(mesto).*

Suburban Trains

Most Moscow train stations have a separate ticket hall for suburban trains, usually called the *prigorodny zal* (Пригородный Зал), which is often tucked away at the side or back of the actual station building. Suburban trains are usually listed on separate timetables and may even depart from a separate group of platforms. These slow trains stop frequently, and have a single class of hard bench seats. You buy your ticket before the train leaves, and there's no capacity limit. *Prigorodny* trains often utilise an electronic ticket reader to enter the platform: be sure to save your ticket as it may be checked on the train or (more likely) as you exit the platform at your destination.

SIGHTS

ABRAMTSEVO MUSEUM-RESERVE MUSEUM, PARK

(Музей-заповедник Абрамцево; ☎495-993 0033; www.abramtsevo.net; Museynaya ul 1, Abramtsevo; grounds R55, all exhibits R295; ⏲10am-6pm Wed-Sun Apr-Sep, 10am-4pm Wed-Sun Oct-Mar) In 1870, Savva Mamontov – railway tycoon and patron of the arts – bought this lovely estate 60km north of Moscow. Here, he hosted a whole slew of painters, who sought inspiration in the gardens and forests: painter Ilya Repin; landscape artist Isaak Levitan; portraitist Valentin Serov; and the quite un-Slavonic painter and ceramicist Mikhail Vrubel. Other artists came to dabble at the woodworking and ceramics workshop, and musicians (including Fyodor Shalyapin, who made his debut here) performed in the private opera.

MANOR HOUSE MUSEUM

Several rooms of the manor house have been preserved intact, complete with artwork by various resident artists. The main attraction is Mamontov's dining room, featuring Repin's portraits of the patron and his wife, and Serov's luminous *Girl with Peaches*. A striking maiolica bench by Vrubel is in the garden.

SAVIOUR CHURCH 'NOT MADE BY HAND' CHURCH

The prettiest building in the grounds is Saviour Church 'Not Made by Hand' (Tserkov Spasa Nerukotvorny). The structure epitomises Mamontov's intentions: it's a carefully researched homage by half-a-dozen artists to 14th-century Novgorod architecture. The iconostasis is by Repin and Vasily Polenov. The tiled stove in the corner, still working, is exquisite.

RUSSIAN ARTISTS OF THE 20TH CENTURY ART MUSEUM

This neoclassical building was a 20th-century addition to the estate and it now houses a collection of paintings and sculptures by 20th-century artists. It started as an exhibit of paintings by the avant-garde 'Knave of Artists' group and afterwards expanded to include pieces by Andrei Vasnetsov, Igor Grabar, Vera Mukhina and others. Many of the featured artists lived at the 'Artist Village' that blossomed on the bank of the nearby Vorya River in the 1930s. The museum was closed for renovations at the time of research.

ARTS & CRAFTS DEPARTMENT ART MUSEUM

(Отдел художественных ремесел; www.abramtsevo.net; Kooperativnaya ul 23; Khotkovo; admission R95; ⏲10am-6pm Wed-Sun Apr-Sep, 10am-4pm Wed-Sun Oct-Mar) Located in one of the outbuildings of the Khotkov Pokrovsky Monastery, this branch of the Abramtsevo Museum is dedicated to the craft of woodcarving. A specific style – known as Abramtsevo-Kudrino woodcarving – was developed at Abramtsevo by artist Vasily Vornoskov. The craft is still practised by artists in the region. At the Arts & Crafts Department, finely carved woodwork by Vornoskov and his contemporaries is on display, along with pieces by their modern-day successors.

Sergiev Posad

Explore

In Russia, it doesn't get any holier than Sergiev Posad (Сергиев Посад), for the place was founded in 1340 by the country's most revered saint. Since the 14th century, seekers have been journeying to this place to pay homage to him. It is still one of the most important spiritual sites in Russia and is usually crowded with pilgrims.

Sergiev Posad is an easy day trip from Moscow and that's how most people visit it. There are a handful of museums and other attractions, but the monastery is the main drawcard and it's more than enough to merit the trip here.

The Best

- **Sight** Trinity Cathedral
- **Place to Eat** Russky Dvorik
- **Place to Drink** Art Café San Marino

Top Tip

Visitors should refrain from photographing the monks. Female visitors should wear headscarves, and men are required to remove hats before entering the churches.

Getting There & Away

Bus Bus 388 to Sergiev Posad from Moscow's VDNKh metro station departs every 10 to 20 minutes from 8.30am to 7.30pm (R145, 70 minutes). Transit buses for Kostroma (R560), Yaroslavl (R400) or Rybinsk pass almost hourly; all these will take you to Pereslavl-Zalessky and Rostov-Veliky (280) if you can get a ticket.

Train The fastest transport option is the express train that departs from Moscow's Yaroslavsky vokzal (R320, one hour, at least twice daily) and continues to Yaroslavl (three hours) via Rostov (two hours). Suburban trains also run every half-hour (R130, 1½ hours); some continue to Aleksandrov where you can change for Yaroslavl.

Need to Know

- **Area code** ☎496
- **Location** Sergiev Posad is 60km north of Moscow.

Sergiev Posad

Sights

1 Bell Tower A2
2 Cathedral of the Assumption A2
3 Chapel-at-the-Well A2
4 Grave of Boris Godunov A2
5 Konny Dvor B1
6 Refectory Church of St Sergius A2
7 Toy Museum A3
8 Trinity Cathedral A2
9 Vestry A2

Eating

10 Russky Dvorik B2

Transport

11 Bus Station B3

SIGHTS

TRINITY MONASTERY OF ST SERGEI — MONASTERY

(Троице-Сергиева Лавра; www.stsl.ru; admission free; ⏲10am-6pm) In 1340, St Sergei of Radonezh founded this monastery, which soon became the spiritual centre of Russian Orthodoxy. St Sergei was credited with providing mystic support to prince Dmitry Donskoy in his improbable victory over the Tatars in the battle of Kulikovo Pole in 1380. Soon after his death at the age of 78, Sergius was named Russia's patron saint.

Nowadays, the monastery is an active religious centre with a visible population of monks in residence. This mystical place is a window into the age-old belief system that has provided Russia with centuries of spiritual sustenance.

TRINITY CATHEDRAL — CHURCH

(Троицкий собор) Built in the 1420s, the squat, dark Trinity Cathedral is the heart of the Trinity Monastery. The tomb of St Sergei stands in the southeastern corner, where a memorial service for St Sergei goes on all day, every day. The icon-festooned interior, lit by oil lamps, is largely the work of the great medieval painter Andrei Rublyov and his students.

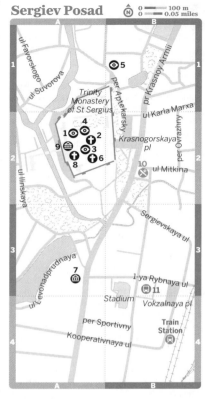

CATHEDRAL OF THE ASSUMPTION CHURCH

(Успенский собор) The star-spangled Cathedral of the Assumption was modelled on the cathedral of the same name in the Moscow Kremlin. It was finished in 1585 with money left by Ivan the Terrible in a fit of remorse for killing his son. Outside the west door is the **grave** of Boris Godunov, the only tsar not buried in the Moscow Kremlin or St Petersburg's SS Peter & Paul Cathedral.

CHAPEL-AT-THE-WELL CHURCH

(Накладезная часовня) Nearby, the resplendent Chapel-at-the-Well was built over a spring that is said to have appeared during the Polish siege. The five-tier baroque **bell tower** took 30 years to build in the 18th century, and once had 42 bells, the largest of which weighed 65 tonnes.

VESTRY MUSEUM

(Ризница; admission R200, students R200; ⌚10am-5.30pm Wed-Sun) The Vestry, behind the Trinity Cathedral, displays the monastery's extraordinarily rich treasury, bulging with 600 years of donations by the rich and powerful – tapestries, jewel-encrusted vestments, solid-gold chalices and more.

REFECTORY CHURCH OF ST SERGEI CHURCH

(Трапезная церковь преподобного Сергия) The huge block with the 'wallpaper' paint job is the Refectory Church of St Sergei, so called because it was once a dining hall for pilgrims. Now it's the Assumption Cathedral's winter counterpart, holding morning services in cold weather. It is closed outside of services, except for guided tours. The green building next door is the metropolitan's residence.

KONNY DVOR MUSEUM

(Конный двор; ul Udarnoy Armii; joint ticket R140; ⌚10am-5pm Wed-Sun) The former monastery stables house three interesting historic and traditional craft exhibitions.

TOY MUSEUM MUSEUM

(Музей игрушек; pr Krasnoy Armii 123; ⌚11am-5pm Wed-Sun) Toys from throughout history and around the world. The museum houses a particularly good collection of nesting dolls, as Sergiev Posad was the centre of *matryoshka* (nesting doll) production before the revolution.

EATING

ART CAFÉ SAN MARINO ITALIAN $$

(pr Krasnoy Armii 138/2; r R220-350) Looking utterly unorthodox in front of the holy site, this little cellar cafe is filled with art and books. Salads and pastas with a few vegetarian options dominate the menu. Live jazz concerts happen regularly. A singing canary bird will keep you awake at other times.

RUSSKY DVORIK RUSSIAN $$

(Русский дворик; www.russky-dvorik.ru; pr Krasnoy Armii 134; meals R300-900; ⌚10am-9pm) This is a charming, kitschy place decked out like a Russian dacha. There is also an affiliated hotel.

Vladimir

Explore

Vladimir (Владимир) may look like another Soviet Gotham-City, until you pass the medieval Golden Gate and spy the cluster of exquisite churches and cathedrals, some of the oldest in Russia. This is your first (and perhaps your only) destination in Vladimir.

Prince Andrei Bogolyubsky chose Vladimir as his capital in 1157, when he invited the best European architects to design the town's landmarks, fusing Western and Kyivan traditions. The style would influence Russian architecture for years to come.

It's possible to visit Vladimir as a day trip from Moscow, but it's better to combine it with a trip to nearby Suzdal (p163) and make a weekend of it. If you do stay, you'll have time to visit one of the interesting museums in the vicinity of the churches.

The Best

- **Sight** Cathedral of St Dmitry
- **Place to Eat** Salmon & Coffee
- **Place to Drink** Traktir

Top Tip

If you intend to visit Vladimir and Suzdal in one trip, plan to spend the night in Suzdal, which offers more (and better) accommodation options.

Getting There & Away

➡ **Bus** Privately run buses (R200, 3½ hours) leave regularly from Kursky and Kazansky vokzaly to Vladimir. They do not run on a timetable but leave as they fill up. The train and bus stations are 500m east of the city centre, on Vokzalnaya ul, at the bottom of the slope.

➡ **Train** The daily express train between Moscow's Kursky vokzal (seat R340, 2½ hours) stops in Vladimir, as do many slower trains.

Need to Know

➡ **Area code** ☎4922

➡ **Location** Vladimir is 178km east of Moscow.

SIGHTS

ASSUMPTION CATHEDRAL CATHEDRAL

(Успенский собор; Sobornaya pl; adult/under 15 R70/30; ⏰7am-8pm Tue-Sun, tourist time 1am-4.45pm) Construction of this white-stone version of Kyiv's brick Byzantine churches began in 1158 – its simple but majestic form was adorned with fine carving, innovative for the time. The cathedral gained the four outer domes when it was extended on all sides after a fire in the 1180s.

Inside the working church, a few restored 12th-century murals of peacocks and prophets can be deciphered about halfway up the inner wall of the outer north aisle; this was originally an outside wall. The real treasures, though, are the **Last Judgment frescoes** by Andrei Rublyov and Daniil

Vladimir

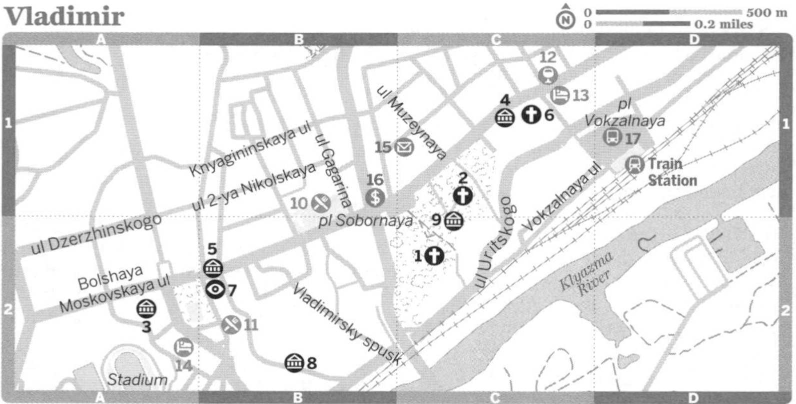

Vladimir

Sights

1 Assumption Cathedral C2
2 Cathedral of St Dmitry C1
3 Crystal, Lacquer Miniatures & Embroidery Exhibition A2
Golden Gate .... (see 5)
4 History Museum C1
5 Military Museum B2
6 Nativity Monastery C1
7 Old City Wall B2
8 Old Vladimir Exhibition B2
9 Palaty C2

Eating

10 Salmon & Coffee B1
11 Traktir B2

Drinking & Nightlife

12 Guinness Pub C1

Sleeping

13 Hotel Vladimir C1
14 Monomakh Hotel A2

Information

15 Post & Telephone Office C1
16 Sberbank B1

Transport

17 Bus Station D1

WORTH A DETOUR

BOGOLYUBOVO

According to legend, when Andrei Bogolyubsky was returning north from Kyiv in the late 1150s, his horses stopped at the site where Bogolyubovo now stands, 11km east of Vladimir. And so Andrei was inspired to build a stone-fortified palace at this strategic spot near the meeting of the Nerl and Klyazma Rivers. Fragments from the palace survive amid a renovated and reopened 18th-century monastery. Driving along the Vladimir–Nizhny Novgorod road, you can't miss the monastery in the middle of Bogolyubovo.

The dominant buildings today are the monastery's 1841 **bell tower** beside the road, and its 1866 **Assumption Cathedral**. Just east of the cathedral there is the arch and tower, on whose stairs – according to a chronicle – Andrei was assassinated by hostile boyars (nobles). The arch abuts the 18th-century **Church of the Virgin's Nativity**.

Nearby, Andrei built the most perfect of all old Russian buildings, the **Church of the Intercession** on the Nerl. The church's beauty lies in its simple but perfect proportions, a brilliantly chosen waterside site (floods aside) and sparing use of delicate carving. Legend has it that Andrei had the church built in memory of his favourite son, Izyaslav, who was killed in battle against the Bulgars. As with the Cathedral of St Dmitry (p161) in Vladimir, King David sits at the top of three facades, the birds and beasts entranced by his music.

To reach this famous little church, walk down Vokzalnaya ul, which is immediately east of the monastery. At the end of the street, cross the railway tracks and follow the cobblestone path 1km across the field. You may be able to catch a ride in a horse-drawn carriage for a small fee.

To get to Bogolyubovo, take trolleybus 1 east from Vladimir and get off at Khimzavod. Walk along the main road for 100m to the bus stop, where you can catch a *marshrutka* (fixed-route minibus) to Bogolyubovo (second stop).

Chyorny, painted in 1408 in the central nave and inner south aisle, under the choir gallery towards the west end.

The church also contains the original coffin of Alexander Nevsky of Novgorod, the 13th-century military leader who was also Prince of Vladimir. He was buried in the former **Nativity Monastery** east of the cathedral, but his remains were moved to St Petersburg in 1724 when Peter the Great awarded him Russian hero status.

Adjoining the cathedral on the northern side are an 1810 **bell tower** and the 1862 **St George's Chapel**. Don't miss the spectacular views over the bluff into the Oka valley.

CATHEDRAL OF ST DMITRY — CATHEDRAL

(Дмитриевский собор; Bolshaya Moskovskaya ul 60; adult/under 15 R50/20) A quick stroll to the east of the Assumption Cathedral is the smaller Cathedral of St Dmitry, built between 1193 and 1197, where the art of Vladimir-Suzdal stone carving reached its pinnacle.

You can enter the church, but the attraction here is the cathedral's exterior walls, covered in an amazing profusion of images. The top centre of the north, south and west walls all show King David bewitching the birds and beasts with music. The Kyivan prince Vsevolod III, who had this church built as part of his palace, appears at the top left of the north wall, with a baby son on his knee and other sons kneeling on each side. Above the right-hand window of the south wall, Alexander the Great ascends into heaven, a symbol of princely might; on the west wall appear the labours of Hercules.

PALATY — MUSEUM

(Палаты; Bolshaya Moskovskaya ul 58; adult/under 15 R150/70; ⏲10am-5pm Tue-Sun, 10am-4pm Tue-Wed) The grand 18th-century court building between the cathedrals is known as Palaty – the Chambers; it contains a children's museum, art gallery and historical exhibition. The former is a welcome diversion for little ones, who may well be suffering from old-church fatigue. The art gallery features art since the 18th century, with wonderful depictions of the Golden Ring towns.

HISTORY MUSEUM MUSEUM

(Bolshaya Moskovskaya ul 64; adult/under 15 R50/20; ⏲10am-5pm Wed-Mon) Across the small street from the Palaty, this museum displays many remains and reproductions of the ornamentation from the Cathedrals of the Assumption and St Dmitry. Reminiscent of Moscow's History Museum (p64), the red-brick edifice was purpose-built in 1902.

GOLDEN GATE TOWN GATE

(Золотые ворота) Vladimir's Golden Gate, part defensive tower, part triumphal arch, was modelled on the very similar structure in Kyiv. Originally built by Andrei Bogolyubsky to guard the western entrance to his city, it was later restored under Catherine the Great. You can climb the narrow stone staircase to check out the **Military Museum** (adult/under 15 R40/20; ⏲10am-6pm Fri-Wed) inside. It's a small exhibit, the centrepiece of which is a diorama of old Vladimir being ravaged by nomadic raiders in 1238 and 1293. Across the street to the south you can see a remnant of the **old city wall** that protected the city.

CRYSTAL, LACQUER MINIATURES AND EMBROIDERY MUSEUM MUSEUM

(Bolshaya Moskovskaya ul 2; admission R60; ⏲10am-4pm Wed-Mon) Housed in the former Old Believers' Trinity Church this museum features the crafts of Gus-Khrustalny and other nearby towns. The shop in the basement has a decent selection of crystal for sale.

EATING & DRINKING

SALMON & COFFEE FUSION $$

(Лосось и кофе; www.losos-coffee.ru; Bolshaya Moskovskaya ul 19a; meals R200-400) Salmon is yet to be found in the Oka, while coffee is not exactly what medieval princes had for breakfast. But instead of hinting at the city's past, this DJ cafe is here to give a cosmopolitan touch to the ancient town. Lots of dark wood, dim lights and magenta-coloured metal railings create a cool, intriguing atmosphere. The menu is divided between European and Japanese dishes. One can only admire the chef's sense of experiment, but some dishes are pretty funky.

TRAKTIR RUSSIAN $$

(Трактир; ☎324 162; Letneperevozinskaya ul 1A; meals R300-500; ⏲11am-last guest) This wooden mega-cottage, serving a simple menu of Russian food, is about the liveliest place in town. In summer, the terrace opens up for cold beer and grilled shashlyk (meat kebab). With live music 8pm to 11.30pm Thursday to Saturday), it's a popular spot for people to congregate and celebrate.

GUINNESS PUB PUB $

(Bolshaya Moskovskaya ul 67; beer R100) Here is a friendly, cheapish and blissfully unauthentic pseudo-Irish pub, its walls adorned with insignia of obscure teams from obscure leagues. Plasma screens show football or hockey nonstop, but a surprising number of regulars come here to play chess.

SLEEPING IN VLADIMIR

Hotel prices include breakfast.

➡ **Voznesenskaya Sloboda** (Вознесенская слобода; ☎4922-325 494; www.vsloboda.ru; ul Voznesenskaya 14b; d R4600; ❄) Perched on a bluff with tremendous views of the valley, this hotel might have the most scenic location in the whole of the Golden Ring area. It is very quiet in this neighbourhood, where old wooden cottages and new villas are dominated by the elegant Ascension church. The interior of this new building is tastefully designed to resemble art nouveau c 1900. The popular restaurant Krucha is in the premises.

➡ **Hotel Vladimir** (Гостиница Владимир; ☎4922-324 447; www.vladimir-hotel.ru; Bolshaya Moskovskaya ul 74; s/d from R2300/2800; @) This hotel near the train station used to be a state-run establishment, but it has successfully survived the transition to a privately owned, efficiently run hotel. All the rooms have been renovated with new bathrooms and furniture, but retaining a hint of old-fashioned Soviet charm in the choice of wallpaper and draperies. It is a big place with a slew of services.

➡ **Monomakh Hotel** (Гостиница Мономах; ☎4922-440 444; www.monomahhotel.ru; ul Gogolya 20; s R2300-2800, d R3500; 🚭❄@📶) Off the main drag, this newish hotel has 16 rooms that are simply decorated but fully equipped.

Suzdal

Explore

The Golden Ring comes with a diamond, and that's Suzdal (Суздаль). If you have only one place to visit near Moscow, come here – even though everyone else will do the same. The place remains largely the same as ages ago – its cute wooden cottages mingle with golden cupolas that reflect in the river, which meanders through gentle hills and flower-filled meadows.

Spend a morning exploring the Kremlin, shopping in Market Square and admiring the rural views over the Klyazma River. In the afternoon, investigate the Saviour Monastery of St Euthymius. Along the way, you'll pass dozens of exquisite churches, colourful log cabins and other photogenic scenes. If you have the time or inclination, the surrounding countryside is a spectacular place for bike riding or horse riding.

The Best

➡ **Sight** Kremlin

➡ **Place to Eat** Salmon & Coffee

➡ **Place to Drink** Graf Suvorov & Mead-Tasting Hall

Top Tip

Most long-distance buses (from Vladimir or Moscow) pass the central square on their way to the Suzdal bus station. Ask the driver to let you out to avoid the 2km trek back into town.

Getting There & Away

➡ **Bus** The bus station is 2km east of the centre on Vasilievskaya ul. Buses run every half-hour to/from Vladimir (R50, one hour). A daily bus goes directly to/from Moscow's Shchyolkovsky bus station (R365, 4½ hours).

Need to Know

➡ **Area code** ☎49231

➡ **Location** Suzdal is 35km north of Vladimir.

SIGHTS

KREMLIN FORTRESS

(Кремль; exhibits each R30-70, joint ticket adult/child R400/100; ⌚10am-6pm Tue-Sun) The 1.4km-long earth rampart of Suzdal's kremlin, founded in the 11th century, encloses a few streets of houses and a handful of churches, as well as the main cathedral group on Kremlyovskaya ul.

NATIVITY OF THE VIRGIN CATHEDRAL CHURCH

(Церковь Казанской иконы Божьей Матери) The Nativity of the Virgin Cathedral, its blue domes spangled with gold, was founded in the 1220s. Only its richly carved lower section is original white stone, though, the rest being 16th-century brick. The inside is sumptuous, with 13th- and 17th-century frescoes and 13th-century damascene (gold on copper) west and south doors.

ARCHBISHOP'S CHAMBERS MUSEUM

(Архиерейские палаты; admission R70; ⌚10am-5pm Wed-Mon) Within the Kremlin, the Archbishop's Chambers houses the **Suzdal History Exhibition**, which includes the original 13th-century door from the cathedral, photos of its interior and a visit to the 18th-century **Cross Hall** (Крестовая палата), which was used for receptions. The tent-roofed 1635 **kremlin bell tower** (звоница) on the east side of the yard contains additional exhibits.

MARKET SQUARE CENTRAL SQUARE

(Торговая площадь) Suzdal's Market Square is dominated by the pillared **Trading Arcades** (1806–11) along its western side. There are four churches in the immediate vicinity, including the **Resurrection Church** (admission R50). Make the precarious climb to the top of the bell tower and be rewarded with wonderful views of Suzdal's gold-domed skyline. The five-domed 1707 **Emperor Constantine Church** in the square's northeastern corner is a working church with an ornate interior. Next to it is the smaller 1787 **Virgin of All Sorrows Church**.

SAVIOUR MONASTERY OF ST EUTHYMIUS MONASTERY

(Спасо-Евфимиев мужской монастырь; exhibits each R20-80, all-inclusive R300, under 15 R150; ⌚10am-6pm Tue-Sun) Founded in the 14th century to protect the town's northern

Suzdal

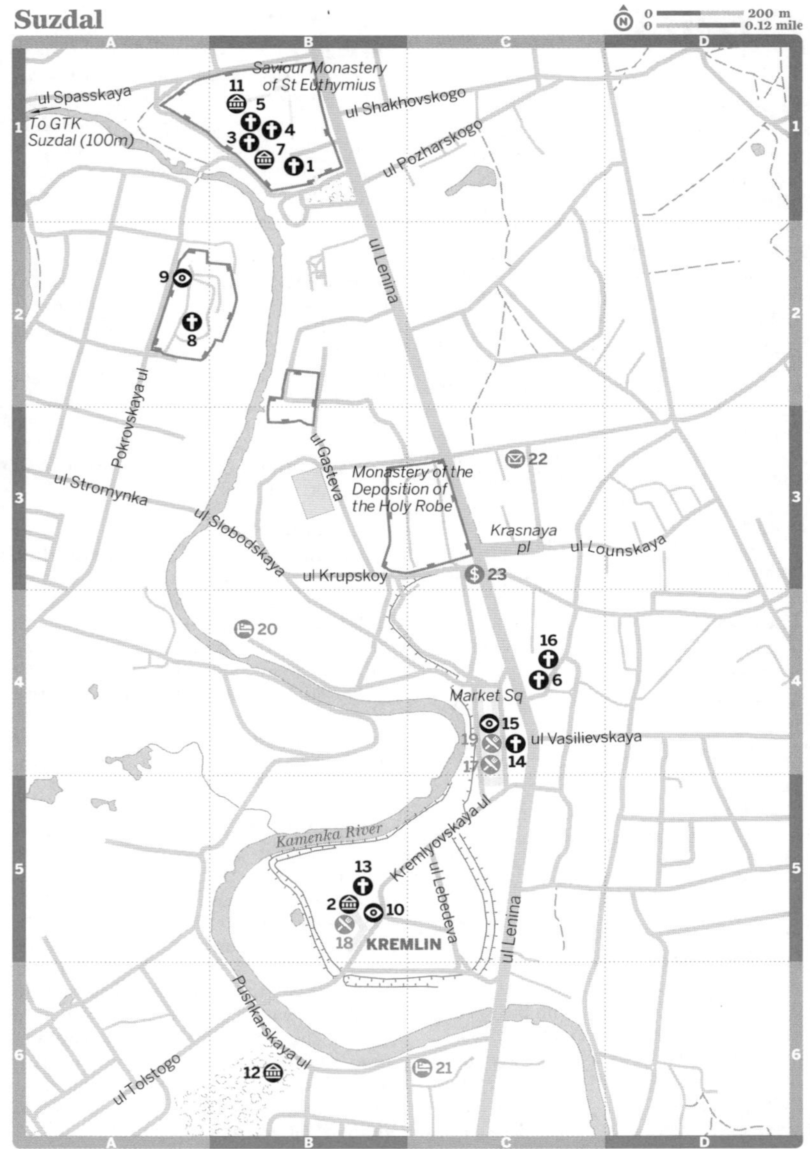

entrance, Suzdal's biggest monastery grew mighty in the 16th and 17th centuries after Vasily III, Ivan the Terrible and the noble Pozharsky family funded impressive new stone buildings, and big land and property acquisitions. It was girded with its great brick walls and towers in the 17th century.

Inside, the **Annunciation Gate-Church** houses an interesting exhibit on Dmitry Pozharsky (1578–1642), leader of the Russian army that drove the Polish invaders from Moscow in 1612.

A tall 16th- to 17th-century **cathedral bell tower** stands before the seven-domed

Suzdal

Sights
1 Annunciation Gate-Church B1
2 Archbishop's Chambers B5
3 Assumption Refectory Church B1
4 Cathedral Bell Tower B1
5 Cathedral of the Transfiguration of the Saviour B1
6 Emperor Constantine Church C4
7 Father Superior's Chambers B1
8 Intercession Cathedral A2
9 Intercession Convent A2
10 Kremlin Bell Tower B5
11 Monastery Prison B1
12 Museum of Wooden Architecture & Peasant Life B6
13 Nativity of the Virgin Cathedral B5
14 Resurrection Church C4
Suzdal History Exhibition .... (see 2)
15 Trading Arcades C4
16 Virgin of All Sorrows Church C4

Eating
17 Graf Suvorov & Mead-Tasting Hall C4
18 Kremlin Trapeznaya B5
19 Salmon & Coffee C4

Sleeping
20 Godzillas Suzdal B4
21 Pushkarskaya Sloboda C6

Information
22 Post & Telephone Office C3
23 Sberbank C3

Cathedral of the Transfiguration of the Saviour. Every hour on the hour from 11am to 5pm a short concert of chimes is given on the bell tower's bells. The cathedral was built in the 1590s in 12th- to 13th-century Vladimir-Suzdal style. Inside, restoration has uncovered some bright 1689 frescoes by the school of Gury Nikitin from Kostroma. The **tomb** of Prince Dmitry Pozharsky is by the cathedral's east wall.

The 1525 **Assumption Refectory Church**, facing the bell tower, adjoins the old **Father Superior's chambers**, which houses a display of Russian icons and the excellent naïive art exhibition showcasing works by Soviet-era amateur painters from local villages.

The old **monastery prison**, set up in 1764 for religious dissidents, is at the north end of the complex. It now houses a fascinating exhibit on the monastery's prison history, including displays of some of the better-known prisoners who stayed here. The combined **hospital** and **St Nicholas Church** (1669) features a rich museum of church gold treasures.

INTERCESSION CONVENT — CONVENT

(Покровский монастырь; Pokrovskaya ul; admission free; 9.30am-4.30pm Thu-Mon) This convent was founded in 1364, originally as a place of exile for the unwanted wives of tsars. Among them was Solomonia Saburova, the first wife of Vasily III, who was sent here in the 1520s because of her supposed infertility. The story goes that she finally became pregnant, but she was too late to avoid being divorced. A baby boy was born in Suzdal. Fearing he would be seen as a dangerous rival to any sons produced by Vasily's new wife, Solomonia secretly had him adopted, pretended he had died and staged a mock burial. This was probably just as well for the boy since Vasily's second wife did indeed produce a son – Ivan the Terrible.

The legend received dramatic corroboration in 1934 when researchers opened a small 16th-century tomb beside Solomonia's in the crypt underneath the **Intercession Cathedral**. They found a silk-and-pearl shirt stuffed with rags, but no bones. The crypt is closed to visitors.

MUSEUM OF WOODEN ARCHITECTURE & PEASANT LIFE — MUSEUM

(Музей деревянного зодчества и крестьянского быта; Pushkarskaya ul; adult/under 15 R150/60; 9.30am-7pm Wed-Mon May-Oct) This open-air museum, illustrating old peasant life in this region of Russia, is a short walk across the river, south of the Kremlin. Besides log houses, windmills, a barn and lots of tools and handicrafts, its highlights are the 1756 **Transfiguration Church** (Преображенская церковь) and the simpler 1776 **Resurrection Church** (Воскресенская церковь).

SPORTS & ACTIVITIES

GTK SUZDAL BICYCLES, HORSES

(ГТК; 23 380, 20 908; ul Korovniki 45; 10am-6pm) The Hotel Tourist Complex rents bicycles, snowmobiles and skis, as well as offering horse-riding tours.

GORYACHIE KLYUCHI STEAM BATH

(Горячие ключи; 24 000; www.parilka.com, in Russian; 11am-1am) Rural Suzdal is a great place to cleanse body and soul in a Russian *banya* (hot bath). Beautiful, lakeside *bani* are available for rental at Goryachie Klyuchi starting at R880 for up to four people. Rooms start at R2100/2500 per single/double.

DVA KOLESA BICYCLES

(Два Колеса; 8-910-186 0252; www.dvakolesa.ru; ul Tolstogo 5) This little guesthouse rents bicycles for R500 per day to those who didn't come on their own bike, unlike most of their guests. Owners lead bicycle excursion through villages surrounding Suzdal. Rooms go for R2000 during the week and R3000 on weekends.

EATING & DRINKING

In addition to the places listed below, all of the hotels have restaurants.

SALMON & COFFEE FUSION **$$**

(Лосось и кофе; ul Lenina 63a, inside Trading Arcades; mains R200-450) Like its sister in Vladimir, Suzdal's S&C is about the best place for an unhurried lunch or a cup of coffee. It is, however, much quainter, with lots of whitewashed wood interior aged to evoke the 'Cherry Orchard' dacha ambience. Despite the name, salmon is not really prominent on the menu, which includes inventive fusion European dishes and sushi.

GRAF SUVOROV & MEAD-TASTING HALL RUSSIAN **$$**

(Граф Суворов и зал дегустаций; ul Lenina 63a, inside Trading Arcade; tasting menu R130-350, mains R150-300) With vaulted ceilings and kitschy wall paintings depicting Russian military hero count Suvorov's exploits in the Alps, this place serves standard Russian food and a few dozen varieties of locally produced *medovukha,* a mildly alcoholic honey ale that was drunk by princes

SLEEPING IN SUZDAL

Suzdal is experiencing a tourist boom, which means there is plenty of choice in the midrange and high-end bracket – from quaint two- to three-room guesthouses to vast holiday resorts. You may save up to R1000 per night if you avoid coming to Suzdal during weekends or holidays. Breakfast is included unless otherwise stated.

➡ **Pushkarskaya Sloboda** (Пушкарская слобода; 49231-23 303; www.sloboda-gk.ru, in Russian; ul Lenina 45; d in inn from R2900, d in village from R3700;) This holiday village has everything you might want from your Disney vacation – accommodation in the log-cabin 'Russian inn' or the reproduction 19th-century 'Gunner's Village'; three restaurants, ranging from the rustic country tavern to a formal dining room; and every service you might dream up. It's an attractive, family-friendly, good-value option, though it might be too well-manicured for some tastes.

➡ **Petrov Dom** (Петров дом; 49231-23 326, 8-919-025 8884, 8-910-188 3108; www.petrovdom.ru; per Engelsa 18; r weekdays R1500, weekends R2000, holidays R2500;) Vlad and Lena offer three nicely furnished and strictly nonsmoking rooms in their wooden dacha-style house with a lovely garden on a quiet street (not to be confused with ul Engelsa), which makes it a great option for travellers with children. A sumptuous breakfast is included. Self-caterers are welcome to use the kitchen and garden grill.

➡ **Godzillas Suzdal** (in Moscow 495-699 4223; www.godzillashostel.com; Naberezhnaya ul 12; per person without breakfast R650-750;) An affiliate of the namesake hostel in Moscow, this big log cabin facility overlooking the river opened just a few years ago, but has already undergone a thorough renovation. Each dorm room has its own bathroom and balcony. Guests can also enjoy the blooming garden and Russian *banya* (hot bath), as well as the chill-out lounge and the bar in the basement.

of old. Go for tasting sets, which include 10 samples each. Apart from the regular one, there are separate sets of berry- and herb-flavoured *medovukha*.

KREMLIN TRAPEZNAYA RUSSIAN **$$**

(Кремлевская трапезная; ☎21 763; meals R300-500; ⌚11am-11pm) The attraction here is the choice location in an old dining hall inside the Archbishop's Chambers. The menu features tasty, filling Russian favourites.

Borodino

EXPLORE

Borodino (Бородино) battlefield is the site of turning-point battles in the Napoleonic War of 1812. Two hundred years later, the rural site presents an amazing, vivid history lesson. Start at the Borodino Museum, which provides a useful overview, then spend the rest of the day exploring the 100-sq-km preserve. If you have your own car, you can see monuments marking the sites of the most ferocious fighting, as well as the headquarters of both French and Russian armies. If you come by train, you'll probably be limited to the monuments along the road between the train station and the museum (which are many).

The rolling hills around Borodino and Semyonovskoe are largely undeveloped, due to their historic status. Facilities are extremely limited; be sure to bring a picnic lunch.

The Best

➡ **Sight** Borodino Field

Top Tip

The first Sunday in September, the museum complex hosts a re-enactment of the historic battle, complete with Russian and French participants, uniforms and weapons. The 200-year anniversary is 2012, so it's bound to be a big one.

Getting There & Away

➡ **Train** Suburban trains leave from Moscow's Belorussky vokzal to Borodino (R200, two hours) at 7.15am, 10.45am and 12.40pm. Trains return to Moscow at 5pm and 8.20pm. There is more frequent transport to/from the nearby village of Mozhaysk, from where you can catch a taxi to Borodino for about R350.

➡ **Car** Since the area is rural and the monuments are spread out, visiting by car is more convenient and probably more rewarding. If driving from Moscow, stay on the M1 highway (Minskoe sh) until the Mozhaysk turn-off, 95km beyond the Moscow outer ring road. It's 5km north to Mozhaysk, then 13km west to Borodino village.

Need to Know

➡ **Area code** ☎49638

➡ **Location** Borodino is 130km west of Moscow.

SIGHTS

BORODINO FIELD

(Бородинское поле) In 1812 Napoleon invaded Russia, lured by the prospect of taking Moscow. For three months the Russians retreated, until on 26 August the two armies met in a bloody battle of attrition at the village of Borodino. In 15 hours more than one-third of each army was killed – over 100,000 soldiers in all. Europe would not know fighting this devastating again until WWI. The French seemed to be the winners, as the Russians withdrew and abandoned Moscow. But Borodino was, in fact, the beginning of the end for Napoleon, who was soon in full, disastrous retreat.

The entire battlefield – more than 100 sq km – is now the **Borodino Field Museum-Preserve** (Бородинский музей-заповедник; www.borodino.ru), basically vast fields dotted with dozens of memorials to specific divisions and generals (most erected at the centenary of the battle in 1912).

The front line was roughly along the 4km road from Borodino village to the train station: as you walk from the station you'll see many monuments close to the road. The hilltop monument about 400m in front of the museum is **Bagration's tomb** (Могила Багратиона), the grave of Prince Bagration, a heroic Georgian infantry general who was mortally wounded in battle.

Borodino

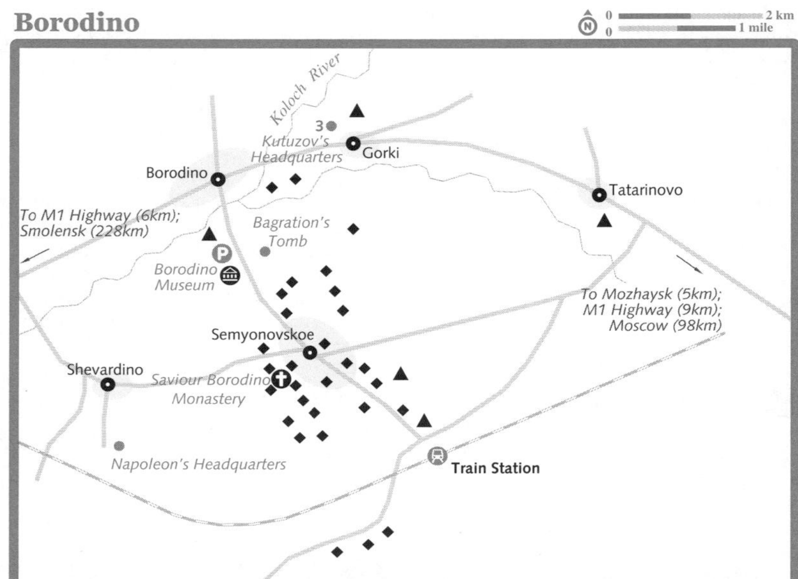

Further south, a concentration of monuments around **Semyonovskoe** marks the battle's most frenzied fighting. Here, Bagration's heroic Second Army, opposing far more numerous French forces, was virtually obliterated. Apparently, Russian commander Mikhail Kutuzov deliberately sacrificed Bagration's army to save his larger First Army, opposing lighter French forces in the northern part of the battlefield. **Kutuzov's headquarters** are marked by an obelisk in the village of Gorky. Another obelisk near Shevardino to the southwest, paid for in 1912 with French donations, marks **Napoleon's camp**.

This battle scene was re-created during WWII, when the Red Army confronted the Nazis on this very site. Memorials to this battle also dot the fields, and **WWII trenches** surround the monument to Bagration. Near the train station are two WWII mass graves.

BORODINO MUSEUM

(Бородинский музей; ☎51 546; www.borodino.ru; admission R50; ⏲10am-6pm Tue-Sun) The museum is an excellent starting place, as you can study a diorama of the battle (and get the big picture) before setting out to see the site in person. Otherwise, the main exhibits feature original objects from the battle, including uniforms, weapons, documents and personal items. The displays, created by soldiers and their contemporaries, demonstrate the perception of the war and the battle at the time. There is also an exhibit dedicated to the WWII battle at this site.

SAVIOUR BORODINO MONASTERY

(Спасо-Бородинский монастырь; ☎51 057; ⏲10am-5pm Tue-Sun) Built by widows of the Afghan War. Among its exhibits is a display devoted to Leo Tolstoy and the events in *War and Peace* that took place at Borodino.

Sleeping

With the world's most expensive average hotel rates, Moscow is not a cheap place. The city is flush with international luxury hotels, but more affordable hotels are few and far between. Fortunately, a slew of hostels have opened in Moscow, so budget travellers have plenty of options. And more midrange options are also appearing, usually in the form of 'mini-hotels.'

Hotels

The most visible type of accommodation in Moscow is the palatial four- or five-star hotel that has proliferated in the last decade. Priced for the business market, they may be prohibitively expensive for some travellers (although many offer far better deals through travel agents and hotel websites).

At the other end of the spectrum is the Soviet *gostinitsa* (hotel). Some of these old-style institutions are now slowly adapting to the needs of the modern traveller. Many of these hotels have undertaken some degree of renovation. As a result, the quality of rooms can vary widely, and prices usually do too (even within the same hotel).

In recent years, some smaller private hotels have opened in Moscow. Many are housed in historic buildings, and their smaller size means they offer more intimacy than the larger chain hotels. However, the level of comfort and service at these smaller hotels is not guaranteed. The high price – and it is higher than you expect – does not necessarily translate into five-star quality.

Mini-Hotels

A concept that started in St Petersburg has finally arrived in Moscow. Privately owned mini-hotels usually occupy one or two floors in an apartment building. The rooms have been renovated to comfortably accommodate guests, but the hotel itself (which might have a dozen rooms or less) does not usually offer other facilities. Considering the shortage of midrange options, mini-hotels are among the best-value accommodation in the city.

Hostels

In recent years, dozens of hostels have opened in Moscow, much to the delight of budget travellers. Many have been converted from flats or *communalky* (communal apartments), so they are often located in innocuous, unmarked buildings on residential streets. All hostels offer English-speaking staff, internet access, linen, kitchens and laundry facilities. Hostel prices do not usually include breakfast.

Serviced Apartments

Entrepreneurial Muscovites have begun renting out apartments on a short-term basis. Flats are equipped with kitchens and laundry facilities and they almost always offer wireless internet access. The rental agency usually makes arrangements for the flat to be cleaned every day or every few days. Often, a good-sized flat is available for the price of a hotel room, or less. It is an ideal solution for travellers in a group, who can split the cost.

Apartments are around R4300 to R8600 per night. Expect to pay more for fully renovated, Western-style apartments. Although there are usually discounts for longer stays, they are not significant, so these services are not ideal for long-term renters.

Cheap Moscow (www.cheap-moscow.com) Heed the disclaimers, but this site has loads of listings for apartments to rent directly from the owner.

Moscow Suites (www.moscowsuites.com) Slick apartments in central locations. Services like airport pick-up and visa support are included in the price, which starts at R6200.

Intermark Serviced Apartments (www.intermarksa.ru) Catering mostly to business travellers, Intermark offers four-star accommodations, starting at R5500 per night.

Rick's Apartments (www.enjoymoscow.com) Rick's apartments are off the Garden Ring between Sukharevskaya and Tsvetnoy Bulvar metro stations. Studios start at R4200, with two-bedroom apartments about R6700.

Evans Property Services (www.evans.ru) Caters mainly to long-term renters, but also offers some apartments for R4800 to R7800 per night.

HOFA (www.hofa.ru) Apartments from R2600 per night and a variety of homestay programs.

Moscow4rent.com (www.moscow4rent.com) Most flats are centrally located, with internet access, satellite TV and unlimited international phone calls. Prices start at US$150 per night.

Longer-Term Rentals

Moscow real estate is among the most expensive in the world, which means you'll pay the price if you want to rent a flat in Moscow. The best source of information about apartments is the expat internet forums, such as **Expat.ru** (www.expat.ru), **Red Tape** (www.redtape.ru) or **Small World** (www.smallworld.com). Finding a flat usually requires working with an agency, which normally charges the renter a fee of one month's rent. Some agencies:

Intermark Savills (www.intermarksavills.ru)

Evans Property Services (www.evans.ru)

City Realty (www.cityrealtyrussia.com)

Fortline Real Estate Agency (www.fortline.ru)

Blackwood Real Estate (www.blackwood.ru)

Penny Lane Realtor (rent.realtor.ru)

Beatrix Real Estate Solutions (www.beatrix.ru)

Room Rates

Moscow doesn't provide much value for money when it comes to the hospitality industry. Luxury hotels are indeed top notch, but they have prices to match. Expect to pay upwards of R10,000 for a night at one of Moscow's top-end hotels. If you can forgo a degree of luxury, you can stay in a classy, comfortable and centrally located hotel for R8000 to R10,000 for a double. Midrange travellers can choose from a range of hotels, which offer decent rooms and amenities for R3000 to R8000 for a double. This wide-ranging category includes a variety of Soviet-era properties that have not come completely into the 21st century, though many are very atmospheric (as reflected in the price). Budget accommodation is usually dorm-style, although there are a few private rooms available for less than R3000.

The hotel market in Moscow caters primarily to business travellers, as you can tell by the ridiculously high prices. It also means that accommodation is harder to find during the week than on weekends, and prices may be lower on Friday and Saturday nights. Prices do not generally fluctuate seasonally, although there are certainly exceptions. All prices listed in this chapter include breakfast, unless otherwise indicated.

Lonely Planet's Top Choices

Home from Home (p175) At once a hostel and a minihotel, this excellent-value place is a comfortable home away from home, right on the old Arbat.

Golden Apple (p173) Contemporary, creative and classy, this boutique hotel also has an unbeatable location.

Artel (p173) Steps from Red Square, this funky place offers artistic and affordable rooms.

Basilica Hotel (p177) The selling point is the atmospheric location overlooking the Moscow River and on the grounds of a charming 19th-century church.

Best by Budget

$

Godzillas Hostel (p174)

Suharevka Mini-Hotel (p178)

Trans-Siberian Hostel (p178)

$$

Red Arrow (p176)

Kitay-Gorod Hotel (p173)

Ozerkovskaya Hotel (p177)

$$$

Ritz-Carlton (p173)

Swissôtel Krasny Holmy (p177)

Hotel Metropol (p173)

Best for Kids

Hotel Volga (p179)

Korston Hotel (p176)

Best Rooms with a View

Hotel Baltschug Kempinski (p177)

Hotel National (p174)

Swissôtel Krasnye Holmy (p177)

Ritz-Carlton Moscow (p173)

Radisson Royal (Hotel Ukraine) (p176)

Korston Hotel (p176)

Best Historical Hotels

Hotel Metropol (p173)

Hotel National (p174)

Radisson Royal (Hotel Ukraine) (p176)

Hilton Moscow Leningradskaya (p178)

Sovietsky Hotel (p174)

Best for Contemporary Cool

Ararat Park Hyatt (p174)

Red Dawn (p176)

Red Arrow (p176)

Swissôtel Krasnye Holmy (p177)

Best Soviet Throwbacks

Sovietsky Hotel (p174)

Arbat Hotel (p175)

Hotel Yunost (p176)

Hotel Sputnik (p176)

Best Hideaways

Red Arrow (p176)

Ozerkovskaya Hotel (p177)

Petrovka Loft (p174)

Sverchkov-8 (p178)

NEED TO KNOW

Price Guide

$$$	over R8000 per night
$$	R3000-8000 per night
$	under R3000

Book Your Stay Online

➡ www.hotels.lonelyplanet.com

➡ www.booking.com

➡ www.moscow-hotels.com

Price Units

Most hotels accept credit cards, but most hostels do not. Many hotels set their prices in *uslovie yedenitsiy* (often abbreviated as 'y.e.'), or standard units, which is usually equivalent to euros. Prices in this chapter are quoted in roubles, as you will always be required to pay in roubles.

Taxes

Prices listed here include the 18% value-added tax (VAT), but not the 5% sales tax, which is charged mainly at luxury hotels.

Reservations

Reservations are highly recommended. Unfortunately, some old-style hotels still charge a reservation fee, usually 20% but sometimes as much as 50% of the first night's tariff.

Where to Stay

Neighbourhood	For	Against
Kremlin & Kitay Gorod	Close to the city's most prominent historic sites, including the Kremlin and Red Square; beautiful and atmospheric location; good transport connections	Touristy; no inexpensive options; heavy traffic in city centre
Basmanny & Taganka	Plenty of dining and entertainment options in Basmanny; easy access to Yaroslavsky vokzal (train station); good transport connections	Taganka can be noisy due to heavy traffic and multiple metro lines
Tverskoy	Excellent dining and entertainment options; easy access to Sheremetyevo from Belorussky vokzal	Can be noisy; heavy traffic
Presnya	Excellent dining and entertainment options; lots of green space	
Arbat & Khamovniki	Close to Pushkin Fine Arts Museum and other art venues; excellent dining and entertainment options; lots of green space	
Dorogomilovo & Sparrow Hills	Easy access to Kievsky vokzal; city views; lots of green space	Limited dining and entertainment options; far away from most sights
Zamoskvorechie	Close to Tretyakov Gallery; excellent dining and entertainment options; easy access to Domodedovo from Paveletskaya vokzal; lots of green space	

Kremlin & Kitay Gorod

FOUR SEASONS HOTEL MOSKVA HISTORIC HOTEL $$$

Map p262 (www.hotel-moskva.com; Manezhnaya pl; MOkhotny Ryad) The story goes that Stalin was shown two possible designs for the Hotel Moskva on Manezhnaya pl. Not realising they were alternatives, he approved both. The builders did not dare point out his error, and so built half the hotel in constructivist style and half in Stalinist style. The incongruous result became a familiar and beloved feature of the Moscow landscape, even gracing the label of Stolichnaya vodka bottles. After years of rumours, the infamous Hotel Moskva was finally demolished in 2003, one in a long list of Soviet-era institutions to bite the dust. The site has since been claimed by Four Seasons, which reconstructed the old building complete with architectural quirks. The new high-class luxury hotel is expected to open in 2012.

HOTEL METROPOL HISTORIC HOTEL $$$

Map p262 (499-501 7800; www.metmos.ru; Teatralny proezd 1/4; s/d from R9700/10,700; MTeatralnaya) Nothing short of an art nouveau masterpiece, the historic Metropol brings an artistic touch to every nook and cranny, from the spectacular exterior (see p70) to the grand lobby, to the individually decorated rooms. The place dates back to 1907, so rooms are small by today's standards; if you need space, upgrade to a suite. Prices vary widely by season and day: call the reservations department for the best price.

KITAY-GOROD HOTEL MINI-HOTEL $$

Map p262 (Отель Китай-Город; 495-991 9971; www.otel-kg.ru; Lubyansky proezd 25; s R3500-4500, d R5500; MKitay-Gorod) Ever since the demolition of the old Hotel Rossiya, it has been impossible for budget-conscious travellers to stay this close to the Kremlin. We're pleased to see that capitalism has brought us full circle in the form of this privately owned mini-hotel on the edge of Kitay Gorod. This place has tiny rooms, but they are fully and comfortably equipped. The hotel's small size guarantees a warm welcome (unlike at the Rossiya).

Tverskoy

TOP CHOICE **ARTEL** MINI-HOTEL $$

Map p260; 495-626 9008; www.artelhotel.ru; Teatralny proezd 3, Bldg 3; s/d economy from R2450/2850, s/d standard 3570/4000; MKuznetsky Most) Tucked into an alley behind the Bolshoi, the Artel has an unbeatable location and an awesome, offbeat atmosphere. Graffiti covers the walls in the stairwell and lobby, while various artists have taken their design skills to some of the (more expensive) rooms. The economy rooms are minute but, the whole place feels very creative and cool. Note the music club Masterskaya (p85) is one floor below, so at times it may *sound* creative and cool, too.

TOP CHOICE **GOLDEN APPLE** BOUTIQUE HOTEL $$$

Map p260 (495-980 7000; www.goldenapple.ru; ul Malaya Dmitrovka 11; r from R12,000; MPushkinskaya) 'Moscow's first boutique hotel'. A classical edifice fronts the street, but the interior is sleek and sophisticated. The rooms are decorated in a minimalist, modern style – subdued whites and greys punctuated by contrasting coloured drapes and funky light fixtures. Comfort is also paramount, with no skimping on luxuries such as heated bathroom floors and down-filled duvets. Check the website for some great promotional discounts.

HOTEL SAVOY BOUTIQUE HOTEL $$$

Map p260 (Отель Савой; 495-620 8500; www.savoy.ru; ul Rozhdestvenka 3; r from R8260; MLubyanka) Built in 1912, the Savoy maintains an atmosphere of prerevolutionary privilege for its guests. It is more intimate and more affordable than the other luxury hotels, with 70 elegant rooms. All rooms are equipped with marble bathrooms and Italian fittings and furnishings. The state-of-the-art health club includes a glass-domed 20m swimming pool, complete with geysers and cascades to refresh tired bodies.

RITZ-CARLTON MOSCOW HOTEL $$$

Map p260 (495-225 8888; www.ritzcarlton.com; Tverskaya ul 3; r from R19,500; MOkhotny Ryad) This beauty opened in 2007 on the site of the much-maligned Soviet-era Intourist Hotel. The Ritz is everything that the Intourist wasn't: the guestrooms are spacious and sumptuous; service is impeccable; and amenities are virtually unlimited.

Note that the Ritz is a few floors taller than its next-door neighbour, the National. That means that rooms on the upper floors enjoy spectacular views, as does the cool rooftop lounge, O2.

ARARAT PARK HYATT HOTEL **$$$**

Map p260 (☎495-783 1234; www.moscow.park.hyatt.com; Neglinnaya ul 4; r from R18,000; ⊖❄📶≋; Ⓜ Teatralnaya) This deluxe hotel is an archetype of contemporary design: its glass-and-marble facade is sleek and stunning, yet blends effortlessly with the classical and baroque buildings in the surrounding area. The graceful, modern appearance extends inside to the atrium-style lobby and the luxurious rooms. Guests enjoy every imaginable amenity, and the service in the Ararat Park is top-notch (twice-daily housekeeping!). Of the hotel's many restaurants, don't miss the Conservatory Lounge, which offers panoramic views of Teatralnaya pl.

HOTEL NATIONAL HISTORIC HOTEL **$$$**

Map p260 (☎495-258 7000; www.national.ru; 15/1 Mokhovaya ul; r from R9528; ⊖❄📶≋; Ⓜ Okhotny Ryad) For over a century, the National has occupied this choice location at the foot of Tverskaya ul, opposite the Kremlin. The handsome building is something of a museum from the early 20th century, displaying frescoed ceilings and antique furniture. Rooms have king-sized beds, flat-screen TVs, down comforters and jewel-toned decor. While the place reeks of history, the service and amenities are up to modern five-star standards.

GODZILLAS HOSTEL HOSTEL **$**

Map p260 (☎495-699 4223; www.godzillashostel.com; Bolshoy Karetny per 6; dm R450-780, d/tr R1960/2600; ⊖❄📶@; Ⓜ Tsvetnoy Bulvar) Godzillas is the biggest and most professionally run hostel in Moscow, with 90 beds spread out over four floors. The rooms come in various sizes, but they are all spacious and light-filled and painted in different colours. To cater to the many guests, there are bathroom facilities on each floor, three kitchens and a big living room with satellite TV. Reminder: don't leave valuables in the luggage-storage facility.

PETROVKA LOFT MINI-HOTEL **$$**

Map p260 (☎495-626 2210; www.petrovkaloft.com; 17/2 ul Petrovka 17/2; s & d from R3500; ⊖❄📶; Ⓜ Teatralnaya) Enter the courtyard and go straight ahead to find the entrance to this 10-room hotel (note the four-storey climb). None of the rooms have en suites, but everything is pretty stylish and clean, and the location is brilliant.

SOVIETSKY HOTEL HISTORIC HOTEL **$$**

off Map p260 (Советский отель; ☎495-960 2000; www.sovietsky.ru; Leningradsky pr 32/2; r from R6080; ⊖❄📶≋; Ⓜ Dinamo) Built in 1952, this historic hotel shows Stalin's tastes in all of its architectural details, starting from the gilded hammer and sickle and the enormous Corinthian columns flanking the front door. The sumptuous lobby is graced with grand, sweeping staircases, crystal chandeliers and plush carpets, and even the simplest rooms have ceiling medallions and other ornamentation. The legendary restaurant Yar (p85), complete with old-fashioned dancing girls, is truly over the top. The location is not super-convenient, but this throwback is still fun for a Soviet-style splurge.

AKVAREL BOUTIQUE HOTEL **$$$**

Map p260 (Акварель; ☎495-502 9430; www.hotelakvarel.ru; Stoleshnikov per 12; s/d R9250/11,000; ⊖❄📶; Ⓜ Chekhovskaya) Set amid the grandeur of Stoleshnikov per is this intimate business-class hotel, offering 23 simple but sophisticated rooms, adorned with watercolour paintings. The friendly Akvarel is tucked in behind Simachyov Boutique & Bar (p88). Reduced rates on weekends.

HOTEL BUDAPEST HOTEL **$$**

Map p260 (Гостиница Будапешт; ☎495-925 3050; www.hotel-budapest.ru; Petrovskie linii 2/18; s/d from R5950/6900; ⊖❄📶; Ⓜ Kuznetsky Most) This 19th-century neoclassical edifice is an atmospheric option to retire to after shopping on ul Petrovka or seeing a ballet at the Bolshoi. Indeed, guests have been doing exactly that for more than a century. The rooms are traditional and comfortable, though nothing fancy, unless you dish out some extra cash for a suite (from R7500).

CHOCOLATE HOSTEL HOSTEL **$**

Map p260 (☎495-971 2046; www.chocohostel.com; Apt 4, Degtyarny per 15; dm R700-800, tw/tr/q R2400/3000/4000; @📶; Ⓜ Pushkinskaya) Chocolate lovers rejoice – this charming, friendly hostel will sooth your craving. Bring your favourite brand from home for their collection. In return you'll get simple friendly accommodations – colourfully painted rooms with metal furniture and old-style parquet floors. Bonus: bikes available for rent!

Presnya

MELODIYA HOTEL BOUTIQUE HOTEL $$

Map p264 (Отель Мелодия; ☎495-660 7178; www.melody-hotel.ru, in Russian; Skaterny per 13; s/d R5100/5600; ⊖✱☜; ⓂArbatskaya) If you like small hotels in quaint neighbourhoods, you will love the Melody Hotel. At least you will want to love it. Service can be spotty and the rooms are rather nondescript, but the place offers good value and the location – tucked into a quiet residential street – is as lovely as a song. Get the best rates on www.booking.com.

NIKITSKAYA HOTEL BOUTIQUE HOTEL $$$

Map p264 (Никицкая гостиница; ☎495-933 5001; www.assambleya-hotels.ru; Bolshaya Nikitskaya ul 12; s/d from R7900/9900, breakfast R500; ⊖✱☜; ⓂOkhotny Ryad) While the building and rooms at the Nikitskaya are freshly renovated, the hotel preserves an old-fashioned atmosphere of cosiness and comfort. And you can't beat the location. Despite its superb location and Russian charm, we can't help feeling that this place is overpriced. Hold out for the discounts that are available at weekends and other low-occupancy times.

PEKING HOTEL HOTEL $$

Map p264 (Гостиница Пекин; ☎495-650 0900; www.hotelpeking.ru; Bolshaya Sadovaya ul 5/1; s/d from R4400/4700; ⊖✱☜; ⓂMayakovskaya) Towering over Triumfalnaya pl, this Stalinist building is blessed with high ceilings, parquet floors and a marble staircase. The rooms vary, but they have all been renovated in attractive jewel tones with modern furniture. The atmosphere is much improved since the closure of the casino on the ground floor; nowadays it houses the raucous Radio City (p100).

Arbat & Khamovniki

TOP CHOICE HOME FROM HOME HOSTEL, MINI-HOTEL $

Map p268 (☎495-229 8018; www.home-fromhome.com; ul Arbat 49, Apt 9; dm R450-700, d R2000; ⊖@; ⓂSmolenskaya) Original art and mural-painted walls create a bohemian atmosphere, which is enhanced by ceiling medallions and exposed brick. For its excellent private en suite rooms, it goes by the name **Bulgakov Hotel** (www.bulgakovhotel.com). There is also a comfy, cosy common area with kitchen facilities. The building is on the Arbat, but you must enter the courtyard from Plotnikov per and look for entrance number 2.

ARBAT HOTEL HOTEL $$$

Map p268 (Гостиница Арбат; ☎499-271 2801; www.president-hotel.net/arbat; Plotnikov per 12; s/d from R10,000/11,500; ⊖✱☜; ⓂSmolenskaya) One of the few hotels that manages to preserve some appealing Soviet camp – from the greenery-filled lobby to the mirrors behind the bar. The guestrooms by contrast are decorated tastefully and comfortably, but the whole place has an anachronistic charm, which is unexpected at this price range. Its location is excellent – a quiet residential street, just steps from the Arbat. Reserve online for the best rates.

KEBUR PALACE HOTEL $$$

Map p270 (Кебур Палас; ☎495-733 9070; www.keburpalace.ru; ul Ostozhenka 32; s/d R11,000/12,040; ⊖✱☜≋; ⓂKropotkinskaya) Georgians know hospitality. The proof is in the fine restaurants, such as the landmark Tiflis (p115), and in this refined four-star hotel under the same management. With 80 rooms, the hotel offers an intimate atmosphere and personalised service. There are also a few small singles (R6000 to R8600) that are cheaper – ask for one with a balcony overlooking the fountain-filled patio.

HOTEL BELGRAD HOTEL $$

Map p268 (Гостиница Белград; ☎495-248 9500; www.hotel-belgrad.ru; Smolenskaya ul 8; s/d/ste R4200/5700/6100, breakfast R580; ✱☜; ⓂSmolenskaya) This big post-Soviet block on Smolenskaya-Sennaya pl is not the most atmospheric place to stay in Moscow. With few guests and a stark lobby, the place has a ghost-town aura. The cheapest rooms are poky but functional; only the more expensive 'tourist' or 'business-class' accommodation (costing R7100 to R8000) has been renovated. The advantage is the location, which can be noisy but is convenient to the western end of ul Arbat. Some of the rooms offer spectacular panoramic views.

HOTEL YUNOST HOTEL **$$**

(Гостиница Юность; ☎499-242 4860; www.hotelyunost.com; ul Khamovnichesky val 34; r from R3100; ; MSportivnaya) Yunost means 'youth', but this place looks decidedly middle-aged (it was built in 1961, after all). The Soviet-style rooms are clean and comfortable, but won't win any design awards; some have been upgraded (R5400). In any case, this place is a decent option for the money, and it's right around the corner from Novodevichy Monastery. Fun fact: back in the day, this hotel was popular with the cosmonaut set, including Yury Gagarin.

Dorogomilovo & Sparrow Hills

RADISSON ROYAL (HOTEL UKRAINE) HISTORIC HOTEL **$$$**

Map p278 (Рэдиссон Ройал Гостиница Украина; ☎495-221 5555; www.ukraina-hotel.ru; Kutuzovsky pr 2/1; r from R10,000; ; MKievskaya) This bombastic beauty sits majestically on the banks of the Moscow River facing the White House. The place reopened in 2010 under the management of Radisson. While the atmosphere of the 1950s is gone, the place has retained its old-fashioned ostentation, with crystal chandeliers, polished marble and a thematic ceiling fresco in the lobby. Heavy drapes, textured wallpaper and reproduction antique furniture give the guestrooms a similar atmosphere of old aristocracy, but all the modern amenities are here.

KORSTON HOTEL HOTEL **$$**

Map p278 (☎495-939 8000; www.korston.ru; ul Kosygina 15; r from R8900; ; MVorobyovy Gory) The location, not far from Moscow State University Sparrow Hills, allows for fantastic views of the Moscow city skyline from some rooms. It's a quiet, green, prestigious residential area – pleasant enough, but a bit of a hike into the centre. Otherwise, the rooms are tastefully decorated and spaciously appointed. There is no longer a casino here, but Korston is still an 'entertainment complex' with bowling, billiards and some 15 bars and restaurants.

HOTEL SPUTNIK HOTEL **$$**

Map p278 (Гостиница Спутник; ☎495-930 2287; www.hotelsputnik.ru; Leninsky pr 38; s/d R4840/5500; ; MLeninsky Prospekt) This hulk of a hotel is rather Soviet, but the rooms are quite attractive, with contemporary Ikea-style furnishings and flat-screen TVs. It's just a short walk to Sparrow Hills and the leafy campus of Moscow State University. Among the many services available, the on-site Indian restaurant, Darbar, is one of the best of its type in Moscow (see p152).

Zamoskvorechie

TOP CHOICE **RED DAWN** BOUTIQUE HOTEL **$$**

Map p276 (Красная Заря; ☎495-980 4774; www.red-zarya.ru; Bersenevsky per 3/10, Bldg 8; r from 7000; ; MKropotkinskaya) With a prime waterfront location on the edge of the Red October chocolate factory, this well-placed hotel offers lovely river views and easy access to the capital's hottest nightlife. Spacious designer rooms are done up in browns and beiges, which should be soothing for your hangover. Prices decrease significantly at the weekend.

RED ARROW MINI-HOTEL **$$**

Map p276 (Красная Стрела; ☎985-928 6000; Bolotnaya nab 7, Bldg 4; r R2500-4000; ; MKropotkinskaya) If you can find this teeny-weeny mini-hotel, you'll enjoy cool, contemporary rooms in Moscow's newest and trendiest area for eating and drinking. Look for a barely marked door in the small courtyard beside Art Akademiya. The seven small rooms exude the post-industrial hipness of the surrounding Red October chocolate factory, with high ceilings, painted brick walls and modern bathrooms. Note that the place is not protected from the nightlife noise, so you might as well go out and join the party!

DANILOVSKAYA HOTEL HOTEL **$$**

off Map p276 (Даниловская гостиница; ☎495-954 0503; www.danilovsky.ru; Bul Starodanilovsky per; s/d/ste R5500/6000/8500; @; MTulskaya) Moscow's holiest hotel is on the grounds of the 12th-century monastery of the same name – the exquisite setting comes complete with 18th-century churches and well-maintained gardens. The modern five-storey hotel was built so that nearly all the rooms have a view of the grounds. The recently renovated rooms are simple but clean, and breakfast is modest: no greed, gluttony or sloth to be found here.

OZERKOVSKAYA HOTEL BOUTIQUE HOTEL $$

Map p276 (Озерковская гостиница; ☎495-953 7644; www.cct.ru; Ozerkovskaya nab 50; s/d from R5900/6900; ; MPaveletskaya) This comfy, cosy hotel has only 27 rooms, including three that are tucked up under the mansard roof. The rooms are simply decorated, but parquet floors and comfortable queen-sized beds rank it above the standard post-Soviet fare. Add in attentive service and a central location (convenient for the express train to Domodedovo airport), and you've got an excellent-value accommodation option.

HOTEL BALTSCHUG KEMPINSKI HISTORIC HOTEL $$$

Map p276 (Балчуг Кемпинский; ☎495-287 2000; www.kempinski-moscow.com; ul Balchug 1; r without/with view from R13,000/16,000; ; MKitay-Gorod or Ploshchad Revolyutsii) If you want to wake up to views of the sun glinting off the Kremlin's golden domes, this luxurious property on the Moscow River is the place for you. It is a historic hotel, built in 1898, with 230 high-ceilinged rooms that are sophisticated and sumptuous in design. The on-site restaurant is famous for its Sunday brunch, or 'linner' if you prefer, as it's served from 12.30pm to 4.30pm. Russian champagne and live jazz accompany an extravagant buffet. Discounts on Friday and Saturday nights make this a great place for a weekend splurge.

SWISSÔTEL KRASNYE HOLMY HOTEL $$$

Map p276 (☎495-787 9800; www.moscow.swissotel.com; Kosmodamianskaya nab 52; r weekends/weekdays from R16,200/19,800; ; MPaveletskaya) The metallic skyscraper towering over the Moscow River is the swish Swissôtel Krasnye Holmy, named for this little-known neighbourhood of Moscow. Rooms are sumptuous, subtle and spacious. The decor is minimalist: rich, dark hardwood floors and a few modernist paintings, but nothing to detract from the striking city skyline. If you don't want to dish out the cash to spend the night, you can still enjoy the views by heading up to the City Space Bar on the 32nd floor.

ALROSA ON KAZACHY BOUTIQUE HOTEL $$$

Map p276 (Алроса на Казачьем; ☎495-745 2190; www.alrosa-hotels.ru; 1-y Kazachy per 4; s/d from R8800/10,400; ; MPolyanka) Set in the heart of Zamoskvorechie, one of the oldest and most evocative parts of Moscow, the Alrosa re-creates the atmosphere of an 18th-century estate. The light-filled atrium, bedecked with a crystal chandelier, and 15 classically decorated rooms provide a perfect setting for old-fashioned Russian hospitality. Reduced rates on weekends.

WARSAW HOTEL HOTEL $$

Map p276 (Гостиница Варшава; ☎495-238 7701; www.hotelwarsaw.ru; Leninsky pr 2/1; s R4300-5800, d R5550-6000; ; MOktyabrskaya) The Warsaw sits at the centre of Oktyabrskaya pl, voted the ugliest square in the city by Muscovites. Nonetheless, the location is the main drawcard here: it offers lots of restaurants, easy access to the metro and a short walk into the heart of Zamoskvorechie. The hotel itself does not exactly add to the aesthetics of the square. However, the interior is fully renovated, as evidenced by the sparkling, space-age lobby, adorned with lots of chrome, blue leather furniture and spiderlike light fixtures. The new rooms are decent value for the location.

IBIS PAVELETSKAYA HOTEL $$

Map p276 (☎495-661 8500; www.ibishotel.com; ul Shchipok 22; r from R3100; ; MPaveletskaya) You know exactly what you're getting when you book a room at the Ibis: affordable, comfortable rooms and professional, reliable service. The Ibis Paveletskaya is no different. For so long, Moscow suffered from a serious deficiency of both of those, so the Ibis is a welcome addition.

Basmanny & Taganka

TOP CHOICE **BASILICA HOTEL** MINI-HOTEL & HOSTEL $$

Map p272 (☎reservations 910-420 3446, front desk 915-462 5575; www.basilicahotel.ru; Serebryanichesky per 1a; s/d from R3000/4000; ; MKitay-Gorod) On the grounds of the 1781 Church of Silver Trinity, this aptly named hotel offers lovely, light-filled rooms with wood floors and contemporary furnishings. In the same building, the **hostel** (www.sweetmoscow.com; dm R700, s/d with shared bathroom from R2300/2400) has similarly decorated four- and six-bed dorm rooms. Besides the brightly painted kitchen and lounge area, there is an inviting outdoor patio. For extra fun, guests can climb to the top of the church's belfry (which is otherwise closed to the public). Breakfast not included.

AIRPORT ACCOMMODATION

Recommended for transit travellers who need to crash between flights, both hotels listed here operate free shuttle buses from their respective airports.

Aerotel Domodedovo (Аэротель Домодедово; ☎495-795 3572; www.airhotel.ru; Domodedovo airport; ❄; s/d R6300/6900) Small but satisfactory rooms, plus a fitness centre and billiards room.

Atlanta Sheremetyevo Hotel (☎498-720 5785; www.atlantahotel.ru; 36/7 Tsentralnaya ul, Sheremetyevsky; ⊖❄📶; r from R4500) Friendly, small and convenient, the Atlanta is an anomaly in the airport world. Reduced rates available for six- and 12-hour layovers.

TRANS-SIBERIAN HOSTEL — HOSTEL $

Map p272 (☎495-916 2030; www.tshostel.com; Barashevsky per 12; dm R630-700, d R2200-3000; ⊖@📶; Ⓜ Kitay-Gorod) If you can snag one of the double rooms in this tiny hostel, you're assured of getting one of the capital's best bargains. While they're no longer the cheapest private rooms in central Moscow, they are still pretty cheap. There are also two dorm rooms, one with four heavy wooden bunks and one with eight. The only common space is the kitchen, but it's spacious and modern. A train-themed decor brightens the place up, starting from the moment you step off the street.

BOULEVARD HOTEL — MINI-HOTEL $$

Map p272 (Отель Бульвар; ☎495-776 7276; www.bulvar-sr.ru; ul Sretenka 1; s R3800-5100, d R4700-6050; ⊖❄📶; Ⓜ Chistye Prudy) On the 2nd floor of a lovely classical building on the Boulevard Ring, this mini-hotel offers simple, individually appointed rooms. They are not too fancy, but they benefit from a few artistic touches, such as boldly painted walls, period furnishings and artistic details. The lower end of the price range is for Friday and Saturday nights.

SVERCHKOV-8 — MINI-HOTEL $$

Map p272 (Сверчков-8; ☎495-625 4978; www.sverchkov-8.ru; Sverchkov per 8; s/d R4800/5200; ⊖❄📶; Ⓜ Chistye Prudy) Situated on a quiet residential lane, this is a tiny 11-room hotel in a graceful 19th-century building. The hallways are lined with green-leafed plants, and paintings by local artists adorn the walls. Though rooms have old-style bathrooms and faded furniture, this place is a rarity for its intimacy and homey feel.

HILTON MOSCOW LENINGRADSKAYA — HISTORIC HOTEL $$$

Map p272 (☎495-627 5550; www.hilton.com; Kalanchevskaya ul 21/40; d from R10,300; ⊖❄📶🏊; Ⓜ Komsomolskaya) Occupying one of the iconic Stalinist skyscrapers (see the boxed text, p211), the old Leningradskaya Hotel has a new life, thanks to Hilton and its multiyear upgrade (completed in 2008). Hilton has maintained the Soviet grandiosity in the lobby, but updated the rooms with contemporary design and state-of-the-art amenities. This is the most convenient option if you are arriving or departing by train, due to its proximity to three stations. This beauty overlooks Komsomolskaya pl, in all its chaotic, commotion-filled glory.

SUHAREVKA MINI-HOTEL — MINI-HOTEL & HOSTEL $

Map p272 (Сухаревка; ☎8-910-420 3446; www.suharevkahotel.ru; Bolshaya Sukharevskaya pl 16/18; dm/r R500/1800; ⊖@📶; Ⓜ Sukharevskaya) This place occupies two side-by-side flats in a big block on the Garden Ring. The 'hostel side' is cramped and cluttered, with no real common space. Some travellers will appreciate the relative spaciousness and serenity across the hall on the 'hotel side'. Although the private rooms are also small, they evoke an atmosphere of old Moscow with high ceilings and rich fabrics. All bathroom facilities are shared.

BENTLEY HOTEL — MINI-HOTEL $$

Map p272 (☎495-917-4436; www.bentleyhotel.ru; ul Pokrovka 28; r R7900-8400; ⊖❄📶🏊; Ⓜ Kitay-Gorod) Upstairs from a popular American-style diner, Bentley goes all out to make its guests feel right at home. Cheeseburgers aside, the mini-hotel is a warm and inviting place, with a dozen spacious and richly decorated rooms. Bonus: guests get a discount on massage and other services at a nearby spa – the perfect way to recover after a day of sightseeing.

HOTEL VOLGA HOTEL **$$**

Map p272 (Апарт-Отель Волга; ☎495-783 9109; www.hotel-volga.ru; Bolshaya Spasskaya ul 4; s/d R6800/7200; ; MSukharevskaya) This characterless but comfortable hotel complex, run by Moscow's city government, is on a quiet corner northeast of the centre. The location is just outside the Garden Ring and not far from the metro. Most of the rooms are actually suites with several rooms or a kitchen, making the Volga ideal for small groups or families. Hey kids, this place also has a playground and a pool table on site!

SRETENSKAYA HOTEL HOTEL **$$$**

Map p272 (Сретенская гостиница; ☎495-933 5544; www.hotel-sretenskaya.ru; ul Sretenka 15; d 12,540; ; MSukharevskaya) Special for its small size and friendly atmosphere, the Sretenskaya boasts a romantic, Russian atmosphere. Rooms have high ceilings and tasteful, traditional decor. This place is welcoming in winter, when you can warm your bones in the sauna, or soak up some sun in the tropical 'winter garden'. Discounts are available on weekends.

NAPOLEON HOSTEL HOSTEL **$**

Map p272 (☎495-628 6695; www.napoleonhostel.ru; Maly Zlatoustinsky per 2, 4th fl; dm R800-1000; ; MKitay-Gorod) Apparently Napoleon stayed in this building in 1812. Nowadays, after a four-storey climb, you'll find a friendly, up-to-date hostel. The light-filled rooms have six to 10 wooden bunks, for a total of 48 beds (but only two toilets and two showers – do the maths), plus a clean kitchen and a comfy common room that is well stocked with board games and a plasma TV. Tea and coffee are free, but there's no breakfast.

COMRADE HOSTEL HOSTEL **$**

Map p272 (☎495-628 3126; www.comradehostel.com; ul Maroseyka 11; dm R500-600; ; MKitay-Gorod) It's hard to find this tiny place – go into the courtyard and look for entrance number 3, where you might spot a computer-printed sign in the 3rd-floor window. Inside, there is a great, welcoming atmosphere, although the place is packed. Ten to 12 beds are squeezed into the dorm rooms, plus there are mattresses on the floor if need be. There is not really any common space, except the small foyer and kitchen, but everybody seems to get along like comrades. Breakfast is not included.

Understand Moscow

Moscow Today

Twenty years into its reign as the capital of the new Russian Federation, Moscow has proven itself. In this short time the city has weathered economic crises and political transitions, building sprees and demolition derbies, terrorist attacks and festive celebrations. Now – with a new mayor at its helm, a newly prosperous middle class and a new look to boot – the city has settled into an upbeat but sustainable rhythm. What Stalin said is finally true: 'Life has become better, comrades. Life has become more joyous.'

Best on Film

Little Vera (1989) A ground-breaking film that caused a sensation with its frank portrayal of a family in chaos.
Farewell (2010) A real-life Cold War–era political thriller with a French twist.
Moscow Doesn't Believe in Tears (1980) Great chick flick that bagged an Oscar for best foreign language film.
My Perestroika (2010) An insightful documentary about coming of age during the *perestroika* era and navigating life in contemporary Moscow.

Best in Print

The Master and Margarita (Mikhail Bulgakov) The most telling fiction to come out of the Soviet Union.
On the Golden Porch (Tatyana Tolstaya) Short stories focusing on big souls in little flats in the 1990s.
Anna Karenina (Leo Tolstoy) A legitimate alternative for readers who don't have time for *War and Peace*.
Children of the Arbat (Anatoly Rybakov) A tragic but vivid portrait of 1930s Russia.

Politics

In September 2010, long-time Moscow mayor Yury Luzhkov lost his job. After 18 years, he was fired by President Medvedev, who issued a formal decree on the matter. The new boss is Sergey Sobyanin, hand-picked by the president in tandem with Prime Minister Putin.

Sobyanin was a surprising choice, as he hails from the Siberian province of Tyumen, although he had previously been working in Moscow as the Head of the Presidential Administration. Analysts theorise that his 'outsider' status and his clean reputation made him an attractive and inoffensive candidate.

Sobyanin's early initiatives have included a crackdown on corruption and a slow-down of construction, both of which were welcomed by many Moscow residents. He also promised to address the city's massive traffic problems.

One year down the line, critics are questioning his effectiveness. His early talk was tough, but preservationists wonder if the new mayor has the power to enforce his policies. The *Moscow Times* quoted one sceptical analyst: 'There are always politicians who like to fight corruption, but it's unlikely that Sobyanin will get rid of it in Moscow. It never works this way.'

Terrorism

Terror continues to rock the Russian capital. The most recent episode (at the time of research) was the January 2011 bomb that exploded in the baggage-claim area at Domodedovo International Airport, killing 37 people. This is just one in a growing list of horrific incidents that remind Muscovites that the conflict in Chechnya is not resolved.

Meanwhile, Chechens and other peoples from the Caucasus claim that they endure increased harassment, both officially and unofficially. They complain of increasing difficulty in obtaining residency permits and of constant unwarranted attention from Moscow police. Predictably, all this has resulted in growing mistrust between Russians and Chechens.

Clean-Up

Moscow has shed its grim and grey demeanour. Two decades of renovations and restorations have much of the old architecture in tip-top shape. The ancient onion domes have been regilded, the imperial palaces have been patched up or rebuilt, the people's parks are blooming, and the Soviet-era skyscrapers are sparkling.

Former mayor Yury Luzhkov was criticised for destroying old buildings and preserving only their facades; in his defence, the facades are beautiful.

Meanwhile, 21st-century builders are leaving their mark: the flashy new International Business Centre, for example, is shooting up along the Moscow River. The complex claims the tallest skyscraper in Russia and in Europe – the 'Moscow Tower' of the double-pronged City of Capitals building.

Other planning measures are also paying dividends. Industry has been removed from the city centre, and many of the former factories and deserted warehouses have been converted into edgy art galleries and underground clubs. Outdoor advertising has been banned from Red Square and other historic areas. And one of Sobyanin's first acts in office was, controversially, to do away with some 2000 kiosks that were scattered over Moscow's streets and squares.

Prosperity

Muscovites are enjoying disposable income like never before – and we're not talking only about the super rich. Over three million cars clog Moscow's streets: plenty of Mercedes, but also old-fashioned Ladas and everything in between. Restaurants include not only upscale eateries, but also bohemian bars and cool cafeterias. Many nightclubs are branded 'elite', but others are 'democratic'. Even eating raw fish has become popular, as sushi finds a place on almost every menu.

But as Muscovites embrace the joys of capitalism, they also grapple with its challenges. Moscow ranks among the world's most expensive cities, and the chasm between rich and poor is widening. Sixteen per cent of the population lives below the poverty line.

Nonetheless, the capital remains upbeat. The optimism is pervasive. It's evident in the ongoing construction of skyscrapers, shopping malls, theme parks and theatres; in the 'world premieres' and 'grand openings'; and on the faces of shoppers, strollers, diners and drinkers in the crowded streets. Indeed, to borrow a communist slogan, 'the future is bright!'.

if Moscow were 100 people

85 would be Russian
1 would be Armenian
2 would be Tatar
3 would be Ukrainian
9 would be other

belief systems

(% of population)

population per sq km

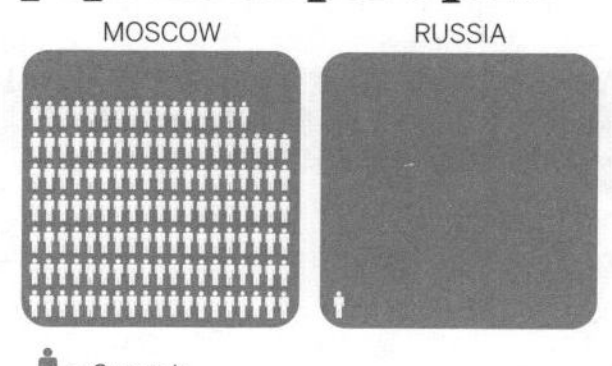

History

'Come to me, brother, please come to Moscow.' With these words, Yury Dolgoruky invited his allies to a celebratory banquet at the fortification he had erected on Borovitsky Hill, at the confluence of two rivers. The year was 1147. The settlement would prosper, eventually gaining power in the region and establishing itself as the capital of Ancient Rus. Nine centuries later – even as Russia has gone through multiple transformations – it is still ruled from the fortress that crowns Borovitsky Hill.

MEDIEVAL MOSCOW

Early Settlement

Moscow began as a trading post, set up by eastern Slav tribes who had migrated eastward from Kyivan Rus. Back in Kyiv, the Grand Prince Vladimir I was anxious to secure his claim of sovereignty over all the eastern Slavs. He made his son Yaroslav the regional vicelord, overseeing the collection of tribute and conversion of pagans.

After Vladimir's death, the descendants of Yaroslav inherited the north-eastern territories of the realm, where they established a series of towns, fortresses and monasteries that is today known as the Golden Ring.

Political power gradually shifted eastward to these new settlements. During the reign of Vladimir Monomakh as Grand Prince, he appointed his youngest son Yury Dolgoruky to look after the region. Legend has it that on his way back to Vladimir from Kyiv, Prince Yury stopped at Moscow. Believing that Moscow's Prince Kuchka had not paid him sufficient homage, Yury put the impudent boyar (high-ranking noble) to death and placed the trading post under his direct rule. Moscow's strategic importance prompted Yury to construct a moat-ringed wooden palisade on the hilltop and install his personal vassal on site.

With its convenient access to rivers and roads, Moscow soon blossomed into a regional economic centre, attracting traders and artisans to the merchant rows just outside the Kremlin's walls. In the early 13th century,

PRINCE DANIIL

Prince Daniil was the first Grand Prince of Moscow at the end of the 13th century. Revered for his humbleness and diplomacy, he was canonised by the Russian Orthodox Church in 1652.

TIMELINE

10th century

Eastern Slav tribes migrate from the Kyivan Rus principality further west, eventually assimilating or displacing the Ugro-Finnic tribes that had previously populated the region.

1015

Vladimir I's realm is divided among his sons, leading to a violent period of family feuds. His son Yaroslavl (and descendents) eventually gain control over the eastern territories.

1113–25

The Vladimir-Suzdal principality becomes a formidable rival in the medieval Russian realm. As Grand Prince, Vladimir appoints his youngest son, Yury Dolgoruky, to look after the region.

BY GEORGE, IT'S ST GEORGE

Visitors to Moscow are likely to notice the unmistakable likeness of St George around town. Indeed, all city properties display the iconic image of the Holy Helper, riding atop a white steed and sticking it to a scaly dragon below. While George is probably better known as the patron saint of England, he holds the same high status for Moscow.

The real-life George was born in Palestine in the 2nd century AD and rose to high rank in the Roman imperial guard. When Emperor Diocletian ordered all Christian soldiers to convert to paganism, George publicly tore up the edict. Neither the enticement of riches nor the pains of torture could make him renounce his faith, and he died a Christian martyr. Returning crusaders spread the legend of St George across Europe, which somehow came to include the slaying of a villainous serpent.

Moscow's founder, Prince Yury Dolgoruky, adopted St George as the city's heavenly protector. Not coincidentally, in the Russian tongue the name George is Yury. Henceforth, St George adorned the coat of arms of the medieval Muscovite principality, featured on coins and stamps. When Catherine the Great ordered all the administrative territories of the empire to design their own heraldic shields, Moscow once again went with the bane of flying reptiles.

But George was eventually knocked off his high horse by the Bolsheviks, who banned old regime regalia. Soviet Moscow was assigned a new city insignia, with proletariat protectors.

When the communist regime fell, Moscow returned St George to his traditional place of prominence. In 1993, then-Mayor Luzhkov – another Yury – officially restored the prerevolutionary St George image to the capital's crest. Perhaps it was a subliminal political message, but Muscovites seemed to like it anyway. A striking St George statue, forged by the city's favourite Georgian sculptor (p112), now presides over Manezhnaya pl next to the Kremlin.

On 23 April 2007, Russia's liberator from red dragons, Boris Yeltsin, died in Moscow. It was the feast day of St George.

Moscow became the capital of a small, independent principality, though it remained a prize contested by successive generations of boyar princes.

The Rise of Muscovy

In the 13th century, Eastern Europe was overwhelmed by the marauding Golden Horde, a Mongol-led army of nomadic tribespeople who appeared out of the eastern Eurasian steppes and were led by Chinggis (Genghis) Khaan's grandson, Batu. The ferocity of the Golden Horde raids was unprecedented, and quickly Russia's ruling princes acknowledged the region's new overlord. The Golden Horde's khan would

1147

Moscow is first mentioned in the historic chronicles when Yury Dolgoruky invites his allies to a banquet there: 'Come to me, brother, please come to Moscow.'

1156

Moscow is fortified with a wooden fence and surrounded by a moat as protection against rival principalities and other attackers from the east.

1237–38

The Mongols raze the city and kill its governor. Their menacing new presence levels the political playing field in the region, creating an opportunity for a small Muscovite principality.

1260s

Alexander Nevsky's youngest son Daniil inherits the territory of Moscow. The settlement is governed by his uncle until the child is old enough to rule.

constrain Russian sovereignty for the next two centuries, demanding tribute and allegiance from the Slavs.

The years of Mongol domination coincided with the rise of medieval Muscovy in a marriage of power and money. The Golden Horde was mainly interested in tribute, and Moscow was conveniently situated to monitor the river trade and road traffic. With Mongol backing, Muscovite officials soon emerged as the chief tax collectors in the region.

The Arbat is one of Moscow's oldest streets, dating back to the 15th century. Linguists believe the word Arbat comes from the Arabic word *arbad*, which means 'outskirts'. The Arabic word might have entered the Russian language by way of the Crimean Khanate, which was frequently attacking Moscow at this time.

As Moscow prospered economically, its political fortunes rose as well. Grand Prince Ivan Danilovich earned the moniker of 'Moneybags' (*Kalita*) because of his remarkable revenue-raising abilities. Ivan Kalita used his good relations with the khan to manoeuvre Moscow into a position of dominance in relation to his rival princes. By the middle of the 14th century, Moscow had absorbed its erstwhile patrons, Vladimir and Suzdal.

Soon Moscow became a nemesis rather than a supplicant to the Mongols. In the 1380 Battle of Kulikovo, Moscow's Grand Prince Dmitry, Kalita's grandson, led a coalition of Slav princes to a rare victory over the Golden Horde on the banks of the Don River. He was thereafter immortalised as Dmitry Donskoy. This feat did not break the Mongols, who retaliated by setting Moscow ablaze only two years later. From this time, however, Moscow acted as champion of the Russian cause.

Towards the end of the 15th century, Moscow's ambitions were realised as the once-diminutive duchy evolved into an expanding autocratic state. Under the long reign of Grand Prince Ivan III, the eastern Slav independent principalities were forcibly consolidated into a single territorial entity.

After a seven-year assault, Ivan's army finally subdued the prosperous merchant principality of Novgorod and evicted the Hansa trading league. After Novgorod's fall, the 'gathering of the lands' picked up pace as the young Muscovite state annexed Tver, Vyatka, Ryazan, Smolensk and Pskov.

In Russian, Ivan IV is called Ivan Grozny, which usually gets translated as 'terrible'. It actually means something like 'dreadfully serious', in reference to the tsar's severity and strictness.

In 1480 Ivan's army faced down the Mongols at the Ugra River without a fight. Ivan now refused outright to pay tribute or deference to the Golden Horde, and the 200-year Mongol yoke was lifted. A triumphant Ivan had himself crowned 'Ruler of all Russia' in a solemn Byzantine-style ceremony, earning him the moniker Ivan the Great.

Ivan the Terrible

At the time of Ivan the Great's death, the borders of Muscovy stretched from the Baltic region in the west to the Ural Mountains in the east and the Barents Sea in the north. The south was still the domain of hostile steppe tribes of the Golden Horde.

1282

On the southern outskirts of Moscow, Daniil founds the town's first monastery as a defensive outpost – now the Danilovsky Monastery.

1303

Having become a monk before his death, Prince Daniil is buried in the cemetery at Danilovsky Monastery.

1326

Moscow emerges as a political stronghold and religious centre. The head of the Russian episcopate departs Vladimir and moves into the Kremlin.

1328

Grand Prince Ivan I (Kalita) gains the right to collect taxes from other Russian principalities, effectively winning control of the Vladimir-Suzdal principality.

CHECK YOUR CALENDAR

For hundreds of years Russia was out of sync with the West. Until 1700 Russia dated its years from 'creation', which was determined to be approximately 5508 years before the birth of Christ. So at that time, the year 1700 was considered the year 7208 in Russia. Peter the Great – westward-looking as he was – instituted a reform to date the years from the birth of Christ, as they did in the rest of Europe.

Things got complicated again in the 18th century, when most of Europe abandoned the Julian calendar in favour of the Gregorian calendar, and Russia did not follow suit. By 1917, Russian dates were 13 days out of sync with European dates. Which explains how the October Revolution could have taken place on November 7.

Finally, the all-powerful Soviet regime made the necessary leap. The last day of January 1918 was followed by 14 February 1918. All dates since 1918 have been identical to dates in the West.

In this book we use dates corresponding to the current Gregorian calendar that is used worldwide. However, even history is not always straightforward, as other accounts may employ the calendars that were the convention at that time. Tell *that* to your history professor.

In the 16th century, however, the Golden Horde fragmented into four Khanates, which continued to raid Russian settlements. At this time, the grandson of Ivan the Great, Ivan IV (the Terrible), led the further expansion and consolidation of the upstart Muscovy state, defeating three out of four Khanates, securing control over the Volga River and opening up a vast wilderness east of the Urals. Ivan was less successful against the Crimean Tatars, who dominated the southern access routes to the Black Sea.

On the home front, the reign of Ivan IV spelt trouble for Moscow. Ivan came to the throne at age three with his mother as regent. Upon reaching adulthood, 13 years later, he was crowned 'Tsar of all the Russias'. (The Russian word 'tsar' is derived from the Latin term 'caesar'.) Ivan's marriage to Anastasia, a member of the Romanov boyar family, was a happy one, unlike the five that followed her early death.

When his beloved Anastasia died, it marked a turning point for Ivan. Believing her to have been poisoned, he started a reign of terror against the ever-intriguing and jealous boyars, earning himself the sobriquet 'the terrible'. Later, in a fit of rage, he even killed his eldest son and heir to the throne.

Ivan suffered from a fused spine and took mercury treatments to ease the intense pain. The cure, however, was worse than the ailment; it gradually made him insane.

Medieval Moscow Sights

Kremlin

Kitay Gorod

St Basil's Cathedral (Kremlin and Kitay Gorod)

1327–33

The first stone structures are built within the Kremlin walls, including three elaborate limestone churches and a bell tower, each topped with a single dome.

1360

The Kremlin is refortified and expanded. As the small village grows into an urban centre, Grand Prince Dmitry replaces the wooden walls with a limestone edifice.

1380

Grand Prince Dmitry mounts the first successful Russian challenge to Tatar authority, earning his moniker Donskoy after defeating the Tatars in the Battle of Kulikovo on the Don River.

1450s

A Russian Orthodox Church is organised, independent of the Greek Church. When Constantinople falls to heathen Turks, Moscow is said to be the 'Third Rome', the rightful heir of Christendom.

The last years of Ivan's reign proved ruinous for Moscow. In 1571 Crimean Tatars torched the city, burning most of it to the ground. Ivan's volatile temperament made matters worse by creating political instability. At one point he vacated the throne and concealed himself in a monastery.

Upon his death, power passed to his feeble-minded son, Fyodor. For a short time, Fyodor's brother-in-law and able prime minister, Boris Godunov, succeeded in restoring order to the realm. By the beginning of the 17th century, however, Boris was dead, Polish invaders occupied the Kremlin, and Russia slipped into a 'Time of Troubles'. Finally, Cossack soldiers relieved Moscow of its uninvited Polish guests and political stability was achieved with the coronation of Mikhail as tsar, inaugurating the Romanov dynasty.

IMPERIAL MOSCOW

The Spurned Capital

Peter I, known as 'Peter the Great' for his commanding frame (reaching over 2m) and equally commanding victory over the Swedes, dragged Russia kicking and screaming into modern Europe. Peter spent much of his youth in royal residences in the Moscow countryside, organising his playmates in war games. Energetic and inquisitive, he was eager to learn about the outside world. As a boy, he spent hours in Moscow's European district; as a young man, he spent months travelling in the West. In fact, he was Russia's first ruler to venture abroad. Peter briefly shared the throne with his half-brother, before taking sole possession of it in 1696.

In 1682 Peter I was installed as tsar, His half-sister, Sophia Alekseyevna, acted as regent, advising from her hiding place behind the throne. This two-seated throne – complete with hidden compartment – is on display at the Kremlin Armoury.

Peter wilfully imposed modernisation on Moscow. He ordered the boyars to shave their beards, imported European advisers and craftspeople, and rationalised state administration. He built Moscow's tallest structure, the 90m-high Sukharev Tower, and next to it founded the College of Mathematics and Navigation.

Yet Peter always despised Moscow for its scheming *boyars* and archaic traditions. In 1712 he startled the country by announcing the relocation of the capital to a swampland, recently acquired from Sweden in the Great Northern War. St Petersburg would be Russia's 'Window on the West' and everything that Moscow was not – modern, scientific and cultured. Alexander Pushkin later wrote that 'Peter I had no love for Moscow, where, with every step he took, he ran into remembrances of mutinies and executions, inveterate antiquity and the obstinate resistance of superstition and prejudice'.

1475–1495

Ivan III launches a rebuilding effort to celebrate his military successes, importing Italian artisans and masons to construct the Kremlin's thick brick walls and imposing watchtowers.

1478–80

Moscow subdues its rival principalities, and the Russian army defeats the Mongols at the Ugra River. Ivan III is crowned Ruler of all Russia, earning him the moniker 'Ivan the Great'.

1505–08

Construction within the Kremlin continues, with the erection of Ivan the Great Bell Tower, which would remain the highest structure in Moscow until the 20th century.

1508–16

Alevizov moat is built outside the eastern wall of the Kremlin. The area outside the moat – present-day Red Square – is the town's marketplace.

THE BATTLE OF MOSCOW – 1812

In 1807 Tsar Alexander I negotiated the Treaty of Tilsit. It left Napoleon emperor of the west of Europe and Alexander emperor of the east, united (in theory) against England. The alliance lasted until 1810, when Russia resumed trade with England. A furious Napoleon decided to crush the tsar with his Grand Army of 700,000 – the largest force the world had ever seen for a single military operation.

The vastly outnumbered Russian forces retreated across their own countryside throughout the summer of 1812, scorching the earth in an attempt to deny the French sustenance, and fighting some successful rearguard actions.

Napoleon set his sights on Moscow. In September, with the lack of provisions beginning to bite the French, Russian general Mikhail Kutuzov finally decided to turn and fight at Borodino (p167), 130km from Moscow. The battle was extremely bloody, but inconclusive, with the Russians withdrawing in good order. More than 100,000 soldiers lay dead at the end of a one-day battle.

Before the month was out, Napoleon entered a deserted Moscow. Defiant Muscovites burned down two-thirds of the city rather than see it occupied by the French invaders. Alexander, meanwhile, ignored Napoleon's overtures to negotiate.

With winter coming and supply lines overextended, Napoleon declared victory and retreated. His badly weakened troops stumbled westward out of the city, falling to starvation, disease, bitter cold and Russian snipers. Only one in 20 made it back to the relative safety of Poland. The tsar's army pursued Napoleon all the way to Paris, which Russian forces briefly occupied in 1814.

The spurned former capital quickly fell into decline. With the aristocratic elite and administrative staff departing for marshier digs, the population fell by more than a quarter in the first 25 years. The city suffered further from severe fires, a situation exacerbated by Peter's mandate to direct all construction materials to St Petersburg.

In the 1770s, Moscow was devastated by an outbreak of bubonic plague, which claimed more than 50,000 lives. It was decreed that the dead had to be buried outside the city limits. Vast cemeteries, including Danilovskoye and Vagankovskoye, were the result. The situation was so desperate that residents went on a riotous looting spree that was violently put down by the army. Empress Catherine II (the Great) responded to the crisis by ordering a new sanitary code to clean up the urban environment and silencing the Kremlin alarm bell that had set off the riots.

By the turn of the 19th century, Moscow had recovered from its gloom; Peter's exit had not caused a complete rupture. The city retained the title of 'First-Throned Capital' because coronations were held there.

JONATHAN SMITH / LONELY PLANET IMAGES ©

Ivan the Great Bell Tower

1524

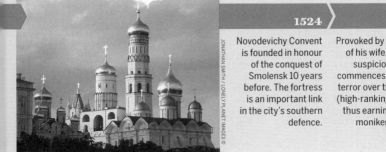

Novodevichy Convent is founded in honour of the conquest of Smolensk 10 years before. The fortress is an important link in the city's southern defence.

1560

Provoked by the death of his wife, the ever-suspicious Ivan IV commences a reign of terror over the boyars (high-ranking nobles), thus earning him the moniker 'Ivan the Terrible'.

When Peter's grandson, Peter III, relieved the nobles of obligatory state service, many returned to Moscow. Moreover, many of the merchants had never left. After the initial shock of losing the capital, their patronage and wealth became visible again throughout the city.

The late 18th century also saw the construction of the first embankments along the Moscow River, which were followed by bridges. Russia's first university and first newspaper were started in Moscow. This new intellectual and literary scene would soon give rise to a nationalist-inspired cultural movement, which would embrace those features of Russia that were distinctly different from the West.

KREMLIN

The Kremlin sat abandoned and empty from 1712 until 1773, when Catherine the Great commissioned a residence there. Construction of the palace did not move forward due to lack of funding. But several years later, architect Matvey Kazakov did build the handsome neoclassical Senate building, which stands today.

Moscow Boom Town

Moscow was feverishly rebuilt in just a few years following the Napoleonic War. Monuments were erected to commemorate Russia's hard-fought victory and Alexander's 'proudest moment'. A Triumphal Arch (p150), inspired by their former French hosts, was placed at the top of Tverskaya ul on the road to St Petersburg. The sculpture of Minin and Pozharsky (p63), who had liberated Moscow from a previous foreign foe, adorned Red Square. And the immensely grandiose Cathedral of Christ the Saviour (p111), which took almost 50 years to complete, went up along the river embankment outside the Kremlin.

The building frenzy did not stop with national memorials. In the city centre, engineers diverted the Neglinnaya River into an underground canal and created two new urban spaces: the Alexander Garden (p61), running alongside the Kremlin's western wall; and Teatralnaya pl, featuring the glittering Bolshoi Theatre and later the opulent Hotel Metropol. The rebuilt Manezh, the 180m-long imperial stables, provided a touch of neoclassical grandeur to the scene.

Meanwhile, the city's two outer defensive rings were replaced with the tree-lined Boulevard Ring and Garden Ring roads. The Garden Ring became an informal social boundary line: on the inside were the abodes and amenities of the merchants, intellectuals, civil servants and foreigners; on the outside were the factories and dosshouses of the toiling, the loitering and the destitute.

A postwar economic boom changed the city forever. The robust recovery was at first led by the big merchants, long the mainstay of the city's economy. In the 1830s, they organised the Moscow Commodity Exchange. By midcentury, industry began to overtake commerce as the city's economic driving force. Moscow became the hub of a network of railroad construction, connecting the raw materials of the east to the manufacturers of the west. With a steady supply of cotton from Central Asia, Moscow became a leader in the textile industry. By 1890, more

1571

Moscow is burned to the ground by Crimean Tatars. As the city rebuilds, a stone wall is erected around the commercial quarters outside the Kremlin.

1592

An earthen rampart is constructed around the city, punctuated by some 50 towers, marking the city limits at the location of the present-day Garden Ring.

1591–1613

Ivan IV dies with no capable heir, leaving the country in chaos. His death ushers in the so-called 'Time of Troubles', when Russia is ruled by a string of pretenders to the throne.

1601–03

Russia suffers from widespread famine, which kills as much as two-thirds of the population. Over 100,000 people are buried in mass graves around Moscow.

than 300 of the city's 660 factories were engaged in cloth production and the city was known as 'Calico Moscow'. While St Petersburg's industrial development was financed largely by foreign capital, Moscow drew upon its own resources. The Moscow Merchant Bank, founded in 1866, was the country's second-largest bank by century's end.

The affluent and self-assured business elite extended its influence over the city. The eclectic tastes of the nouveau riche were reflected in the multiform architectural styles of the mansions, salons and hotels. The business elite eventually secured direct control over the city government, removing the remnants of the old boyar aristocracy. In 1876, Sergei Tretyakov, artful entrepreneur and art patron, started a political trend when he became the first mayor who could not claim noble lineage.

The increase in economic opportunity in the city occurred simultaneously with a decline in agriculture and the emancipation of the serfs. As a result, the city's population surged, mostly driven by an influx of rural job seekers. In 1890, Moscow claimed over one million inhabitants. The population was growing so rapidly that the number increased by another 50% in less than 20 years. Moscow still ranked second to St Petersburg in population, but unlike the capital, Moscow was a thoroughly Russian city – its population was 95% ethnic Russian.

By 1900, more than 50% of the city's inhabitants were first-generation peasant migrants. They settled in the factory tenements outside the Garden Ring and south of the river in the Zamoskvorechie district. The influx of indigents overwhelmed the city's meagre social services and affordable accommodation. At the beginning of the 20th century, Moscow's teeming slums were a breeding ground for disease and discontent. The disparity of wealth among the population grew to extremes. Lacking a voice, the city's less fortunate turned an ear to the outlawed radicals.

Tolstoy's most famous novel *War and Peace* is a historical novel about five aristocratic families in the lead-up to the Napoleonic invasion. The author used letters, journals, interviews and other first-hand materials to create the realist masterpiece, which includes some 160 real-life historical characters.

RED MOSCOW

Revolutionary Moscow

The tsarist autocracy staggered into the new century. In 1904 the impressionable and irresolute Tsar Nicholas II was talked into declaring war on Japan over some forested land in the Far East. His imperial forces suffered a decisive and embarrassing defeat, touching off a nationwide wave of unrest.

Taking their cue from St Petersburg, Moscow's workers and students staged a series of demonstrations, culminating in the October 1905 general strike, forcing political concessions from a reluctant Nicholas. In

Imperial Moscow Sights

- *Cathedral of Christ the Saviour (Khamovniki)*
- *Bolshoi Theatre (Tverskoy)*
- *Triumphal Arch (Dorogomilovo)*

1610–12

The army of the Polish-Lithuanian Commonwealth occupies Moscow, until the arrival of a Cossack army, led by Dmitry Pozharsky and Kuzma Minin, which expels the Poles.

1613

The *zemsky sobor*, a sort of parliament, elects Mikhail Romanov tsar. He is rescued from his exile in Kostroma and crowned, inaugurating the Romanov dynasty.

1600s

In the first half of the 17th century, the capital's population doubles to approximately 200,000 as settlements grow up outside the ramparts.

1648

Angry peasants and townsfolk rise up in rebellion when a new tax is instituted on salt. Insurgents set fire to the city, ransack houses and execute two tsarist officials.

December the attempt by city authorities to arrest leading radicals provoked a new round of confrontation, which ended in a night of bloodshed on hastily erected barricades in the city's Presnya district.

Vladimir Ilych Ulyanov (Lenin) later called the failed 1905 Revolution the 'dress rehearsal for 1917'. He had vowed that next time Russia's rulers would not escape the revolutionary scourge. Exhausted by three years of fighting in WWI, the tsarist autocracy meekly succumbed to a mob of St Petersburg workers in February 1917. Unwilling to end the war and unable to restore order, the provisional government was itself overthrown in a bloodless palace coup, orchestrated by Lenin's Bolshevik Party.

In Moscow, regime change was not so easy, as a week of street fighting left more than 1000 dead. Radical socialism had come to power in Russia.

Red Moscow Sights

Lenin's Tomb (Kremlin and Kitay Gorod)

Moscow Metro

All-Russia Exhibition Centre (Ostankino)

Fearing a German assault, Lenin ordered that the capital return to Moscow. In March 1918, he set up shop in the Kremlin and the new Soviet government expropriated the nicer city hotels and townhouses to conduct affairs. The move unleashed a steady stream of favour-seeking sycophants on the city. The new communist-run city government authorised the redistribution of housing space, as scores of thousands of workers upgraded to the dispossessed digs of the bourgeoisie.

The revolution and ensuing civil war, however, took its toll on Moscow. Political turmoil fostered an economic crisis. In 1921 the city's factories were operating at only 10% of their prewar levels of production. Food and fuel were in short supply. Hunger and disease stalked the darkened city. The population dropped precipitously from two million in 1917 to just one million in 1920. Wearied workers returned to their villages in search of respite, while the old elite packed up its belongings and moved beyond the reach of a vengeful new regime.

Stalin's Moscow

In May 1922 Lenin suffered the first of a series of paralysing strokes that removed him from effective control of the Party and government. He died, aged 54, in January 1924. His embalmed remains were put on display in Moscow (p64), St Petersburg was renamed Leningrad in his honour, and a personality cult was built around him – all orchestrated by Josef Stalin.

The most unlikely of successors, Stalin outwitted his rivals and manoeuvred himself into the top post of the Communist Party. Ever-paranoid, Stalin later launched a reign of terror against his former party rivals, which eventually consumed nearly the entire first generation of Soviet officialdom. Hundreds of thousands of Muscovites were systematically executed and secretly interred on the ancient grounds of the old monasteries.

1654–62

Wars with Poland and Sweden spur financial crisis. The production of copper coinage causes further economic hardship, sparking a massive uprising of 10,000 people on the streets.

1682

A power struggle between two clans stirs up unrest among the Kremlin guard, which spreads to the Moscow mobs. Afterwards Sophia Alekseyevna is installed as regent for her two brothers.

1712

Peter I (the Great) surprises the country by moving the Russian capital from Moscow to St Petersburg.

1700s

Moscow falls into decline in the first half of the century, when bureaucrats and aristocrats relocate to the north. By mid-century the population has dropped to 130,000.

THE BATTLE OF MOSCOW – 1941

In the 1930s Stalin's overtures to enter into an anti-Nazi collective security agreement were rebuffed by England and France. Vowing that the Soviet Union would not be pulling their 'chestnuts out of the fire', Stalin signed a nonaggression pact with Hitler instead.

Thus, when Hitler launched Operation Barbarossa in June 1941, Stalin was caught by surprise and did not emerge from his room for three days.

The ill-prepared Red Army was no match for the Nazi war machine, which advanced on three fronts. History repeated itself with the two armies facing off at Borodino (p167). By December, the Germans were just outside Moscow, within 30km of the Kremlin. Only an early, severe winter halted the advance. A monument now marks the spot, near the entrance road to Sheremetyevo airport, where the Nazis were stopped in their tracks. Staging a brilliant counteroffensive, Soviet war hero General Zhukov staved off the attack and pushed the invaders back.

In the early 1930s, Stalin launched Soviet Russia on a hell-bent industrialisation campaign. The campaign cost millions of lives, but by 1939 only the USA and Germany had higher levels of industrial output. Moscow set the pace for this rapid development. Political prisoners became slave labourers. The building of the Moscow-Volga Canal was overseen by the secret police, who forced several hundred thousand 'class enemies' to dig the 125km-long ditch.

The brutal tactics employed by the state to collectivise the countryside created a new wave of peasant immigrants who flooded into Moscow. Around the city, work camps and bare barracks were erected to shelter the huddling hordes who shouldered Stalin's industrial revolution. At the other end, Moscow also became a centre of a heavily subsidised military industry, whose engineers and technicians enjoyed a larger slice of the proletarian pie. The party elite, meanwhile, moved into new spacious accommodation such as the Dom na Naberezhnoy (p126), on the embankment opposite the Kremlin.

Under Stalin, a comprehensive urban plan was devised for Moscow. On paper, it appeared as a neatly organised garden city; unfortunately, it was implemented with a sledgehammer. Historic cathedrals and bell towers were demolished in the middle of the night. The Kitay Gorod wall (p66) was dismantled for being 'a relic of medieval times'. Alexander's Triumphal Arch and Peter's Sukharev Tower likewise became victims of unsympathetic city planners, eager to wrench Moscow into a proletarian future.

1746

The road to Tver becomes the road to St Petersburg, or Peterburskoye shosse, connecting the two capitals.

1755

At the instigation of Mikhail Lomonosov and Minister of Education Ivan Shuvalov, Empress Elizabeth establishes Moscow State University (MGU), the first university in Russia.

JONATHAN SMITH / LONELY PLANET IMAGES ©

Statue of Mikhail Lomonosov

1756

The country's first newspaper – the *Moscow News (Moskovskiye Vedemosti)* – is published at the new university, coming out on a weekly basis.

New monuments marking the epochal transition to socialism went up in place of the old. The first line of the marble-bedecked metro was completed in 1935. The enormous Cathedral of Christ the Saviour was razed with the expectation of erecting the world's tallest building, upon which would stand an exalted 90m statute of Lenin. This scheme was later abandoned and the foundation hole instead became the world's biggest municipal swimming pool. Broad thoroughfares were created and neo-Gothic skyscrapers (p211) girded the city's outer ring.

In the 1940s, the medieval Zaryadie district in Kitay Gorod was razed to make room for a massive wedding cake–style skyscraper. The 'Eighth Sister' was never built, and the foundation eventually became the base of the gargantuan Hotel Rossiya (now demolished).

Post-Stalinist Moscow

When Stalin died, his funeral procession brought out so many gawkers that a riot ensued and scores of mourners were trampled to death. The system he built, however, lived on, with a few changes.

First, Nikita Khrushchev, a former mayor of Moscow, tried a different approach to ruling. He curbed the powers of the secret police, released political prisoners, introduced wide-ranging reforms and promised to improve living conditions. Huge housing estates grew up around the outskirts of Moscow; many of the hastily constructed low-rise projects were nicknamed *khrushchoby,* after *trushchoby* (slums). Khrushchev's populism and unpredictability made the ruling elite a bit too nervous and he was ousted in 1964.

Next came the long, stagnant reign of ageing Leonid Brezhnev. Overlooking Lenin's mausoleum, he presided over the rise of a military superpower and provided long-sought-after political stability and material security.

Many of Moscow's 'historic' sights are new buildings modelled after structures that had been destroyed in the past. Kazan Cathedral and the Cathedral of Christ the Saviour were built in the 1990s, while the Great Wooden Palace at Kolomenskoe and the Great Palace at Tsaritsyno are both 21st-century constructions.

During these years, the Cold War shaped Moscow's development as the Soviet Union enthusiastically competed with the USA in the arms and space races. The aerospace, radio-electronics and nuclear weapons ministries operated factories, research laboratories and design institutes in and around the capital. By 1980 as much as one-third of the city's industrial production and one-quarter of its labour force was connected to the defence industry. Moscow city officials were not privy to what went on in these secretly managed facilities. As a matter of national security, the KGB discreetly constructed a second subway system, Metro-2, under the city.

Still, the centrally planned economy could not keep pace with rising consumer demands. While the elite lived in privilege, ordinary Muscovites stood in line for goods. For the Communist Party, things became a bit too comfortable. Under Brezhnev the political elite grew elderly and corrupt, while the economic system slid into a slow, irreversible decline. And the goal of turning Moscow into a showcase socialist city was quietly abandoned.

1770–80

The bubonic plague breaks out in Moscow, killing as many as 50,000 people. By the end of the decade, the population of St Petersburg surpasses that of Moscow.

1810–12

Russia defies its treaty with France, provoking Napoleon and his Grand Army to invade Russia. According to some accounts, Muscovites burn down their own city in anticipation of the invasion.

1824

The Bolshoi Theatre and the Maly Theatre are built on the aptly named Theatre Square, with the inauguration of the historic venues taking place the following year.

1839–60

To celebrate the heroic victory over France in the Napoleonic Wars, the Cathedral of Christ the Saviour is built on the banks of the Moscow River.

LENIN UNDER GLASS

Red Square is home to the world's most famous mummy, that of Vladimir Ilych Lenin. When he died of a massive stroke on 22 January 1924, aged 53, a long line of mourners patiently gathered in the depths of winter for weeks to glimpse the body as it lay in state. Inspired by the spectacle, Stalin proposed that the father of Soviet communism should continue to serve the cause as a holy relic. So the decision was made to preserve Lenin's corpse for perpetuity, against the vehement protests of his widow, as well as Lenin's own expressed desire to be buried next to his mother in St Petersburg.

Boris Zbarsky, a biochemist, and Vladimir Voribov, an anatomist, were issued a political order to put a stop to the natural decomposition of the body. The pair worked frantically in a secret laboratory in search of a long-term chemical solution. In the meantime the body's dark spots were bleached, and the lips and eyes sewn tight. The brain was removed and taken to another secret laboratory, to be sliced and diced by scientists for the next 40 years in the hope of uncovering its hidden genius.

In July 1924 the scientists hit upon a formula to successfully arrest the decaying process, a closely guarded state secret. This necrotic craft was passed on to Zbarsky's son, who ran the Kremlin's covert embalming lab for decades. After the fall of communism, Zbarsky came clean: the body is wiped down every few days and then, every 18 months, thoroughly examined and submerged in a tub of chemicals, including paraffin wax. The institute has now gone commercial, offering its services and secrets to wannabe immortals for a mere million dollars.

In the early 1990s Boris Yeltsin expressed his intention to heed Lenin's request and bury him in St Petersburg, setting off a furore from the political left as well as more muted objections from Moscow tour operators. It seems that the mausoleum, the most sacred shrine of Soviet communism, and the mummy, the literal embodiment of the Russian Revolution, will remain in place for at least several more years.

Nonetheless, Moscow enjoyed a postwar economic boom. The city underwent further expansion, accommodating more and more buildings and residents. Brezhnev showed a penchant for brawny displays of modern architecture. Cavernous concrete-and-glass slabs, such as the now defunct Hotel Rossiya, were constructed to show the world the modern face of the Soviet Union. The cement pouring reached a frenzy in the build-up to the 1980 Summer Olympics. However, Russia's invasion of Afghanistan caused many nations to boycott the Games and the facilities mostly stood empty.

Appreciation for Moscow's past began to creep back into city planning. Most notably, Alexander's Triumphal Arch (p150) was reconstructed, though plans to re-erect Peter's tall Sukharev Tower were not

1861

The 'liberator tsar' Alexander II enacts the Emancipation Reform, which liberates the serfs. Moscow's population surges as thousands of peasants descend on the big city.

1862

Ivan Turgenev's novel *Fathers and Sons* kicks off the nihilist movement, an early forerunner of populism, anarchism and eventually Bolshevism.

1905

Upon institution of the new position of 'city governor', the tsar appoints Alexander Adrianov as the first Mayor of Moscow.

1905

The unpopular Russo-Japanese War provokes general strikes in Moscow and St Petersburg. In Moscow street barricades are set up, and fighting takes place in present-day Presnya.

realised. Residential life continued to move further away from the city centre, which was increasingly occupied by the governing elite. Shoddy high-rise apartments went up on the periphery and metro lines were extended outward.

The attraction for Russians to relocate to Moscow in these years was, and continues to be, very strong. City officials tried desperately to enforce the residency permit system, but to no avail. In 1960 the population topped six million, and by 1980 it surpassed eight million. The spillover led to the rapid growth of Moscow's suburbs. While industry, especially the military industry, provided the city's economic foundation, many new jobs were created in science, education and public administration. The city became a little more ethnically diverse, particularly with the arrival of petty-market traders from Central Asia and the Caucasus.

TRANSITIONAL MOSCOW

The Communist Collapse

History Museums

State History Museum (Kremlin and Kitay Gorod)

Contemporary History Museum (Tverskoy)

Gulag Museum (Tverskoy)

The Soviet leadership showed it was not immune to change when Mikhail Gorbachev came to power in March 1985 with a mandate to revitalise the ailing socialist system. Gorbachev soon launched a multifaceted program of reform under the catchphrase *'perestroika'* (restructuring). Gorbachev recognised that it would take more than bureaucratic reorganisations and stern warnings to reverse economic decline. He believed that the root of the economic crisis was society's alienation from the socialist system. Thus, he sought to break down the barrier between 'us' and 'them'.

His reforms were meant to engage the population and stimulate initiative. *Glasnost* (openness) gave new voice to both a moribund popular culture and a stifled media. Democratisation introduced multicandidate elections and new deliberative legislative bodies. Cooperatives brought the first experiments in market economics in over 50 years. Gorbachev's plan was to lead a gradual transition to reform socialism, but in practice, events ran ahead of him. Moscow set the pace.

In 1985 Gorbachev promoted Boris Yeltsin from his Urals bailiwick into the central leadership as the new head of Moscow. Yeltsin was given the assignment of cleaning up the corrupt Moscow party machine and responded by sacking hundreds of officials. His populist touch made him an instant success with Muscovites, who were often startled to encounter him riding public transport or berating a shopkeeper for not displaying his sausage. During Gorbachev's ill-advised anti-alcohol

1914–17

Russia suffers immeasurably from losses in WWI. By 1916, Russia has sustained as many as 1.6 million casualties. High prices and food shortages affect the populace on the homefront.

1917

Tsar Nicholas II succumbs to a mob of workers in St Petersburg and abdicates the throne. A provisional government is set up in an attempt to restore order.

1918

The Bolshevik Party seizes power from the ineffective provisional government. In fear of a German attack, Vladimir Ilych Ulyanov (Lenin) moves the capital back to Moscow.

1922–24

Lenin dies after a series of strokes and he is succeeded by Josef Stalin. Nearly one million mourners arrive to pay their respects while Lenin lies in state.

campaign, Yeltsin saved Moscow's largest brewery from having to close its doors.

More importantly, Yeltsin embraced the more open political atmosphere. He allowed 'informal' groups, unsanctioned by the Communist Party, to organise and express themselves in public. Soon Moscow streets, such as those in the Arbat district, were hosting demonstrations by democrats, nationalists, reds and greens. Yeltsin's renegade style alienated the entire party leadership, one by one. He was summarily dismissed by Gorbachev in 1987, though he would be heard from again.

Gorbachev's political reforms included elections to reformed local assemblies in the spring of 1990. By this time, communism had already fallen in Eastern Europe and events in the Soviet Union were becoming increasingly radical. In their first free election in 88 years, Muscovites turned out in large numbers at the polls and voted a bloc of democratic reformers into office.

The new mayor was economist Gavril Popov, and the vice-mayor was Yury Luzhkov. Popov immediately embarked on the 'decommunisation' of the city, selling off housing and state businesses and restoring prerevolutionary street names. He clashed repeatedly with the Soviet leadership over the management of city affairs. Popov soon acquired a key ally when Yeltsin made a political comeback as the elected head of the new Russian Supreme Soviet.

On 18 August 1991, the city awoke to find a column of tanks in the street and a 'Committee for the State of Emergency' claiming to be in charge. This committee was composed of leaders from the Communist Party, the KGB and the military. They had already detained Gorbachev at his Crimean dacha and issued directives to arrest Yeltsin and the Moscow city leadership.

But the ill-conceived coup quickly went awry and confusion ensued. Yeltsin, Popov and Luzhkov made it to the Russian parliament building, the so-called White House (p96), to rally opposition. Crowds gathered at the White House, persuaded some of the tank crews to switch sides and started to build barricades. Yeltsin climbed on a tank to declare the coup illegal and call for a general strike. He dared the snipers to shoot him, and when they didn't, the coup was over.

The following day, huge crowds opposed to the coup gathered in Moscow. Coup leaders lost their nerve, one committed suicide, some fell ill and the others simply got drunk. On 21 August, the tanks withdrew; the coup was foiled. Gorbachev flew back to Moscow to resume command, but his time was up as well. On 23 August, Yeltsin banned the Communist Party in Russia.

In the 1970s, Moscow's most devastating social problem was alcoholism, cited as the major factor behind the high rate of absenteeism, abuse and truancy. Alcoholism was so rampant that Gorbachev tried to limit consumption to two bottles of vodka per week per family, which was not a popular policy initiative.

JONATHAN SMITH / LONELY PLANET IMAGES ©

Lenin's Tomb

1930s

Stalin launches a campaign of modernisation and a reign of terror. Moscow becomes an industrial city, complete with impoverished workers, billowing factories and new construction.

1931

The massive Cathedral of Christ the Saviour is destroyed by dynamite to make way for the Palace of Soviets, a Lenin-topped monument to socialism.

1935

Members of the Komsomol pitch in to construct their Komsomolskaya metro station, earning them the Order of Lenin. The first line of the metro, the Sokolniki line, starts operation.

Gorbachev embarked on a last-ditch bid to save the Soviet Union with proposals for a looser union of independent states. Yeltsin, however, was steadily transferring control over everything that mattered from Soviet hands into Russian ones. On 8 December, Yeltsin and the leaders of Ukraine and Belarus, after several rounds of vodka toasts, announced that the USSR no longer existed. They proclaimed a new Commonwealth of Independent States (CIS), a vague alliance of fully independent states with no central authority. Gorbachev, a president without a country or authority, formally resigned on 25 December, the day the white, blue and red Russian flag replaced the Soviet red flag over the Kremlin.

Rebirth of Russian Politics

Buoyed by his success over Gorbachev and the coup plotters, Yeltsin (now Russia's president) was granted extraordinary powers by the parliament to find a way out of the Soviet wreckage. Yeltsin used these powers to launch radical economic reforms and rapprochement with the West. In so doing, he polarised the political elite. As Yeltsin's team of economic reformers began to dismantle the protected and subsidised command economy, the parliament finally acted in early 1992 to seize power back from the president. A stalemate ensued that lasted for a year and a half.

Historic Estates

Kolomenskoe
Tsaritsyno
Izmailovsky Park
Ostankino Palace

The executive-legislative conflict at the national level was played out in Moscow politics as well. After the Soviet fall, the democratic bloc that had brought Popov to power came apart. In Moscow a property boom began, as buildings and land with no real owners changed hands at a dizzying rate with dubious legality. Increasingly, the mayor's office was at odds with the city council, as well as the new federal government. Popov began feuding with Yeltsin, just as he had previously with Gorbachev.

In June 1992 the impulsive Popov resigned his office in a huff. Without pausing to ask him to reconsider, Vice-Mayor Yury Luzhkov readily assumed the mayor's seat. The city council passed a vote of no confidence in Luzhkov and called for new elections, but the new mayor opted simply to ignore the resolution.

Throughout 1993, the conflict between President Yeltsin and the Russian parliament intensified. Eight different constitutional drafts were put forward and rejected. In September 1993 parliament convened with plans to remove many of the president's powers. Before it could act, Yeltsin issued a decree that shut down the parliament and called for new elections.

1941

Hitler defies a German-Soviet nonaggression pact and launches an attack on Russia.

1944

The Nazi advance on Moscow is halted by a severe Russian winter, allowing the embattled Red Army to fight them back.

1953

Stalin dies and is entombed on Red Square. Nikita Khrushchev becomes first secretary. His main rival, Lavrenty Beria, is arrested, tried for treason and executed.

1956

Khrushchev makes a 'secret speech' at the Party Congress, denouncing Stalin's repressive regime and justifying his execution of Beria three years earlier.

Events turned violent. Yeltsin sent troops to blockade the White House, ordering the members to leave it by 4 October. Many did, but on 2 and 3 October, a National Salvation Front appeared, in an attempt to stir popular insurrection against the president. They clashed with the troops around the White House and tried to seize Moscow's Ostankino TV Tower (p82).

The army, which until this time had sought to remain neutral, intervened on the president's side and blasted the parliament into submission. In all, 145 people were killed and another 700 wounded – the worst such incident of bloodshed in the city since the Bolshevik takeover in 1917. Yeltsin, in conjunction with the newly subjugated parliament, put together the 1993 constitution that created a new political system organised around strong central executive power.

Throughout the 1990s Yeltsin suffered increasingly from heart disease. But come 1996, he was not prepared to step down from his 'throne'. It has been widely reported that in the time surrounding the 1996 presidential election, Russia's newly rich financiers, who backed Yeltsin's campaign, were rewarded with policy-making positions in the government and with state-owned assets in privatisation auctions. In a scene reminiscent of the medieval boyars, the power grabs of these 'oligarchs' became more brazen during Yeltsin's prolonged illness.

Economic Prosperity

In the new Russia, wealth was concentrated in Moscow. While the rest of Russia struggled to survive the collapse of the command economy, Moscow emerged quickly as an enclave of affluence and dynamism. By the mid-1990s Moscow was replete with all the things Russians had expected capitalism to bring, but which had yet to trickle down to the provinces: banks, shops, restaurants, casinos, BMWs, bright lights and nightlife.

The city provided nearly 25% of all tax revenues collected by the federal government. Commercial banks, commodity exchanges, big businesses and high-end retailers all set up headquarters in the capital. By the late 1990s, Moscow had become one of the most expensive cities in the world.

When the government defaulted on its debts and devalued the currency in 1998, it appeared that the boom had gone bust. But as the panic subsided, it became clear that it was less a crisis and more a correction for a badly overvalued rouble. In the aftermath Russian firms became more competitive and productive with the new exchange rate. Wages started to be paid again and consumption increased.

History Books

Alexander Rodchenko: The New Moscow (Margarita Tupitsyn)

The Greatest Battle (Andrew Nagorski)

Lenin's Tomb (David Remnick)

Midnight Diaries (Boris Yeltsin)

1961

Stalin is removed from the mausoleum on Red Square and buried in the Kremlin wall.

1950s

In response to the post-war housing crisis, Khrushchev oversees the construction of thousands of prefabricated high-rise apartment blocks on the outskirts of Moscow.

1958

Nearly three decades after the destruction of the Cathedral of Christ the Saviour, the massive hole in the ground becomes the world's largest swimming pool.

1964

A coup against Khrushchev brings Leonid Brezhnev to power, ushering in the so-called 'years of stagnation'.

MILLENNIUM MOSCOW

Cops in the Kremlin

In December 1999 Boris Yeltsin delivered his customary televised New Year's greeting to the nation. On this occasion the burly president shocked his fellow countryfolk yet again by announcing his resignation from office and retirement from politics. The once-combative Yeltsin had grown weary from a decade full of political adversity and physical infirmity.

Yeltsin turned over the office to his recently appointed prime minister, Vladimir Putin. As an aide to the president, Putin had impressed Yeltsin with his selfless dedication, shrewd mind and principled resolve. It was Yeltsin's plan to spring this holiday surprise on the unprepared political opposition to bolster Putin's chances in the upcoming presidential election. The plan worked. In March 2000 Putin became the second president of the Russian Federation.

Mystery surrounded the cop in the Kremlin: he was a former KGB chief, but an ally of St Petersburg's democratic mayor; well versed in European culture, but nostalgic for Soviet patriotism; diminutive in stature, but a black belt in karate.

In his first term, Putin's popular-approval ratings shot through the onion domes. He brought calm and stability to Russian politics after more than a decade of crisis and upheaval. The economy finally bottomed out and began to show positive growth. The improved economic situation led to budget surpluses for the first time since the 1980s and wages and pensions were paid in full and on time.

Putin vowed to restore the authority of the Moscow-based central state, engineering a constitutional reform to reduce the power of regional governors and launching a second war against radical Chechen separatists. His main opponent in the 2000 election, Moscow Mayor Yury Luzhkov, took note and hastily allied his political machine with Putin's new 'Unity' party.

Putin was reelected in 2004. His second term accelerated the disturbing trend toward a more authoritarian approach to politics. Former police officials were named prime minister and speaker of the parliament. Restraints on mass media, civil society and nongovernmental agencies were further tightened. Russia's big business tycoons were cowed into submission after independent-minded oil magnate Mikhail Khodorkovsky was jailed for tax evasion.

Where Russia's young tycoons failed, its senior citizens succeeded. Putin's 2005 attempt to scrap the existing system of subsidised social services was met with unexpected resistance from protesting pension-

1979–80

Russia invades Afghanistan to support its communist regime against US-backed Islamic militants.

1979–80

Relations between the superpowers deteriorate and the USA and 61 other nations boycott the Olympic Games held in Moscow.

1982–84

Brezhnev's death ushers in former KGB supremo Yury Andropov as president for 15 months until his death in 1984.

1985

Brezhnev's successor, the doddering 72-year-old Konstantin Chernenko, hardly makes an impact before dying 13 months later.

ers. Thousands filled Moscow's streets, denouncing the pension reforms and forcing Putin to back down from his plan.

As Russia emerged from the 1990s, it was no longer fearful of incurring Western wrath. Diplomatic disputes and territorial takings meant Russia's relationship with the Brits and the Yanks, in particular, had become fraught.

Terror in the Capital

Though the origins of the Russian-Chechen conflict date to the 18th century, it is only in recent times that Moscow has felt its consequences so close to home. In September 1999 mysterious explosions in the capital left more than 200 people dead. Chechen terrorists were blamed for the bombings, although the evidence was scant. Conspiracy theorists had a field day.

In 2002 Chechen rebels wired with explosives seized a popular Moscow theatre, demanding independence for Chechnya. Nearly 800 theatre employees and patrons were held hostage for three days. Russian troops responded by flooding the theatre with immobilising toxic gas, disabling hostage-takers and hostages alike and preventing the worst-case scenario. The victims' unexpectedly severe reaction to the gas and a lack of available medical facilities resulted in 120 deaths and hundreds of illnesses. The incident refuelled Russia's campaign to force the Chechens into capitulation

Chechen terrorists responded i.n kind, with smaller-scale insurgencies taking place regularly over the next several years. Between 2002 and 2005, suicide bombers in Moscow made strikes near Red Square, on the metro, in airplanes and at rock concerts, leaving hundreds of people dead and injured. One of the worst incidents in Moscow proper was in February 2004, when a bomb exploded in a metro carriage travelling between Avtozavodskaya and Paveletskaya stations, killing 39 and injuring over 100.

Other incidents served as unnerving reminders of the ongoing conflict, including a series of attacks that coincided with a horrific school siege in Beslan, which resulted in 331 deaths. A couple of days before that, in late August 2004, two planes that took off from Moscow exploded almost simultaneously in midair, killing all 90 passengers, including the suicide bombers on board. Soon after, a suicide bomber failed to enter Rizhskaya metro station, but still managed to kill 10 and injure 50 people on the street.

After that, things quieted down for a few years, but the terror was not over. Toward the end of the decade, attacks resumed in full force, occurring on an annual basis in and around the capital. In 2009, a bomb

Post-Soviet Moscow Sights

Art Muzeon (Zamoskvorechie)

White House (Presnya)

Hotel Moskva (Kremlin and Kitay Gorod)

1985

Mikhail Gorbachev is elected general secretary of the Communist Party. Intent on reform he institutes policies of *perestroika* (restructuring) and *glasnost* (openness).

1985-87

Boris Yeltsin is appointed first secretary (mayor) of Moscow, earning him a place on the Politburo. Frustrated by the slow pace of reform, Yeltsin is at odds with Gorbachev.

1991

A failed coup in August against Gorbachev seals the end of the USSR. Gorbachev resigns and Yeltsin takes charge as the first popularly elected president of the Russian Federation.

1992

The former Chairman of the Moscow City Council, Yury Luzhkov is appointed Mayor of Moscow, replacing his patron Gavril Papov.

exploded on the Nevsky Express, a high-speed train travelling between Moscow and St Petersburg. At least 26 people died.

The following year, the metro scenario repeated itself, this time with bombs detonating at Park Kultury and Lubyanka metro stations. For maximum impact, the bombs went off during rush hour, killing about 40 people and injuring over 100.

In January 2011, a bomb went off in the arrivals hall at Domodedovo International Airport, killing 37 people and injuring 180. And the list goes on. Federal officials promise retribution and city officials increase security, and the violence continues.

The Party After the Party

While Russia's transition to a market economy produced prosperity for some, it also came at enormous social cost. The formerly subsidised sectors of the economy, such as education, science and healthcare, were devastated. For many dedicated professionals, it became close to impossible to eke out a living in their chosen profession. Sadly, many of the older generation, whose hard-earned pensions were reduced to a pittance, paid the price for this transformation. Many were forced to beg and scrimp on the margins of Moscow's new marketplace.

Starting from 1999, however, Russia recorded positive economic growth. After the devaluation of the rouble, domestic producers became more competitive and more profitable. A worldwide shortage of energy resources heaped benefits on the economy. The Russian oil boom, going strong since 2000, enabled the government to run budget surpluses, pay off its foreign debt and lower tax rates.

In 2005, Yelena Baturina, property magnate and wife of Mayor Luzhkov, became Russia's first female billionaire.

Moscow, in particular, prospered. The city's congested roadways were replete with luxury vehicles. The new economy spawned a small group of 'New Russians', who were alternately derided and envied for their garish displays of wealth.

Following decades of an austere and prudish Soviet regime, Muscovites revelled in their new-found freedom. Liberation, libation, defiance and indulgence were all on open display. Those reared in a simpler time were no doubt shocked by the immodesty of the younger generation.

In 2007 Mayor Luzhkov was reappointed for his fifth term in office. Under his stewardship, the city continued to undergo a massive physical transformation, with industry emptying out of the historic centre and skyscrapers shooting up along the Moscow River. The population continued to climb, as fortune seekers arrived from the provinces and other parts of the former Soviet Union. And Moscow – political capital, economic powerhouse and cultural innovator – continued to lead the way as the most fast-dealing, free-wheeling city in Russia.

1993

In a clash of wills with the Russian parliament, Yeltsin sends in troops to deal with dissenters at Moscow's White House and Ostankino TV Tower. It is Russia's most violent political conflict since 1917.

1997

To celebrate the 850th anniversary of the founding of Moscow, the Cathedral of Christ the Saviour is rebuilt in its original location.

TIM MAKINS / LONELY PLANET IMAGES ©

Cathedral of Christ the Saviour

HEAT WAVE

It was summer 2010 and the mercury was rising. The heat wave was felt across the Northern Hemisphere, and in Moscow the problem was compounded by drought, forest fires and smog. The head of the Russian weather agency declared it was the worst heat in 1000 years.

The season started with an unusually warm spring. At the end of June, temperatures upwards of 30°C gave an indication of what was to come. Indeed, the hot weather persisted throughout the month of July, coinciding with a drought that ravaged crops across the country. On July 29, Moscow temperatures climbed to 39°C – the hottest day on record in the capital. Moscow recorded more than 14,000 deaths during the month of July – some 30% more than the same month in the previous year. Heat stroke was one culprit, and many others drowned while trying to cool off (often under the influence of alcohol).

By the end of July, the unrelenting heat was wreaking havoc in the countryside around Moscow. In three days or less, hundreds of forest fires spread across the land, giving residents a new appreciation for the expression 'spread like wildfire'. After a week of burning, the fires consumed almost 2000 sq km of land.

Smog blanketed the capital. Scientists reported levels of carbon monoxide that were nearly seven times the norm, and residents wore face masks to avoid the poison. At the peak of the crisis, the city recorded nearly 700 deaths a day, twice as many as usual.

President Medvedev issued a call to action as quoted in Simon Shuster's *Time* magazine article in August 2010: 'What's happening with the planet's climate right now needs to be a wake-up call to all of us, meaning all heads of state, all heads of social organisations, in order to take a more energetic approach to countering the global changes to the climate.'

Finally, in mid-August, the weather broke. Heavy thunderstorms brought relief from the heat and dispersed the smog. Life in the capital gradually returned to normal. But not before thousands of lives and billions of roubles were lost to the heat.

Moscow Under Medvedev

In 2008 Putin's second term as president came to an end. Some Russian lawmakers volunteered to amend the constitution so that the president could run for a third consecutive term. But Putin said that would not be in the spirit of democracy, and he stepped aside. Or did he?

Putin's hand-picked presidential successor was law professor and Deep Purple fan Dmitry Medvedev, whose nomination was ratified by 70% of voters. Although he hailed from the same St Petersburg cohort as Putin and his police pals, Medvedev worked as a lawyer before jumping into postcommunist politics. In the Russian political system, power

1998

An artificially high exchange rate and fiscal deficit bring on a financial crisis, resulting in the devaluation of the rouble and the Russian government's default on international loans.

1999

On New Year's Eve, in a move that catches everyone by surprise, Yeltsin announces his immediate resignation, entrusting the caretaker duties of president to Prime Minister Vladimir Putin.

2002

Chechen rebels wired with explosives seize a Moscow theatre, holding 800 people hostage for three days. Russian troops flood the theatre with toxic gas, resulting in hundreds of deaths.

2004

Terrorism continues to rock the capital as suicide bombers in Moscow make strikes on the metro, in airplanes and at rock concerts, leaving hundreds of people dead and injured.

LUZHKOV VERSUS SOBYANIN

Many have observed that the appointment of Sergei Sobyanin as mayor of Moscow was consistent with a more general trend in the refashioning of power and wealth since Putin came to power. Free-wheeling democracy and freebooter capitalism have given way to well-ordered oligarchy and corporate control. In this regard, a comparison of Luzhkov and Sobyanin makes for a revealing study in contrasts:

	LUZHKOV	SOBYANIN
Age (2011)	75 years	53 years
Hails From	Moscow	Siberia
Political Patron	Gavril Popov (from the democratic movement)	Vladimir Putin (from the KGB)
Political Approach	Can-do populist	Managerial technocrat
Policy Initiative	Free public transport for the elderly	Privatisation of social benefits for the elderly
Fashion Statement	Worker's cap	Executive pompadour
Wife's Occupation	Billionaire	School teacher
Urban Plan	Build, build, build!	Historical preservation
Hobby	Tennis	Hunting
Leadership Style	Brash	Brass

is concentrated in the office of the president, so people were curious to see what Medvedev would do with it. The answer – as it turned out – was 'nothing radical'.

The 2008 election did not cause a turnover in administration; rather the same dozen guys changed seats around the Kremlin table. As Vladimir Isachenkov and Lynn Berry wrote in the *Huffington Post*, 'Although Putin departed the Kremlin in 2008 due to term limits...in a sense he never left at all. He cannily used Russia's state-controlled national TV channels to remain the country's pre-eminent political figure.'

All eyes turned to the 2012 presidential election. In 2011, Putin announced that he would run for President the following year. His first and strongest endorsement came from his main man Medvedev. The former president is widely considered to be a shoo-in for his previous post, while Medvedev will likely take over as Prime Minister. As opined in a *New York Times* editorial, 'Mr Putin proved again that he is really the one in charge.'

2005

Mikhail Khodorkovsky is sentenced to nine years in jail for fraud and tax evasion. This is seen by Western critics as a pretext for the government to dismantle his company, Yukos Oil.

2008

A former chairperson of Gazprom, Dmitry Medvedev, succeeds Putin as Russia's third elected president. One of his first acts is to install his predecessor as prime minister.

2008-09

A worldwide financial crisis hits Russia hard. The economic recession is exacerbated by the falling price of oil and military entanglements with Georgia.

2009–11

Chechen terrorists continue their deadly campaign. A series of attacks claim hundreds of victims, as bombs are detonated on trains, in metro stations and at the airport.

A New Era

Since the time that mayor of Moscow became a full-time bureaucratic job, instead of an honorary aristocratic title, no one held the position longer than Yury Luzhkov. And certainly no one was more influential in shaping postcommunist Moscow than the 'mayor in the cap'. During Luzhkov's 18-year run, Moscow realised its claim of being a global centre of power and wealth. The skyline was transformed, the economy boomed and international culture thrived. In the tradition of urban political bosses, Luzhkov provided plenty of bread and circuses, bluster and cronyism.

The downfall of the Grand Patron of Moscow was a long time coming. Back in 1999, Luzhkov's rival political bloc threatened to upset Boris Yeltsin's plans to turn over power to Vladimir Putin. Although Luzhkov eventually joined forces with Putin, Moscow city still operated like an autonomous fiefdom beyond Kremlin control. As long as the mayor displayed deference to the president and things went well in the city, this arrangement worked. But in 2010 both personal relations and urban affairs became heated.

Under Medvedev, the Kremlin began to encroach on local matters that heretofore were considered to be in the mayor's domain. Luzhkov responded by airing negative opinions about the new president. The summer of 2010 offered the opportunity for Medvedev to go on the attack when Luzhkov went off on vacation while the capital was engulfed in a deadly heat wave. State-run media ran a series of exposés on corruption and incompetence in the city administration. Luzhkov rejected the suggestion that he take responsibility and resign.

In late September, making use of presidential appointment powers, Medvedev simply fired the unrepentant chieftain. Just to make sure that all knew it was personal, Medvedev's decree explained that the mayor had 'lost the trust of the president'.

In postcommunist Russia's feudal-like mosaic of big businesses and bureaucracies, the Moscow city administration is among the most coveted possessions. It is testimony to Luzhkov's impressive political skills that he was able to remain mayor for so long.

His replacement, Sergei Sobyanin, is the former head of the presidential administration under Putin. Like other prized possessions in Putin's Russia, Moscow now belongs to the Kremlin.

POPULATION

Moscow is estimated to be the world's seventh-largest city by population. The 2011 land deal will make the Russian capital the world's seventh-largest city by geographic area, too.

2010

A deadly heat wave sweeps across Russia. High temperatures are compounded by forest fires and horrific smog, all of which claims thousands of lives.

2010

The long-serving, popular mayor Yury Luzhkov is finally removed from office after running afoul of Kremlin officials. He is replaced by Sergei Sobyanin.

2011

Moscow negotiates a land deal, whereby the city acquires a huge tract of sparsely populated land, more than doubling its geographic area.

2011

Putin announces that he will run for president again in 2012. After receiving Medvedev's endorsement, he recommends his colleague as his replacement as prime minister.

Art & Architecture

The Russian capital is an endless source of amusement and amazement for the art and architecture aficionado. Moscow has great visual appeal, from the incredible Moscow Baroque and Russian Revival architecture to the world-famous collections of Russian and Impressionist art. But now the capital city is experiencing a burst of creative energy and artists and architects are experimenting with integrating old and new forms in this timeless city.

VISUAL ARTS

Art is busting out all over Moscow, with the opening of two new collections of icons, the planned expansion of the Pushkin Fine Arts Museum and the countless new contemporary art galleries that are taking over the city's former industrial spaces.

PUSHKIN

The Pushkin Fine Arts Museum is Moscow's premier venue for European art, including the fantastic collection of Impressionist and post-Impressionist paintings that hang in the Gallery of European and American Art of the 19th–20th Centuries.

Icons

Up until the 17th century, religious icons were Russia's key art form. Originally painted by monks as a spiritual exercise, icons are images intended to aid the veneration of the holy subjects they depict, and are sometimes believed able to grant luck, wishes or even miracles. They're most commonly found on the iconostasis (screen) of a church.

Traditional rules decreed that only Christ, the Virgin, angels, saints and scriptural events could be depicted by icons – all of which were supposed to be copies of a limited number of approved prototype images. Christ images include the Pantokrator (All-Ruler) and the Mandilion, the latter called 'not made by hand' because it was supposedly developed from the imprint of Christ's face on St Veronica's handkerchief. Icons were traditionally painted in tempera (inorganic pigment mixed with a binder such as egg yolk) on wood.

The beginning of a distinct Russian icon tradition came when artists in Novgorod started to draw on local folk art in their representation of people, producing sharply outlined figures with softer faces and introducing lighter colours, including pale yellows and greens. The earliest outstanding painter was Theophanes the Greek (1340–1405), or Feofan Grek in Russian. Working in Byzantium, Novgorod and Moscow, Theophanes brought a new delicacy and grace to the form. His finest works are in the Annunciation Cathedral of the Moscow Kremlin (p57).

Andrei Rublyov (1370–1430), a monk at the Trinity Monastery of St Sergius and Andronikov Monastery, was the greatest Russian icon painter. His most famous work is the dreamy *Old Testament Trinity,* in Moscow's Tretyakov Gallery (p123).

The layperson Dionysius, the leading late-15th-century icon painter, elongated his figures and refined the use of colour. Sixteenth-century icons grew smaller and more crowded, their figures more realistic and Russian-looking. In 17th-century Moscow, Simon Ushakov (1626–86) moved towards Western religious painting with the use of perspective and architectural backgrounds.

Besides the outstanding collection at the Tretyakov Gallery and the Rublyov Museum of Early Russian Culture & Art (p139), there are impressive private collections on display at the Dom Ikony on Spiridonovka (p92) and the Museum of the Russian Icon (p139), not to mention the many churches around town.

Peredvizhniki & Russian Revival

The major artistic force of the 19th century was the Peredvizhniki (Society of Wanderers) movement, which saw art as a vehicle for promoting national awareness and social change. The movement gained its name from the touring exhibitions with which it widened its audience. These artists were patronised by the brothers Pavel and Sergei Tretyakov (after whom the Tretyakov Gallery is named). The artists included Vasily Surikov (1848–1916), who painted vivid Russian historical scenes; Nikolai Ghe (1831–94), who depicted biblical and historical scenes; and Ilya Repin (1884–1930), perhaps the best loved of all Russian artists, whose works ranged from social criticism *(Barge Haulers on the Volga)* to history *(Zaporozhie Cossacks Writing a Letter to the Turkish Sultan)* to portraits. Many Peredvizhniki masterpieces are on display at the Tretyakov Gallery (p123).

Later in the century, industrialist Savva Mamontov was a significant patron of the arts, promoting a Russian revivalist movement. His Abramtsevo estate (p156) near Moscow became an artists' colony. Victor Vasnetsov (1848–1926) was a Russian-revivalist painter and architect who is famous for his historical paintings with fairy-tale subjects. In 1894, Vasnetsov designed his own house in Moscow, which is now a small museum (p78). He also designed the original building for the Tretyakov Gallery. Nikolai Rerikh (1874–1947) – known internationally as Nicholas Roerich – was an artist whose fantastical artwork is characterised by rich, bold colours, primitive style and mystical themes. His paintings are on display at the Rerikh Museum (p111) and the Museum of Oriental Art (p109).

The late-19th-century genius Mikhail Vrubel (1856–1910) was unique in form and style. He was inspired by sparkling Byzantine and Venetian mosaics. His panels on the sides of Hotel Metropol are some of his best work (see the boxed text, p70).

Avant-Garde

In the 20th century, Russian art became a mishmash of groups, styles and 'isms', as it absorbed decades of European change in a few years. It finally gave birth to its own avant-garde futurist movements.

Mikhail Larionov (1881–1964) and Natalya Goncharova (1881–1962) developed neoprimitivism, a movement based on popular arts and primitive icons. Just a few years later, Kazimir Malevich (1878–1935) announced the arrival of Suprematism. His utterly

RUSSIAN ART & ARCHITECTURE

1405

Andrei Rublyov paints the icons in the Annunciation Cathedral in the Kremlin and in the Assumption Cathedral in Vladimir, representing the peak of Moscow iconography.

1555

Churches with tent-roofs and onion domes represent a uniquely Russian architectural style, the pinnacle of which is St Basil's Cathedral on Red Square.

1757

The Imperial Academy of Art is established to support romantic and classical painting and sculpture.

1870

After boycotting the Imperial Academy of Arts, a group of rebellious art students form the Peredvizhniki (Society of Wanderers), whose work focuses on social and political issues.

1900–03

Fyodor Shekhtel fuses Russian Revival and art nouveau to create architectural masterpieces like Yaroslavsky station and Ryabushinksy Mansion (now the Gorky House).

1915–20

Kazimir Malevich publishes a treatise on Supremitism, as exemplified by his iconic painting *The Black Square*. Constructivist artists and architects explore the idea of art with a social purpose.

abstract geometrical shapes (with the black square representing the ultimate 'zero form') freed art from having to depict the material world and made it a doorway to higher realities. Another famed futurist, who managed to escape subordinate 'isms', was Vladimir Mayakovsky, who was also a poet (see p214). Works by all of these artists are on display at the New Tretyakov Gallery (p124), as well as the Moscow Museum of Modern Art (p75).

Icons

Tretyakov Gallery (Zamoskvorechie)

Museum of the Russian Icon (Taganka)

Dom Ikony on Spiridonovka (Presnya)

An admirer of Malevich, Alexander Rodchenko (1891–1956) was one of the founders of the constructivist movement. He was a graphic designer, sculptor and painter, but he is best known for his innovative photography. Rodchenko often took his photos from unexpected or unusual angles to give his viewers a new perspective on the subject. His first published photomontage was an illustration of a Mayakovsky poem, the first of many collaborations with the artist-poet. Rodchenko's influence on graphic design is immeasurable, as many of his techniques were used widely later in the 20th century.

Soviet Era Art

Futurists turned to the needs of the revolution – education, posters and banners – with enthusiasm. They had a chance to act on their theories of how art shapes society. But, at the end of the 1920s, abstract art fell out of favour and was branded 'formalist'. The Communist Party wanted 'socialist realism', or realist art that advanced the goals of the glorious socialist revolution. Images of striving workers, heroic soldiers and inspiring leaders took over from abstraction. Plenty of examples of this realism are on display at the New Tretyakov Gallery (p124). Two million sculptures of Lenin and Stalin dotted the country. Malevich ended up painting penetrating portraits and doing designs for Red Square parades; Mayakovsky committed suicide.

After Stalin, an avant-garde 'conceptualist' underground was allowed to form. Ilya Kabakov (1933–) painted, or sometimes just arranged the debris of everyday life, to show the gap between the promises and realities of Soviet existence. The 'Sotsart' style of Erik Bulatov (1933–) pointed to the devaluation of language by ironically reproducing Soviet slogans and depicting words disappearing over the horizon. It became common practice for these artists to officially work as book illustrators and graphic designers, but to do their own more abstract work in secret.

Art Museums

Museum of Private Collections (Khamovniki)

New Tretyakov Gallery (Zamoskvorechie)

Pushkin Fine Arts Museum (Khamovniki)

Rerikh Museum (Khamovniki)

Tretyakov Gallery (Zamoskvorechie)

Contemporary Art

In the immediate post-Soviet years contemporary painters of note abandoned Russia for the riches of the West. Today, with increased economic prosperity, many of the most promising young artists are choosing to stay put. There is unprecedented interest in contemporary art, as entrepreneurs are investing their new-found wealth in established and up-and-coming artists. Industrial space is being converted into art galleries such as Winzavod (p137) and Garage Centre for Contemporary Culture (p78). The former Red October chocolate factory (p126) is packed with galleries and studio space.

The best-known artists in Russia today are individuals that have been favoured by politicians in power, meaning that their work appears in public places. You might not know the name Alexander Burganov (1935–), but you will certainly recognise his sculptures, which grace the Arbat and other locales. More notorious than popular is the artist and architect Zurab Tsereteli (1934–), whose monumental buildings and statues are ubiquitous in Moscow – see p112 and p112.

Religious painter Ilya Glazunov (1930–; see p110) has been a staunch defender of the Russian Orthodox cultural tradition, while Alexander

Shilov (1943–; see p110) is famous for his insightful portraits of contemporary movers and shakers.

The most intriguing aspect of Moscow's contemporary art scene is not the established artists with their own named galleries but rather the up-and-coming creatives who are stashed at the city's art centres. Artists are now freer than they ever were in the past to depict all aspects of Russian life, with even the government pitching in to fund prestigious events such as the Moscow Biennale of Contemporary Art (p21). That said, contemporary artists and curators risk prosecution, especially if they tackle such sensitive topics as the war in Chechnya, the Russian Orthodox Church or the Russian government.

1934

Avant-garde ideas are officially out of favour with the institution of Socialist Realism. Architecture tends toward bombastic neoclassicism.

1985

The policy of *glasnost*, or openness, gradually allows for more freedom of expression by artists and architects, who begin to explore diverse styles and themes.

ARCHITECTURE

Moscow's streets are a textbook of Russian history, with churches, mansions, theatres and hotels standing as testament to the most definitive periods. Despite the tendency to demolish and rebuild (exhibited both in the past and in the present), Moscow has managed to preserve an impressive array of architectural gems.

Medieval Moscow

Moscow's oldest architecture has its roots in Kyivan Rus. The quintessential structure is the Byzantine cross-shaped church, topped with vaulted roofs and a central dome. In the 11th and 12th centuries, Russian culture moved north from Kyiv to principalities further northeast. These towns – now comprising the so-called 'Golden Ring' – copied the Kyivan architectural design, developing their own variations on the pattern. Roofs grew steeper to prevent the crush of heavy snow; windows grew narrower to keep out the cold.

In many cases, stone replaced brick as the traditional building material. For example the white stone Assumption Cathedral (p160) and Golden Gate (p162), both in Vladimir, are close copies of similar brick structures in Kyiv. In some cases, the stone facade became a tableau for a glorious kaleidoscope of carved images, such as the Cathedral of St Dmitry (p161) in Vladimir and the Church of the Intercession on the Nerl (p161) in Bogolyubovo.

Early church-citadel complexes required protection, so all of these settlements had sturdy, fortress-style walls replete with fairy-tale towers – Russia's archetypal kremlins. They are still visible in Suzdal (p163) and of course Moscow (see the boxed text, p67).

At the end of the 15th century, Ivan III imported architects from Italy to build two of the three great cathedrals in the Moscow Kremlin: Assumption Cathedral (p52) and Archangel Cathedral (p56). Nonetheless, the outsider architects looked to Kyiv for their inspiration, again copying the Byzantine design.

It was not until the late 16th century that architects found inspiration in the tent roofs and onion domes on the wooden churches in the north of Russia. Their innovation was to construct these features out of brick, which contributed to a new, uniquely Russian style of architecture. The iconic illustration is St Basil's Cathedral (p62), although there are other examples around Moscow, such as the Ivan the Great Bell Tower (p55) in the Kremlin, and the Ascension Church (p127) at Kolomenskoe.

The centrepiece of the former Red October chocolate factory is the Strelka Institute for Media, Architecture and Design (www.strelkainstitute.com), an exciting and innovative organisation that hosts all kinds of cultural events and activities for public consumption.

In the 17th century, merchants financed smaller churches bedecked with tiers of *kokoshniki* (gables), colourful tiles and brick patterning. The Church of St Nicholas in Khamovniki (p113) and the Church of the Trinity in Nikitniki (p68) are excellent examples, as are most of the churches in Suzdal. Patriarch Nikon outlawed such frippery shortly after the construction of the Church of the Nativity of the Virgin in Putinki (p76).

Imperial Moscow

Embellishments returned at the end of the 17th century with the Western-influenced Moscow baroque. This style featured ornate white detailing against red-brick walls, such as at the Epiphany Cathedral (p66) in the monastery with the same name in Kitay Gorod. Zamoskvorechie is a treasure chest of Moscow baroque churches.

In 1962, the Moscow artist union celebrated the post-Stalin thaw with an exhibit of previously banned 'unofficial' art. The cautious reformer Khrushchev was aghast by what he saw, declaring the artwork to be 'dog shit'. The artists returned to the underground.

In 1714 it all came to a halt. Peter the Great's edict banned stone construction in Moscow and everywhere else in Russia, as all the resources were needed for the new city of St Petersburg. But frequent fires and a general outcry from Moscow's wealthy elite meant that the order was rescinded in 1722.

Tsar Alexander I favoured the grandiose Russian Empire style, commissioning it almost exclusively. Moscow abounds with Empire-style buildings, since much of the city had to be rebuilt after the fire of 1812. The flamboyant decorations of earlier times were used on the huge new buildings erected to proclaim Russia's importance, such as the Triumphal Arch (p149) and the Bolshoi Theatre (p75).

The Russian revival of the end of the 19th century extended to architecture. The Cathedral of Christ the Saviour (p111) was inspired by Byzantine Russian architecture. The State History Museum (p64) and the Leningradsky vokzal (Leningrad station) were inspired by medieval Russian styles. The extraordinary Kazansky vokzal (Kazan station) embraces no fewer than seven earlier styles.

Meanwhile, Russia's take on art nouveau – Style Moderne – added wonderful curvaceous flourishes to many buildings across Moscow. Splendid examples include Yaroslavsky vokzal and the Hotel Metropol (p173).

Soviet Moscow

The revolution gave rise to young constructivist architects, who rejected superficial decoration; they designed buildings whose appearance was a direct function of their uses and materials – a new architecture for a new society. They used lots of glass and concrete in uncompromising geometric forms.

Contemporary Art

- *Red October (Zamoskvorechie)*
- *Garage Centre for Contemporary Culture (Tverskoy)*
- *Winzavod (Basmanny)*
- *Proekt-Fabrika (Basmanny)*
- *Central House of Artists (Zamoskvorechie)*

Konstantin Melnikov was probably the most famous constructivist, and his own house (p109) off ul Arbat is one of the most interesting and unusual examples of the style. The former bus depot that now houses the Garage Centre for Contemporary Culture (p78) is a more utilitarian example. In the 1930s, constructivism was denounced, as Stalin had much grander predilections.

Stalin favoured neoclassical architecture, which echoed ancient Athens ('the only culture of the past to approach the ideal', according to Anatoly Lunacharsky, the first Soviet Commissar of Education). Stalin also favoured building on a gigantic scale to underline the might of the Soviet state. Monumental classicism inspired a 400m-high design for Stalin's pet project, a Palace of Soviets, which (mercifully) never got off the ground.

STALIN'S SEVEN SISTERS

The foundations for seven large skyscrapers were laid in 1947 to mark Moscow's 800th anniversary. Stalin had decided that Moscow suffered from a 'skyscraper gap' when compared to the USA, and ordered the construction of these seven behemoths to jump-start the city's skyline.

One of the main architects, Vyacheslav Oltarzhevsky, had worked in New York during the skyscraper boom of the 1930s, and his experience proved essential. (Fortunately, he'd been released from a Gulag in time to help.)

In addition to the 'Seven Sisters' listed here, there were plans in place to build an eighth Stalinist skyscraper in Zaryadie (near Kitay Gorod). The historic district was razed in 1947 and a foundation was laid for a 32-storey tower. It did not get any further than that – for better and for worse – and the foundation was later used for the gargantuan Hotel Rossiya (demolished in 2006).

With their widely scattered locations, the towers provide a unique visual reference for Moscow. Their official name in Russia is *vysotky* (high-rise) as opposed to *neboskryob* (foreign skyscraper). They have been nicknamed variously the 'Seven Sisters', the 'wedding cakes', 'Stalin's sisters' and more.

Foreign Affairs Ministry (Map p268; Smolenskaya-Sennaya pl 32/34; M Smolenskaya)

Hilton Moscow Leningradskaya (Map p272; Kalanchevskaya ul 21/40; M Komsomolskaya) See p178.

Radisson Royal (Hotel Ukraine) (Map p278; Kutuzovsky pr 2/1; M Kievskaya) See p176.

Kotelnicheskaya apartment block (Map p271; Kotelnicheskaya nab 17/1; M Taganskaya) The Illuzion cinema (p144) is here.

Kudrinskaya apartment block (Map p264; Kudrinskaya pl 1; M Barrikadnaya) The Real McCoy (p100) and Tsentralny Restaurant House (p98) is here.

Moscow State University (Map p278; Universitetskaya pl 1; M Universitetskaya) See p150.

Transport Ministry (Map p272; ul Sadovaya-Spasskaya; M Krasnye Vorota)

Stalin's architectural excesses reached their apogee in the seven wedding-cake-style skyscrapers that adorn the Moscow skyline, also known as the 'Seven Sisters'.

In 1955 a schizophrenic decree ordered architects to avoid 'excesses'. A bland modern style was introduced, stressing function over form. The State Kremlin Palace (p49) is representative of this period. The White House (p96) was built later, but harks back to this style.

Contemporary Planning & Development

At the end of the Soviet Union, architectural energies and civic funds were initially funnelled into the restoration of decayed churches and monasteries, as well as the rebuilding of structures such as the Cathedral of Christ the Saviour and Kazan Cathedral (p65).

In more recent years Moscow has been a hotbed of development. Skyscrapers and steeples are changing the city skyline; the metro is expanding in all directions; and office buildings, luxury hotels and shopping centres are going up all over the city. Just like in times past, many of the grandest projects have come to a standstill since the 2008 economic slow-down, but many others are still moving forward.

The most visible urban development is in Moskva-City, the flashy new International Business Centre that is sprouting up along the Moscow River in Presnya. Former Mayor Luzhkov had planned to move the

Iconic Moscow Architecture

- *Epiphany Catheral (Kremlin & Kitay Gorod)*
- *St Basil's Cathedral (Kremlin & Kitay Gorod)*
- *Kazansky vokzal (Basmanny)*
- *Melnikov House (Arbat)*
- *Moscow Tower (Presnya)*

city administration to a new building in this complex, but the project has been stalled due to lack of funding and lack of will in the new administration.

Even without the mayor on board, the complex is impressive, with shiny glass-and-metal buildings on either side of the Moscow River and a cool pedestrian bridge connecting them. The **Moscow Tower** of the double-pronged City of Capitals building gained the status of tallest building in Europe at its 2009 opening. The 302m tower is a shiny structure of glass and steel, housing an entertainment complex, offices and luxury apartments. More, taller skyscrapers are in the works, so Moscow Tower will not hold the record for long.

Moskva-City is the first of many dramatic developments, some of which are still in the planning stages. On the southern outskirts of the city, the Norman Foster–designed US$4 billion Crystal Island complex will be the world's largest building – 2.5 sq km – when (if) completed. Muscovites are still waiting with great expectations to see what will become of the site of the former Hotel Rossiya in Kitay Gorod.

Endangered Architecture

The urban development taking place in Moscow is an exciting sign of the city's prosperity and possibility. It is also a source of contention among architects, historians and other critics, who claim that Moscow is losing its architectural heritage.

The nonprofit group **Moscow Architectural Preservation Society** (MAPS; www.maps-moscow.com) estimates that more than 1000 buildings have been razed since the collapse of communism, including as many as 200 buildings of historical interest. The latter are supposed to be protected by federal law, but critics claim that the laws are useless in the face of corruption and cash.

Sidelined Development Projects

Reconstruction of the Rossiya Hotel (Kremlin & Kitay Gorod)

Expansion of Pushkin Fine Arts Museum (Khamovniki)

Crystal Island (Southern Moscow)

New City Hall & Duma (Presnya)

Activists go so far as to compare former Mayor Yury Luzhkov to Stalin when it comes to development, claiming that the city has lost more buildings during the contemporary period than any time since the 1930s. That the ex-mayor's wife is a prominent developer who made millions from city contracts only adds fuel to their fire.

Preservationists are distressed about the tendency to tear down and build up, as opposed to preserve. Many buildings might look old, but they are mere replicas, such as some of the buildings along the Arbat. Or developers maintain the historic facade, but destroy the building behind it, such as the complex that houses Café Pushkin (p96) and Turandot (p98). Luzhkov's Moscow has been called 'a Disneyland of sham replicas, giant advertising hoardings and neon signs' by journalist Clementine Cecil on www.opendemocracy.net.

In 2011, there is a sense – or at least a hope – that the tide is turning. The city's artists and architects have started to explore the possibilities of recycling instead of rebuilding. Prominent projects include Winzavod, an art centre housed in a former wine factory, and the Garage Centre of Contemporary Culture, housed – you guessed it – in a former garage. Most prominently, the Red October chocolate factory – occupying a prime spot opposite the Kremlin – has been revamped into a vibrant space for art, entertainment and nightlife, with an emphasis on preserving the historic building.

When Mayor Sobyanin was appointed in 2010, he promised to halt all construction in the centre and stop all demolition of historic buildings. Preservationists lauded his efforts to clear the kiosks and billboards from the city streets. But the demolition has continued, and critics wonder if the new mayor has the power to defy the cycle of destruction and construction.

Literature & Cinema

Of Russia's rich cultural offerings, none is more widely appreciated than her traditions of literature and cinema, much of which originates in Moscow. The classics – *War and Peace* by Leo Tolstoy, *Battleship Potemkin* by Sergei Eisenstein – are masterpieces that have earned the awe and admiration of international audiences across the ages. Contemporary Russian culture may be lesser known, but the electric atmosphere in the creative capital continues to stimulate innovative and insightful literature and film.

LITERATURE

The love of literature is an integral part of Russian culture, as most Ivans and Olgas will wax rhapsodic on the Russian classics without hesitation. With the end of Soviet censorship, the literati are gradually figuring out what to do with their new-found freedom and new authors have emerged, exploring literary genres from historical fiction to science fiction.

Literary Sights

Tolstoy Estate-Museum (Khamovniki)

Bulgakov House-Museum (Presnya)

Gogol House (Arbat)

Dostoevsky House-Museum (Tverskoy)

Mayakovsky Museum (Kremlin & Kitay Gorod)

Chekhov House-Museum (Presnya)

Romanticism in the Golden Age

Among the many ways that Peter the Great and Catherine the Great Westernised and modernised Russia was through the introduction of a modern alphabet. As such, during the Petrine era, it became increasingly acceptable to use popular language in literature. This development paved the way for two centuries of Russian literary prolificacy.

Romanticism was a reaction against the strict social rules and scientific rationalisation of previous periods, exalting emotion and aesthetics. Nobody embraced Russian romanticism more than the national bard, Alexander Pushkin (1799–1837). Pushkin was born in Moscow. Here, he met his wife Natalia Goncharova. The two were wed at the Church of Grand Ascension and lived for a time on ul Arbat (p110).

Pushkin's most celebrated drama, *Boris Godunov,* takes place in medieval Muscovy. As per the title, the plot centres on the historical events leading up to the Time of Troubles and its resolution with the election of Mikhail Romanov as tsar. The epic poem *Yevgeny Onegin* is set, in part, in imperial Moscow. Pushkin savagely ridicules its foppish, aristocratic society, despite being a fairly consistent fixture of it himself.

Tolstoy is one of the most celebrated novelists, not only in Russia but in the world. The depth of his characters and the vividness of his descriptions evoke 19th-century Russia. His novels *War and Peace* and *Anna Karenina*, both of which are set in Moscow, express his scepticism with rationalism, espousing the idea that history is the sum of an infinite number of individual actions. This theme – that human beings can only cope with, but not control, the events of their lives – is consistent with his Buddhist-influenced world view.

In the course of writing these great works, Tolstoy underwent a conversion to Christianity and his later works reflect this change. His final novel, *Resurrection,* is the tale of a nobleman who seeks redemption for earlier sins.

Tolstoy spent most of his time at his estate in Yasnaya Polyana, but he also had property in Moscow (p113), and he was a regular parishioner at the Church of St Nicholas of Khamovniki (p113).

Although Fyodor Dostoevsky (1821–81) is more closely associated with St Petersburg, he was actually born in Moscow (p78). He was among the first writers to navigate the murky waters of the human subconscious, blending powerful prose with psychology, philosophy and spirituality. Dostoevsky's best-known works, such as *Crime and Punishment,* were all written (and to a large degree set) in his adopted city of St Petersburg. But bibliophiles assert that his early years in Moscow profoundly influenced his philosophical development.

Irony of Fate (1975) is a classic that is still screened on TV every New Year's Eve. After a mind-bending party in Moscow, the protagonist wakes up in St Petersburg, where his key fits into the lock of an identical building at the same address in a different town. Comedy ensues.

Amid the epic works of Pushkin, Tolstoy and Dostoevsky, an absurdist short-story writer such as Nikolai Gogol (1809–52) sometimes gets lost in the annals of Russian literature. But his troubled genius created some of Russian literature's most memorable characters, including Akaki Akakievich, tragicomic hero of *The Overcoat.*

Gogol spent most of his years living abroad, but it was his hilarious satire of life in Russia that earned him the respect of his contemporaries. *Dead Souls* is his masterpiece. This 'novel in verse' follows the scoundrel Chichikov as he attempts to buy and sell deceased serfs, or 'dead souls', in an absurd money-making scam.

After the novel's highly lauded publication in 1841, Gogol suffered from poor physical and mental health. While staying at the Gogol House (p109), in a fit of depression, he threw some of his manuscripts into the fire, including the second part of *Dead Souls,* which was not recovered in its entirety (the novel ends midsentence). The celebrated satirist died shortly thereafter and he is buried at Novodevichy Cemetery (p104).

Symbolism in the Silver Age

The late 19th century saw the rise of the symbolist movement, which emphasised individualism and creativity, and maintained that artistic endeavours were exempt from the rules that bound other parts of society. The outstanding figures of this time were the novelists Vladimir Solovyov (1853–1900), Andrei Bely (1880–1934) and Alexander Blok (1880–1921), as well as the poets Sergei Yesenin (1895–1925) and Vladimir Mayakovsky (1893–1930).

Anton Chekhov describes his style: 'All I wanted was to say honestly to people: have a look at yourselves and see how bad and dreary your lives are! The important thing is that people should realise that, for when they do, they will most certainly create another and better life for themselves.'

Although Bely lived in Moscow for a time (p110), he is remembered for his mysterious novel *Petersburg.* He was also respected for his essays and philosophical discourses, making him one of the most important writers of the symbolist movement.

Mayakovsky was a futurist playwright and poet, and he acted as the revolution's official bard. He lived near Lyubyanskaya pl, where his flat is now a museum (p70). He devoted his creative energy to social activism and propaganda on behalf of the new regime. But the romantic soul was unlucky in love and life. As is wont to happen, he became disillusioned with the Soviet Union, as reflected in his satirical plays. In one of his last letters, he wrote, 'She did devour me, lousy, snuffling dear Mother Russia, like a sow devouring her piglet'. He shot himself in 1930 and is buried at Novodevichy Cemetery. He is memorialised at Triumfalnaya pl, site of Mayakovskaya metro.

Revolutionary Literature

The immediate aftermath of 1917 saw a creative upswing in Russia. Inspired by social change, writers carried over these principles into their work, pushing revolutionary ideas and ground-breaking styles.

The trend was temporary, of course. The Bolsheviks were no connoisseurs of culture, and the new leadership did not appreciate literature unless it directly supported the goals of communism. Some writers managed to write within the system, penning some excellent poetry and plays in the 1920s; however, most found little inspiration in the prevailing climate of art 'serving the people'. Stalin announced that writers were 'engineers of the human soul' and as such had a responsibility to write in a partisan direction.

The clampdown on diverse literary styles culminated in the late 1930s with the creation of socialist realism, a literary form created to promote the needs of the state, praise industrialisation and demonise social misfits. Alexey Tolstoy (1883–1945), for example, wrote historical novels comparing Stalin to Peter the Great and recounting the glories of the Russian civil war.

Vasily Pichul's ground-breaking film *Little Vera* (1988), produced by the Gorky Film Studio, caused a sensation with its frank portrayal of a family in chaos (exhausted wife, drunken husband, rebellious daughter) and with its sexual frankness – mild by Western standards but startling to the Soviet audience.

Literature of Dissent

While Stalin's propaganda machine was churning out novels with titles such as *How the Steel Was Tempered,* the literary community was secretly writing about life under a tyranny. Many accounts of Soviet life were printed in *samizdat* (underground) publications and secretly circulated among the literary community. Now-famous novels such as Rybakov's *Children of the Arbat* were published in Russia only with the loosening of censorship under *glasnost.*

Meanwhile, the Soviet Union's most celebrated writers were silenced in their own country, while their works received international acclaim. *Dr Zhivago,* for example, was published in 1956, but it was officially printed in the Soviet Union only 30 years later.

Boris Pasternak (1890–1960) lived in a country estate on the outskirts of Moscow. *Dr Zhivago's* title character is torn between two lovers, as his life is ravaged by the revolution and the civil war. The novel was unacceptable to the Soviet regime, not because the characters were antirevolutionary but because they were apolitical, valuing their individual lives over social transformation. The novel was awarded the Nobel Prize for Literature in 1958, but Pasternak was forced to reject it.

Mikhail Bulgakov (1890–1940) was a prolific playwright and novelist who lived near Patriarch's Ponds (p95). He wrote many plays that were performed at the Moscow Art Theatre, some of which were apparently enjoyed by Stalin. But later his plays were banned, and he had difficulty finding work. Most of his novels take place in Moscow, including *Fatal Eggs, Heart of a Dog* and, most famously, *The Master and Margarita.*

The post-*glasnost* era of the 1980s and 1990s uncovered a huge library of work that had been suppressed during the Soviet period. Authors such as Yevgeny Zamyatin, Daniil Kharms, Anatoly Rybakov, Venedict Erofeev and Andrei Bitov – banned in the Soviet Union – are now recognised for their cutting-edge commentary and significant contributions to world literature.

Explore Moscow alongside Professor Woland, Bohemoth and Margarita using the interactive map at www.masterandmargarita.eu.

Written in 1970 by Venedict Erofeev, *Moscow to the End of the Line* recounts a drunken man's train trip to visit his lover and child on the outskirts of the capital. As the journey progresses, the tale becomes darker and more hallucinogenic. *Moscow Stations,* by the same author, is another bleakly funny novella recounting alcohol-induced adventures.

Contemporary Literature

Russia's contemporary literary scene is largely based in Moscow and, to some degree, abroad, as émigré writers continue to be inspired and disheartened by their motherland.

Check out what your neighbour is reading as she rides the metro: more than likely, it's a celebrity rag or a murder mystery. Action-packed thrillers and detective stories have become wildly popular in the 21st century, with Darya Dontsova, Alexandra Marinina and Boris Akunin ranking among the best-selling and most widely translated authors. *The Winter Queen,* by Akunin, is just one in the series of popular detective novels featuring the foppish Erast Fandorin as a member of the 19th-century Moscow police force. Several of these are now being made into movies.

Realist writers such Ludmilla Petrushevskaya engage readers with their moving portraits of everyday people living their everyday lives. Tatyana Tolstaya has been celebrated for her collection of short stories *On the Golden Porch.* Her lesser-known novel *The Slynx* is set in a post-nuclear-war Moscow that seems strangely similar to Moscow in the 1990s. In this dystopia, an uneducated scribe learns enough history to start his own revolution.

Besides being an accomplished writer of fiction, Tatyana Tolstaya hosts the popular TV talk show *The School for Scandal*. Her son is the founder and owner of Art Lebedev Studio in Art Lebedev Studio and Cafe in Presnya.

Meanwhile, social critics continue the Soviet literary tradition of using dark humour and fantastical storylines to provide scathing social commentary. In *Homo Zapiens,* Viktor Pelevin tells the tale of a literature student who takes a job as a copywriter for New Russian gangsters, offering a darkly comic commentary on contemporary Russia. Pelevin won the 1993 Russian 'Little Booker' Prize for short stories. *Russian Beauty,* by Viktor Erofeyev, is the tale of a wily beauty from the provinces who sleeps her way to the top of the Moscow social scene. She finds herself pregnant just about the same time she finds God. Caustically funny and overtly bawdy, this best seller in Russia has been translated into 27 languages. *Day of the Oprichnik,* by Vladimir Sorokin, describes Russia in the year 2028 as a nationalist country ruled with an iron fist that has shut itself off from the West by building a wall.

CINEMA

In the Hollywood hills they have Leo the MGM lion, and in Sparrow Hills they have the iconic socialist sculpture, 'Worker and Peasant Woman', the instantly recognisable logo of Mosfilm. Russia's largest film studio has played a defining role in the development of Soviet and Russian cinema.

Revolutionary Cinema

During the Soviet period, politics and cinema were always closely connected. The nascent film industry received a big boost from the Bolshevik Revolution, as the proletarian culture needed a different kind of canvas. Comrade Lenin recognised that motion pictures would become the new mass medium for the new mass politics. By government decree, the film studio Mosfilm was officially founded in 1923, under the leadership of Alexander Khanzhokov, the pioneer of Russian cinema.

Film buffs can see the history of Soviet cinema – as well as contemporary movie sets – at Mosfilm Studio in Sparrow Hills.

In this golden age, Soviet film earned an international reputation for its artistic experimentation and propaganda techniques. Legendary director Sergei Eisentein, a socialist true believer, popularised a series of innovations, such as fast-paced montage editing and mounted tracking cameras, to arouse emotional response from the audience that could be used to shape political views. His *Battleship Potemkin* (1925) remains one of film history's most admired and most studied silent classics. Its famous Odessa Steps sequence has been recreated in many other films, most notably Brian de Palma's *The Untouchables*. Charlie Chaplin described *Battleship Potemkin* as 'the best film in the world'.

Socialist Realism

Under Stalin, the cinematic avant-garde was kept on a tight leash. Stylistic experimentation was repressed, and Socialist Realism was promoted. There was no mistaking the preferred social values of the

MFF 2011

In 2011, the Moscow film world was talking about *Chapiteau-Show*. The film by director Sergei Loban did not take the top prize at the Moscow Film Festival, but it was awarded the jury's special prize, the Silver St George, which is the festival's second honour. The tragicomic film consists of four loosely connected stories, each a dissertation on a different kind of relationship. Love, friendship, respect and collaboration are addressed by four pairs of individuals visiting a seaside town. The individuals reappear as minor characters in the other vignettes. Just like real life, the heroes are the stars of their own story, though barely visible in others' stories. Deception and devastation are the common themes underlying the relationships, but the outsider, ie the viewer, is privy to the absurdity of their behaviour.

political regime. Characters and plot lines were simple; the future looked bright. In the typical commie kitsch ending, a collective farm peasant woman gave up her true love and rode off into the sunset, atop a new modern tractor. Stalin personally preferred private screenings of forbidden American Westerns and gangster films, but these were not for mass consumption.

Some directors were assigned 'partners' to ensure that they did not get too creative and stray into formalism. During this period, Eisenstein produced award-winning historical dramas such as *Alexander Nevsky* (1938) and *Ivan the Terrible* (1946).

When Stalin departed the scene, directors responded with more honest depictions of Soviet daily life and more creative styles. Russian productions again received international acclaim, earning top honours at all the most prestigious cinematic venues. During this period, the Academy Award for Best Foreign Language Film went to Mosfilm works multiple times, for films such as *War and Peace* (1968), *The Brothers Karamazov* (1969), *Tchaikovsky* (1971), *Dersu Ozala* (1975) and *Moscow Doesn't Believe in Tears* (1980).

However, getting past the censors at home still posed challenges. The fate of any movie was decided by the risk-averse Goskino, the vast Moscow-based bureaucracy that funded and distributed films.

Elem Klimov's comedies were thinly veiled critiques of contemporary society. They were not exactly banned, but they were not exactly promoted. The dark and rather disturbing *Adventures of a Dentist* (1965) was shown in less than 100 theatres. Klimov's war drama *Come and See* was on the shelf for eight years before it was finally released in 1985 to commemorate the 40th anniversary of the Soviet victory in WWII.

Andrei Tarkovsky earned worldwide recognition for his films, including his first feature film *Ivan's Childhood* (1962), which won in Venice, and *Andrei Rublyov* (1965), which won in Cannes. The latter film was cut several times before a truncated version was finally released in the Soviet Union in 1971.

FILM FESTIVAL

Every year in June, the Moscow International Film Festival (p21) offers a venue for directors of independent films from Russia and abroad to compete for international recognition.

Glasnost & Transition

During a 1986 congress of Soviet filmmakers held in Moscow, *glasnost* touched the USSR's movie industry. By a large vote the old and conservative directors were booted out of the leadership and renegades demanding more freedom were put in their place.

Over 250 previously banned films were released. As such, some of the most politically daring and artistically innovative works finally made it off the shelf and onto the big screen for audiences to see for the first time. By the end of the Soviet regime, Mosfilm was one of Europe's largest and most prolific film studios, with over 2500 films to its credit.

INDIE

In this age of corporate-sponsored cinema, some Russian directors are still turning out stimulating art-house films.

➡ In 2003 Moscow director Andrei Zvyagintsev came home from Venice with the Golden Lion, awarded for his moody thriller *The Return*. His follow-up film, *The Banishment,* refers to the end of paradise for a couple whose marriage is falling apart.

➡ In 2006 stage director Ivan Vyrypaev won the small Golden Lion for his cinematic debut, the tragic love story *Euphoria*.

➡ Director Valery Todorovsky had fun with the playful musical *Stilyagi* (2008), or 'Hipsters'. Taking place in 1950s Moscow, the film brilliantly uses colour (and lack thereof) to emphasise the bleakness of the era and the bright spirit of the hipster youth.

With the collapse of the Soviet Union, the film industry fell on hard times. Funding had dried up during the economic chaos of the early 1990s and audiences couldn't afford to go to the cinema anyway. Mosfilm was finally reorganised into a quasi-private concern, although it continued to receive significant state patronage.

At this low point, ironically, Mosfilm produced one of its crowning achievements – the Cannes Grand Prize and Academy Award-winning film *Burnt by the Sun* (1994), featuring the work of actor and director Nikita Mikhailkov. The story of a loyal apparatchik who becomes a victim of Stalin's purges, the film demonstrated that politics and cinema were still inextricably linked.

Contemporary Cinema

Moscow's film industry has made a remarkable comeback since the lull in the 1990s. Mosfilm is one of the largest production companies in the world, producing almost all of Russia's film, TV and video programming (see p150). Moscow is indeed the Russian Hollywood. Unfortunately, just like its American counterpart, the industry does not leave much room for artsy, independent films that are not likely to be blockbusters.

In 2010 Nikita Mikhailkov used the largest production budget ever seen in Russian cinema to make the sequel to his 1994 masterpiece. *Burnt by the Sun II* received universally negative reviews and was a box-office flop.

But there is no shortage of blockbusters. *The Turkish Gambit,* a drama set during the Russo-Turkish War, broke all post-Soviet box-office records in 2005. Another historical drama, *The State Counsellor* (2005), was based on a novel by Boris Akunin and produced by Mikhailkov.

In 2007, the super-prolific Mikhailkov directed *12,* a film based on Sidney Lumet's *12 Angry Men*. The Oscar-nominated film follows a jury deliberating over the trial of a Chechen teenager accused of murdering his father, who was an officer in the Russian army. Vladimir Putin is quoted as saying that it 'brought a tear to the eye'.

The glossy vampire thriller *Night Watch* (2004) struck box-office gold both at home and abroad, leading to an equally successful sequel, *Day Watch* (2006), and to Kazakhstan-born director Timur Bekmambetov being lured to Hollywood. The final part of the trilogy *Twilight Watch* is supposedly in the works.

Bekmambetov also directed *Irony of Fate: Continuation* (2007), a follow-up to the classic 1970s comedy. Simultaneously released on 1000 screens across the nation, the movie was poorly reviewed but widely watched. The *Lord of the Rings*-style *Wolfhound* (2007) became an instant cult classic among Russian fantasy fanatics.

Kandahar (2010) is a thrilling action-adventure flick about a Russian flight crew that escaped from the Taliban. The film used the pilot's diary to re-create this historical story.

Performing Arts

Moscow has always been known for the richness of its culture, ranging from the traditional to the progressive. Whether a Tchaikovsky opera or an Ostrovsky drama, the classical performing arts in Moscow are among the best (and cheapest) in the world. But New Russia comes with new forms of art and entertainment. This bohemian side of Moscow – be it a beatnik band or experimental theatre – provides a glimpse of Russia's future.

MUSIC

The classics never go out of style. This is certainly true for music in Moscow, where Mussorgsky, Stravinsky and especially Tchaikovsky still feature in concert halls on an almost daily basis. The atmosphere in these places is a little stuffy, but the musicianship is first rate and the compositions are timeless. Music in Moscow takes many forms, however, and these days rock, blues and jazz are also ubiquitous in the capital, while you can also hear alternative contemporary styles like funk, ska, house, hip hop, trip-hop and more.

Classical & Opera

The defining period of Russian classical music was from the 1860s to 1900. As Russian composers (and painters and writers) struggled to find a national identity, several influential schools formed, from which some of Russia's most famous composers and finest music emerged. The so-called Group of Five, which included Modest Mussorgsky (1839–81) and Nikolai Rimsky-Korsakov (1844–1908), believed that a radical departure from Europe was necessary, and they looked to *byliny* (folk music) for themes. Mussorgsky penned *Pictures at an Exhibition* and the opera *Boris Godunov;* Rimsky-Korsakov is best known for *Scheherazade.*

Pyotr Tchaikovsky (1840–93) also embraced Russian folklore and music, as well as the disciplines of Western European composers. Tchaikovsky is widely regarded as the father of Russian national composers. His output, including the magnificent *1812 Overture;* his concertos and symphonies; the ballets *Swan Lake, Sleeping Beauty* and *The Nutcracker;* and his opera *Yevgeny Onegin* are among the world's most popular classical works. They are certainly the shows that are staged most often at the Bolshoi and other theatres around Moscow.

Following in Tchaikovsky's romantic footsteps was Sergei Rachmaninov (1873–1943) and the innovative Igor Stravinsky (1882–1971). Both fled Russia after the revolution. Stravinsky's *The Rite of Spring,* which created a furore at its first performance in Paris, and *The Firebird* were influenced by Russian folk music. Sergei Prokofiev (1891–1953), who also left Soviet Russia but returned in 1934, wrote the scores for Sergei Eisenstein's films *Alexander Nevsky* and *Ivan the Terrible,* the ballet *Romeo and Juliet,* and *Peter and the Wolf,* so beloved by music teachers of young children. His work, however, was condemned for 'formalism' towards the end of his life.

Similarly, Dmitry Shostakovich (1906–75) was alternately praised and condemned by the Soviet government. He wrote brooding, bizarrely

Classical Music Venues

Tchaikovsky Concert Hall (Presnya)

Moscow Tchaikovsky Conservatory (Presnya)

Moscow International House of Music (Zamoskvorechie)

dissonant works, in addition to more accessible traditional classical music. After official condemnation by Stalin, Shostakovich's *7th Symphony* (also known as the *Leningrad Symphony*) brought him honour and international standing when it was performed by the Leningrad Philharmonic during the Siege of Leningrad. The authorities changed their minds again and banned his formalist music in 1948, then 'rehabilitated' him after Stalin's death.

Classical opera was performed regularly during the Soviet period, and continues to be popular. Nowadays, the top theatres – especially the Bolshoi – are attempting to showcase new works by contemporary composers, as well as unknown works that were censored or banned in the past.

In March 2005 the Bolshoi premiered *Rosenthal's Children,* with music by Leonid Desyatnikov and words by Vladimir Sorokin, its first new opera in 26 years; and 2007 saw the previously unknown 'second version' of Mussorgsky's *Boris Godunov.* More often, though, Moscow theatres and performance halls feature classics from the 19th and 20th centuries that Russians know and love.

Contemporary

Russian music is not all about classical composers. Ever since the 'bourgeois' Beatles filtered through in the 1960s, Russians both young and old have been keen to sign up for the pop revolution. Starved of decent equipment and the chance to record or perform to big audiences, Russian rock groups initially developed underground. All music was circulated by illegal tapes known as *magizdat,* passed from listener to listener; concerts were held in remote halls in city suburbs. By the 1970s – the Soviet hippie era – such music had developed a huge following among the disaffected, distrustful youth.

Contemporary Music Venues

Sixteen Tons (Presnya)

Chinese Pilot Szhao-Da (Kremlin & Kitay Gorod)

Rhythm Blues Cafe (Arbat)

Andrei Makarevich was the leader of Mashina Vremeni (Time Machine), now considered one of the patriarch groups of Soviet rock. Inspired by the Beatles, the band formed in 1968, playing simple guitar riffs and singable melodies. Even today, Mashina Vremeni remains popular across generations.

The god of *russky rok,* though, was Viktor Tsoy, front person of the group Kino; the band's classic album is 1988's *Gruppa Krovi* (Blood Group). Tsoy's early death in a 1990 car crash sealed his legendary status. To this day, there is a graffiti-covered wall on ul Arbat that is dedicated to Tsoy, and fans gather on the anniversary of his death (15 August) to play his music.

Many contemporary favourites on the Russian rock scene have been playing together since the early days. One of the most notable Moscow bands (originally from Vladivostok) is Mumiy Troll, led by the androgynous Ilya Lagushenko. After 25 years, the band continues to produce innovative stuff. Its latest studio album, *Redkie Zemli,* was released in 2010.

Gaining worldwide renown is Bi-2, whose members Shura and Leva have lived in Israel and Australia. Their popularity soared with the release of their namesake album in 2000. The duo is famed for their collaborations with other Russian rock stars. Several years and several records later, this 'post-punk' duo often appears at Moscow rock festivals.

Also based in Moscow, Deti Picasso is an Armenian-Russian folk-rock band whose beautiful lead singer, Gaya Arutyunyan, has a haunting voice. The unique sound blends the vocals with acoustic guitar and a string quartet, adding in the occasional Armenian chant. Also making a name for herself in the folk scene, art-rock-folk vocalist Pelageya is

MOSCOW ALBUMS

- **200km/h in the Wrong Lane** The English-language debut of the sexy, pseudo-lesbian duo tATu earned the Moscow natives the devotion of sugar-sweet pop lovers around the world.
- **Best of the Red Army Choir** The two-disc album uses classic folk songs and a few Soviet gems to show off the impressive vocals of Russia's celebrated choral group.
- **Eto bylo tak davno** (That was so long ago) The first studio recording of Moscow musicians Mashina Vremeni (Time Machine) made the legendary group the tsars of 'russky rock'.
- **Glubina** The breakout album by Armenian folk-fusion stars Deti Picasso got rave reviews from Russian and international critics.
- **Horowitz in Moscow** Both emotionally moving and musically magnificent, this live recording showcases the performance of world-renowned pianist Vladimir Horowitz when he returned to his homeland after almost 60 years away.
- **Mergers & Acquisitions** The insightful Ilya Lagushenko leads Moscow band Mumiy Troll in this album, providing sharp commentary and social criticism.
- **Moscow** The live album of heavy-metal rocker Valery Kipelov, who once fronted the group Aria, known as the 'Russian Iron Maiden'.
- **Peter & the Wolf** Each character in this children's classic is represented by a particular instrument and musical theme. Sergei Prokofiev wrote the masterpiece in 1936, after he returned to Moscow to live out his final years.

apparently Putin's favourite. The Irish-Russian duo Melnitsa fuses the two folk traditions (including the sounds of an Irish harp) with acoustic pop/rock themes.

Arkona represent the incongruous pagan metal movement – heavy metal music that incorporates Russian folklore, Slavic mythology and other pre-Christian rites. Arkona employs traditional Russian instruments and their lead singer is renowned for her death-growl singing style.

Other oddities of the Moscow music scene include the art-fusion EXIT Project; bio-organic chemists by day, musicians by night Disen Gage; and the virtual band Dvar.

The likes of techno-pop girl duo tATu and pretty-boy singer Dima Bilan (winner of 2008's Eurovision Song Contest) are the tame international faces of Russia's contemporary music scene. The former is from Moscow, host of the 2009 Eurovision Song Contest.

Meanwhile, Moscow clubs are filled with garage bands, new wave, punk, hard-rock and many Beatles cover bands.

BALLET & DANCE

Ballet in Russia evolved as an offshoot of French dance combined with Russian folk and peasant dance techniques. As a part of his efforts towards Westernisation, Peter the Great invited artists from France to perform this new form of dance. In 1738 French dance master Jean Baptiste Lande established a school of dance in St Petersburg's Winter Palace, the precursor to the famed Vaganova School of Choreography. The Bolshoi Opera & Ballet Company was founded a few years later in 1776.

But the father of Russian ballet is considered to be the French dancer and choreographer Marius Petipa (1819–1910), who acted as principal dancer and premier ballet master of the Imperial Theatre. All told he produced more than 60 full ballets, including the classics *Sleeping Beauty* and *Swan Lake*.

At the turn of the 20th century, Sergei Diaghilev's Ballets Russes took Europe by storm. The stage decor was unlike anything seen before. Painted by artists such as Alexander Benois, Mikhail Larianov, Natalia Goncharova and Leon Bakst, it suspended disbelief and shattered the audience's sense of illusion.

Bolshoi Ballet

During Soviet rule ballet enjoyed a privileged status, which allowed companies such as the Bolshoi to maintain a level of lavish production and high performance standards. In the 1960s, Yury Grigorovich emerged as a bright, new choreographer, with *Spartacus, Ivan the Terrible* and other successes.

BOLSHOI

The main stage at the Bolshoi Theatre was closed for several years for renovation, and was reopened to much acclaim in the autumn of 2011.

Grigorovich directed the company for over 30 years, but not without controversy. In the late 1980s he came to loggerheads with some of his leading dancers. Stars such as Maya Plisetskaya, Ekaterina Maximova and Vladimir Vasiliev resigned, accusing him of being 'brutal' and 'Stalinist'. With encouragement from President Yeltsin, Grigorovich finally resigned in 1995, prompting his loyal dancers to stage the Bolshoi's first-ever strike.

In the next decade, the Bolshoi would go through three different artistic directors, all of them promising, but none able to pry Grigorovich's grasp from the company. Finally, in 2004, the rising star Alexei Ratmansky was appointed artistic director. Born in 1968 in Ukraine, Ratmansky was young but accomplished. Most notably, *The Bright Stream* – which received a National Dance Award in 2003 – earned him the promotion.

Ratmansky's productions were well received, even when he stretched the traditionally narrow focus of the Bolshoi. In 2006, in honour of the 100th anniversary of Dmitry Shostakovich's birthday, the Bolshoi ballet premiered the composer's ballet *Bolt*. Prior to that, the ballet was performed exactly once – in 1931 – before it was banned for its 'most serious formalist errors'. Ratmansky earned the Golden Mask in 2007 for his staging of *Jeu de Cartes*. In 2008, he re-created the revolutionary ballet *Flames of Paris,* which was originally performed in the 1930s.

At the end of the 2008 season Ratmansky resigned. Ratmansky was succeeded by Yury Burlaka, who is known for reconstructing classical ballets. The Bolshoi administration also appointed Yury Grigorovich as staff ballet master. Burlaka was a discreet presence in the Bolshoi, but he succeeded in carrying on Ratmansky's legacy, promoting promising young dancers and directing innovative programming.

Prima ballerina Svetlana Zakharova starred in the 2009 one-act ballet *Zakharova Supergame*. The unusual piece was an on-stage video game by Italian choreographer Francesco Ventriglia.

The 2010 season opened with a ballet by French choreographer Angolin Preljocaj. Entitled *And then, 1000 Years Peace – Creation 2010,* the abstract piece was composed specially for the Bolshoi dancers. It was not your traditional ballet, as there is no storyline, but it was a cool, contemporary creation, with music by Laurent Garnier and costumes by Igor Chapurin.

In 2011, a handful of Bolshoi ballerinas also trained with the top contemporary choreographers from around the world, as a part of a collaboration with the Orange County Performing Arts Centre known as *Reflections*. The unique assemblage premiered in the US, followed by a Russian premier at the Bolshoi and a tour in London.

Burlaka's contract expired in 2011. Around the same time, the director of the company, Gennady Yanin, also resigned suddenly amid scandal, when a website full of erotic photos (featuring Yanin) became public knowledge. Without a director or an artistic director, the Bolshoi administration acted quickly: soloist Yan Godovsky was named as director, while Sergei Filin – previously director of the Stanislavsky and Nemirovich-Danchenko dance company – was appointed artistic director. The show must go on.

Other Dance Companies

The Bolshoi is Moscow's most celebrated (and therefore most political) ballet company, but other companies in the city have equally talented dancers and directors. Both the Kremlin Ballet Theatre (p72) and the Stanislavsky and Nemirovich-Danchenko Musical Theatre (p86) stage excellent performances of the Russian classics.

The New Ballet (p144), directed by Aida Chernova and Sergei Starukhin, stages a completely different kind of dance. Dubbed 'plastic ballet', it combines dance with pantomime and drama. Productions vary widely, incorporating elements such as folk tales, poetry and improvised jazz. This bizarre, playful performance art is a refreshing addition to Moscow's dance scene.

Dance Venues

Bolshoi Theatre (Tverskoy)

Stanislavsky & Nemirovich-Danchenko Musical Theatre (Tverskoy)

New Ballet (Basmanny)
Kremlin Ballet Theatre (Kremlin & Kitay Gorod)

THEATRE

Moscow's oldest theatre, the Maly Theatre, was established in 1756 upon the decree of Empress Elizabeth. But Russia's theatre really started to flourish under the patronage of drama-lover Catherine the Great, who set up the Imperial Theatre Administration and herself penned several plays. During her reign Moscow playwright Denis Fonvizin wrote *The Brigadier* (1769) and *The Minor* (1791), satirical comedies that are still performed today.

Alexander Ostrovsky (1823–86) was a prominent playwright who lived in Zamoskvorechie (see p126) and based many of his plays on the merchants and nobles who were his neighbours. As the director of the Maly Theatre, he is credited with raising the reputation of that institution as a respected drama theatre and school. Other 19th-century dramatists included Alexander Pushkin, whose drama *Boris Godunov* (1830) later was used as the libretto for the Mussorgsky opera; Nikolai Gogol, whose tragic farce *The Government Inspector* (1836) was said to be a favourite play of Nicholas I; and Ivan Turgenev, whose languid *A Month In The Country* (1849) laid the way for the most famous Russian playwright of all: Anton Chekhov (1860–1904).

Chekhov lived on the Garden Ring in Presnya (see p95), though he spent much of his time at his country estate in Melikhovo. In 1898 Konstantin Stanislavsky implemented his innovative approach of method acting and made Chekhov a success (see the boxed text, p86). Chekhov's *The Seagull, The Three Sisters, The Cherry Orchard* and *Uncle Vanya,* all of which take the angst of the provincial middle class as their theme, owed much of their success to their 'realist' productions at the Moscow Art Theatre.

Through the Soviet period, theatre remained popular, not least because it was one of the few areas of artistic life where a modicum of freedom of expression was permitted. Stalin famously said of Mikhail Bulgakov's play *White Guard* that, although it had been written by an enemy, it still deserved to be staged because of the author's outstanding talent. Bulgakov is perhaps the only person dubbed an 'enemy' by Stalin and never persecuted.

Drama Theatres

Moscow Art Theatre (Tverskoy)

Fomenko Studio Theatre (Dorogomilovo)

Taganka Theatre (Taganka)

Others were not so fortunate. The rebellious director of the Taganka Theatre, Yury Lyubimov, was sent into exile as a result of his controversial plays (see the boxed text, p145). The avant-garde actor-director Vsevolod Meyerhold suffered an even worse fate. Not only was his Moscow theatre closed down but he was imprisoned and later tortured and executed as a traitor.

Today, Moscow's theatre scene is as lively as those in London and New York. The capital hosts over 40 theatres, which continue to entertain and provoke audiences. Notable directors include Kama Gingkas, who works with the Moscow Art Theatre (p85), and Pyotr Fomenko, who heads up the Fomenko Studio Theatre (p152).

Gaining an international reputation are brothers Oleg and Vladimir Presnyakov, who cowrite and direct their plays under the joint name Presnyakov Brothers; they've been praised for their plays' natural-sounding dialogue and sardonic wit. *Terrorism,* their best-known work, has played around the world.

CIRCUS

While Western circuses grow smaller and scarcer, the Russian versions are like those from childhood stories – prancing horses with acrobats on their backs, snarling lions and tigers, heart-stopping high-wire artists and hilarious clowns. No wonder the circus remains highly popular, with around half the population attending a performance once a year.

The Russian circus has its roots in the medieval travelling minstrels *(skomorokhi),* and circus performers today still have a similar lifestyle. The Russian State Circus company, RosGosTsirk, assigns its members to a particular circus for a performance season, then rotates them around to other locations. What the members give up in stability they gain in job security. RosGosTsirk ensures them employment throughout their circus career.

Circus

Nikulin Circus on Tsvetnoy Bulvar (Tverskoy)

Bolshoi Circus on Vernadskogo (Sparrow Hills)

Many circus performers find their calling not by chance but by ancestry. It is not unusual for generations of one family to practice the same circus skill, be it tightrope walking or lion taming. As one acrobat explained quite matter of factly: 'We can't live without the circus. There are very few who leave.'

Moscow is home to several circuses, including the acclaimed Nikulin Circus on Tsvetnoy bulvar (p86). Its namesake is the beloved clown Yury Nikulin, who is described as 'the honour and conscience of the Russian circus'.

Speaking of honour and conscience, most of the major troupes have cleaned up their act with regard to the treatment of animals. In Moscow circuses, it is unlikely you will see animals treated cruelly or forced to perform degrading acts.

Survival Guide

Transport

GETTING TO MOSCOW

Most travellers arrive in Moscow by air, flying into one of the city's three airports. The vast majority of international flights go in and out of Domodedovo and Sheremetyevo International Airports, both of which are about an hour from the city centre by car or train.

All three airports are accessible by the convenient **Aeroexpress train** (☎8-800-700 3377; www.aeroexpress.ru; business/standard R550/320) from the city centre. On some airlines, you can check into your flight (and check your luggage) at the train station no later than two hours before your flight departure time.

If you have a lot of luggage and you wish to take a taxi (p227), book in advance to take advantage of the fixed rates offered by most companies (usually R1000 to R1500 to/from any airport). Driving times vary wildly depending on traffic.

Rail riders will arrive at one of the more central train stations: Kievsky or Belorussky vokzal if you're coming from Europe; Leningradsky vokzal if you're coming from St Petersburg; and Yaroslavsky or Kazansky vokzal if you're coming from the east. All of the train stations are located in the city centre, with easy access to the metro. Alternatively, most taxi companies offer a fixed rate of R300 to R500 for a train station transfer.

Domodedovo International Airport

Since 2003, **Domodedovo** (Домодедово; www.domodedovo.ru), located about 48km south of the city, has undergone extensive upgrades and has become the city's largest and most efficient international airport. The Aeroexpress train leaves Paveletsky vokzal every half-hour between 6am and midnight for the 45-minute trip to Domodedovo.

Sheremetyevo-1 & -2

The other main international airport is **Sheremetyevo-2** (Шереметьево; http://svo.aero), 30km northwest of the city centre. **Sheremetyevo-1** services flights to/from St Petersburg, the Baltic states, Belarus and northern European Russia. The two terminals are across the runways from each other, but they are connected by a free shuttle bus. The new Aeroexpress train departs from Belorussky vokzal every half-hour from 5.30am to 12.30am for the 35-minute trip to Sheremetyevo.

Vnukovo Airport

About 30km southwest of the city centre, **Vnukovo** (Внуково; www.vnukovo-airport.ru) serves most flights to/from the Caucasus, Moldova and Kaliningrad. This airport has also undergone substantial renovation and is expanding its services significantly, specifically catering to budget airlines like SkyExpress (see p228). The Aeroexpress train makes the 35-minute run from Kievsky vokzal to Vnukovo airport every hour from 6am to 11pm.

Leningradsky vokzal

Located at busy Komsomolskaya pl, **Leningrad Station** (Ленинградский вокзал; off Map p272; www.leningradskiy.info, in Russian; Komsomolskaya pl; ⓂKomsomolskaya) serves Tver, Novgorod, Pskov, St Petersburg, Vyborg, Murmansk, Estonia and Helsinki. Note that sometimes this station is referred to on timetables and tickets by its former name, Oktyabrsky.

Belorussky vokzal

At the top of Tverskaya ul, **Belarus Station** (Белорусский вокзал; Map p260; www.belorusskiy.info, in Russian; Tverskaya Zastava pl; ⓂBelorusskaya) serves trains to/from northern and central Europe, as well as suburban trains to/from the west, including Mozhaysk and Borodino.

Kievsky vokzal

Located in Dorogomilovo, **Kiev Station** (Киевский вокзал; Map p278; www.kievskiy.info, in Russian; Kievskaya pl; MKievskaya) serves Kyiv and western Ukraine, as well as points further west, such as Moldova, Slovakia, Hungary, Austria, Prague, Romania, Bulgaria, Croatia, Serbia and Greece.

Yaroslavsky vokzal

The main station for Trans-Siberian trains, **Yaroslav Station** (Ярославский вокзал; off Map p272; http://yaroslavsky.dzvr.ru, in Russian; Komsomolskaya pl; MKomsomolskaya) serves Yaroslavl, Arkhangelsk, Vorkuta, the Russian Far East, Mongolia, China, North Korea; some trains to/from Vladimir, Nizhny Novgorod, Kostroma, Vologda, Perm, the Urals, Siberia; and suburban trains to/from the northeast, including Abramtsevo and Sergiev Posad.

Kazansky vokzal

The third station at Komsomolskaya pl is **Kazan Station** (Казанский вокзал; Map p272; www.kazansky.info; Komsomolskaya pl; MKomsomolskaya), which serves trains to/from Kazan and points southeast, as well as some trains to/from Vladimir, Nizhny Novgorod, the Ural Mountains and Siberia.

GETTING AROUND

Metro

The **Moscow metro** (www.mosmetro.ru) is by far the easiest, quickest and cheapest way of getting around Moscow. Plus, many of the elegant stations are marble-faced, frescoed, gilded works of art (see the Tour of the Metro, p38). The trains are generally reliable: you will rarely wait on a platform for more than three minutes. Nonetheless, they do get packed, especially during the city's rush hour.

The 150-plus stations are marked outside by large 'M' signs. Magnetic tickets (R28) are sold at ticket booths. Queues can be long, so it's useful to buy a multiple-ride ticket (10 rides for R265 or 20 rides for R520). The ticket is actually a contactless smart card, which you must tap on the reader before going through the turnstile.

Stations have maps of the system at the entrance and signs on each platform showing the destinations. The maps are generally in Cyrillic and Latin script, although the signs are usually only in Cyrillic. The carriages also have maps inside that show the stops for that line in both Roman and Cyrillic letters.

Interchange stations are linked by underground passages, indicated by *perekhod* signs, usually blue with a stick figure running up the stairs. Be aware that when two or more lines meet, the intersecting stations often have different names.

Taxi

The safest and most reliable way to get a taxi is to order one by phone. Normally, the dispatcher will ring you back within a few minutes to provide a description and licence number of the car. Most companies will send a car within 60 minutes of your call. Offering online scheduling, some reliable taxi companies include the following:

Central Taxi Reservation Office (Центральное бюро заказов такси; ☎495-627 0000; www.6270000.ru; per 30min R400)

Detskoe Taxi (Детское такси; ☎495-765 1180; www.detskoetaxi.ru; per 10km R500) 'Children's Taxi' has smoke-free cars and car seats for your children.

SAMPLE TRAINS FROM MOSCOW TO ST PETERSBURG

NAME & NO	DEPARTURE	DURATION	FARE
2 Krasnaya Strela	11.55pm	8hr	R2600-3000
4 Ekspress	11.59pm	8hr	R2600-3000
6 Nikolaevsky Express	11.30pm	8hr	R2600-3000
54 Grand Express	11.40pm	9hr	R2700-3400
152 Sapsan	6.45am	4hr	1st-/2nd-class R5056/2612
158 Sapsan	1.30pm	4hr	1st-/2nd-class R4645/2354
162 Sapsan	4.30pm	4hr	1st-/2nd-class R5460/2870
166 Sapsan	7.45pm	4hr	1st-/2nd-class R5530/2870

Diligence Taxi Service (Дилижанс; ☎495-966 5214; www.the-taxi.ru; per 40min R500)

New Yellow Taxi (Новое жёлтое такси; ☎495-940 8888; www.nyt.ru; per km R22-30)

Taxi Bistro (☎495-961 0041; www.taxopark.ru; per 20min R300-400)

Taxi Blues (☎495-105 5115; www.taxi-blues.ru; per 20min R300)

Almost any car in Moscow could be a taxi if the price is right, so if you're stuck, get on the street and stick your arm out. Many private cars cruise around as unofficial taxis, known as 'gypsy cabs', and other drivers will often take you if they're going in roughly the same direction. Expect to pay R200 to R400 for a ride around the city centre.

Don't hesitate to wave on a car if you don't like the look of its occupants. As a general rule, it's best to avoid riding in cars that already have a passenger. Be particularly careful taking a

GOING TO ST PETERSBURG

Train

All trains to St Petersburg depart from Leningradsky vokzal. Take your pick from the standard overnight trains or the new super-fast Sapsan trains. (Sample schedules and fares are provided in the table.)

Overnight There are about 10 overnight trains travelling between Moscow and St Petersburg. Most depart between 10pm and midnight, arriving in the northern capital the following morning between 6am and 8am. On the more comfortable *firmenny* trains, a 1st-class *lyuks* ticket (two-person cabin) costs R5200 to R6000, while a 2nd-class kupe (four-person cabin) is R2000 to R3000.

Sapsan These high-speed trains travel at speeds of 200km per hour to reach their destination in four hours or less. Trains depart throughout the day. Comfortable 2nd-class seats are R2300 to R2800, while super-spacious 1st-class seats run R5000 to R5600.

Airplane

All airlines fly into Pulkovo Airport in St Petersburg. Book in advance and you can get tickets as cheap as R2200 one way, although normally prices are between R3000 and R3600.

Aeroflot (www.aeroflot.ru) Flies out of Sheremetyevo up to 10 times a day.

Rossiya Airlines (www.rossiya-airlines.com) Based in St Petersburg, this airline flies out of Domodedovo and operates about eight flights per day between the two cities.

Sky Express (www.skyexpress.ru) Russia's first no-frills budget airline flies out of Vnukovo, operating two or three daily flights to Petersburg. Sky Express is the cheapest way to go if you book far enough in advance. In-flight food, beverages, entertainment and other services incur additional costs.

Boat

There are numerous cruise boats plying the routes between Moscow and St Petersburg, many stopping at some of the Golden Ring cities on the way. Boat operators and agencies include the following:

Infoflot (www.infoflot.com, in Russian) Cruises range from seven to 12 days, some stopping in Yaroslavl, Uglich, Valaam and other towns.

Mosturflot (www.mosturflot.ru, in Russian) Ships cruise between the two cities in seven days.

Orthodox Cruise Company (www.cruise.ru) Catering to foreigners, the good ship *Anton Chekhov* spends 10 days cruising between the cities, stopping in Uglich, Yaroslavl, Goritsy, Kizhi and Mandroga.

Rechturflot (www.rtflot.ru, in Russian) Offers a 12-day round-trip option.

Vodohod (www.bestrussiancruises.com) Cruises ranging from 10 to 13 days make stops in Uglich, Kostroma, Yaroslavl, Goritsy, Kizhi, Mandroga and Svirstroy along the way.

CLIMATE CHANGE & TRAVEL

Every form of transport that relies on carbon-based fuel generates CO_2, the main cause of human-induced climate change. Modern travel is dependent on aeroplanes, which might use less fuel per kilometre per person than most cars but travel much greater distances. The altitude at which aircraft emit gases (including CO_2) and particles also contributes to their climate change impact. Many websites offer 'carbon calculators' that allow people to estimate the carbon emissions generated by their journey and, for those who wish to do so, to offset the impact of the greenhouse gases emitted with contributions to portfolios of climate-friendly initiatives throughout the world. Lonely Planet offsets the carbon footprint of all staff and author travel.

taxi that is waiting outside a nightclub or bar.

Bus

Buses, trolleybuses and trams might be necessary for reaching some sights away from the city centre (as indicated in the relevant reviews). They can also be useful for a few crosstown or radial routes that the metro misses. Tickets (R28) are usually sold on the vehicle by a conductor or by the driver.

Boat

For new perspectives on Moscow's neighbourhoods, fine views of the Kremlin, or just good old-fashioned transport, a boat ride on the Moscow River is one of the city's highlights. The main route runs between the boat landings at Kievsky vokzal (Map p278) and Novospassky most (Map p271), 1km west of Proletarskaya metro (near the Novospassky Monastery). There are six intermediate stops: Vorobyovy Gory landing (Map p278), at the foot of Sparrow Hills; Frunzenskaya, towards the southern end of Frunzenskaya nab; Gorky Park (Map p276); Krymsky most (Map p276); Bolshoy Kamenny most (Map p276), opposite the Kremlin; and Ustinsky most (Map p276), near Red Square.

The boats are operated by the **Capital Shipping Company** (Столичная Судоходная Компания; ☎495-225 6070; www.cck-ship.ru, in Russian) and run from May to September (adult/child R400/150, 1½ hours, every 20 minutes). Alternatively, you can buy a ticket for the full day (adult/child R800/200), which allows you to get on and off at will.

Car & Motorcycle

There's little reason for travellers to rent a car for getting around Moscow, as public transport is quite adequate. However, you might want to consider car rental for trips out of the city. Be aware that driving in Russia is truly an unfiltered Russian experience. Poor roads, maddeningly inadequate signposting, low-quality petrol and keen highway patrollers can lead to frustration and dismay.

Driving

To drive in Russia, you must be at least 18 years old and have a full driving licence. In addition, you may be asked to present an International Driving Permit with a Russian translation of your licence, or a certified Russian translation of your full licence (you can certify translations at a Russian embassy or consulate).

For your own vehicle, you will also need registration papers and proof of insurance. Be sure your insurance covers you in Russia. Finally, a customs declaration, promising that you will take your vehicle with you when you leave, is also required.

As of 2008, the maximum legal blood-alcohol content is 0.03%. Prior to this change it was practically illegal to drive after consuming *any* alcohol at all, and this rule was strictly enforced. In any case, it is not advisable to drink and drive in Russia, even a small amount.

Officers of the Road Patrol Service *(Dorozhno-Patrulnaya Sluzhba)*, better known as DPS, skulk about on the roadsides all around Moscow waiting for miscreant drivers. They are authorised to stop you (by pointing their striped stick at you and waving you towards the side) and to issue on-the-spot fines. The DPS also hosts the occasional speed trap. If you are required to pay a fine, pay in roubles only and make sure you get a receipt.

Moscow has no shortage of petrol stations that sell all grades of petrol. Most are open 24 hours and can be found on the major roads in and out of town.

Hire

While driving around Moscow is an unnecessary hassle, renting a car may be a reasonable option for trips out of the city. Be aware that some firms won't let you take their cars out of the Moscow Oblast (Moscow Region).

The major international rental firms have outlets in Moscow (at either Sheremetyevo or Domodedovo airport, as well as in the city centre). Prices start at R1700 per day, although you may be able to cut this price by reserving in advance. The major car-rental agencies will usually pick up or drop off the car at your hotel for an extra fee.

Avis (off Map p272; ☎495-578 8425; www.avis.com; Komsomolskaya pl 3; ⏰10am-8pm; Ⓜ Komsomolskaya) Located at Leningradsky vokzal.

Europcar (☎495-926 6373; www.europcar.ru; 4-y Dobryninsky per 8; ⏰10am-7pm; Ⓜ Oktyabrskaya) Cars prohibited from leaving Moscow Oblast. From Oktyabrskaya metro station, walk two blocks south on Mytnaya ul and turn left on 4-y Dobryninsky per.

Hertz (Map p260; ☎495-232 0889; www.hertz.ru, in Russian; 1-ya Brestskaya ul 34; ⏰9am-9pm; Ⓜ Belorusskaya)

Thrifty (☎495-788 6888; www.thrifty.ru) Outer North (Leningradskoe sh 65, Bldg 3; ⏰9am-9pm; Ⓜ Rechnoy Vokzal); Outer South (ul Obrucheva 27, Bldg 1; ⏰8am-8pm; Ⓜ Kaluzhskaya) Mileage limited to 200km per day. The outer north branch is about 1km north of Rechnoy Vokzal metro station. To reach the outer south branch walk one block west on ul Obrucheva from Kaluzhskaya metro station and turn right on Starokaluzhskoe sh.

Bicycle

There are more and more bicycles on the streets and sidewalks of Moscow. Cycling in the centre of Moscow is still a dangerous prospect, as the streets are overcrowded with fast-moving cars, whose drivers probably do not expect bikes on the road. That said, there are a few parks and other off-road areas that are suitable for pleasure riding, including Gorky Park, Vorobyovy Gory Nature Preserve, Ostankino Park and the All-Russia Exhibition Centre.

Bicycles are not allowed on the metro (with the exception of folding bikes). They are permitted on long-distance trains, but you must buy a special ticket to bring your bike on the *elektrichka* (suburban commuter train). Bicycles are allowed on intercity passenger trains as long as your total luggage does not exceed the weight limit (36kg). You should disassemble and package the bike to ensure that you will be able to find space to store it.

The **Russian Cycle Touring Club** (www.rctc.ru) organises weekend rides around Moscow and longer-distance bicycle tours around Russia, including a popular tour of the Golden Ring.

Hire

Bike rental is still a new concept in Moscow, although there are a few hire outfits near parks that have off-road cycling. Another great option is **Oliver Bikes** (Map p121; ☎926-803 0606; www.bikerentalmoscow.com; Pyatnitskaya ul 3/4; per hour/day R200/600; ⏰10am-10pm; Ⓜ Novokuznetskaya), which offers folding bikes, road bikes, mountain bikes and – yes – tandem bikes! Also organises occasional free tours.

RUSSIAN STREET NAMES

We use the Russian names of all streets and squares in this book to help you when deciphering Cyrillic signs and asking locals the way. The following abbreviations are used in the text and on the maps:

bul (*bulvar;* бульвар) – boulevard

nab (*naberezhnaya;* набережная) – embankment

per (*pereulok;* переулок) – lane or side street

pl (*ploshchad;* площадь) – square

pr (*prospekt;* проспект) – avenue

ul (*ulitsa;* улица) – street

sh (*shosse;* шоссе) – highway

TOURS

When on an organised tour, tipping your guide – generally R200 to R500 – is an accepted practice. Small gifts, such as a box of chocolates, a CD or a souvenir from home are also appropriate and appreciated.

Walking Tours

Capital Tours (Map p262; ☎495-232 2442; www.capitaltours.ru; Gostiny Dvor, ul Ilinka 4; Ⓜ Kitay-Gorod) This spin-off of Patriarshy Dom offers a daily Kremlin tour (adult/child R1550/775, 2pm Fri-Wed). Also on offer: Metro tour (adult/child 700/500, 11am Sat and Sun); walking tour of Lubyanka and the Gulag Museum (adult/child R1000/800, 2pm Thu); Kolomenskoe tour (adult/child R1000/800, 10.30am Thu). Tours depart from the tour office in Gostiny Dvor.

Moscow Mania (☎903-234 9540; www.mosmania.com) Young and enthusiastic history scholars have organised more than 50 walking routes around Moscow, covering the top sights and many lesser-known destinations.

Patriarshy Dom Tours (Map p264; ☎495-795 0927; http://russiatravel-pdtours.netfirms.com; Vspolny per 6, Moscow school No 1239; ⓜBarrikadnaya) Provides unique English-language tours on just about any specialised subject; some provide access to otherwise closed museums. Day tours within Moscow range from R500 to R1000 per person, while trips out of the city are usually more expensive. Look for the monthly schedule at Western hotels and restaurants or online.

Boat Tours

Both boat-tour companies follow the same route, from Kievsky vokzal or Hotel Ukraine in Dorogomilovo to Novospassky Monastery in Taganka. Highlights of the trip are Novodevichy Convent, MGU, Gorky Park, the Cathedral of Christ the Saviour and the Kremlin.

Capital Shipping Co (Столичная Судоходная Компания; ☎495-225 6070; www.cck-ship.ru, in Russian; adult/child R400/150; ⓜKievskaya) Ferries ply the Moscow River from May to September (every 20 minutes). Traditionally, this was simply a way to get from point-A to point-B, but visitors to Moscow realised that riding the entire route (1½ hours) was a great way to see the city. Alternatively, you can buy a ticket for the full day (adult/child R800/200), which allows you to get on and off at will. CCK also offers boat excursions out of central Moscow, such as to the Nikolo-Ugreshsky Monastery in the eastern suburb of Dzerzhinsky.

Radisson River Cruises (Map p278; www.radisson-cruise.ru; adult/children R800/600; ⓜKievskaya) The Radisson operates big river boats that cart 140 people up and down the Moscow River from the dock near the former Hotel Ukraine. In summer, ferries depart twice a day from Monday to Thursday and five times on Saturday and Sunday. Boats are enclosed (and equipped with ice cutters), so the cruises run year-round, albeit less frequently in winter.

Bus Tours

Besides the walking tours, **Capital Tours** (Map p262; ☎495-232 2442; www.capitaltours.ru; Gostiny Dvor, ul Ilinka 4; ⓜKitay-Gorod) also operates a hop-on-hop-off bus service (adult/child R1000/500, 10.30am, 1.30pm & 3.30pm) that departs from the Bolshoi, with 13 stops around the city.

Directory A–Z

Business Hours

Government offices Open at 9am or 10am and close at 5pm or 6pm on weekdays.

Banks and other services Hours vary. Large branches in busy commercial areas are usually open from 9am to 6pm weekdays, with shorter hours on Saturday; smaller bank branches have shorter hours, and will often close for a one-hour break *(pereriv)* in the middle of the day.

Shops Most are open daily, often from 10am to 8pm or 9pm. Smaller shops might close on Sunday. Department stores and food shops are usually open from 8am to 8pm daily. These days, many larger food shops stay open *kruglosutochno* (around the clock).

Restaurants Typically open from noon to midnight, although – again – it is not unusual for them to stay open for 24 hours a day. Bars may stay open until 2am, while some restaurants, bars and clubs are open until 5am or 6am on weekends.

Museums Opening hours change often, as do their weekly days off. Recently, many museums have instituted evening hours one day a week, usually until 8pm or 9pm. Most museums shut their entrance doors 30 minutes or an hour before closing time. Many also close for a 'sanitary day' during the last week of every month.

Customs Regulations

Even though searches beyond the perfunctory are quite rare, clearing customs can be a lengthy process (though usually not when departing through Moscow). Apart from the usual restrictions, bringing in and out large amounts of cash is limited, although the amount at which you have to go through the red channel changes frequently. Currently, visitors are allowed to bring in and take out under US$3000 (or its equivalent) in currency, and goods of a value under R65,000, weighing less than 50kg, without making a customs declaration.

As long as you don't exceed this limit, the only time

PRACTICALITIES

TV

TV channels include Channel 1 (Pervy Kanal; www.1tv.ru); NTV (www.ntv.ru); Rossiya (www.rutv.ru); Kultura; Sport; RenTV (www.ren-tv.com); and Russia Today (http://rt.com), an English-language satellite channel.

Radio

Radio is broken into three bands: AM, UKV (66MHz to 77MHz) and FM (100MHz to 107MHz). A Western-made FM radio usually won't go lower than 85MHz.

Weights & Measurements

Russia uses the metric system. Menus often list food and drink servings in grams: a teacup is about 200g, a shot-glass 50g. The unit for items sold by the piece, such as eggs, is *shtuka* ('thing' or 'piece') or *sht*.

Smoking

Smoking is widespread. Nowadays, most hotels have nonsmoking rooms and many restaurants offer a non-smoking area, though the latter may or may not be protected from second-hand smoke. Most clubs and bars do not restrict smoking.

it's worth filling in a customs declaration form is if you're bringing into the country any major equipment, antique, art work or musical instrument (including a guitar) that you plan to take out with you. Get your declaration stamped in the red channel of customs to avoid any problems on leaving Russia with the same goods.

For information on restrictions and requirements for taking art and antiques out of the country, see p36.

Embassies

It's wise to register with your embassy, especially if you'll be in Russia for a long stay.

Australia (Map p272; ☎495-956 6070; www.russia.embassy.gov.au; Podkolokolny per 10A/2; Ⓜ Kitay-Gorod)

Belarus (Map p272; ☎495-777 6644; www.embassybel.ru, in Russian; ul Maroseyka 17/6; Ⓜ Kitay-Gorod)

Canada (Map p270; ☎495-925 6000; http://russia.gc.ca; Starokonyushenny per 23; Ⓜ Kropotkinskaya)

China (Map p278; ☎499-783 0867, consular 499-143 1540; http://ru.china-embassy.org, in Russian; ul Druzhby 6; Ⓜ Universitet)

France (Map p276; ☎495-937 1500; www.ambafrance-ru.org; ul Bolshaya Yakimanka 45; Ⓜ Oktyabrskaya)

Germany (Map p278; ☎495-937 9500; www.moskau.diplo.de; Mosfilmovskaya ul 56; Ⓜ Universitet) Take bus 119 or trolleybus 34 from Universitet or Kievskaya metro station.

Ireland (Map p260; ☎495-937 5911; www.embassyofireland.ru; Grokholsky per 5; Ⓜ Prospekt Mira)

Mongolia (Map p268; ☎495-690 6792; Borisoglebsky per 11; Ⓜ Arbartskaya); consular section (Map p268; Spasopeskovsky per 7/1; Ⓜ Smolenskaya)

Netherlands (Map p268; ☎495-797 2900; www.netherlands-embassy.ru; Kalashny per 6; Ⓜ Arbatskaya)

UK (Map p268; ☎495-956 7200; www.greatbritain.ru; Smolenskaya nab 10; Ⓜ Smolenskaya)

Ukraine (Map p260; ☎495-629 9742; www.mfa.gov.ua/russia; Leontevsky per 18; Ⓜ Pushkinskaya)

USA (Map p264; ☎495-728 5000; http://moscow.usembassy.gov; Bol Devyatinsky per 8; Ⓜ Barrikadnaya)

Emergency

Ambulance ☎03

Fire ☎01

Police ☎02

Russia is in the process of implementing a new **Universal Emergency Number** (☎112), which is supposed to be functional in 2012.

Electricity

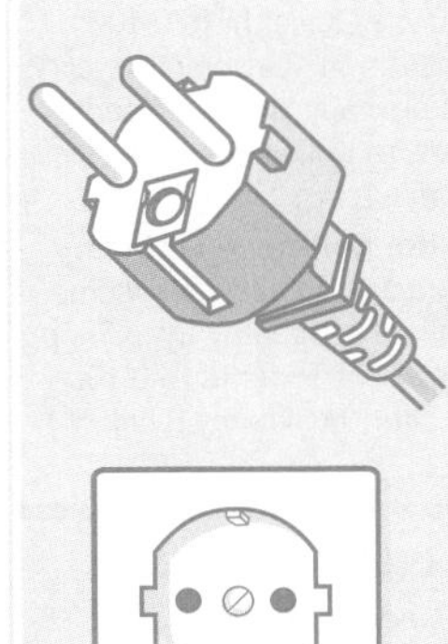

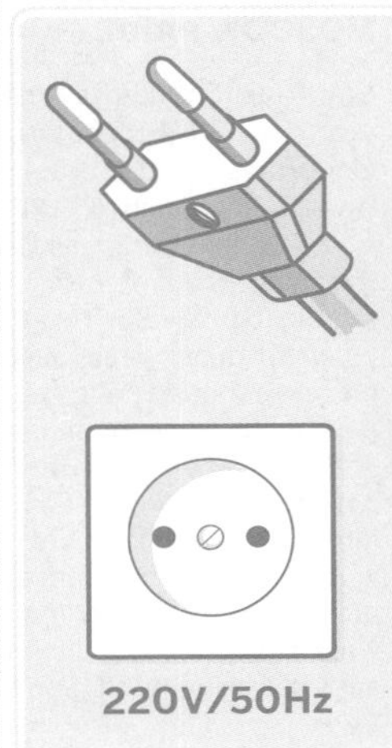

Gay & Lesbian Travellers

Moscow is the most cosmopolitan of Russian cities, and the active gay and lesbian scene reflects this attitude. Newspapers such as the *Moscow Times* feature articles about gay and lesbian issues, as well as listings of gay and lesbian clubs. Some other useful resources:

www.gay.ru/english Includes updated club listings, plus information on gay history and culture in Russia.

www.gayrussia.ru An advocacy group also involved with the organisation of Gay Pride.

www.gaytours.ru Dmitry is a gay-friendly face in Moscow and his site is still a wealth of information about gay life in the city.

www.lesbi.ru An active site for lesbian issues; in Russian only.

For details on gay and lesbian venues, see the list on p30.

MOSCOW PRIDE

Gay Pride Parades have been held in Moscow every year since 2006, despite bureaucratic obstacles, popular protests and sporadic violence. **Moscow Pride** (www.moscowpride.ru, in Russian) takes place in May.

In 2010 the European Court of Human Rights fined the government of Russia for human rights violations related to previous Pride Parades. Nonetheless, in 2011 officials refused yet again to grant the right to assemble (even though antigay protesters were able to obtain permits for their counter-rally on the same day).

The event went forward as planned, even without permits. After only a few minutes, the parade was interrupted by a group of religious protestors, some of whom wore T-shirts that said 'God is with us' as they attacked the peaceful marchers. A few dozen people were arrested, including three high-profile gay-rights activists from the US and France.

Internet Access

Almost all hotels and hostels offer wi-fi, as do many bars, restaurants and cafes. It isn't always free, but it is ubiquitous. Look for the 📶 icon in the listings for hotels, restaurants, bars and cafes that offer wireless access. If you are not travelling with your own computer, there are plenty of internet cafes around the city, offering excellent, fast and generally affordable internet access. You can also look for the internet icon @ in this book's listings for general internet access in hotels.

Biblioteca Internet Lounge (Map p268; www.internet-lounge.ru; Novinsky bul 8, 6th fl; 10am-10pm; M Smolenskaya; 📶) This lounge inside the Lotte Plaza is an internet cafe for fancy people, complete with face control.

Cafemax – Dorogomilovo (Map p278; Bryanskaya ul 5; per hr R100; 24hr; M Kievskaya; 📶) Discounts available late at night and early in the morning.

Cafemax – Zamoskvorechie (Map p276; Pyatnitskaya ul 25; per hr R100; 24hr; M Novokuznetskaya; 📶)

Internet Club (Map p260; Kuznetsky most 12; 9am-midnight; M Kuznetsky most)

Playground.ru (Map p264; 495-980 1020; Tishinskaya pl 1; per hr R50; 24hr; M Belorusskaya) This computer-gaming club is inside the Tishinka shopping centre.

Time Online – Leningradsky vokzal (off Map p272; 495-266 8351; Komsomolskaya pl 3; per hr R70-100; 24hr; M Komsomolskaya; 📶) Offers copy and photo services, as well as over 100 zippy computers.

Time Online – Okhotny Ryad (Map p262; www.timeonline.ru; Okhotny Ryad Shopping Centre; per hr R70-100; 24hr; M Okhotny Ryad; 📶)

Legal Matters

It's not unusual to see police officers *(militsia)* randomly stopping people on the street to check their documents. Such checks have become more frequent since the terrorist attacks in Moscow in recent years. Often, the *militsiya* targets individuals who look like they come from the Caucasus, and other people with darkish skin. But officers have the right to stop anyone, and they do exercise it.

Technically, everyone is required to carry a passport *(dokumenty)* at all times. Unfortunately, some readers have complained about police pocketing their passports and demanding bribes. The best way to avoid such unpleasantness is to carry a photocopy of your passport, visa and registration, and present them when an officer demands to see your *dokumenty*. A photocopy is sufficient, despite what the officer may argue.

Medical Services

Hospitals

Both of the international medical facilities listed here accept health insurance from major international providers.

American Medical Centre (Map p260; 495-933 7700; www.amcenter.ru; Grokholsky per 1; M Prospekt Mira) Offers 24-hour emergency service, consultations and a full range of medical specialists, including paediatricians and dentists. There is also an on-site pharmacy with English-speaking staff.

Botkin Hospital (Боткинская больница; 495-945 0045; www.botkinmoscow.ru, in Russian; 2-y Botkinsky proezd 5; M Begovaya) The best Russian facility. From Begovaya metro station, walk 1km northeast on Khoroshevskoe sh and Begovoy pr. Turn left on Begovaya ul and continue to 2-y Botkinsky proezd.

European Medical Centre (Map p264; 495-933 6655; www.emcmos.ru; Spirodonevsky per 5; M Mayakovskaya) Includes medical and dental facilities, which are open around the clock for emergencies. The staff speak 10 languages.

Pharmacies

A chain of 24-hour pharmacies called **36.6** (☎495-797 6366; www.366.ru) has many branches all around the city, including the following:

Arbat (Map p268; ul Novy Arbat 15; Ⓜ Arbatskaya)

Basmanny (Map p272; ul Pokrovka 1/13; Ⓜ Kitay-Gorod)

Tverskoy (Map p260; Tverskaya ul 25/9; Ⓜ Tverskaya)

Zamoskvorechie (Map p260; Klimentovsky per 12; Ⓜ Tretykovskaya)

Money

Russian currency is the rouble, written as рубль or abbreviated as руб. There are 100 kopecks (копеек or коп) in the rouble and these come in small coins that are worth one, five, 10 and 50 kopecks. Roubles are issued in coins in amounts of one, two and five roubles. Banknotes come in values of 10, 50, 100, 500 and 1000 roubles. Small stores, kiosks and many other vendors have difficulty changing large notes, so save those scrappy little ones.

The rouble has been relatively stable since it was revalued in 1998. See www.xe.com for up-to-date exchange rates.

ATMs

Automatic teller machines (ATMs), linked to international networks such as Amex, Cirrus, Eurocard, MasterCard and Visa, are now common throughout Moscow. Look for signs that say bankomat (БАНКОМАТ). Using a credit or debit card, you can always obtain roubles and often US dollars or euros.

Changing Money

US dollars and euros are now widely accepted at exchange bureaus around Moscow. Other currencies will undoubtedly cause more hassle than they are worth. Whatever currency you bring should be in pristine condition. Banks and exchanges do not accept old, tatty bills with rips or tears. With US dollars, make certain that, besides looking and smelling newly minted, they are of the new design, with the large off-set portrait.

When you visit an exchange office, be prepared to fill out a lengthy form and show your passport. The receipt is for your own records, as customs officials no longer require documentation of your currency transactions.

Credit Cards

Credit cards, especially Visa and MasterCard, are widely accepted at upmarket hotels, as well as restaurants and stores and some hostels. You can also use your credit card to get a cash advance at most major banks in Moscow.

Travellers Cheques

The process of changing travellers cheques can be lengthy, involving trips to numerous cashiers in the bank, each responsible for a different part of the transaction. Expect to pay 1% to 2% commission. If you do bring travellers cheques, make sure they are Amex, Thomas Cook or Visa, as other names are rarely accepted.

Newspapers & Magazines

All of the following English-language publications can be found at hotels, restaurants and cafes around town that are frequented by tourists. *Afisha* is a glossy magazine in Russian that comes out biweekly with lots of information about pop culture and entertainment events.

element (www.elementmoscow.ru) This oversized newsprint magazine comes out weekly with restaurant reviews, concert listings and art exhibits. Also publishes a seasonal supplement highlighting Moscow's hottest restaurants.

Moscow News (www.moscownews.ru) This long-standing Russian news weekly – now in English too – focuses on domestic and international politics and business.

Moscow Times (www.themoscowtimes.com) This first-rate daily is the undisputed king of the hill for locally published English-language news, covering Russian and international issues, as well as sport and entertainment. The Friday edition is a great source for information about what's happening at the weekend.

Passport Magazine (www.passportmagazine.ru) An excellent monthly lifestyle magazine that includes restaurant listings, book, music and film reviews and articles on culture and business in the capital.

Post

Although the service has improved dramatically in recent years, the usual warnings about delays and disappearances of incoming and outgoing mail apply to Moscow. Airmail letters take two to three weeks from Moscow to the UK, and three to four weeks to the USA or Australasia.

Should you decide to send mail to Moscow, or try to receive it, note that addresses should be written in reverse order: Russia, postal code, city, street address and then name.

Central telegraph (Map p260; Tverskaya ul 7; ⏲post 8am-10pm, telephone 24hr;

Ⓜ Okhotny Ryad) This convenient office offers telephone, fax and internet services.

Main post office (Map p272; Myasnitskaya ul 26; ⊙8am-8pm Mon-Fri, 9am-7pm Sat & Sun; Ⓜ Chistye Prudy) Moscow's main post office is on the corner of Chistoprudny bul.

Express Services

Many companies, hotels and even individuals use private mail services:

DHL Worldwide Express (☎495-956 1000; www.dhl.ru) Air courier services. Call for information on drop-off locations and to arrange pick ups.

FedEx (☎495-788 8881; www.fedex.com/ru)

UPS (☎495-961 2211; www.ups.com)

Public Holidays

New Year's Day 1 January

Russian Orthodox Christmas 7 January

International Women's Day 8 March

International Labour Day/Spring Festival 1 and 2 May

Victory (1945) Day 9 May

Russian Independence 12 June

Day of Reconciliation and Accord (formerly Revolution Day) 7 November

Safety

Unfortunately, street crime targeting tourists has increased in recent years, although Moscow is not as dangerous as paranoid locals might have you think. As in any big city, be on your guard against pickpockets and muggers. Be particularly careful at or around metro stations, especially at Kurskaya and Partizanskaya, where readers have reported specific incidents. Always be cautious about taking taxis late at night, especially near bars and clubs that are in isolated areas. Never get into a car that already has two or more people in it.

Watch out for gangs of children (generally referred to as 'gypsy kids'), who are after anything they can get their hands on.

Some police officers can be bothersome, especially to dark-skinned or foreign-looking people. Other members of the police force target tourists, though reports of tourists being hassled about their documents and registration have declined. However, it's still wise to carry a photocopy of your passport, visa and registration stamp. If stopped by a member of the police force, do not hand over your passport! It is perfectly acceptable to show a photocopy instead.

The most common hazards are violent or xenophobic drunks, and overly friendly drunks.

Taxes & Refunds

The value-added tax (VAT, in Russian NDS) is 18% and is usually included in the price listed for purchases. Moscow also has a 5% sales tax that is usually only encountered in top hotels.

Telephone

Phone Codes

Russia's country code is ☎7. There are now two area codes operating within Moscow (see box, p237). The most common code is ☎495, while some numbers – especially on the outskirts – use ☎499. If calling Moscow from abroad, dial the entire code.

To make an intercity call from Moscow, dial ☎8 plus the area code and number. To call internationally from Moscow, dial ☎810 plus the country code, city code and phone number.

Some places use a subscription service that requires the caller to dial a special operator code before entering the long-distance or international number. Your hotel or apartment will provide detailed instructions if this service is in place.

In any case, the method of placing calls is expected to change in the near future (☎0 for intercity and ☎00 for international).

Public Phones

The **central telegraph** (Map p260; Tverskaya ul 7, Tverskoy District; ⊙24hr) is convenient for phone calls and doubles as a post office. For calls, you leave a deposit with an attendant and are assigned a private booth where you dial your number directly. You might have to press the button with the speaker symbol or ответ (answer) when your party answers the phone.

In some other offices, you may have to give your number to an attendant, who dials the number and then sends you to a booth to take the call. You can collect change from your deposit when you leave. Rates are similar to home services.

The telegraph office is also the place at which you can send a fax.

Mobile Phones

Mobile (or cell) phones *(sotovye telefony)* are now ubiquitous in the capital, as Muscovites bypass the antiquated landline system. When trying to reach a mobile phone, it's necessary to dial ☎8 plus a 10-digit number (as when making an intercity/international call).

If you bring a cell phone from home, you can purchase a SIM card when you arrive in Moscow. It is a simple procedure to set up a 'pay-as-you-go' account with a local provider. Stores and kiosks all over the city have automated tellers that credit units to your telephone number. Units are consumed faster or slower depending on whether you call domestic or international numbers or within the same mobile-phone network. Most networks charge significant roaming charges when you leave the city. Note that you spend your units both when you dial and when you receive calls.

Several companies offer such services:

Beeline (www.beeline.ru)

Megafon (www.megafon.ru)

MTS (www.mts.ru)

Buy your SIM card and sign up for service at **Euroset** (www.euroset.ru), which has a zillion outlets around the city.

HOW TO DIAL THE TELEPHONE

It's more complicated than you would think. There are now two area codes functioning within the city: ☎495 and ☎499. Dialling patterns for the two area codes are different:

- Within the ☎495 area code, dial seven digits, with no area code.
- Within the ☎499 area code, dial 10 digits (including ☎499).
- From ☎495 to ☎499 (or vice versa), dial ☎8 plus 10 digits (including appropriate area code). Although this looks like an intercity call, it is charged as a local call.

The addition of mobile phones also complicates matters, as mobile-phone numbers have a completely different area code (usually ☎915, 916 or 926). To call a mobile phone from a landline (or vice versa) you must dial ☎8 plus 10 digits.

Phonecards

Most payphones require prepaid phonecards, which are available from metro token booths and from kiosks. Cards can be used for local and domestic or international long-distance calls and are available in a range of units; international calls require at least 100 units. The only trick is to remember to press the button with the speaker symbol when your party answers the phone.

Time

Russians use the 12-hour clock and the 24-hour clock interchangeably. As of 2011, Moscow time is GMT/UTC plus four hours. So when it is noon in Moscow, it is 8am in London, 3am in New York, midnight in San Francisco and 7pm in Vladivostok. Daylight Savings Time is no longer observed in Moscow.

Toilets

Pay toilets are identified by the words платный туалет *(platny tualet)*. In any toilet Женский or Ж stands for women's *(zhensky)*, while Мужской or М stands for men's *(muzhskoy)*.

Plastic-cabin portable loos are scattered around Moscow in public places, but other public toilets are rare. Where they do exist, they are often dingy and uninviting. These days, though, the toilets in hotels, restaurants and cafes are usually modern and clean, so public toilets need only be used for emergencies. Toilet paper is not the rarity it once was, but it's still wise to carry your own supply, as there is no guarantee it will be there when you need it.

Travellers with Disabilities

Inaccessible transport, lack of ramps and lifts, and no centralised policy for people with physical limitations make Russia a challenging destination for wheelchair-bound visitors. More mobile travellers will have an easier time, but keep in mind that there are obstacles along the way. Toilets are frequently accessed from stairs in restaurants and museums, distances are great, public transport is extremely crowded and many footpaths are in a poor condition.

This situation is changing (albeit very slowly) as buildings undergo renovations and become more accessible. Most upscale hotels (especially those belonging to Western chains) offer accessible rooms. Some local organisations that might be useful for disabled travellers include the following:

All-Russian Society for the Blind (www.vos.org.ru) Provides info and services for visually impaired people, including operating holiday and recreation centres.

All-Russian Society for the Deaf (http://vog.deafnet.ru, in Russian) Organises cultural activities and recreational facilities for its members.

All-Russian Society of Disabled People (☎495-930 6877; Lomonosovsky pr 15; Ⓜ Universitet) Does not offer any services to travellers, but may provide publications (in Russian) on legal issues or local resources. Located 500m south of Universitet metro station.

Visas

All foreigners visiting Russia need visas. A Russian visa can either be a passport-sized paper document that is separate from your passport or a sticker in your passport. The visa lists entry and exit dates, your passport number, any children travelling with you and visa type. It's an exit permit too, so if you lose it (or overstay), leaving the country can be harder than getting in.

There are five types of visa available to foreign visitors, as listed following.

Tourist Visas

These are the most straightforward but most inflexible Russian visas available. They allow a stay of up to 30 days in the country. It is not possible to extend a tourist visa.

In addition to the items listed in the boxed text, below, you'll also need a voucher issued by the travel agency that provided your invitation. Note that Russian consulates reserve the right to see your return ticket or some other proof of onward travel when you apply for a visa.

Business Visas

A single-entry business visa is valid for up to three months, while a multiple-entry visa may be valid for up to 12 months. Both of these allow complete freedom of movement once you arrive in Russia.

A business visa requires the same documentation listed in the boxed text, below, but the invitation from a Russian company is usually more expensive. Also, the Russian consulate may require the original copy of this invitation. In addition to these documents, travellers applying for a visa for more than three months must submit an HIV-AIDS test certificate.

Note that your visa registration may or may not be included in the price of your invitation. If you are not planning to stay at a hotel, be sure that the company issuing the invitation can register your visa once you arrive in Moscow.

FIVE VISA ESSENTIALS

You will need the following for all visas:

- **Passport** Valid for at least six months beyond your return date.
- **Two or three passport-sized (4cm by 4.5cm) full-face photos** Must not be more than one year old. Vending-machine photos with white background are fine if they're identical.
- **Completed application form** Including entry and exit dates. US citizens must fill out a special, longer application form that is available from the appropriate consulate.
- **Handling fee** Usually in the form of a company cheque or money order. The fee varies depending on your citizenship: US citizens pay the most, in retaliation for high fees for American visas.
- **Visa-support letter or letter of invitation** This letter is not required for a transit visa. For business and tourist visas, most hostels and apartment rental agencies can provide this letter, as can any number of online services. Some companies offering visa support include **Visa House** (www.visahouse.ru), **Visa to Russia** (www.visatorussia.com) and **Way to Russia** (www.waytorussia.net).

Transit Visas

This is for 'passing through', which is loosely interpreted. For transit by air, it's usually good for 48 hours. For a nonstop Trans-Siberian Railway journey it's valid for 10 days, giving westbound passengers a few days in Moscow; those heading east, however, are not allowed to linger in Moscow. To obtain a transit visa, you will need to show the itinerary for your entire trip, as well as any visa needed for your onward journey.

'Private' Visas

This is the visa you get for a visit by personal invitation, and it's also referred to as an 'ordinary' visa by some authorities. The visa itself is as easy to get as a tourist visa, but getting the invitation is a complex matter.

The person who is inviting you must go to his or her local visa office of the Russian Ministry of Internal Affairs (RMIA) – sometimes still referred to as OVIR – and fill out an invitation form that asks for approval of the invitation. Approval, which takes several weeks, comes in the form of a notice of permission *(izveshchenie)*, good for one year, which the person inviting you must send to you. You will need this invitation approval notice, together with the standard application form, to apply for the visa, which is valid for up to 60 days in your host's town. On arrival in Russia you will also have to go to the local visa office to register your visa (see Registration, p239).

Even if you plan to stay in a private residence in Moscow, it is practical (and easy) to obtain a tourist or business visa instead of a private visa.

Student Visas

Student visas are flexible and extendable. You'll need an invitation from the Ministry of Internal Affairs, which the

Russian school or university will help you obtain (after paying upfront for the tuition, no doubt). To obtain a visa valid for more than three months, you must submit an HIV-AIDS test certificate.

When & Where to Apply

Technically, you must apply for your Russian visa in your country of residence. Other restrictions may apply. For example, US residents must apply to the Russian consulate that covers their geographic region within the US. Most Russian consulates have their own requirements regarding the application process, so it's very important to contact the consulate where you will be applying for your visa.

Apply for a visa as soon as you have all the documents you need (but not more than two months ahead). Business, tourist, private and student visas all take the same amount of time to process once you have the paperwork. Processing time ranges from 24 hours to two weeks, depending on how much you are willing to pay. Transit visas normally take seven working days, but may take as little as a few hours at the Russian embassy in Beijing.

It's possible to apply at your local Russian consulate by dropping off all the necessary documents with the right payment. Some consulates accept application documents by mail, but others (such as New York) require the applicant to use a local visa service if they cannot come in person.

When you receive the visa, be sure to check it carefully, especially the expiry, entry and exit dates and any restrictions on entry or exit points.

Registration

When you check in at a hotel, you surrender your passport and visa so the hotel can register you with the local visa office. You'll get your documents back the next morning, if not the same day. Alternatively, your hostel, or the tourist agency that issued your visa, can make arrangements for your registration (usually for an extra fee). *All* Russian visas must be registered with the local visa office within seven business days of your arrival in Moscow. If you are in Moscow for less than seven business days, you are exempt. If you leave Moscow, you must register again in any city in which you stay seven days or longer.

Women Travellers

Although sexual harassment on the streets is rare, it is common in the workplace, in the home and in personal relations. Discrimination and domestic violence are hard facts of life for many Russian women. Some estimate that as many as 12,000 to 16,000 women throughout Russia die at the hands of their partners every year. Alcoholism and unemployment are related problems.

Activists ridicule as hypocritical the Women's Day celebrations (8 March) in Russia while such problems continue. Others say it is the one day in the year that men have to be nice to their mates.

Foreign women are likely to receive some attention, mostly in the form of genuine, friendly interest. An interested stranger may approach you out of the blue and ask: *'Mozhno poznokomitsa?'* (May we become acquainted?). Of course you can answer *'da'*, but you can also give a gentle, but firm, *'nyet'*. The conversation usually goes no further, although drunken men may be more persistent. The best way to lose an unwelcome suitor is to enter an upmarket hotel or restaurant, where ample security will come to your aid. Women should avoid taking private taxis alone at night.

Russian women dress up and wear lots of make-up on nights out. If you are wearing casual gear, you might feel uncomfortable in an upmarket restaurant, club or theatre.

The following websites provide useful information about women's organisations in Moscow:

www.iwcmoscow.ru The International Women's Club is an active group of expat women. It is involved in organising social and charity events.

www.womnet.ru The Women Information Network (WIN) site, in Russian only, is updated regularly. It has news items, local events, book reviews and information on grants for women's organisations.

Language

Russian belongs to the Slavonic language family and is closely related to Belarusian and Ukrainian. It has more than 150 million speakers within the Russian Federation and is used as a second language in the former republics of the USSR, with a total number of speakers of more than 270 million people.

Russian is written in the Cyrillic alphabet (see the opposite page), and it's well worth the effort familiarising yourself with it so that you can read maps, timetables, menus and street signs. Otherwise, just read the coloured pronunciation guides given next to each Russian phrase in this chapter as if they were English, and you'll be understood. Most sounds are the same as in English, and the few differences in pronunciation are explained in the alphabet table. The stressed syllables are indicated with italics.

BASICS

Hello.	Здравствуйте.	*zdrast*·vuy·tye
Hi.	Привет.	priv·*yet*
Goodbye.	До свидания.	da svi·*da*·nya
Excuse me.	Простите.	pras·*ti*·tye
Sorry.	Извините.	iz·vi·*ni*·tye
Please.	Пожалуйста.	pa·*zhal*·sta
Thank you.	Спасибо.	spa·*si*·ba
You're welcome.	Пожалуйста.	pa·*zhal*·sta
Yes.	Да.	da
No.	Нет.	nyet

WANT MORE?

For in-depth language information and handy phrases, check out Lonely Planet's *Russian phrasebook*. You'll find it at **shop.lonelyplanet.com**, or you can buy Lonely Planet's iPhone phrasebooks at the Apple App Store.

How are you?
Как дела? — kak di·*la*

Fine, thank you. And you?
Хорошо, спасибо. А у вас? — kha·ra·*sho* spa·*si*·ba a u vas

What's your name?
Как вас зовут? — kak vas za·*vut*

My name is ...
Меня зовут ... — mi·*nya za*·vut ...

Do you speak English?
Вы говорите по-английски? — vi ga·va·*ri*·tye pa·an·*gli*·ski

I don't understand.
Я не понимаю. — ya nye pa·ni·*ma*·yu

ACCOMMODATION

Where's a ...?	Где ...?	gdye ...
boarding house	пансионат	pan·si·a·*nat*
campsite	кемпинг	*kyem*·ping
hotel	гостиница	ga·*sti*·ni·tsa
youth hostel	общежитие	ap·shi·*zhih*·ti·ye

Do you have a ... room?	У вас есть ...?	u vas yest' ...
single	одноместный номер	ad·na·*myest*·nih *no*·mir
double	номер с двуспальней кроватью	*no*·mir z dvu·*spal'*·nyey kra·*va*·tyu

How much is it for ...?	Сколько стоит за ...?	*skol'*·ka *sto*·it za ...
a night	ночь	noch'
two people	двоих	dva·*ikh*

The … isn't working.	… не работает.	… ne ra·*bo*·ta·yit
heating	Отопление	a·ta·*plye*·ni·ye
hot water	Горячая вода	ga·*rya*·cha·ya va·*da*
light	Свет	svyet

DIRECTIONS

Where is …?
Где …? gdye …

What's the address?
Какой адрес? ka·*koy a*·dris

Could you write it down, please?
Запишите, пожалуйста. za·pi·*shih*·tye pa·*zhal*·sta

Can you show me (on the map)?
Покажите мне, пожалуйста (на карте). pa·ka·*zhih*·tye mnye pa·*zhal*·sta (na *kar*·tye)

Turn …	Поверните …	pa·vir·*ni*·tye …
at the corner	за угол	za *u*·gal
at the traffic lights	на светофоре	na svi·ta·*fo*·rye
left	налево	na·*lye*·va
right	направо	na·*pra*·va

behind …	за …	za …
far	далеко	da·li·*ko*
in front of …	перед …	*pye*·rit …
near	близко	*blis*·ka
next to …	рядом с …	*rya*·dam s …
opposite …	напротив …	na·*pro*·tif …
straight ahead	прямо	*prya*·ma

EATING & DRINKING

I'd like to reserve a table for …	Я бы хотел/хотела заказать столик на … (m/f)	ya bih khat·*yel*/khat·*ye*·la za·ka·*zat'* *sto*·lik na …
two people	двоих	dva·*ikh*
eight o'clock	восемь часов	*vo*·sim' chi·*sof*

What would you recommend?
Что вы рекомендуете? shto vih ri·ka·min·*du*·it·ye

What's in that dish?
Что входит в это блюдо? shto *fkho*·dit v *e*·ta *blyu*·da

That was delicious!
Было очень вкусно! *bih*·la *o*·chin' *fkus*·na

Please bring the bill.
Принесите, пожалуйста счёт. pri·ni·*sit*·ye pa·*zhal*·sta shot

I don't eat …	Я не ем …	ya nye yem …
eggs	яиц	*ya*·its
fish	рыбы	*rih*·bih
poultry	птицы	*ptit*·sih
red meat	мяса	*mya*·sa

CYRILLIC ALPHABET

Cyrillic	Sound	
А, а	a	as in 'father' (in a stressed syllable); as in 'ago' (in an unstressed syllable)
Б, б	b	as in 'but'
В, в	v	as in 'van'
Г, г	g	as in 'god'
Д, д	d	as in 'dog'
Е, е	ye	as in 'yet' (in a stressed syllable and at the end of a word);
	i	as in 'tin' (in an unstressed syllable)
Ё, ё	yo	as in 'yore' (often printed without dots)
Ж, ж	zh	as the 's' in 'measure'
З, з	z	as in 'zoo'
И, и	i	as the 'ee' in 'meet'
Й, й	y	as in 'boy' (not transliterated after **ы** or **и**)
К, к	k	as in 'kind'
Л, л	l	as in 'lamp'
М, м	m	as in 'mad'
Н, н	n	as in 'not'
О, о	o	as in 'more' (in a stressed syllable);
	a	as in 'hard' (in an unstressed syllable)
П, п	p	as in 'pig'
Р, р	r	as in 'rub' (rolled)
С, с	s	as in 'sing'
Т, т	t	as in 'ten'
У, у	u	as the 'oo' in 'fool'
Ф, ф	f	as in 'fan'
Х, х	kh	as the 'ch' in 'Bach'
Ц, ц	ts	as in 'bits'
Ч, ч	ch	as in 'chin'
Ш, ш	sh	as in 'shop'
Щ, щ	shch	as 'sh-ch' in 'fresh chips'
Ъ, ъ	–	'hard sign' meaning the preceding consonant is pronounced as it's written
Ы, ы	ih	as the 'y' in 'any'
Ь, ь	'	'soft sign' meaning the preceding consonant is pronounced like a faint y
Э, э	e	as in 'end'
Ю, ю	yu	as the 'u' in 'use'
Я, я	ya	as in 'yard' (in a stressed syllable);
	ye	as in 'yearn' (in an unstressed syllable)

Key Words

bottle	бутылка	bu·*tihl*·ka
bowl	миска	*mis*·ka
breakfast	завтрак	*zaf*·trak
cold	холодный	kha·*lod*·nih
dinner	ужин	*u*·zhihn
dish	блюдо	*blyu*·da
fork	вилка	*vil*·ka
glass	стакан	sta·*kan*
hot (warm)	жаркий	*zhar*·ki
knife	нож	nosh
lunch	обед	ab·*yet*
menu	меню	min·*yu*
plate	тарелка	tar·*yel*·ka
restaurant	ресторан	ris·ta·*ran*
spoon	ложка	*losh*·ka
with	с	s
without	без	byez

Meat & Fish

beef	говядина	gav·*ya*·di·na
caviar	икра	i·*kra*
chicken	курица	*ku*·rit·sa
duck	утка	*ut*·ka
fish	рыба	*rih*·ba
herring	сельдь	syelt'
lamb	баранина	ba·*ra*·ni·na
meat	мясо	*mya*·sa
oyster	устрица	*ust*·rit·sa
pork	свинина	svi·*ni*·na
prawn	креветка	kriv·*yet*·ka
salmon	лососина	la·sa·*si*·na
turkey	индейка	ind·*yey*·ka
veal	телятина	til·*ya*·ti·na

Signs

Вход	Entrance
Выход	Exit
Открыт	Open
Закрыт	Closed
Справки	Information
Запрещено	Prohibited
Туалет	Toilets
Мужской (М)	Men
Женский (Ж)	Women

Fruit & Vegetables

apple	яблоко	*yab*·la·ka
bean	фасоль	fa·*sol'*
cabbage	капуста	ka·*pu*·sta
capsicum	перец	*pye*·rits
carrot	морковь	mar·*kof'*
cauliflower	цветная капуста	tsvit·*na*·ya ka·*pu*·sta
cucumber	огурец	a·gur·*yets*
fruit	фрукты	*fruk*·tih
mushroom	гриб	grip
nut	орех	ar·*yekh*
onion	лук	luk
orange	апельсин	a·pil'·*sin*
peach	персик	*pyer*·sik
pear	груша	*gru*·sha
plum	слива	*sli*·va
potato	картошка	kar·*tosh*·ka
spinach	шпинат	shpi·*nat*
tomato	помидор	pa·mi·*dor*
vegetable	овощ	*o*·vash

Other

bread	хлеб	khlyep
cheese	сыр	sihr
egg	яйцо	yeyt·*so*
honey	мёд	myot
oil	масло	*mas*·la
pasta	паста	*pa*·sta
pepper	перец	*pye*·rits
rice	рис	ris
salt	соль	sol'
sugar	сахар	*sa*·khar
vinegar	уксус	*uk*·sus

Drinks

beer	пиво	*pi*·va
coffee	кофе	*kof*·ye
champagne	шампанское	sham·*pan*·ska·ye
(orange) juice	(апельсин-овый) сок	(a·pil'·*si*·na·vih) sok
milk	молоко	ma·la·*ko*
tea	чай	chey
(mineral) water	(минеральная) вода	(mi·ni·*ral'*·na·ya) va·*da*
wine	вино	vi·*no*

EMERGENCIES

Help!	Помогите!	pa·ma·*gi*·tye
Call ...!	Вызовите ...!	*vih*·za·vi·tye ...
a doctor	врача	vra·*cha*
the police	милицию	mi·*li*·tsih·yu

Leave me alone!
Приваливай! pri·*va*·li·vai

There's been an accident.
Произошёл несчастный случай. pra·i·za·*shol* ne·*shas*·nih *slu*·chai

I'm lost.
Я заблудился/заблудилась. (m/f) ya za·blu·*dil*·sa/za·blu·*di*·las'

Where are the toilets?
Где здесь туалет? gdye zdyes' tu·al·*yet*

I'm ill.
Я болен/больна. (m/f) ya *bo*·lin/bal'·*na*

It hurts here.
Здесь болит. zdyes' ba·*lit*

I'm allergic to (antibiotics).
У меня алергия на (антибиотики). u min·*ya* a·lir·*gi*·ya na (an·ti·bi·*o*·ti·ki)

SHOPPING & SERVICES

I need ...
Мне нужно ... mnye *nuzh*·na ...

I'm just looking.
Я просто смотрю. ya *pros*·ta smat·*ryu*

Can I look at it?
Покажите, пожалуйста. pa·ka·*zhih*·tye pa·*zhal*·sta

How much is it?
Сколько стоит? *skol'*·ka *sto*·it

That's too expensive.
Это очень дорого. e·ta *o*·chen' *do*·ra·ga

There's a mistake in the bill.
Меня обсчитали. min·*ya* ap·shi·*ta*·li

bank	банк	bank
market	рынок	*rih*·nak
post office	почта	*poch*·ta
telephone office	телефонный пункт	ti·li·*fo*·nih punkt

Question Words

What?	Что?	shto
When?	Когда?	kag·*da*
Where?	Где?	gdye
Which?	Какой?	ka·*koy*
Who?	Кто?	kto
Why?	Почему?	pa·chi·*mu*

TIME, DATES & NUMBERS

What time is it?
Который час? ka·*to*·rih chas

It's (10) o'clock.
(Десять) часов. (*dye*·sit') chi·*sof*

morning	утро	*ut*·ra
afternoon	после обеда	*pos*·lye ab·*ye*·da
evening	вечер	*vye*·chir
yesterday	вчера	vchi·*ra*
today	сегодня	si·*vod*·nya
tomorrow	завтра	*zaft*·ra
Monday	понедельник	pa·ni·*dyel'*·nik
Tuesday	вторник	*ftor*·nik
Wednesday	среда	sri·*da*
Thursday	четверг	chit·*vyerk*
Friday	пятница	*pyat*·ni·tsa
Saturday	суббота	su·*bo*·ta
Sunday	воскресенье	vas·kri·*syen*·ye
January	январь	yan·*var'*
February	февраль	fiv·*ral'*
March	март	mart
April	апрель	ap·*ryel'*
May	май	mai
June	июнь	i·*yun'*
July	июль	i·*yul'*
August	август	*av*·gust
September	сентябрь	sin·*tyabr'*
October	октябрь	ak·*tyabr'*
November	ноябрь	na·*yabr'*
December	декабрь	di·*kabr'*
1	один	a·*din*
2	два	dva
3	три	tri
4	четыре	chi·*tih*·ri
5	пять	pyat'
6	шесть	shest'
7	семь	syem'
8	восемь	*vo*·sim'
9	девять	*dye*·vyat'
10	десять	*dye*·syat'
20	двадцать	*dva*·tsat'
30	тридцать	*tri*·tsat'
40	сорок	*so*·rak
50	пятьдесят	pi·dis·*yat*
60	шестдесят	shihs·dis·*yat*
70	семьдесят	*syem'*·dis·yat

80	восемьдесят	*vo*·sim'·di·sit
90	девяносто	di·vi·*no*·sta
100	сто	sto
1000	тысяча	*tih*·si·cha

TRANSPORT

Public Transport

A ... ticket (to Novgorod).	Билет ... (на Новгород).	bil·*yet* ... (na *nov*·ga·rat)
one-way	в один конец	v a·*din* kan·*yets*
return	в оба конца	v *o*·ba kan·*tsa*

bus	автобус	af·*to*·bus
train	поезд	*po*·ist
tram	трамвай	tram·*vai*
trolleybus	троллейбус	tra·*lyey*·bus

first	первый	*pyer*·vih
last	последний	pas·*lyed*·ni
metro token	жетон	zhi·*ton*
platform	платформа	plat·*for*·ma
(bus) stop	остановка	a·sta·*nof*·ka
ticket	билет	bil·*yet*
ticket office	билетная касса	bil·*yet*·na·ya *ka*·sa
timetable	расписание	ras·pi·*sa*·ni·ye

When does it leave?
Когда отправляется? kag·*da* at·prav·*lya*·it·sa

How long does it take to get to ...?
Сколько времени нужно ехать до ...? *skol'*·ka *vrye*·mi·ni *nuzh*·na *ye*·khat' da ...

Does it stop at ...?
Поезд останавливается в ...? *po*·yist a·sta·*nav*·li·va·yit·sa v ...

Please stop here.
Остановитесь здесь, пожалуйста! a·sta·na·*vit*·yes' zdyes' pa·*zhal*·sta

Driving & Cycling

I'd like to hire a ...	Я бы хотел/ хотела взять ... на прокат. (m/f)	ya bih kha·*tyel*/ kha·*tye*·la vzyat' ... na pra·*kat*
4WD	машину с полным приводом	ma·*shih*·nu s *pol*·nihm pri·*vo*·dam
bicycle	велосипед	vi·la·si·*pyet*
car	машину	ma·*shih*·nu
motorbike	мотоцикл	ma·ta·*tsikl*

KEY PATTERNS

To get by in Russian, mix and match these simple patterns with words of your choice:

When's (the next bus)?
Когда (будет следующий автобус)? kag·*da* (*bu*·dit *slye*·du·yu·shi af·*to*·bus)

Where's (the station)?
Где (станция)? gdye (*stant*·sih·ya)

Where can I (buy a padlock)?
Где можно (купить нависной замок)? gdye *mozh*·na (ku·*pit'* na·vis·*noy* za·*mok*)

Do you have (a map)?
Здесь есть (карте)? zdyes' yest' (*kart*·ye)

I'd like (the menu).
Я бы хотел/ хотела (меню). (m/f) ya bih khat·*yel*/ khat·*ye*·la (min·*yu*)

I'd like to (hire a car).
Я бы хотел/ хотела (взять машину). (m/f) ya bih khat·*yel*/ khat·*ye*·la (vzyat' ma·*shih*·nu)

Can I (come in)?
Можно (войти)? mozh·na (vey·ti)

Could you please (write it down)?
(Запишите), пожалуйста. (za·pi·*shiht*·ye) pa·*zhal*·sta

Do I need (a visa)?
Нужна ли (виза)? nuzh·*na* li (*vi*·za)

I need (assistance).
Мне нужна (помощь). mnye nuzh·*na* (*po*·mash)

diesel	дизельное топливо	*di*·zil'·na·ye *to*·pli·va
regular	бензин номер 93	ben·*zin* *no*·mir di·vi·*no*·sta tri
unleaded	очищенный бензин	a·*chi*·shi·nih bin·*zin*

Is this the road to ...?
Эта дорога ведёт в ...? e·ta da·*ro*·ga vid·*yot* f ...

Where's a petrol station?
Где заправка? gdye za·*praf*·ka

Can I park here?
Здесь можно стоять? zdyes' *mozh*·na sta·*yat'*

I need a mechanic.
Мне нужен автомеханик. mnye *nu*·zhihn af·ta·mi·*kha*·nik

The car has broken down.
Машина сломалась. ma·*shih*·na sla·*ma*·las'

I have a flat tyre.
У меня лопнула шина. u min·*ya* lop·*nu*·la *shih*·na

I've run out of petrol.
У меня кончился бензин. u min·*ya* *kon*·chil·sa bin·*zin*

GLOSSARY

avtovokzal – bus terminal

bankomat – ATM
banya – Russian bathhouse, similar to a sauna
bilet, bilety – ticket, tickets
boyar – high-ranking noble
bufet – snack bar
bulvar – boulevard

dacha – country cottage or summer house
devushka or **devushki** (pl) – young woman
dom – house, building
DPS (Dorozhno-Patrulnaya Sluzhba) – Road Patrol Service
duma – parliament

elektrichka – slow, suburban train

firmeny poezd – a fancy, fast train, often with a special name

glasnost – literally 'openness'; used in reference to the free-expression aspect of the Gorbachev reforms in the 1980s
gostinitsa – hotel

kamera khraneniya – left-luggage
kassa – cash register or ticket office
kremlin – fort, usually a town's foundation
kruglosutochno – around the clock, 24 hours a day, usually used in reference to opening hours
kupeyny or **kupe** – 2nd class on a train; usually four-person couchettes

lyux – luxury or 1st class; often refers to a sleeping car on a train or rooms in a hotel

magazin – shop
maly – small
matryoshka – painted wooden nesting doll
mesto – place, as in seat on a train
MKAD (Moskovskaya Koltsevaya Avtomobilnaya Doroga) – Moscow Automobile Ring Road; refers to the outermost highway around the city
most – bridge
muzey – museum

naberezhnaya – embankment

passazhirsky poezd – slow, intercity passenger train
perekhod – cross walk, often underground
pereriv – break period, often in the middle of the day, when stores close
perestroika – literally 'restructuring'; refers to Gorbachev's economic reforms of the 1980s
pereulok – lane or side street
platskartny – 3rd class, general seating on an intercity train
ploshchad – square
prigorodny poezd – slow, suburban train
proezd – passage
prospekt – avenue

rynok – market
ryumochnaya – bar

sad – garden
samizdat – underground publishing during the Soviet period
shampanskoye – Russian sparkling wine
shapka – fur hat
shosse – highway
skory poezd – fast train
spalny vagon (SV) – sleeping car
stolovaya – canteen or cafeteria

tsarevitch – son of the tsar, successor to the throne
tsarina – wife of the tsar
tserkov – church

ulitsa – street
uslovie yedenitsiy (y.e.) – standard unit that usually equates to €s or US dollars; sometimes used to quote prices in upmarket restaurants and hotels

vagon – train carriage
val – rampart
vokzal – train station

MENU DECODER

bliny – crêpes блины
borsch – beetroot soup борщ
buterbrod – open-faced sandwich бутерброд

garnir – garnish, or side dish гарнир

ikra (chyornaya, krasnaya) – caviar (black, red) икра (чёрная, красная)

kartoshki – potatoes картошки
kasha – porridge каша

kefir – sour yogurt-like drink кефир
khleb – bread хлеб
kvas – mildly alcoholic fermented-rye-bread drink квас

lapsha – noodle soup лапша

losos – salmon лосось

mineralnaya voda (gazirovannaya, negazirovannaya) – water (sparkling, still) минеральная вода (газированная, негазированная)

moloko – milk молоко

morozhenoye – ice cream мороженое

myaso – meat мясо

obed – midday meal обедь

okroshka – cold cucumber soup with a *kvas* base окрошка

ovoshchi – vegetables овощи

ovoshnoy salat – tomato and cucumber salad, literally 'vegetable salad' овошной салат

pelmeni – dumplings filled with meat or vegetables пельмени

pirog or **pirogi** (pl) – pie пирог, пироги

pivo (svetloe, tyomnoe) – beer (light, dark) пиво (светлое, тёмное)

ptitsa – poultry птица

ris – rice рис

ryba – fish рыба

salat olivier – see *stolichny salat* салат Оливье

seld pod shuboy – salad with herring, potatoes, beets and carrots, literally 'herring in a fur coat' сельдь под шубой

shashlyk (myasnoy, kuriny, rybnoy) – kebab (meat, chicken, fish) шашлык (мясной, куриный, рыбной)

shchi – cabbage soup щи

solyanka – a tasty meat soup with salty vegetables and hint of lemon солянка

svekolnik – cold beet soup свекольник

sok – juice сок

stolichny salat – 'capital salad', which contains beef, potatoes and eggs in mayonnaise; also called *salat olivier* столичный салат

tvorog – soft sweet cheese similar to ricotta творог

uzhin – dinner ужин

zavtrak – breakfast завтрак

zakuski – appetisers закуски

Behind the Scenes

SEND US YOUR FEEDBACK

We love to hear from travellers – your comments keep us on our toes and help make our books better. Our well-travelled team reads every word on what you loved or loathed about this book. Although we cannot reply individually to postal submissions, we always guarantee that your feedback goes straight to the appropriate authors, in time for the next edition. Each person who sends us information is thanked in the next edition – and the most useful submissions are rewarded with a free book.

Visit **lonelyplanet.com/contact** to submit your updates and suggestions or to ask for help. Our award-winning website also features inspirational travel stories, news and discussions.

Note: We may edit, reproduce and incorporate your comments in Lonely Planet products such as guidebooks, websites and digital products, so let us know if you don't want your comments reproduced or your name acknowledged. For a copy of our privacy policy visit lonelyplanet.com/privacy.

OUR READERS

Many thanks to the travellers who used the last edition and wrote to us with helpful hints, useful advice and interesting anecdotes:

Lucy Baird, Rudi Blacker, Graciela Canamero, Cristian Canton, Romelle Castle, Kathleen Conti, Simon Cordall, Magdalena Cross, Francesco Garofalo, Cheryl Kern, Vivian Kerr, Su Mace, Lucy Norman, Dan Panshin, Johan Poels, Vetle Roeim, Christina Rupsch, Craig Schlozman, Wanda Serkowska, Becky Towndrow, Marloes Van Rens, Redmer Van Delden, Yvonne Warners, Michael York

AUTHOR THANKS

Mara Vorhees

Moscow with one-year-old twins requires an extra set of thank-yous to everyone who helped the monkeys settle into life in the Russian capital. Our awesome babysitter tops that list – Спасиба дорогоя Маша! My regular crew of Muscovite contacts was ever helpful, especially Tim O'Brien and Mirjana Vinsentin. Special thanks to Laura Bridge and Campbell Bethwaite for the 'local knowledge'. And a million kisses to Jerry, Shay and Van for coming along for the ride.

ACKNOWLEDGMENTS

Climate map data adapted from Peel MC, Finlayson BL & McMahon TA (2007) 'Updated World Map of the Köppen-Geiger Climate Classification', *Hydrology and Earth System Sciences*, 11, 163344. Illustration pp50-1 by Javier Zarracina. Cover photograph: St Basil's Cathedral, Red Square, Moscow, Günter Gräfenhain/Huber/4Corners.

Many of the images in this guide are available for licensing from Lonely Planet Images: www.lonelyplanetimages.com.

THIS BOOK

This 5th edition of Lonely Planet's *Moscow* guidebook was researched and written by Mara Vorhees. Leonid Ragozin researched and wrote text for the Golden Ring towns. The previous three editions were also written by Mara Vorhees. Ryan Ver Berkmoes wrote the 1st edition. This guidebook was commissioned in Lonely Planet's London office, and produced by the following:

Commissioning Editors Heather Howard, Anna Tyler

Coordinating Editors Jeanette Wall, Simon Williamson

Coordinating Cartographer Xavier Di Toro

Coordinating Layout Designer Paul Iacono

Senior Editor Angela Tinson

Managing Editor Brigitte Ellemor

Managing Cartographers Shahara Ahmed, Adrian Persoglia, Anthony Phelan

Managing Layout Designer Jane Hart

Assisting Editors Rebecca Chau, Anne Mulvaney, Ross Taylor

Assisting Cartographer Ildiko Bogdanovits

Cover Research Naomi Parker

Internal Image Research Aude Vauconsant

Language Content Branislava Vladisavljevic

Thanks to Jo Cooke, Janine Eberle, Catherine Eldridge, Ryan Evans, Will Gourlay, Liz Heynes, Laura Jane, David Kemp, Valentina Kremenchutskaya, Annelies Mertens, Wayne Murphy, Trent Paton, Piers Pickard, Lachlan Ross, Michael Ruff, Julie Sheridan, Laura Stansfeld, John Taufa, Gerard Walker, Clifton Wilkinson, Wendy Wright

See also separate subindexes for:
EATING P254
DRINKING & NIGHTLIFE P254
ENTERTAINMENT P255
SHOPPING P255
SLEEPING P256

Index

Sights p000
Map Pages **p000**
Photo Pages **p000**

Sights p000
Map Pages **p000**
Photo Pages p000

EATING

DRINKING & NIGHTLIFE

ENTERTAINMENT

SHOPPING

 SLEEPING

Sights p000
Map Pages **p000**
Photo Pages **p000**

Moscow Maps

Map Legend

Sights
- Beach
- Buddhist
- Castle
- Christian
- Hindu
- Islamic
- Jewish
- Monument
- Museum/Gallery
- Ruin
- Winery/Vineyard
- Zoo
- Other Sight

Eating
- Eating

Drinking & Nightlife
- Drinking & Nightlife
- Cafe

Entertainment
- Entertainment

Shopping
- Shopping

Sports & Activities
- Diving/Snorkelling
- Canoeing/Kayaking
- Skiing
- Surfing
- Swimming/Pool
- Walking
- Windsurfing
- Other Sports & Activities

Sleeping
- Sleeping
- Camping

Information
- Bank
- Embassy/ Consulate
- Hospital/Medical
- Internet
- Police
- Post Office
- Telephone
- Toilet
- Tourist Information
- Other Information

Transport
- Airport
- Border Crossing
- Bus
- Cable Car/ Funicular
- Cycling
- Ferry
- Metro
- Monorail
- Parking
- S-Bahn
- Taxi
- Train/Railway
- Tram
- Tube Station
- U-Bahn
- Other Transport

Routes
- Tollway
- Freeway
- Primary
- Secondary
- Tertiary
- Lane
- Unsealed Road
- Plaza/Mall
- Steps
- Tunnel
- Pedestrian Overpass
- Walking Tour
- Walking Tour Detour
- Path

Boundaries
- International
- State/Province
- Disputed
- Regional/Suburb
- Marine Park
- Cliff
- Wall

Geographic
- Hut/Shelter
- Lighthouse
- Lookout
- Mountain/Volcano
- Oasis
- Park
- Pass
- Picnic Area
- Waterfall

Hydrography
- River/Creek
- Intermittent River
- Swamp/Mangrove
- Reef
- Canal
- Water
- Dry/Salt/ Intermittent Lake
- Glacier

Areas
- Beach/Desert
- Cemetery (Christian)
- Cemetery (Other)
- Park/Forest
- Sportsground
- Sight (Building)
- Top Sight (Building)

MAP INDEX

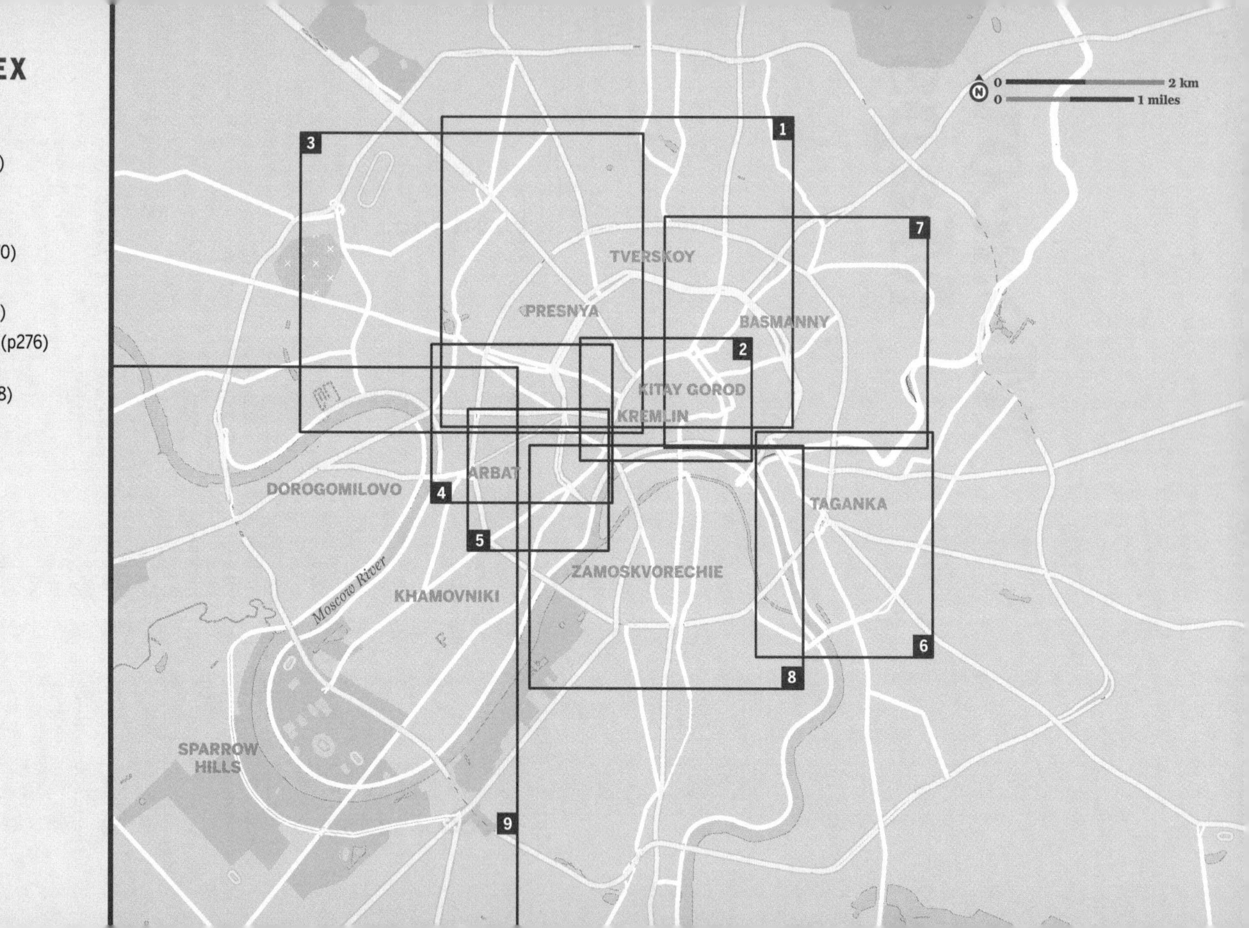

N
0
2 km
0
1 miles
1
2
3
4
5
6
7
8
9
TVERSKOY
PRESNYA
BASMANNY
KITAY GOROD
KREMLIN
ARBAT
DOROGOMILOVO
TAGANKA
ZAMOSKVORECHIE
KHAMOVNIKI
Moscow River
SPARROW HILLS

TVERSKOY *Map on p260*

Top Sights (p75)
Bolshoi Theatre E6

Sights (p75)
1 Central Museum of the Armed Forces E1
2 Church of SS Kosma & Damian E5
3 Church of the Nativity of the Virgin in Putinki D4
4 Contemporary History Museum C4
5 Dostoevsky House-Museum E1
6 Glinka Museum of Musical Culture C3
7 Gulag History Museum E5
8 House of Unions E6
9 M'ARS Contemporary Art Centre F4
10 Moscow Mayor's Office D5
11 Moscow Museum of Modern Art (ul Petrovka) E4
12 Museum of Decorative & Folk Art E3
13 State Duma E6
14 Upper St Peter Monastery E4
15 Vasnetsov House-Museum F2
16 Yury Dolgoruky Statue D5

Eating (p79)
17 Akademiya E6
18 Baltisky Khleb D4
19 Barashka E5
20 Courvoisier Cafe G3
21 Delicatessin D3
22 Dodo E5
23 Druzhba C2
Dzhondzholi .... (see 30)
24 Filimonova & Yankel Fish House C4
25 Galereya E4
26 Jagannath F5
27 Kitezh E5
28 Korchma Taras Bulba E4
29 Maki Café D5
30 Mi Piace D4
31 Mi Piace B3
32 Prime Star E6
33 Service Entrance E5
Sisters Grimm .... (see 41)
34 Starlite Diner (Tverskoy) D4
35 Trattoria Venezia D5
36 Uzbekistan F4
Varvary .... (see 34)

Drinking & Nightlife (p84)
37 12 Volts D5
38 ArteFAQ E5
39 Bavarius C4
Café Mart .... (see 11)
40 Chaikhona No 1 .... D3
41 Gogol E5
42 Kukly Pistolety C1
43 Pilsner C4
Simachyov .... (see 67)

Entertainment (p85)
44 BB King E3
45 Dome Cinema F1
46 Durov Animal Theatre F2
47 Lenkom Theatre D4
48 Maly Theatre F6
49 Masterskaya F6
50 Moscow Art Theatre (MKhT) E6
51 Nikulin Circus on Tsvetnoy Bulvar E4
52 Novaya Opera D3
53 Obraztsov Puppet Theatre & Museum E3
54 Sanduny Baths F5
55 Stanislavsky & Nemirovich-Danchenko Musical Theatre D5

Shopping (p87)
56 Atlas F5
57 Bustier E5
58 Detsky Mir F6
59 Dom Farfora B3
60 Dom Inostrannoy Knigi F5
61 K Faberge F5
62 Karpov Chess B2
63 Khudozhestvenny Salon E5
64 Masterskaya Rosemarie F5
65 Podium Concept Store F5
66 Respublika C3
Room Arterium .... (see 31)
Russian Bronze .... (see 61)
67 Simachyov Boutique & Bar E5
68 Transylvania E6
69 TsUM E5
70 Yekaterina E5
71 Yeliseev Grocery D5

Sleeping (p173)
Akvarel .... (see 67)
72 Ararat Park Hyatt F6
Artel .... (see 49)
73 Chocolate Hostel D4
74 Godzillas Hostel E4
75 Golden Apple D4
76 Hotel Budapest E5
77 Hotel National E6
78 Hotel Savoy F6
79 Petrovka Loft E5
80 Ritz-Carlton Moscow E6

Information (p233)
81 Irish Embassy G2

Key on p259

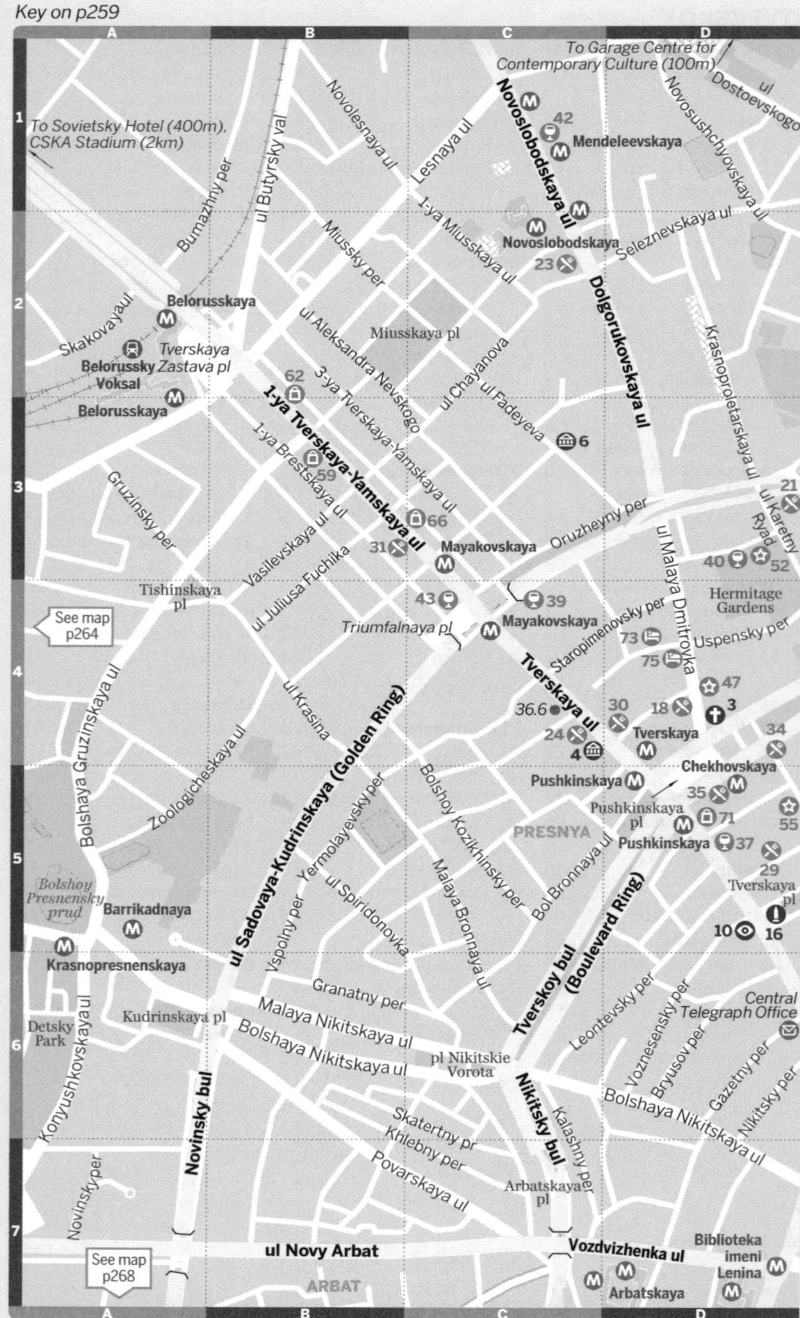

TVERSKOY
To Sovietsky Hotel (400m), CSKA Stadium (2km)
To Garage Centre for Contemporary Culture (100m)
ul Dostoevskogo
Novosushchyovskaya ul
Novoslobodskaya ul
Mendeleevskaya
Novoslobodskaya
Seleznevskaya ul
Lesnaya ul
Novolesnaya ul
ul Butyrsky val
Bumazhny per
Miussky per
1-ya Miusskaya ul
Dolgorukovskaya ul
Krasnoproletarskaya ul
Skakovaya ul
Belorusskaya
Belorussky Voksal
Tverskaya Zastava pl
Miusskaya pl
ul Aleksandra Nevskogo
3-ya Tverskaya-Yamskaya ul
ul Chayanova
ul Fadeyeva
1-ya Tverskaya-Yamskaya ul
1-ya Brestskaya ul
Gruzinsky per
Vasilevskaya ul
ul Juliusa Fuchika
Mayakovskaya
Oruzheyny per
ul Malaya Dmitrovka
ul Karetny Ryad
Hermitage Gardens
Tishinskaya pl
See map p264
Triumfalnaya pl
Staropimenovsky per
Uspensky per
Tverskaya ul
Bolshaya Gruzinskaya ul
ul Krasina
ul Sadovaya-Kudrinskaya (Golden Ring)
Zoologicheskaya ul
36.6
Tverskaya
Chekhovskaya
Pushkinskaya
Pushkinskaya pl
PRESNYA
Bolshoy Kozikhinsky per
Yermolayevsky per
Bol Bronnaya ul
Tverskoy bul (Boulevard Ring)
Malaya Bronnaya ul
ul Spiridonovka
Vspolny per
Bolshoy Presnensky prud
Barrikadnaya
Krasnopresnenskaya
Tverskaya pl
Granatny per
Malaya Nikitskaya ul
Kudrinskaya pl
Bolshaya Nikitskaya ul
pl Nikitskie Vorota
Leontevsky per
Voznesensky per
Bryusov per
Central Telegraph Office
Gazetny per
Nikitsky per
Detsky Park
Konyushkovskaya ul
Novinsky bul
Skaterny pr
Khlebny per
Povarskaya ul
Nikitsky bul
Kalashny per
Arbatskaya pl
Novinsky per
ul Novy Arbat
Vozdvizhenka ul
Biblioteka imeni Lenina
Arbatskaya
ARBAT
See map p268
42
23
62
59
66
31
6
21
40
52
43
39
73
75
47
30
18
3
24
4
34
35
71
55
37
29
10
16

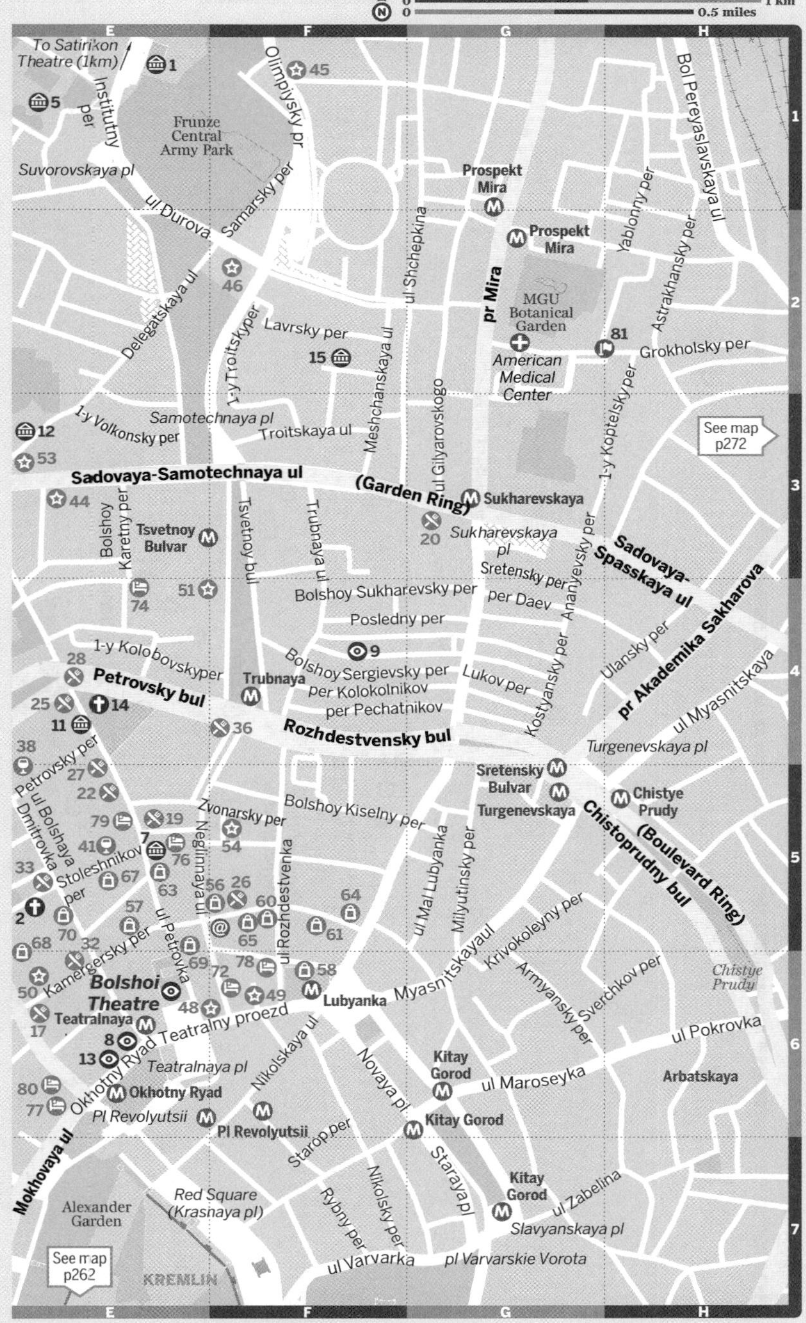

TVERSKOY
To Satirikon Theatre (1km)
Frunze Central Army Park
Suvorovskaya pl
Institutny per
ul Durova
Samarsky per
Olimpiysky pr
Delegatskaya ul
1-y Troitsky per
Lavrsky per
Meshchanskaya ul
ul Shchepkina
Prospekt Mira
pr Mira
MGU Botanical Garden
American Medical Center
Grokholsky per
Bol Pereyaslavskaya ul
Yablonny per
Astrakhansky per
1-y Koptelsky per
Samotechnaya pl
1-y Volkonsky per
Troitskaya ul
ul Gilyarovskogo
See map p272
Sadovaya-Samotechnaya ul
(Garden Ring)
Sukharevskaya
Sukharevskaya pl
Bolshoy Karetny per
Tsvetnoy Bulvar
Tsvetnoy bul
Trubnaya ul
Sretensky per
per Daev
Ananyevsky per
Sadovaya-Spasskaya ul
pr Akademika Sakharova
Bolshoy Sukharevsky per
Posledny per
1-y Kolobovsky per
Petrovsky bul
Trubnaya
Bolshoy Sergievsky per
per Kolokolnikov
per Pechatnikov
Lukov per
Kostyansky per
Ulansky per
ul Myasnitskaya
Rozhdestvensky bul
Turgenevskaya pl
Petrovsky per
Sretensky Bulvar
Turgenevskaya
Chistye Prudy
Chistoprudny bul
(Boulevard Ring)
ul Bolshaya Dmitrovka
Zvonarsky per
Bolshoy Kiselny per
Neglinnaya ul
Stoleshnikov per
ul Rozhdestvenka
ul Mal Lubyanka
Milyutinsky per
Krivokoleny per
Kamergersky per
ul Petrovka
Bolshoi Theatre
Teatralnaya
Teatralny proezd
Lubyanka
Myasnitskaya ul
Armyansky per
Sverchkov per
Chistye Prudy
Okhotny Ryad
Teatralnaya pl
Nikolskaya ul
Novaya pl
Kitay Gorod
ul Pokrovka
ul Maroseyka
Arbatskaya
Pl Revolyutsii
Mokhovaya ul
Starop per
Staraya pl
Red Square (Krasnaya pl)
Rybny per
Nikolsky per
ul Zabelina
Alexander Garden
Slavyanskaya pl
See map p262
KREMLIN
ul Varvarka
pl Varvarskie Vorota
0 1 km
0 0.5 miles

KREMLIN & KITAY GOROD

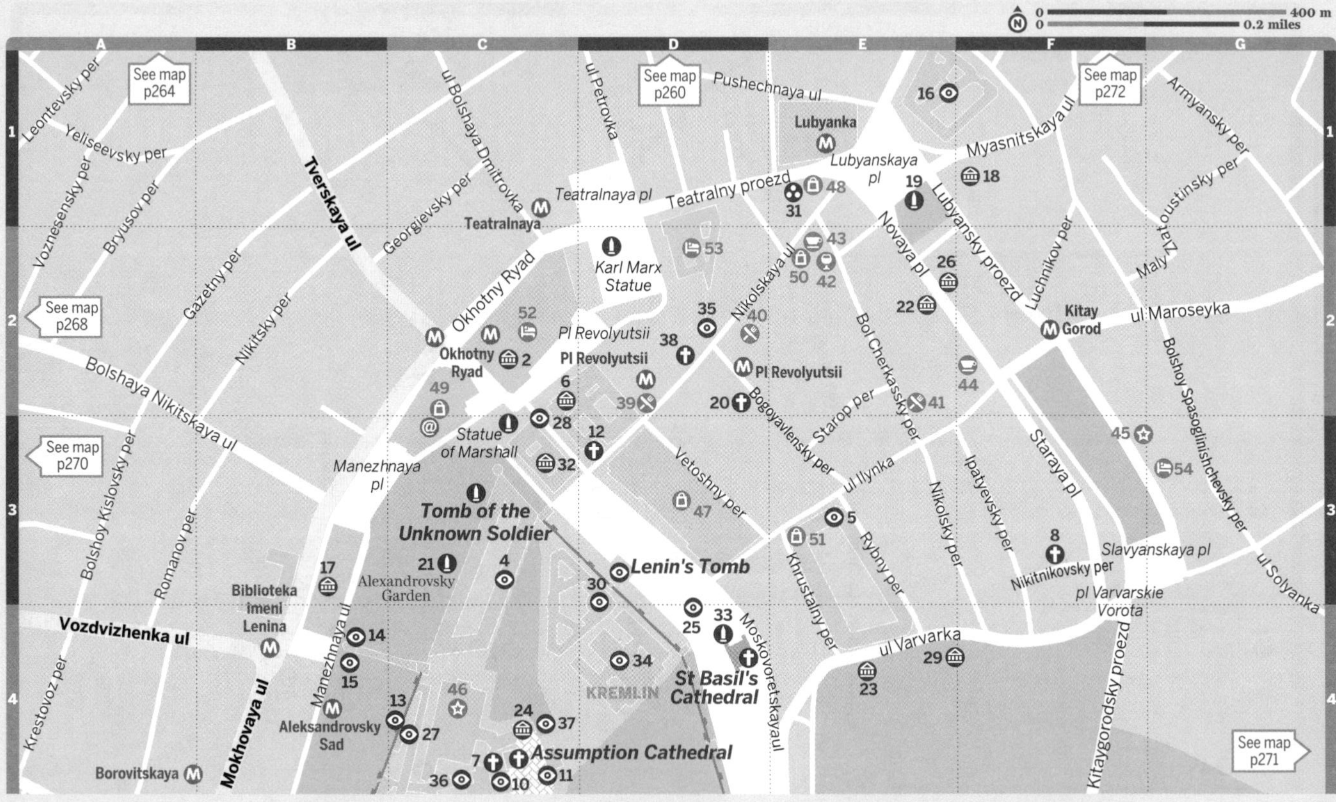

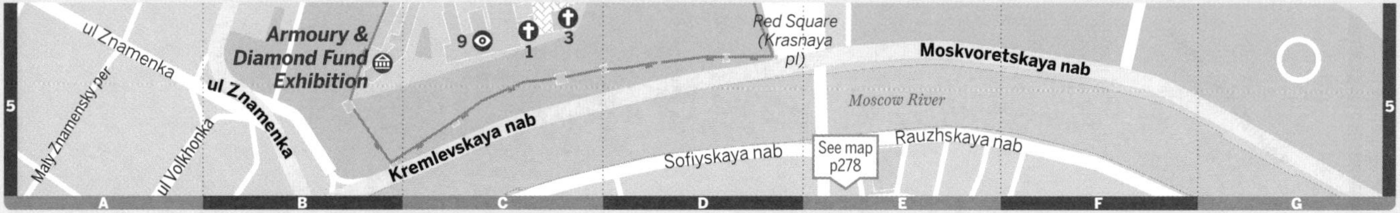

KREMLIN & KITAY GOROD

Top Sights **(p48)**

Armoury & Diamond Fund Exhibition ... B5
Assumption Cathedral ... C4
Lenin's Tomb ... D3
St Basil's Cathedral ... D4
Tomb of the Unknown Soldier ... C3

Sights **(p66)**

1 Annunciation Cathedral ... C5
2 Archaeological Museum ... C2
3 Archangel Cathedral ... C5
4 Arsenal ... C3
5 Capital Tours ... E3
6 Central Lenin Museum ... C2
Chapel of the Iverian Virgin ... (see 28)
7 Church of the Deposition of the Robe ... C4
8 Church of the Trinity in Nikitniki ... F3
Church of the Twelve Apostles ... (see 24)
9 Great Kremlin Palace ... C5
GUM ... (see 47)
10 Hall of Facets ... C4
11 Ivan the Great Bell Tower ... C4
12 Kazan Cathedral ... D3
13 Kremlin Excursions Office ... C4
14 Kremlin Ticket Office ... B4
15 Left-luggage Office ... B4
16 Lubyanka Prison ... E1
17 Manezh Exhibition Centre ... B3
18 Mayakovsky Museum ... F1
19 Memorial to the Victims of Totalitarianism ... E1
20 Monastery of the Epiphany ... D2
21 Monument to Revolutionary Thinkers ... C3
22 Moscow City History Museum ... E2
23 Old English Court ... E4
24 Patriarch's Palace ... C4
25 Place of Skulls ... D4
26 Polytechnical Museum ... E2
27 Poteshny Palace ... C4
28 Resurrection Gate ... C3
29 Romanov Chambers in Zaryadie ... E4
30 Senate ... D3
31 Starye Polya ... E1
32 State History Museum ... C3
State Kremlin Palace ... (see 46)
33 Statue of Kuzma Minin & Dmitry Pozharsky ... D4
34 Supreme Soviet ... D4
35 Synod Printing House ... D2
36 Terem Palace ... C4
Tsar Bell ... (see 11)
37 Tsar Cannon ... C4
38 Zaikonospassky Monastery ... D2

Eating **(p70)**

Bosco Cafe ... (see 47)
39 Drova ... D2
Loft Café ... (see 48)
40 Pelmeshka ... D2
Stolovaya 57 ... (see 47)
Sushi Vyosla ... (see 48)
41 Syrnaya Dyrka ... E2

Drinking & Nightlife **(p71)**

Chinatown Café ... (see 45)
42 Club Che ... E2
43 Cup & Cake Cafe ... E2
Dissident Vinoteca ... (see 48)
Kitaysky Lyotchik Dzhao-Da (see 45)
44 Neutral Territory ... F2

Entertainment **(p71)**

45 Chinese Pilot ... F3
46 Kremlin Ballet Theatre ... C4

Shopping **(p71)**

Alena Akhmadullina Boutique (see 43)
47 GUM (Gosudarstvenny Univermag) ... D3
Gus-Khrustalny Factory Store (see 51)
48 Nautilus Shopping Centre ... E1
49 Okhotny Ryad ... C2
50 Vladimir Mikhailov ... E2
51 Vologda Linen ... E3

Sleeping **(p173)**

52 Four Seasons Hotel Moskva ... C2
53 Hotel Metropol ... D2
54 Kitay Gorod Hotel ... G3

Key on p266

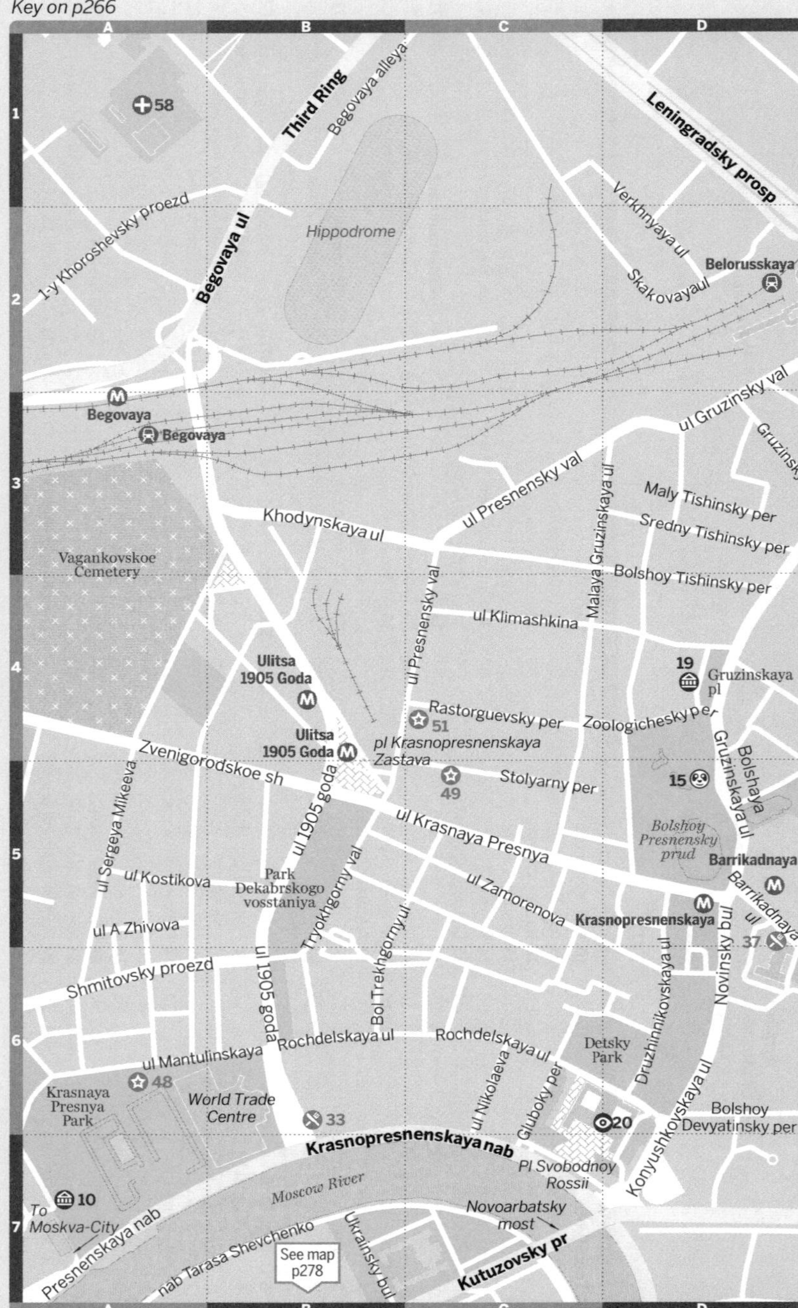
A
B
C
D
1
2
3
4
5
6
7
58
Third Ring
Begovaya alleya
Leningradsky prosp
Hippodrome
Verkhnyaya ul
1-y Khoroshevsky proezd
Begovaya ul
Belorusskaya
Skakovaya ul
Begovaya
Begovaya
ul Gruzinsky val
Gruzinsky
ul Presnensky val
Malaya Gruzinskaya ul
Maly Tishinsky per
Sredny Tishinsky per
Khodynskaya ul
Vagankovskoe Cemetery
Bolshoy Tishinsky per
ul Presnensky val
ul Klimashkina
Ulitsa 1905 Goda
19
Gruzinskaya pl
Rastorguevsky per
51
Zoologichesky per
Ulitsa 1905 Goda
pl Krasnopresnenskaya Zastava
Gruzinskaya ul
Bolshaya
Zvenigorodskoe sh
49
Stolyarny per
15
ul Sergeya Mikeeva
ul 1905 goda
ul Krasnaya Presnya
Bolshoy Presnensky prud
Barrikadnaya
ul Kostikova
Park Dekabrskogo vosstaniya
Tryokhgorny val
ul Zamorenova
Barrikadnaya ul
Krasnopresnenskaya
ul A Zhivova
Bol Trekhgornyul
Druzhinnikovskaya ul
37
Novinsky bul
Shmitovsky proezd
ul 1905 goda
Rochdelskaya ul
Rochdelskaya ul
Detsky Park
ul Mantulinskaya
ul Nikolaeva
Gluboky per
Konyushkovskaya ul
48
Krasnaya Presnya Park
World Trade Centre
33
20
Bolshoy Devyatinsky per
Krasnopresnenskaya nab
Pl Svobodnoy Rossii
10
Moscow River
To Moskva-City
Novoarbatsky most
Presnenskaya nab
nab Tarasa Shevchenko
Ukrainsky bul
See map p278
Kutuzovsky pr
A
B
C
D

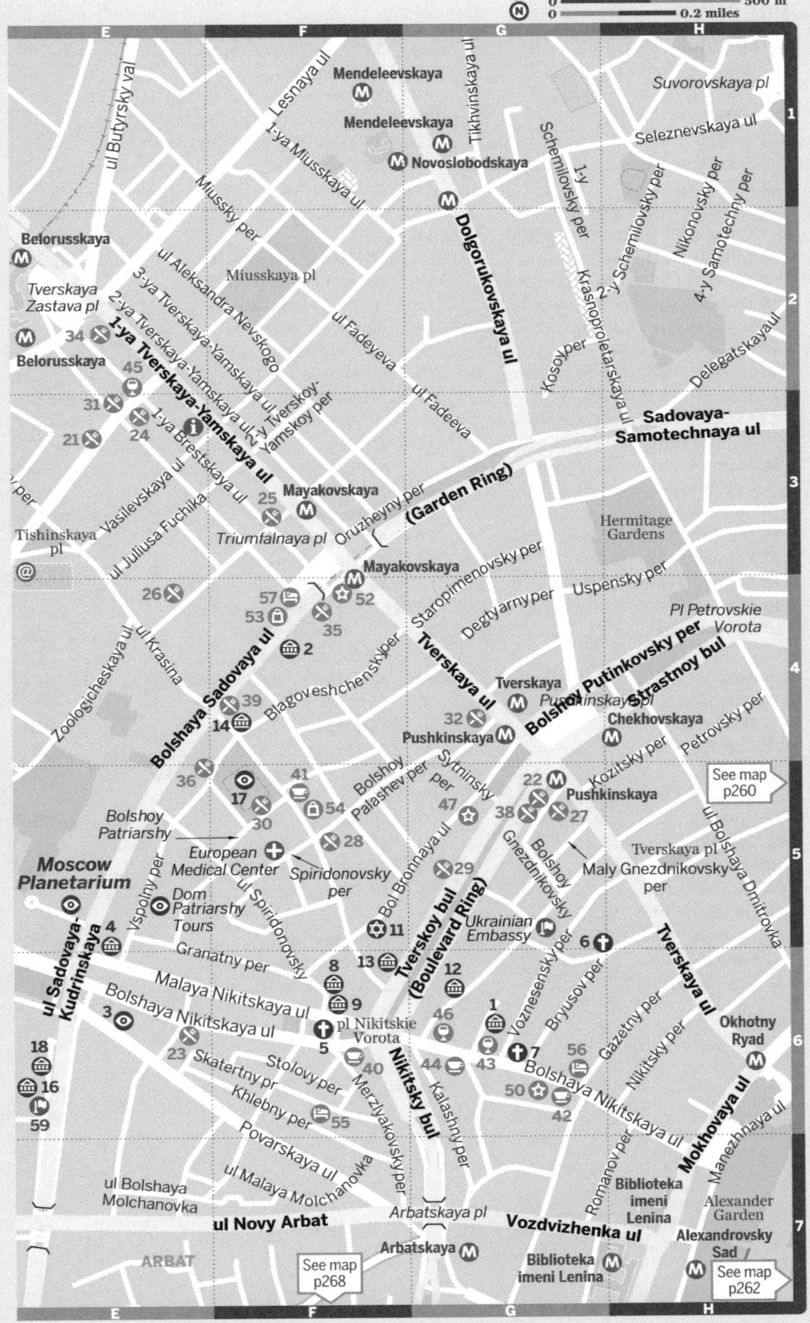

PRESNYA
0 500 m
0 0.2 miles
Mendeleevskaya
Mendeleevskaya
Novoslobodskaya
Belorusskaya
Tverskaya Zastava pl
Belorusskaya
Miusskaya pl
Hermitage Gardens
Tishinskaya pl
Mayakovskaya
Triumfalnaya pl
Mayakovskaya
(Garden Ring)
Sadovaya-Samotechnaya ul
Suvorovskaya pl
Seleznevskaya ul
Dolgorukovskaya ul
Tverskaya ul
Tverskaya
Pushkinskaya pl
Pushkinskaya
Chekhovskaya
Pushkinskaya
Pl Petrovskie Vorota
Bolshoy Patriarshy
European Medical Center
Moscow Planetarium
Dom Patriarshy Tours
Ukrainian Embassy
Tverskaya pl
Maly Gnezdnikovsky per
pl Nikitskie Vorota
Okhotny Ryad
Biblioteka imeni Lenina
Alexander Garden
Alexandrovsky Sad
Arbatskaya pl
ul Novy Arbat
Vozdvizhenka ul
Arbatskaya
Biblioteka imeni Lenina
ARBAT
See map p260
See map p268
See map p262

PRESNYA *Map on p264*

Top Sights (p93)
Moscow Planetarium E5

Sights (p92)
1 Art4.ru G6
2 Bulgakov House F4
3 CDL E6
4 Chekhov House-Museum E5
5 Church of the Grand Ascension F6
6 Church of the Resurrection G5
7 Church of the Small Ascension G6
8 Dom Ikony on Spiridonovka F6
9 Gorky House-Museum F6
10 Ice Sculpture Gallery A7
11 Lyubavicheskaya Synagogue F5
12 Matryoshka Museum G6
13 Moscow Museum of Modern Art (Tverskoy bul) F6
14 Moscow Museum of Modern Art (Yermolayevsky per) F4
15 Moscow Zoo D5
16 Narkomfin E6
17 Patriarch's Ponds F5
18 Shalyapin House-Museum E6
19 Tsereteli Studio-Museum D4
20 White House D6

Eating (p96)
21 Botanika E3
Bulka .... (see 31)
22 Café Pushkin G5
23 Chagall E6
24 Corner Burger E3
25 Correa's F3
26 Correa's E4
27 Khachapuri G5
28 Mari Vanna F5
29 Nedalny Vostok G5
30 Pavilion F5
31 Ragout E3
32 Scandinavia G4
33 Shinok B6
34 Soup Cafe E2
35 Starlite Diner F4
36 Suliko E5
37 Tsentralny restoranny dom D5
38 Turandot G5
Upside Down Cake Co .... (see 24)
39 Volkonsky F4

Drinking & Nightlife (p99)
40 Art Lebedev Cafe F6
41 Cafe Margarita F5
42 Coffee Mania G6
43 Kvartira 44 .... G6
44 Mayak G6
Radio City .... (see 57)
Real McCoy .... (see 37)
45 Red E2
46 Ryumochnaya G6

Entertainment (p100)
47 Club Forte G5
48 Imperia Lounge A6
49 Krasnopresnensky Bani C5
50 Moscow Tchaikovsky Conservatory G6
51 Sixteen Tons C4
52 Tchaikovsky Concert Hall F4

Shopping (p101)
53 Mostok F4
54 Podarky, Dekor & Podarky F5

Sleeping (p175)
55 Melodiya Hotel F6
56 Nikitskaya Hotel G6
57 Peking Hotel F4

Information (p233)
58 Botkin Hospital A1
59 US Embassy E6

ARBAT *Map on p268*

Sights (p109)

1 Bulat Okudzhava statue C5
2 Church of the Grand Ascension E2
3 Foreign Affairs Ministry C6
4 Gogol House F3
5 House of Friendship with Peoples of Foreign Countries G3
6 Lermontov House-Museum E3
7 Melnikov House D5
Memorial Apartment of Andrey Bely .... (see 9)
8 Museum of Oriental Art F2
9 Pushkin House-Museum C5
Tochka-G Museum of Erotic Art .... (see 21)

Eating (p113)

10 Akademiya F4
11 Balkon C4
12 Cafe Sindibad F2
13 Genatsvale on Arbat E4
14 Jean-Jacques F3
15 Kishmish D3
16 Moo-Moo D5
17 Prime Star F4
18 Shashlyk Mashlyk C5
19 Shesh-Besh C3
20 Vostochny Kvartal D5
Yolki-Palki .... (see 22)

Drinking & Nightlife (p117)

21 Maximilian's Brauerei D4
22 Zhiguli Beer Hall E4

Entertainment (p118)

23 Gelikon Opera E4
24 Rhythm Blues Café H4

Shopping (p118)

Army Store .... (see 32)
25 Bukle E5
26 Chocolate Salon D2
27 Confael Chocolate F2
28 Dom Knigi E3
29 Russian Embroidery & Lace E5
30 Russkie Chasovye Traditsii (Arbat 11) F4
31 Russkie Chasovye Traditsii (Arbat 25) E5
32 Skazka C5
33 Vassa & Co F3

Sleeping (p175)

34 Arbat Hotel D6
Bulgakov Hotel .... (see 35)
HM Hostel .... (see 10)
35 Home from Home Hostel C5
36 Hotel Belgrad B6

Information (p233)

37 Mongolian Embassy D3
38 Mongolian Embassy (Visa Section) C4
39 Netherlands Embassy G3
40 UK Embassy A4

Key on p267

ARBAT

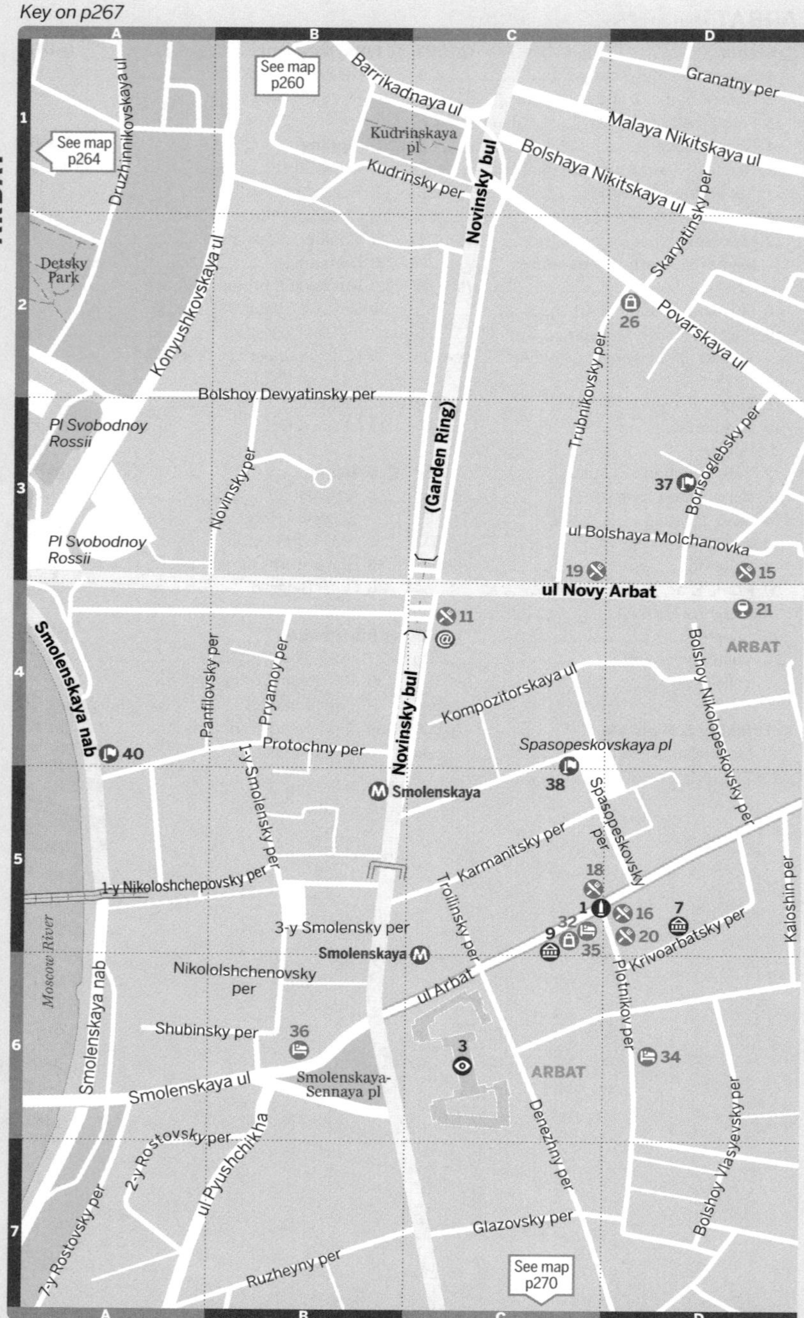

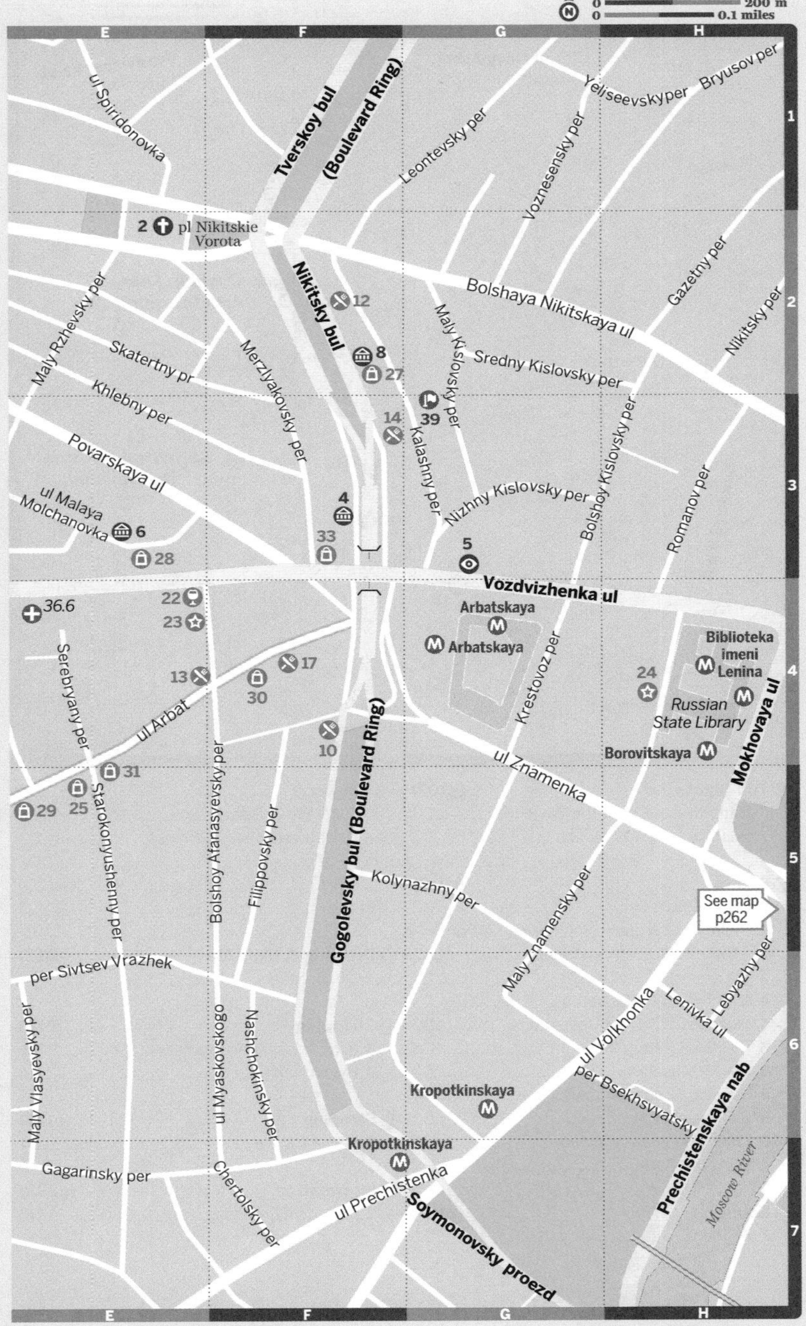
200 m
0.1 miles
ul Spiridonovka
Tverskoy bul
(Boulevard Ring)
Leontevsky per
Yeliseevsky per
Bryusov per
Voznesensky per
2 pl Nikitskie Vorota
Nikitsky bul
Bolshaya Nikitskaya ul
Gazetny per
Nikitsky per
Maly Rzhevsky per
Skatertny per
Merzlyakovsky per
12
8
27
Maly Kislovsky per
Sredny Kislovsky per
Khlebny per
14
39
Kalashny per
Bolshoy Kislovsky per
Povarskaya ul
Romanov per
ul Malaya Molchanovka
6
28
4
33
Nizhny Kislovsky per
5
Vozdvizhenka ul
36.6
22
23
Arbatskaya
Arbatskaya
Biblioteka imeni Lenina
Serebryany per
13
17
30
Krestovoz per
24
Russian State Library
Borovitskaya
Mokhovaya ul
ul Arbat
10
Gogolevsky bul (Boulevard Ring)
ul Znamenka
31
29
25
Starokonyushenny per
Bolshoy Afanasyevsky per
Filippovsky per
Kolymazhny per
See map p262
Maly Znamensky per
per Sivtsev Vrazhek
Lebyazhy per
Lenivka ul
ul Volkhonka
Maly Vlasyevsky per
ul Myaskovskogo
Nashchokinsky per
per Bsekhsvyatsky
Kropotkinskaya
Kropotkinskaya
Prechistenskaya nab
Moscow River
Gagarinsky per
Chertolsky per
ul Prechistenka
Soymonovsky proezd

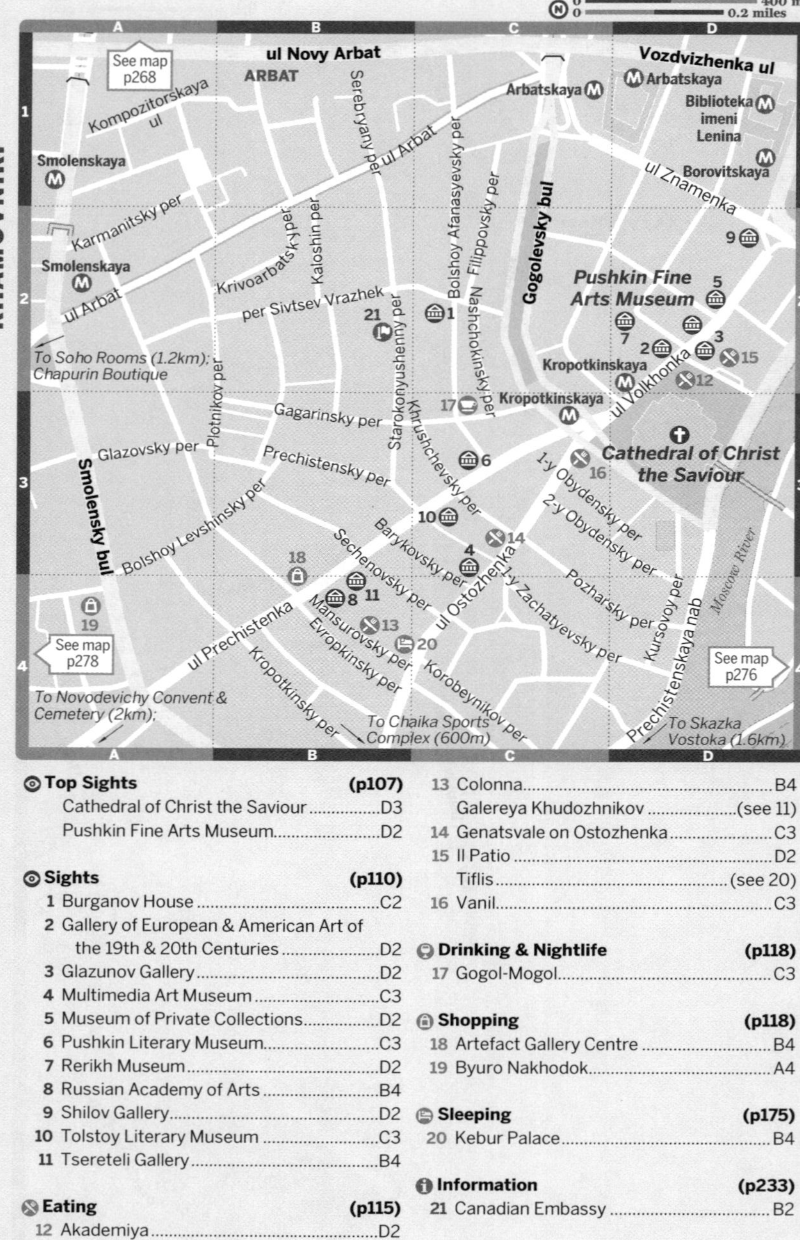

Top Sights (p107)
- Cathedral of Christ the Saviour....D3
- Pushkin Fine Arts Museum....D2

Sights (p110)
1. Burganov House....C2
2. Gallery of European & American Art of the 19th & 20th Centuries....D2
3. Glazunov Gallery....D2
4. Multimedia Art Museum....C3
5. Museum of Private Collections....D2
6. Pushkin Literary Museum....C3
7. Rerikh Museum....D2
8. Russian Academy of Arts....B4
9. Shilov Gallery....D2
10. Tolstoy Literary Museum....C3
11. Tsereteli Gallery....B4

Eating (p115)
- 12 Akademiya....D2
- 13 Colonna....B4
- Galereya Khudozhnikov....(see 11)
- 14 Genatsvale on Ostozhenka....C3
- 15 Il Patio....D2
- Tiflis....(see 20)
- 16 Vanil....C3

Drinking & Nightlife (p118)
- 17 Gogol-Mogol....C3

Shopping (p118)
- 18 Artefact Gallery Centre....B4
- 19 Byuro Nakhodok....A4

Sleeping (p175)
- 20 Kebur Palace....B4

Information (p233)
- 21 Canadian Embassy....B2

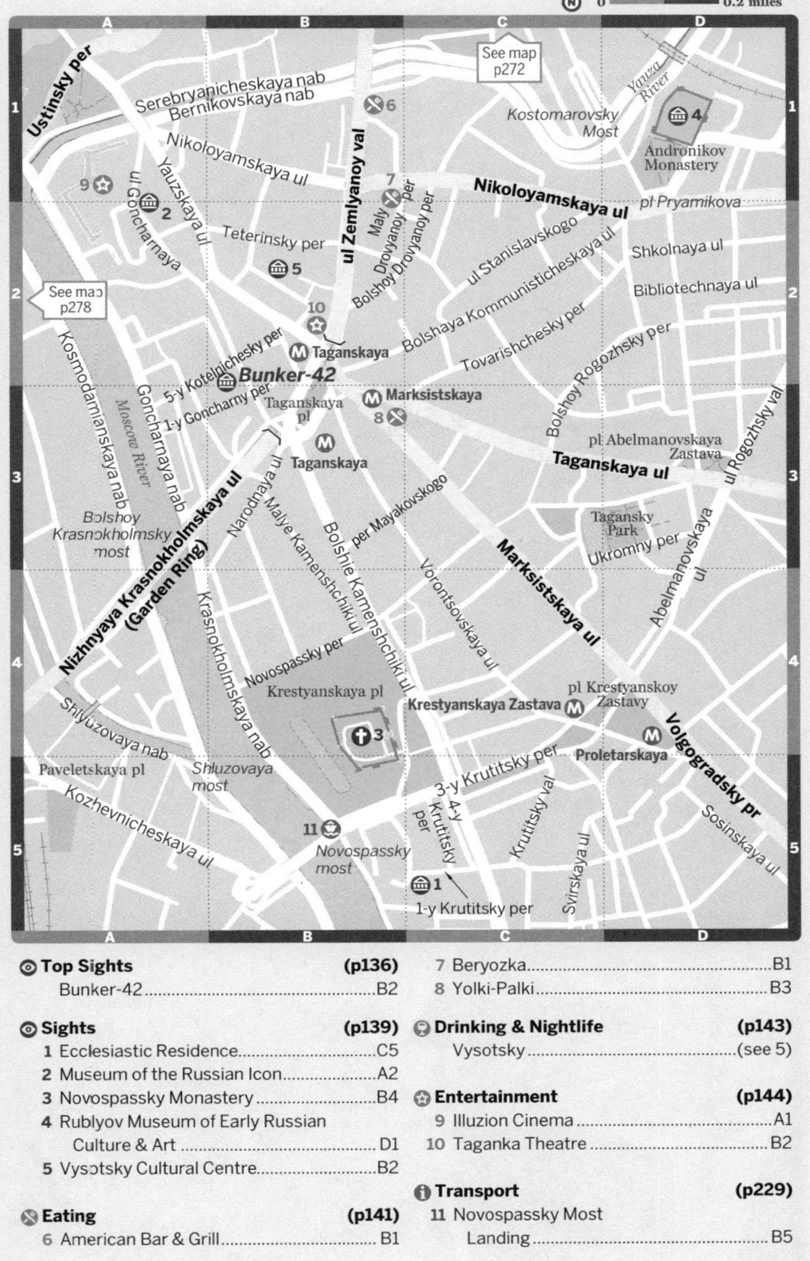

Top Sights (p136)
Bunker-42 B2

Sights (p139)
1 Ecclesiastic Residence C5
2 Museum of the Russian Icon A2
3 Novospassky Monastery B4
4 Rublyov Museum of Early Russian Culture & Art D1
5 Vysotsky Cultural Centre B2

Eating (p141)
6 American Bar & Grill B1
7 Beryozka B1
8 Yolki-Palki B3

Drinking & Nightlife (p143)
Vysotsky (see 5)

Entertainment (p144)
9 Illuzion Cinema A1
10 Taganka Theatre B2

Transport (p229)
11 Novospassky Most Landing B5

Key on p274

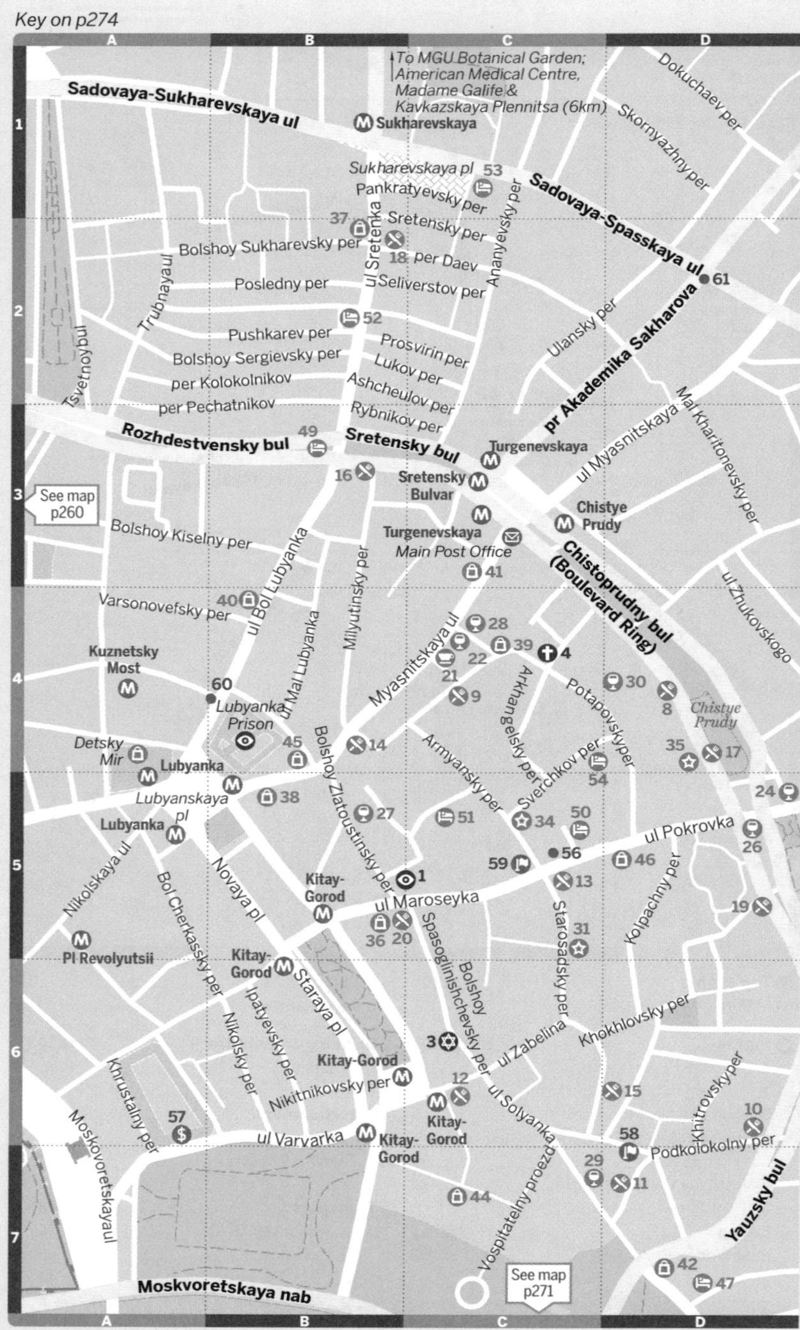

To MGU Botanical Garden; American Medical Centre, Madame Galife & Kavkazskaya Plennitsa (6km)
Sadovaya-Sukharevskaya ul
Sukharevskaya
Dokuchaev per
Skornyazhny per
Sukharevskaya pl
Pankratyevsky per
Sadovaya-Spasskaya ul
Sretensky per
Bolshoy Sukharevsky per
ul Sretenka
per Daev
Ananyevsky per
Trubnaya ul
Posledny per
Seliverstov per
Pushkarev per
Prosvirin per
Bolshoy Sergievsky per
Lukov per
per Kolokolnikov
Ashcheulov per
per Pechatnikov
Rybnikov per
Tsvetnoy bul
Ulansky per
pr Akademika Sakharova
Mal Kharitonevsky per
Rozhdestvensky bul
Sretensky bul
Turgenevskaya
ul Myasnitskaya
Sretensky Bulvar
Chistye Prudy
See map p260
Bolshoy Kiselny per
Turgenevskaya
Main Post Office
Chistoprudny bul (Boulevard Ring)
ul Bol Lubyanka
Milyutinsky per
ul Zhukovskogo
Varsonofevsky per
ul Mal Lubyanka
Myasnitskaya ul
Kuznetsky Most
Lubyanka Prison
Arkhangelsky per
Potapovsky per
Chistye Prudy
Detsky Mir
Bolshoy Zlatoustinsky per
Armyansky per
Sverchkov per
Lubyanka
Lubyanskaya pl
Lubyanka
ul Pokrovka
Nikolskaya ul
Bol Cherkassky per
Novaya pl
Kitay-Gorod
ul Maroseyka
Spasoglinishchevsky per
Starosadsky per
Kolpachny per
Pl Revolyutsii
Kitay-Gorod
Staraya pl
Ipatyevsky per
Nikolsky per
Bolshoy
ul Zabelina
Khokhlovsky per
Kitay-Gorod
Khrustalny per
Nikitnikovsky per
ul Solyanka
Khitrovsky per
Moskvoretskaya ul
ul Varvarka
Kitay-Gorod
Kitay-Gorod
Podkolokolny per
Vospitatelny proezd
Yauzsky bul
See map p271
Moskvoretskaya nab

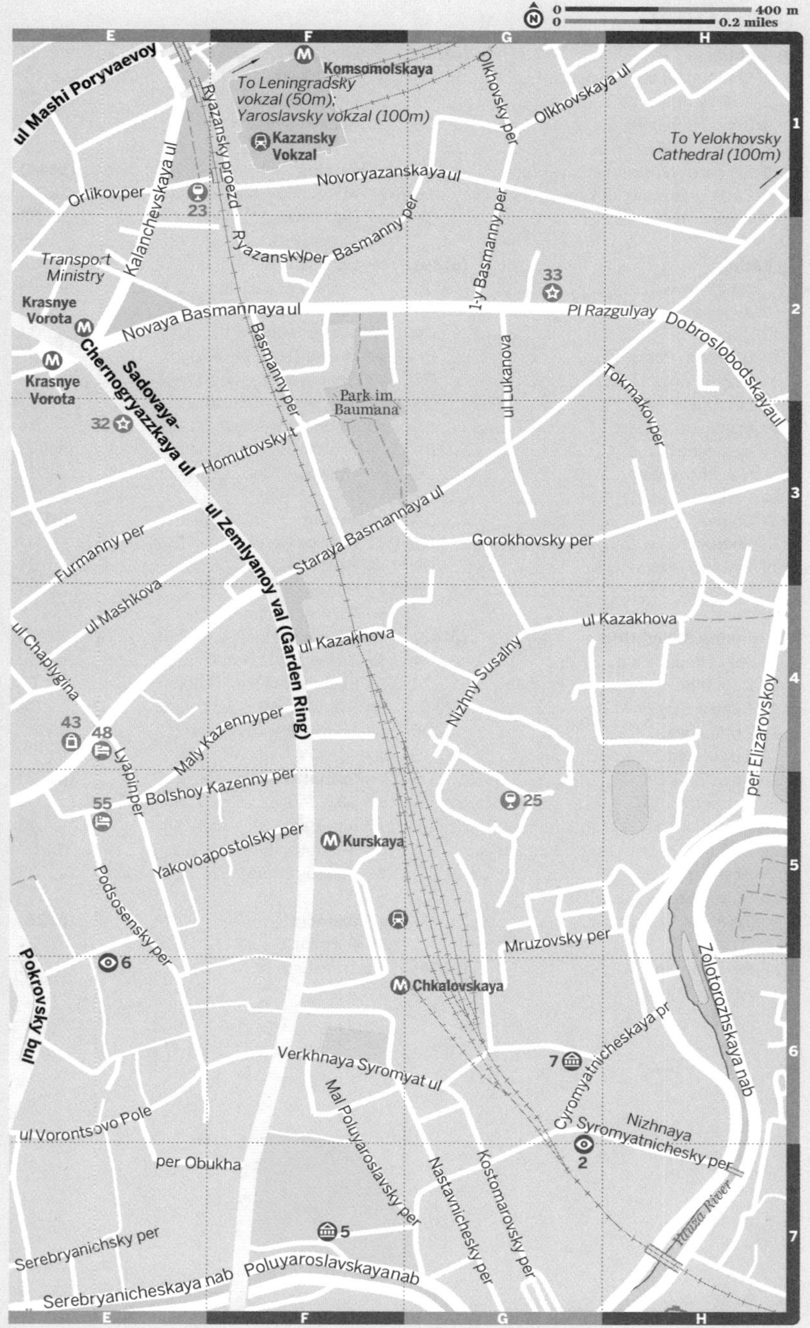
400 m
0.2 miles
E
F
G
H
Komsomolskaya
To Leningradsky vokzal (50m); Yaroslavsky vokzal (100m)
Kazansky Vokzal
ul Mashi Poryvaevoy
Ryazansky proezd
Olkhovsky per
Olkhovskaya ul
To Yelokhovsky Cathedral (100m)
Kalanchevskaya ul
Orlikovper
Novoryazanskaya ul
23
Ryazanskyper
Basmanny per
1-y Basmanny per
Transport Ministry
33
Krasnye Vorota
Novaya Basmannaya ul
Pl Razgulyay
Dobroslobodskaya ul
Krasnye Vorota
Sadovaya-Chernogryazzkaya ul
Basmanny per
Park im Baumana
ul Lukanova
Tokmakov per
32
Homutovsky t
ul Zemlyanoy val (Garden Ring)
Staraya Basmannaya ul
Furmanny per
Gorokhovsky per
ul Mashkova
ul Kazakhova
ul Kazakhova
ul Chaplygina
Nizhny Susalny
43
48
Maly Kazennyper
Lyapinper
per Elizarovskoy
Bolshoy Kazenny per
55
25
Yakovoapostolsky per
Kurskaya
Podsosensky per
Mruzovsky per
6
Pokrovsky bul
Chkalovskaya
Zolotorozhskaya nab
Cyromyatnicheskaya pr
7
Verkhnaya Syromyat ul
Mal Poluyaroslavsky per
ul Vorontsovo Pole
Nizhnaya Syromyatnichesky per
2
per Obukha
Nastavnichesky per
Kostomarovsky per
Yauza River
5
Serebryanichsky per
Poluyaroslavskayanab
Serebryanicheskaya nab
BASMANNY

BASMANNY *Map on p272*

ZAMOSKVORECHIE *Map on p276*

Top Sights (p123)

New Tretyakov Gallery B4
Tretyakov Gallery D3

Sights (p126)

1 Art Muzeon Sculpture Park C4
2 Bakhrushin Theatre Museum G5
3 Church of St John the Warrior C5
4 Church of the Resurrection at Kadashi E2
5 Dom na Naberezhnoy C2
Igor Kormyshev (see 9)
6 Lumiere Brothers Photography Centre C3
7 Ostrovsky Estate-Museum Schelykovo E3
8 Peter the Great Statue C3
Pobeda Gallery (see 25)
9 Red October C3

Eating (p129)

10 Correa's E4
11 Grably E2
12 Korchma Taras Bulba E2
13 Pancho Villa C5
14 Prime Star E2
15 Produkty C3
16 Shesh-Besh E3
17 Sok D3
18 Starlite Diner D6
19 Suliko D5

Drinking & Nightlife (p130)

Bar Strelka (see 30)
20 Chaikhona No 1 A6
Coffee Bean (see 14)
21 GQ Bar E1
Kvartira 44 (see 27)
22 Lebedinoe Ozero A7
23 Pilsner D5
24 Progressive Daddy & Daddy's Terrace C3
25 Rolling Stone C3

Entertainment (p132)

26 Dome C3
27 Garage Club D4
28 Gorky Park Skating Rink B6
29 Moscow International House of Music H4
30 Strelka Institute for Architecture, Media & Design C2

Shopping (p133)

31 Art Market B5
32 Central House of Artists (TsDKh) B4
33 Poradky E5
Russkaya Ulitsa (see 9)
Zazki-Petski (see 25)

Sports & Activities (p230)

34 Oliver Bikes E2

Sleeping (p176)

35 Alrosa on Kazachy E4
36 Hotel Baltschug Kempinski E1
37 Ibis Paveletskaya F7
38 Ozerkovskaya Hotel G4
39 Red Arrow C3
40 Red Dawn C2
41 Swissôtel Krasnye Holmy H5
42 Warsaw Hotel C6

Information (p233)

43 36.6 E3
44 Cafemax E3
45 French Embassy C5

Key on p275

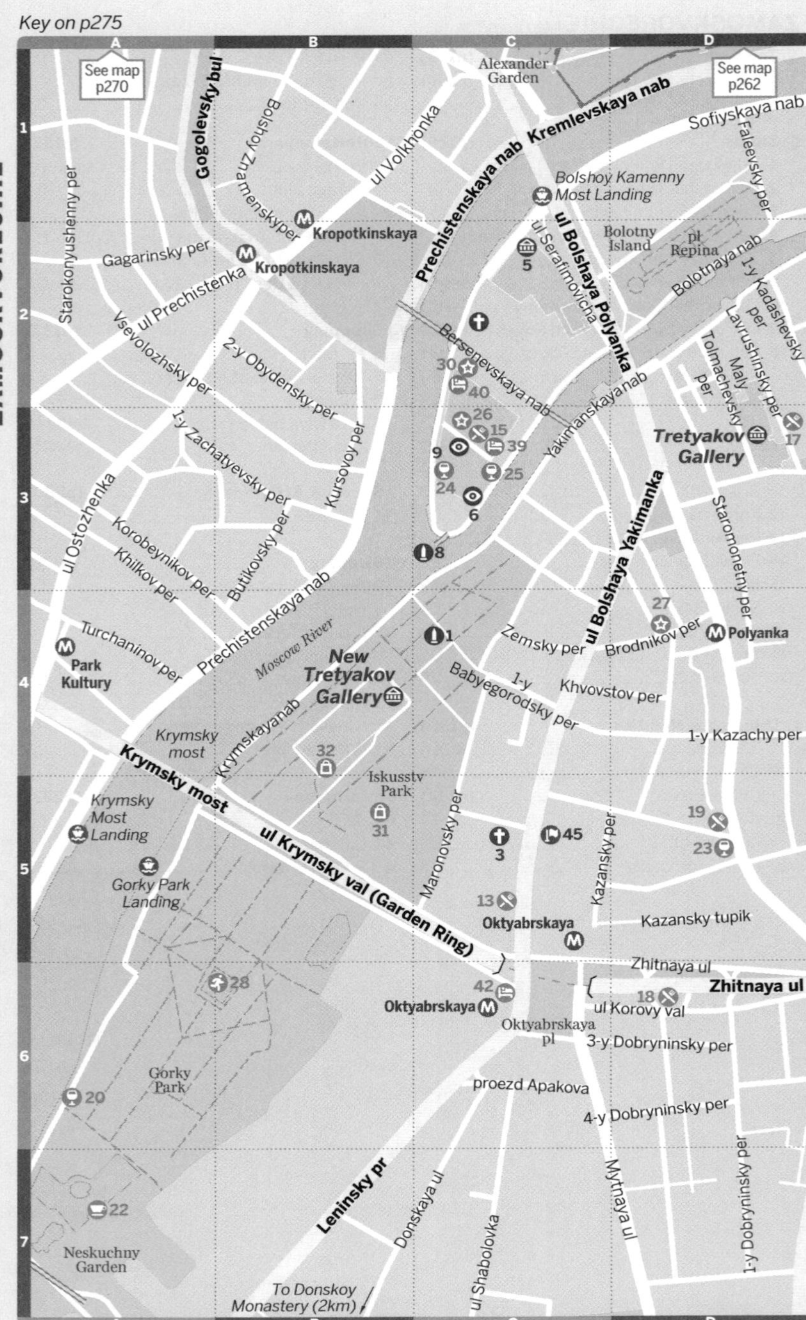

ZAMOSKVORECHIE
See map p270
See map p262
Alexander Garden
Gogolevsky bul
Bolshoy Znamenskyper
ul Volkhonka
Kremlevskaya nab
Sofiyskaya nab
Faleevsky per
Prechistenskaya nab
Bolshoy Kamenny Most Landing
ul Bolshaya Polyanka
ul Serafimovicha
Bolotny Island
pl Repina
Bolotnaya nab
1-y Kadashevsky per
Lavrushinsky per
Maly Tolmachevsky per
Starokonyushenny per
Kropotkinskaya
Gagarinsky per
ul Prechistenka
Vsevolozhsky per
2-y Obydensky per
Bersenevskaya nab
Yakimanskaya nab
Tretyakov Gallery
1-y Zachatyevsky per
Kursovoy per
Butikovsky per
ul Ostozhenka
Korobeynikov per
Khilkov per
Prechistenskaya nab
ul Bolshaya Yakimanka
Staromonetny per
Turchaninov per
Park Kultury
Moscow River
New Tretyakov Gallery
Zemsky per
Brodnikov per
Polyanka
1-y Babyegorodsky per
Khvovstov per
1-y Kazachy per
Krymsky most
Krymskaya nab
Iskusstv Park
Krymsky Most Landing
Gorky Park Landing
ul Krymsky val (Garden Ring)
Maronovsky per
Kazansky per
Kazansky tupik
Oktyabrskaya
Zhitnaya ul
ul Korovy val
Oktyabrskaya pl
3-y Dobryninsky per
proezd Apakova
4-y Dobryninsky per
Gorky Park
Leninsky pr
Donskaya ul
ul Shabolovka
Mytnaya ul
1-y Dobryninsky per
Neskuchny Garden
To Donskoy Monastery (2km)

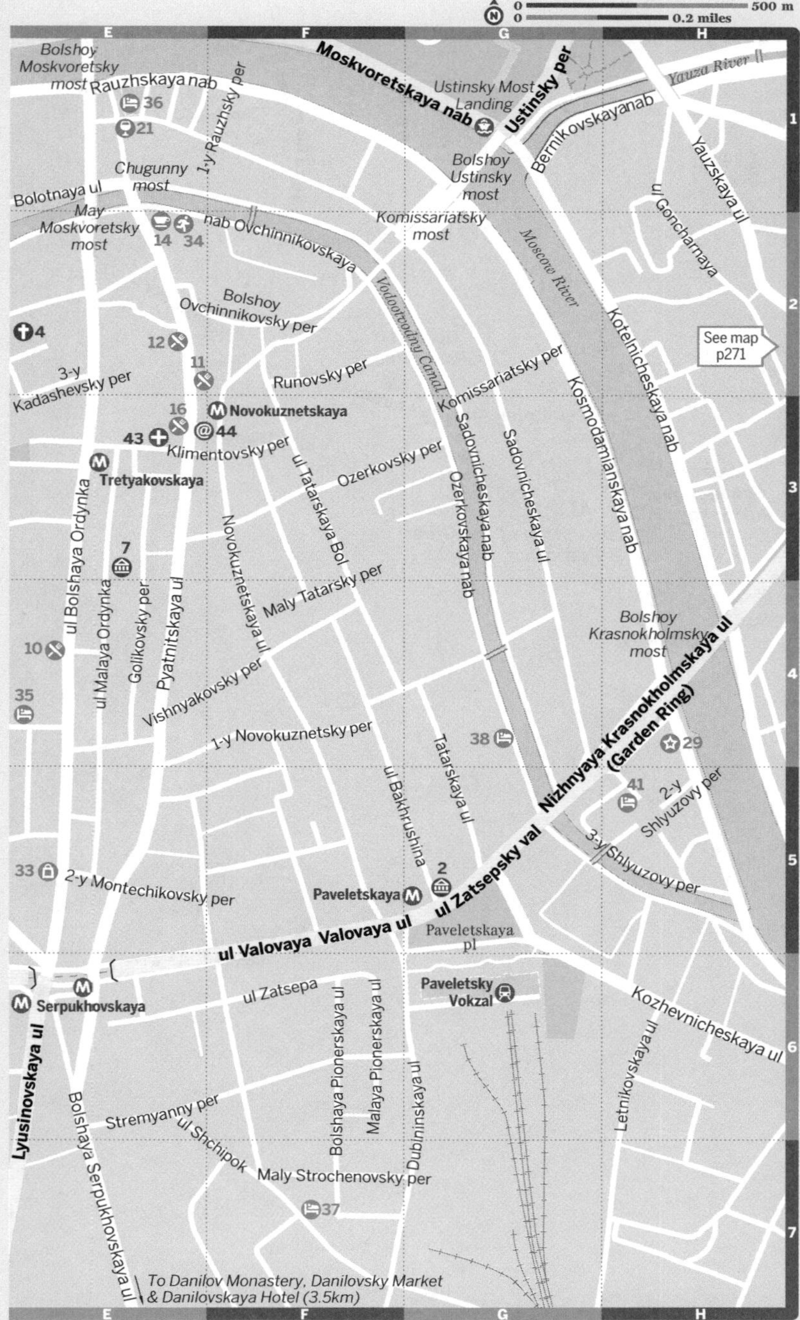

0 500 m
0 0.2 miles
E
F
G
H
1
2
3
4
5
6
7
ZAMOSKVORECHIE
Bolshoy Moskvoretsky most
Rauzhskaya nab
Moskvoretskaya nab
Ustinsky per
Ustinsky Most Landing
Yauza River
Bernikovskaya nab
1-y Rauzhsky per
Chugunny most
Bolotnaya ul
May Moskvoretsky most
nab Ovchinnikovskaya
Bolshoy Ustinsky most
Komissariatsky most
Yauzskaya ul
ul Goncharnaya
Moscow River
Vodootvodny Canal
Bolshoy Ovchinnikovsky per
Kotelnicheskaya nab
See map p271
3-y Kadashevsky per
Runovsky per
Komissariatsky per
Novokuznetskaya
Kosmodamianskaya nab
Klimentovsky per
Tretyakovskaya
ul Tatarskaya Bol
Ozerkovsky per
Sadovnicheskaya nab
Sadovnicheskaya ul
Ozerkovskaya nab
Novokuznetskaya ul
ul Bolshaya Ordynka
ul Malaya Ordynka
Golikovsky per
Pyatnitskaya ul
Maly Tatarsky per
Vishnyakovsky per
Bolshoy Krasnokholmsky most
Nizhnyaya Krasnokholmskaya ul (Garden Ring)
1-y Novokuznetsky per
Tatarskaya ul
ul Bakhrushina
2-y Shlyuzovy per
3-y Shlyuzovy per
ul Zatsepsky val
2-y Montechikovsky per
Paveletskaya
ul Valovaya
Valovaya ul
Paveletskaya pl
Paveletsky Vokzal
ul Zatsepa
Serpukhovskaya
Kozhevnicheskaya ul
Lyusinovskaya ul
Bolshaya Pionerskaya ul
Malaya Pionerskaya ul
Dubininskaya ul
Letnikovskaya ul
Bolshaya Serpukhovskaya ul
Stremyanny per
ul Shchipok
Maly Strochenovsky per
To Danilov Monastery, Danilovsky Market & Danilovskaya Hotel (3.5km)
36
21
14
34
4
12
11
16
43
44
7
10
35
38
29
41
33
2
37

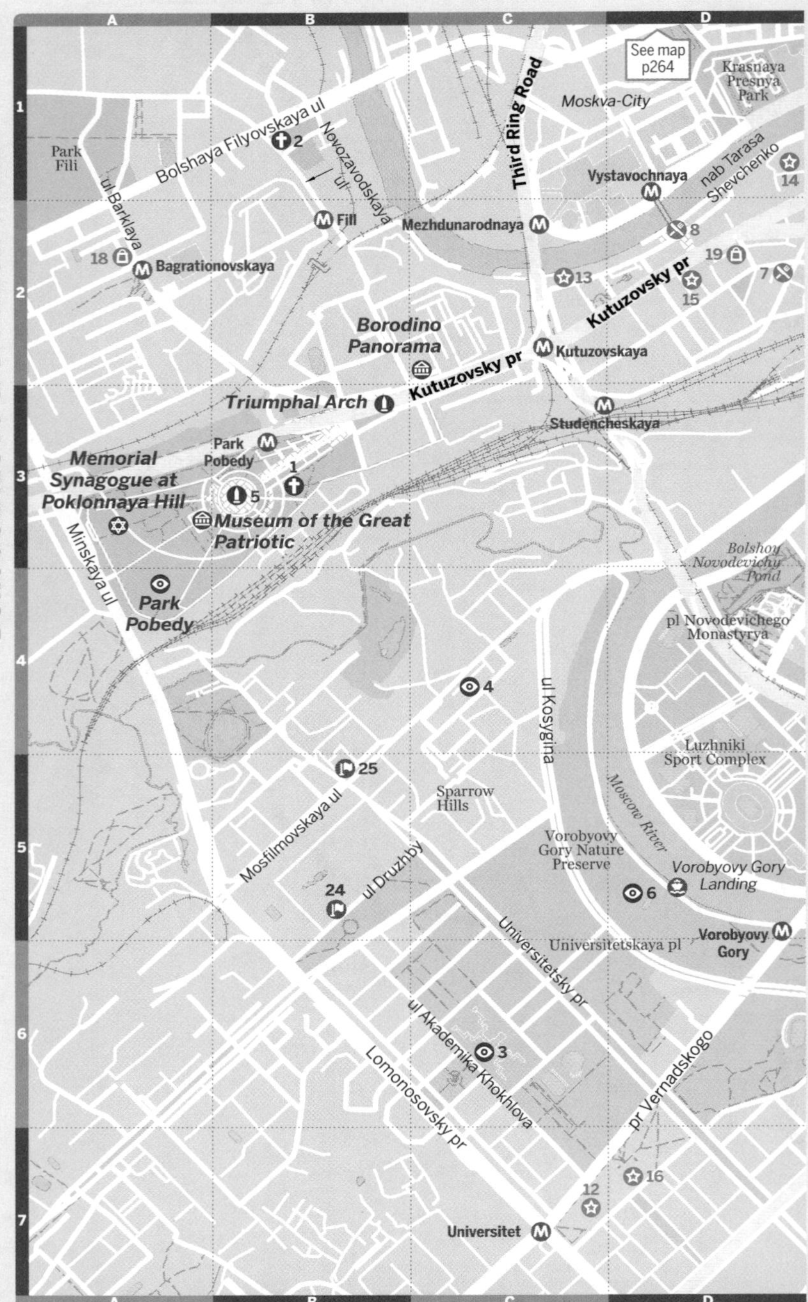

A
B
C
D
1
2
3
4
5
6
7
See map p264
Krasnaya Presnya Park
Moskva-City
Third Ring Road
Park Fili
Bolshaya Filyovskaya ul
Novozavodskaya ul
ul Barklaya
Fili
Vystavochnaya
nab Tarasa Shevchenko
Mezhdunarodnaya
Bagrationovskaya
Kutuzovsky pr
Borodino Panorama
Kutuzovskaya
Triumphal Arch
Studencheskaya
Park Pobedy
Memorial Synagogue at Poklonnaya Hill
Museum of the Great Patriotic
Minskaya ul
Park Pobedy
Bolshoy Novodevichy Pond
pl Novodevichego Monastyrya
ul Kosygina
Luzhniki Sport Complex
Moscow River
Sparrow Hills
Mosfilmovskaya ul
ul Druzhby
Vorobyovy Gory Nature Preserve
Vorobyovy Gory Landing
Vorobyovy Gory
Universitetskaya pl
Universitetsky pr
ul Akademika Khokhlova
Lomonosovsky pr
pr Vernadskogo
Universitet

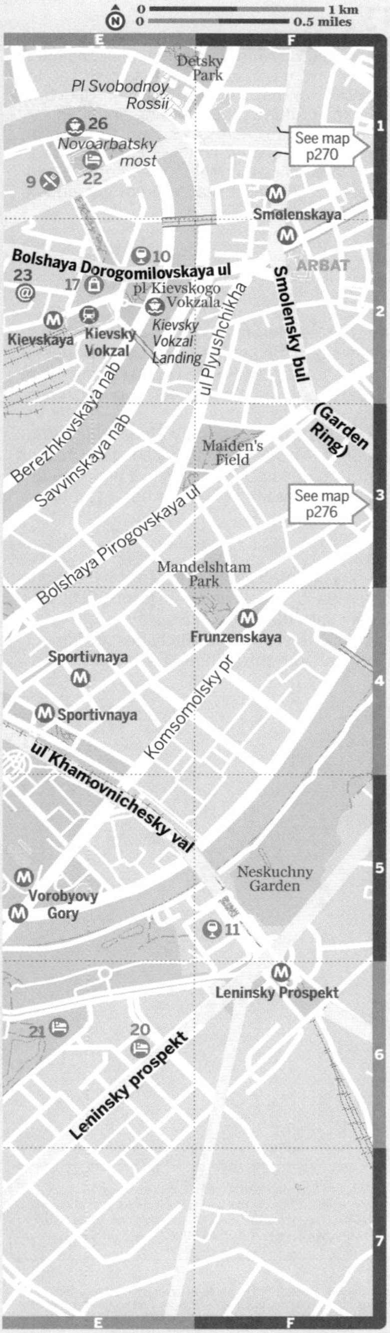

Top Sights **(p149)**

Borodino Panorama C2
Memorial Synagogue at Poklonnaya Hill... A3
Museum of the Great Patriotic War A3
Park Pobedy A4
Triumphal Arch B3

Sights **(p150)**

1 Church of St George B3
2 Church of the Intercession at Fili B1
3 Moscow State University (MGU) C6
4 Mosfilm C4
5 Obelisk B3
6 Vorobyovy Gory Nature Preserve D5

Eating **(p151)**

Darbar .... (see 20)
7 Dorogomilovsky Market D2
Evropeysky Shopping Centre .... (see 17)
8 Pinocchio Bar & Cafe D2
9 Pinocchio on Kutuzovsky E1

Drinking & Nightlife **(p152)**

10 Probka E2
11 Sky Lounge F5

Entertainment **(p152)**

12 Bolshoi Circus on Vernadskogo C7
Evropeysky Skating Rink .... (see 17)
13 Fomenko Studio Theatre C2
14 Krysha Mira D1
15 Kuklachev Cat Theatre D2
16 Moscow Children's Musical Theatre D7

Shopping **(p152)**

17 Evropeysky Shopping Centre E2
18 Gorbushka Shopping Centre A2
19 Valentin Yudashkin Boutique D2

Sleeping **(p176)**

20 Hotel Sputnik E6
21 Korston Hotel E6
22 Radisson Royal (Hotel Ukraine) E1

Information **(p233)**

23 Cafemax E2
24 Chinese Embassy B5
25 German Embassy B5

Transport **(p231)**

26 Radisson River Cruises E1

Our Story

A beat-up old car, a few dollars in the pocket and a sense of adventure. In 1972 that's all Tony and Maureen Wheeler needed for the trip of a lifetime – across Europe and Asia overland to Australia. It took several months, and at the end – broke but inspired – they sat at their kitchen table writing and stapling together their first travel guide, *Across Asia on the Cheap*. Within a week they'd sold 1500 copies. Lonely Planet was born.

Today, Lonely Planet has offices in Melbourne, London and Oakland, with more than 600 staff and writers. We share Tony's belief that 'a great guidebook should do three things: inform, educate and amuse'.

Our Writers

Mara Vorhees

Coordinating Author Mara's first visit to Moscow was in 1990, when the lines inside GUM were dwarfed only by the lines outside Lenin's Tomb. She witnessed the postcommunist transition from her vantage point in the Urals. During those years in the Wild East, the capital was a frequent destination for 'recovery trips', which usually required a recovery afterwards.

The pen-wielding traveller has worked on dozens of Lonely Planet titles, including *Russia* and *Trans-Siberian Railway*. Her stories about Russia have appeared in magazines and newspapers around the world. When not roaming around Russia, Mara lives in a pink house in Somerville, Massachusetts, with her husband, two kiddies and two kitties. Follow her adventures at www.maravorhees.com.

Leonid Ragozin

Leonid Ragozin devoted himself to beach dynamics when he studied geology in Moscow. Despite a want of really nice beaches in Russia, he helped gold miners in Siberia and sold InterRail tickets before embarking on a journalistic career. After eight years with the BBC, he became a foreign correspondent for the *Russian Newsweek* – the job that took him to such unlikely destinations as Bhutan and Ecuador. Now back at the BBC, he has plunged into the turbulent sea of TV news. Leonid contributed to the Day Trips chapter.

Published by Lonely Planet Publications Pty Ltd
ABN 36 005 607 983
5th edition – March 2012
ISBN 978 1 74179 564 6

© Lonely Planet 2012 Photographs © as indicated 2012

10 9 8 7 6 5 4 3
Printed in China

Although the authors and Lonely Planet have taken all reasonable care in preparing this book, we make no warranty about the accuracy or completeness of its content and, to the maximum extent permitted, disclaim all liability arising from its use.

All rights reserved. No part of this publication may be copied, stored in a retrieval system, or transmitted in any form by any means, electronic, mechanical, recording or otherwise, except brief extracts for the purpose of review, and no part of this publication may be sold or hired, without the written permission of the publisher. Lonely Planet and the Lonely Planet logo are trademarks of Lonely Planet and are registered in the US Patent and Trademark Office and in other countries. Lonely Planet does not allow its name or logo to be appropriated by commercial establishments, such as retailers, restaurants or hotels. Please let us know of any misuses: lonelyplanet.com/ip.